Native Paths to Volunteer Trails

Native Paths to Volunteer Trails

Hiking and Trail Building on Oʻahu

Stuart M. Ball, Jr.

A Latitude 20 Book

University of Hawaiʻi Press
Honolulu

© 2012 University of Hawai'i Press
All rights reserved
Printed in the United States of America

17 16 15 14 13 12   6 5 4 3 2 1

Library of Congress Cataloging-in-Publication Data
Ball, Stuart M.
  Native paths to volunteer trails : hiking and trail building on O'ahu /
Stuart M. Ball, Jr.
      p. cm.
  "A latitude 20 book."
  Includes index.
  ISBN 978-0-8248-3560-6 (pbk. : alk. paper)
  1. Hiking—Hawaii—Oahu—Guidebooks. 2. Trails—Hawaii—Oahu—History.
    3. Trails—Hawaii—Oahu—Guidebooks. I. Title.
  GV199.42.H32O142 2012
  919.69'3—dc23
                                                    2011045356

University of Hawai'i Press books are printed on acid-free paper and meet the guidelines for permanence and durability of the Council on Library Resources.

Designed by Mardee Melton
Printed by Sheridan Books, Inc.

DEDICATED TO

Trail historian
Lorin T. Gill
and
Trail builder
Richard H. (Dick) Davis

Contents

Acknowledgments ix
Introduction xi

Hawaiian Trails (pre-1810) 1
    Kaliuwaʻa (Sacred) Falls 4
    Tom Tom 11
    Kūmaipō 15
    Dupont 19
    Mākua-Kawaihāpai 26

Kamaʻāina and Club Trails (1842–1922) 29
    Castle-Olympus 38
    Mānoa Cliff and Kalāwahine 44
    Kaʻau Crater 48
    Lanipō 54
    Olomana 56
    Kaʻala-Schofield 60
    Pālehua-Palikea 64

Sugar Plantation Trails (1898–1917) 70
    Waiawa and Waiāhole 72
    ʻŌpaeʻula and Kawaiiki 78
    Kawainui 82
    Castle (Pig God) 84
    Waimano 91
    Waimalu 98

Army and Territorial Forestry Division Trails (1909–1933) 102
- Schofield-Waikāne 111
- Bowman 117
- Pūpūkea-Kahuku 120
- Pe'ahināi'a 126
- Mālaekahana 132
- Piko 136
- Ma'akua Ridge and Hau'ula 140
- Kaunala 145

Civilian Conservation Corps Trails (1933–1942) 149
- Poamoho 160
- Mokulē'ia 165
- Keālia 169
- Kawailoa 172
- Kīpapa 176
- 'Aiea Loop and Ridge 181
- Lā'ie 186
- Hālawa 189
- Ko'olau Summit 193
- Honouliuli 209

Volunteer Trails (1945–1998) 215
- Likeke 220
- Mānana 223
- 'Aihualama 225
- Nahuina, Moleka, and 'Ualaka'a 228
- Nu'uanu 231
- Maunawili and Maunawili Falls 233

Notes 239
Index 271

Acknowledgments

Mahalo to reviewers Lorin T. Gill, John B. Hall, William Gorst, and Mehana Kaiama. Their helpful suggestions and constructive criticism made this a better book. Lorin reviewed the manuscript as I wrote it, chapter by chapter, over a period of several years.

Mahalo to these trail *kupuna*, who provided a glimpse into the hiking past: Richard H. Davis, Richard Booth, and Joseph Neilson of the Hawaiian Trail and Mountain Club, Colonel Thomas J. Wells of the Piko Club, Lorin T. Gill of the Sierra Club, Hawai'i Chapter, and Mary Judd, daughter-in-law of forester Charles S. Judd.

Mahalo to the following outdoor enthusiasts, who shared their hiking or working experiences on the trails and/or helped gather the maps and photographs: Vince Costello, Curt Cottrell, Andrea Gill, William Gorst, John B. Hall, Nancy Hoffman, Art Isbell, H. Kapua Kawelo, Mabel Kekina, Joyce Oka, Jesse Palmer, Patrick Rorie, Richard Schmidt, Gwen Sinclair, Vince Soeda, Talbert Takahama, Dayle K. Turner, Jim Yuen, Nathan Yuen, Wes Williams, and Merlin Wollenzein.

Finally, *mahalo* to these librarians or archivists, who patiently pointed me in the right direction: Judy Bowman at the U.S. Army Museum of Hawai'i, DeSoto Brown at the Bishop Museum, Linda Hee at the Tropic Lightning Museum, Patricia Lai at the Hawai'i State Archives, Patrick McNally at the Hawai'i State Library, and Marilyn Reppun at the Mission Houses Museum.

Introduction

For such a small, populous island, Oʻahu has a varied, extensive, and distinctive network of mountain trails. Who developed those trails, and why and how did they build them? The story starts with the birth of the island and ends with trail crews of enthusiastic volunteers.

Two volcanoes, Koʻolau and Waiʻanae, created Oʻahu several million years ago. Their rugged remnants remain as two parallel mountain ranges that dominate the topography and restrict human habitation to the lowlands. Early Hawaiians lived in the coastal areas and their associated watersheds. The current population of about a million is still concentrated near the shore or on the gentle upland between the two ranges.

Through the years Oʻahu inhabitants developed trails into and across the mountain barriers for various reasons. Early Hawaiians blazed ridge and valley routes for travelers, plant gatherers, bird catchers, and woodcutters. Sugar plantations constructed trails to access ditches that tapped stream water for their thirsty cane. The U.S. Army built trails for training and island defense against enemy attack. The Territorial Forestry Division and the Civilian Conservation Corps constructed trails for reforestation, wild pig control, and unemployment reduction. Volunteers and hiking clubs created additional routes solely for recreation.

The result of all that varied activity is a network of just over a hundred trails, a precious and special resource on our crowded island. The people of Oʻahu are fortunate indeed to be able to enjoy a relaxing or challenging outing in the wild mountains so close to home.

This volume compiles the history of fifty of those trails. Most of them still exist, and many are open to the public for hiking; others are closed, and a few are long gone. Not included are numerous trails whose written and oral history is sketchy or whose route has become a paved automobile road.

The trails included are arranged in chronological chapters by the group or organization that built them. The history thus starts with Hawaiian trails before 1800 and ends with volunteer trails of the 1990s. Each chapter has an overview section that describes the background and purpose of the trail building during the period covered. Each trail history is self-contained, recording the major events from construction through 2010.

If you are particularly interested in O'ahu trail history, by all means read the book from cover to cover. Otherwise, use this volume as you would a guidebook. Before hiking a particular trail, look up its history and then peruse the accompanying overview section. Over the years you may eventually read the entire book.

Native Paths to
Volunteer Trails

Hawaiian Trails
(pre-1810)

> Perhaps it would be well to follow the Honolulu trails of about 1810, that they may be known, and to determine whether the houses were many or few. Let us begin looking.
>
> —John Papa Ii, *Fragments of Hawaiian History*

Early Hawaiians developed trails to travel between *ahupuaʻa* (land divisions) and to fish, farm, and gather within the *ahupuaʻa*, each of which was self-sufficient and extended from the uplands to the ocean. Coastal routes connecting the land divisions were used by chiefs, commoners, and tax collectors. The *konohiki* (land manager) collected the annual tax, often of feathers, *kapa* (tapa) cloth, *kalo* (taro), or *puaʻa* (pig), and placed it along the trail on an *ahupuaʻa* (rock altar with a pig image) marking the boundary of the land division. As the coastal routes were usually rough and hot, chiefs and other high-ranking persons preferred to travel by canoe.

Trails also provided access to the *mauka* (inland) resources of the *ahupuaʻa* in the valleys and ridges of the Koʻolau and Waiʻanae mountain ranges. Commoners collected plants for food, medicines, and decoration. They also caught the colorful native birds for their feathers and cut wood for canoes, houses, and *heiau* (religious sites).[1]

In a series of articles for the Hawaiian newspaper *Kuokoa*, historian John Papa Ii described the leeward trails existing on Oʻahu in 1810. West of Honolulu, the main trail went through the *ahupuaʻa* of Kalihi, ʻAiea, and Waimano, passed Puʻu o Kapolei, and headed up the Waiʻanae coast. After reaching Mākua, the route continued around Kaʻena Point to Waialua. From there another major trail crossed the center of the island through the Wahiawā *ahupuaʻa* to Waiawa, where it joined the coast route. Connecting trails traversed the Waiʻanae Range at Pōhākea and Kolekole passes, Kaʻala,

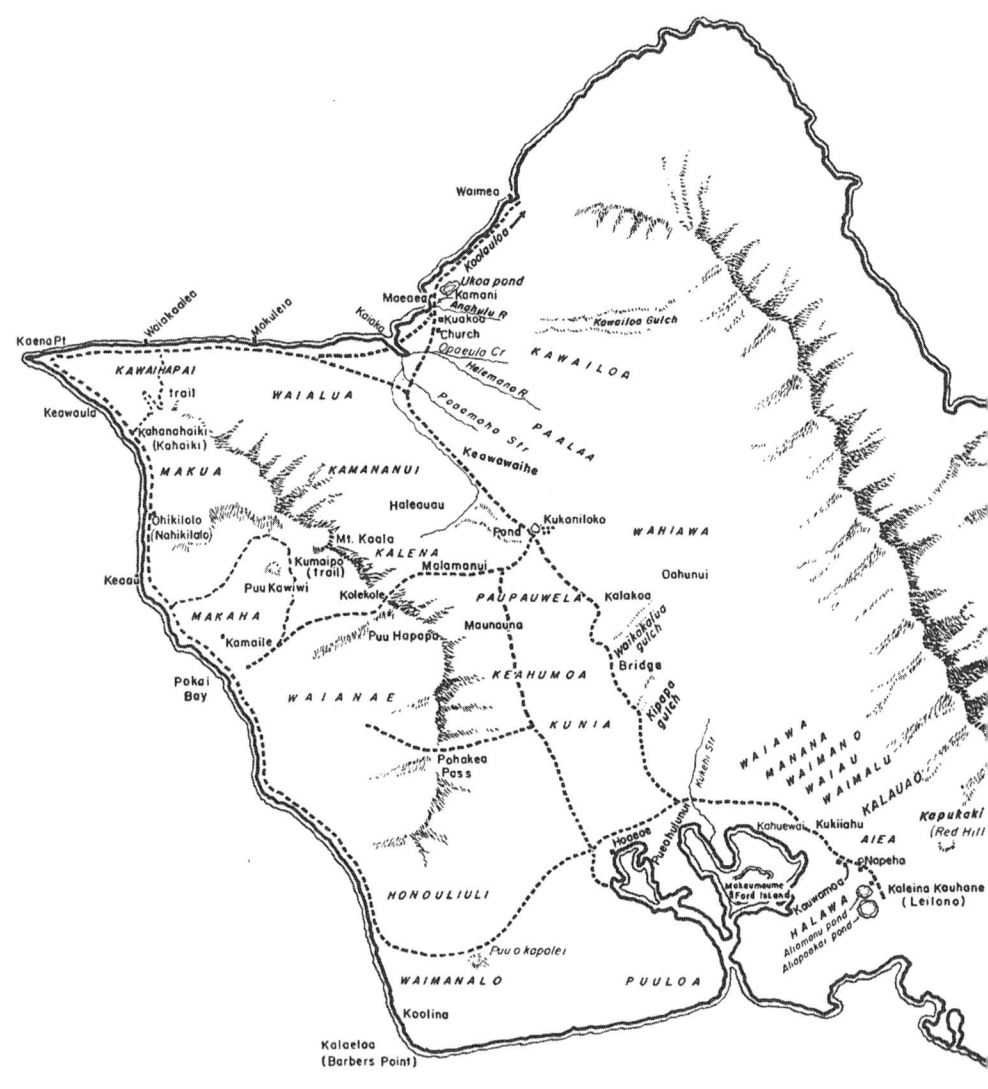

Trails of leeward O'ahu, map by Paul Rockwood from *Fragments of Hawaiian History*. (Bishop Museum Press)

and Kawaihāpai. East of Honolulu the main trail passed through Kaimukī on the way to Maunalua and Makapuʻu. Side trails led to Waikīkī, around Diamond Head, and into Mānoa and Pālolo Valleys.[2]

Hawaiian routes to the windward side had to traverse the formidable Koʻolau Range, with its sheer *pali* (cliff) more than a thousand feet high. While visiting Oʻahu in 1813, John B. Whitman noted in his journal:

> There are but three passes through the mountains, two of which are intricate and dangerous and very seldom attempted. One is at Whyteetee [Waikīkī] and the other at Auhi [Kalihi?]. The middle pass called by the natives New Anu [Nuʻuanu] is at the head of a valley of Hanoruru [Honolulu].[3]

In 1821 Reverend Daniel Tyerman left London on the whaling ship *Tuscan* bound for the Pacific. As a member of the London Missionary Society, he planned to visit the missionary stations on the islands there. After arriving in Honolulu, he walked up Nuʻuanu Valley on April 28, 1822. Near the head of the valley Tyerman found several makeshift stills brewing *ʻōkolehao,* a liquor made from the roots of the *kī* (ti) plant. At Nuʻuanu Pali he observed Hawaiians placing flowers or foliage on four distinct boulders, one of which was covered with *kapa* (tapa) cloth: "their protection is sought by those who clamber these perilous cliffs, that they may be preserved from slips and broken bones in returning," Tyerman later commented.[4] The reverend was not impressed with either the four "idols" at the *pali* or the distillery back in the valley.

On May 6, 1825, HMS *Blonde*, commanded by Captain George A. (Lord) Byron, docked at Honolulu to return the bodies of King Kamehameha II and Queen Kamamalu, who had both died of measles while visiting London. On June 1, a party from the ship took the winding trail up Nuʻuanu Valley. The path followed the stream past *loʻi* (terraces) of *kalo* (taro) and cultivated fields, then through a dense forest to the Nuʻuanu Pali. In his journal Lord Byron later wrote,

> The descent to this plain [windward side], which, like that of Honoruru, extends to the sea, is the most fearful imaginable. In many places the path consists of little more than holes cut into the rock for the hands and feet; and, where most commodius, it lies along narrow ledges, where a false step would be inevitable destruction.[5]

In 1833, Frederick D. Bennett arrived on Oʻahu on the whaler *Tuscan* from London via Cape Horn. A Fellow of the Royal College of Surgeons,

Bennett was studying the anatomy and habits of southern whales, particularly the sperm whale. While in Honolulu, he explored Kalihi Valley and later noted,

> Kalihi has a pass to the vale of Kolau [Koʻolau] similar to the pari of Anuana [Nuʻuanu Pali], though more precipitous and only employed by a few islanders who convey fish from Kolau [Koʻolau] to Honoruru. I descended it in company with a native guide, but found the task difficult, and scarcely practicable without the aid afforded by boughs of trees.[6]

During the first half of the 1800s, the extensive network of Hawaiian foot trails on Oʻahu began to disappear because of changes in transportation and the decimation of the native population from Western diseases and cultural disruption. Over the next hundred years the major Hawaiian trails became horse paths, carriage ways, and eventually paved automobile roads. The mountain routes, abandoned and largely forgotten, gradually disappeared under encroaching vegetation, except for Kaliuwaʻa (Sacred Falls) and a few other popular paths. Army surveyors and club hikers later rediscovered some of the lost routes, which have become some of the finest hiking trails on the island, including Tom Tom, Kūmaipō, and Dupont.

....
Kaliuwaʻa (Sacred) Falls

O Kama hoi paha oe,
O kanaka o ka pali ku,
O ka pali moe
O ka pali ku-hoho
O ka pali kaʻa o ka pohaku . . .

Thou art indeed Kama
The man of the high cliffs,
Of the low lying cliffs,
Of the steep cliffs,
Of the cliffs of the rolling stones . . .

—old Hawaiian chant, Pele speaking to Kamapuaʻa

In the windward Koʻolauloa district just north of Punaluʻu Valley was the *ahupuaʻa* (land division) of Kaluanui. In the level *makai* (seaward) portion, early Hawaiians grew *kalo* (taro) in *loʻi* (terraces) watered by Kaluanui Stream and its two small tributaries Waimanamana and Kuʻumi.[7] *Mauka* (inland) the valley narrowed to a rugged gulch framed by high, steep cliffs. Confined to the canyon, the stream rushed headlong toward the ocean in a series of rapids and cascades. Hawaiians developed a route up the gulch to the first waterfall, called Kaliuwaʻa (canoe leak), and spoke of a powerful and enduring legend about the surrounding ravine.

Kaliuwaʻa was the abode of Kamapuaʻa, a demigod who took the form of a man or a pig. As a hog, he frequently stole chickens from the nearby Kahana and Punaluʻu lands of Olopana, chief of Oʻahu. While coming home late one night from foraging, Kamapuaʻa met a supernatural chicken, who betrayed him to the chief's guards. Olopana quickly organized a search party from the men of Kaluanui, Punaluʻu, and Kahana. More than eight hundred strong, they easily captured the surprised pig, tied him to a pole, and began carrying him back to Kahana. In Punaluʻu, Kamaunuaniho, the grandmother of Kamapuaʻa, saw the procession and chanted in honor of her grandson. The pig merely answered with a grunt, but in Kahana he burst the ropes and killed all his captors except one, who fled to tell Olopana.

The legend goes on to repeat the capture and escape cycle three more times. Each time the search party grew in size, and the chant became more powerful. For the fifth attempt Olopana recruited the entire male population of the island. All were armed with clubs, spears, or daggers and were dressed for battle in feather cloaks and helmets. When Kamapuaʻa heard the army coming up the gulch, he leaned against the high *pali* (cliff) on the Punaluʻu side just before Kaliuwaʻa Falls. His family and servants then scrambled up his hog back out of the steep ravine. His grandmother, however, declined to brave the bristly back of her grandson, so Kamapuaʻa pressed into the *pali* facing outward, and she climbed up his soft teats to safety. When Olopana's warriors arrived below the falls, all they saw was a long gouge in the face of the cliff.[8]

In early 1838, Edwin O. Hall left Honolulu on an eleven-day tour around Oʻahu on horseback. He undertook the journey to relax and become better acquainted with the Hawaiian people and their language. After traveling to Waiʻanae and over Kolekole Pass to Waialua, he decided to visit well-known Kaliuwaʻa Falls on his way down the windward coast. Hall and his native guide rode horses about two miles into Kaluanui Valley and then continued up the narrowing gulch on foot. As the walls closed in, the two men crossed the rushing stream several times under a lovely canopy of ʻōhiʻa ʻai (mountain apple) and kukui trees. Farther in, the guide pointed out the gouge left by Kamapua'a and undoubtedly retold the famous legend. At the trail end, Hall viewed the waterfall, which

> is from eighty to one hundred feet high, and the water compressed into a very narrow space just where it breaks forth from the rock above.[9]

At the base of the fall was a large, circular pool said to be bottomless. The guide also told Hall about two upper falls, one of which was two to three hundred feet high and visible from the road along the shore. During the entire walk Hall marveled at the wild beauty and romance of the gorge.

> A scene where the sublime is mingled with the beautiful, and the bold and striking with the delicate and sensitive; where every sense is gratified, the mind calmed, and the whole soul delighted.[10]

Needless to say, Kaliuwa'a was one of the highlights of his trip.

In 1875, Queen Emma, widow of King Kamehameha IV, asked an old friend, John A. Cummins, to accompany her on a tour around O'ahu. Cummins, the future owner of Waimanalo Sugar Company, readily agreed and began preparation for a lavish and leisurely fifteen-day excursion. On November 5, Cummins, the queen, and her large retinue left Honolulu on horseback bound for Waimānalo. The cavalcade included 140 women riders dressed in colorful *pā'u* (skirts). The party spent the first three nights at Mauna Rose, Cummins' spacious plantation house. Each evening he treated his guests to a sumptuous *lū'au* and *hula* dancing lasting well into the night. Reluctantly leaving Waimānalo, the group slowly proceeded up the windward coast, stopping at Kāne'ohe, Waikāne, Kahana, and Punalu'u. On November 13 near Hau'ula, Cummins and Queen Emma took a wild surf ride in a canoe drawn by two horses racing along the beach. Totally soaked, the two were carried up to Kaliuwa'a Falls to wash off the salt, change clothes, and enjoy refreshments. A large crowd gathered by the pool, where many jumped or dived into its deep, cool water. After the Kaliuwa'a outing, the queen's party continued up the coast to Waialua and eventually returned to Honolulu through Wahiawā.[11] Twenty-three years later, on October 22, 1898, Company H of the U.S. Army First Regiment of New York Volunteers visited Kaliuwa'a Falls as part of a rigorous training hike around the island.[12] Undoubtedly the soldiers enjoyed the fall and pool as much as Cummins and Queen Emma had.

In 1906, windward sugar baron James B. Castle leased the *makai* portion of Kaluanui Valley from the B. P. Bishop Estate. He built a horse trail, later known as the Castle Trail, from Punalu'u Valley to the upper Kaluanui drainage to measure the stream flow. He then diverted much of the lower stream into a ditch to irrigate sugar cane and rice fields.[13] He also built a mountain house in the gulch near a stream gauging station at an elevation of 250 feet. In 1917 the *mauka* portion became part of the Hau'ula Forest Reserve. On August 8 of that year, superintendent of forestry Charles S. Judd hiked up to the falls while inspecting the forest.[14]

By the late 1910s, Kaliuwa'a Falls had become a popular destination for *kama'āina* (island-born) and tourist hikers. They observed Hawaiians carefully placing a leaf, twig, or flower along the path, usually on a boulder and kept in place by a stone. Those simple offerings to Kamapua'a ensured a safe trip without injury from falling rocks or from slipping in the stream.[15] Non-Hawaiian hikers often followed that ritual and soon began calling the cascade Sacred Falls. In the 1920s, one *haole* (white) hiker neglected to leave an offering, fell into the stream several times, and then asked if the place was called Sacred Falls because each fall was more sacred than the last.[16]

On June 27, 1920, the Hawaiian Trail and Mountain Club (HTMC) scheduled Sacred Falls as part of an around-the-island autobus trip. About sixty hikers enjoyed lunch on the beach at Hau'ula and then headed for the falls. They followed the tracks of the Koolau Railway and soon swung right, through cane fields into the gulch, where they crossed the stream eight times. Presumably some of the group left an offering because they all came out safely and continued the tour up the windward coast.[17]

In early 1934, Kermit Kosch decided to explore the upper waterfalls along Kaluanui Stream. One morning he and his friend David Hague hiked the old Castle Trail from Punalu'u Valley and then began rock-hopping downstream toward the ocean. In short order the two reached the top of a first waterfall, which dropped about a hundred feet. After some searching, the men found a steep, treacherous route around the fall. They swam across the pool at its base and continued downstream past several smaller cascades. Suddenly the stream narrowed to a deep channel flanked by vertical cliffs and spilled thirty feet into the forbidden pool,

> a capacious, deep circular contour so named by me on account of its stymie position, shutting off further advance toward the head of the [next] falls.[18]

Without ropes for rappelling, Kosch and Hague could not safely negotiate the pool and the waterfall just beyond, and so reluctantly turned back.

On December 10, 1934, Honolulu mayor George F. Wright met with Bishop Estate trustee Albert F. Judd to discuss making Sacred Falls a city park. The estate proposed to turn over 350 acres in Kaluanui Valley to the

HTMC hikers at Kaliuwa'a (Sacred) Falls, March 16, 1924. (Photo by R. J. Baker, courtesy of Joyce Oka)

city in exchange for property elsewhere. The city and county would then build an access road into the valley and upgrade the trail to the falls.[19] On December 15, territorial forester Charles Judd met with the trustees to discuss the proposal, as the road and trail entered the Hau'ula Forest Reserve.[20] The three parties involved, however, never reached agreement, and the idea died.

After World War II, Sacred Falls became trail number 15 on the 1947 forestry hiking map. That same year HTMC resumed hiking to the falls. In 1952 the club erected signs showing hikers the correct route up the valley.[21] In 1954 workers under the Hawaii Employment Program rerouted the trail to eliminate all but two of the stream crossings, at a cost of $2,544.66.[22]

During the 1960s, the Sacred Falls trail continued to be very popular with the hiking public. In 1963, however, *Paradise of the Pacific* magazine railed against the creeping commercialization of the area in an editorial titled "Nothing Sacred at Sacred Falls." A concessionaire charged fifty cents for parking and sold soda pop and candy at a small stand near the entrance. Even worse, no one could start hiking after 4 p.m.

We were staggered to think that a god's domain could be opened and shut like an amusement arcade at the mere whim of an attendant.[23]

In early May 1963, HTMC member Richard H. (Dick) Davis and four others attempted to descend the upper Kaluanui waterfalls. Over several days they climbed the Castle Trail and rappelled down several good-sized cascades before being stopped by a waterfall so high it took their breath away. Davis later decided to climb upstream starting at Sacred Falls. On November 3, he reached its top by driving pitons into the rock and rigging fixed ropes. On November 10, Davis and seven companions ascended Sacred Falls and camped along the stream for the night. The next day the group rock-hopped upstream and climbed past two smallish falls. At the base of a one-hundred-foot cascade, they ran out of pitons. Just beyond was the immense waterfall reported to be more than three hundred feet high.[24]

In 1977, Sacred Falls officially became a state park. The HTMC soon visited the new park as part of their outing of February 25, 1978, and continued to schedule the hike as a Saturday outing for novices and families through 1985.[25] Hordes of tourists and locals also walked the trail to marvel at Kamapua'a's gouge, admire the lovely falls, and swim in the bottomless pool. Some still placed an offering on a boulder to ensure their immunity from the occasional falling rock.

In 1995, HTMC developed a difficult outing starting from Sacred Falls State Park. Called Kamapua'a, the hike climbed the steep divide between Kaluanui Valley and Punaiki Gulch just *mauka* of Pu'u Waiahilahila. The hikers then followed the rugged ridge to a junction with the Castle Trail well above Kaluanui Stream and the last waterfall. On March 24, 1996, Michael J. (Mike) Mottl led the first Kamapua'a hike; no one reached the Castle junction.[26]

On Sunday afternoon, May 9, 1999, about sixty people were relaxing around the pool at the base of Sacred Falls. Around 2:30 p.m. a small section of the cliff five hundred feet above the pool on the Punalu'u side broke away and slid down a dry waterfall chute. Airborne for the last 150 feet, the rocks and debris smashed into the streambed just below the pool, killing eight people and injuring thirty-two. The state immediately closed the park. A U.S. Geological Survey team later investigated the site and determined that the rock fall was caused by the long-term degrading of the slope, an ongoing process in the gulch. The team recommended that the park be closed permanently as there was no way to lessen the hazard without totally destroying the aesthetic of the hike.[27] As of 2010, Sacred Falls State Park remained closed, although several proposals have surfaced to reopen a portion of it.

After viewing photographs of the two highest waterfalls taken from a helicopter, Merlin Wollenzein, a database specialist at Brigham Young University–Hawaiʻi, decided to attempt the descent of the upper Kaluanui falls in 2006. On September 15, he and two companions followed the Maʻakua Ridge Trail and climbed the ridge separating Papali and Maʻakua gulches to a saddle, known in the 1930s as the "pig wire." There the three men took the Castle Trail down to Kaluanui Stream, where they camped for the night. The next morning the group headed downstream and easily rappelled the first waterfall, a hundred feet high. The three then negotiated the short drop into the forbidden pool and descended a second cascade, eighty feet high. At its base Wollenzein decided to turn around because of continuing rain, high water, and a shortage of rope.

On October 6, Wollenzein made a second attempt to reach the "big drops" under much drier conditions. He and three friends took the same route and again camped where the Castle Trail crossed the stream. The next day they quickly descended the first three waterfalls, the last two by jumping, after setting up ropes. The group bypassed the fourth cascade by crossing over a side ridge and rappelled down the fifth, 110 feet high, using their next to last rope. Soon the four reached a precipice where the stream dropped more than seven hundred feet in two long cascades. Wollenzein started down and later wrote,

> As I was descending I was astounded by the sheer magnitude of the drop. The rappel was thrilling, the view was awesome, and the splash of the cool water felt good in the warm sun.[28]

He reached the bottom with no rope to spare, and one other joined him there. After the two climbed back up the waterfall using ascenders, the group backtracked up the remaining five waterfalls and headed for home.

On April 7, 2007, Wollenzein attempted to descend the Kaluanui waterfalls and hike out the Sacred Falls Trail all in one day. His team included seven members: David Paddock and Jenne Anderson, both veterans of the second trip, Jared Halterman, Yo Phetsomphou, brothers Adam and Nate Wadsworth, both experts in ropes, knots, and anchoring techniques, and their friend Jeff. The seven men and one woman left the Maʻakua trailhead at 5:15 a.m. and had breakfast at the campsite by the stream. The group then methodically descended the six known waterfalls, jumping the low ones and rappelling the high ones. At the top of the huge seventh cascade, the team carefully set up their gear. Seven members then descended the 510-foot drop without incident. Wollenzein, the last to go, was 300 feet down the chute when he felt the rope detach. He crashed into the wall twice before free falling 100 feet into the plunge pool at the base of the falls. After surfacing with only minor injuries, Wollenzein yelled to his worried companions, "That sucks!" With daylight running out, the shaken group settled down and descended two more waterfalls, 50 and 140 feet high, and finally 87-foot Sacred Falls. Wollenzein and Adam Wadsworth jumped Kaliuwaʻa because they didn't want to wait for the rope. The entire team made it out safely sometime after dark.

Tom Tom

Hikers Find Old Hawaiian Trail, Long Forgotten

—*Pacific Commercial Advertiser,* February 6, 1922, page 1 headline

In the middle 1800s and earlier, Hawaiians journeying between Maunalua and Waimānalo *ahupuaʻa* (land divisions) sometimes climbed directly over the Koʻolau Range rather than walking along the coast through the gap at Makapuʻu. The shortcut started at the head of Keahupua-o-Maunalua (shrine of baby mullet), a broad, shallow estuary also known as Kuapā and used by the Hawaiians as a fish pond. From a small settlement there, the route ascended gradually through Kamilonui Valley past sweet potato patches. The trail reached the Koʻolau crest at a small saddle and then turned west along the summit ridge. At the second knoll the path descended precipitously down a narrow buttress ridge into Waimānalo. Despite its steep sections, the cross-Koʻolau route was traveled regularly up to the early 1800s, when Western diseases and cultural disruption decimated the nearby Hawaiian populations. Gradually the trail fell into disuse and was all but forgotten.[29]

In the early 1920s, Thomas R. L. McGuire, part-Hawaiian forest ranger and Hawaiian Trail and Mountain Club (HTMC) member, heard about the Maunalua-Waimānalo route. He slowly pieced together vague and sometimes conflicting information about the trail from various sources. On Sunday, February 5, 1922, while the regular club group hiked around Hanauma Bay, McGuire and fellow HTMC members Thomas P. Cadle, Christopher B. Olsen, and Don M. Lillie headed into Kamilonui Valley and up to the Koʻolau summit. After some searching, the four found the correct side ridge down the *pali* (cliff).[30] Starting the descent, the men were in for a pleasant surprise.

> The ropes they brought were of no use. The other side of the mountain toward Waimanalo was very steep, yet the descent was very good and they had no trouble getting down to the ground below.[31]

Forest ranger Thomas McGuire, circa 1930. (Courtesy of Noel McCully)

HTMC first hiked the rediscovered route on June 4 and initially called it the Waimānalo-Koko Head Trail. For the next outing on December 3, the club named the Hawaiian route Tom Tom, after Tom McGuire and Tom Cadle. That morning twenty-four hikers boarded an autobus at the Armed Forces YMCA in downtown Honolulu and drove to the wireless receiving station on the Koko Head side of Kuapā pond. After completing the trail, the group walked through the cane fields of the Waimanalo Sugar Company to the beach for a refreshing swim in the ocean. The hikers then continued along the coast and climbed the gap at Makapu'u to the waiting bus.[32]

In 1926, the HTMC built a clubhouse a block from the beach at Waimānalo. In the late 1920s and early 1930s, members hiked the Tom Tom Trail to the clubhouse, where they spent the night and the following day relaxing. On December 11, 1932, a group hiked the steep windward portion from the clubhouse in the morning and then attended an afternoon lecture titled "Life in the Philippines." Perhaps the talk was interesting enough to keep everyone awake![33]

On September 19, 1934, territorial forester Charles S. Judd and ranger Tom McGuire hiked the Kamilonui section of Tom Tom to hunt fourteen feral goats reported along the summit ridge. The two made slow progress up the valley as the path was heavily overgrown with prickly lantana and other shrubs. At the top the men spent several hours searching for goats without success.[34]

In addition to Tom Tom, the old Hawaiian route had another name, Marconi Pass Trail, probably bestowed by the U.S. Army.[35] The pass was the small saddle on the Ko'olau crest at the head of Kamilonui Valley. Marconi was the inventor of wireless communication, and the rediscovered trail started near the radio receiving station by the shore of Kuapā pond. On the 1938 *Sales Builder* map, the Hawaiian route was listed as trail number 18, Tom Tom (Marconi).

After World War II, the HTMC resumed scheduling the Marconi–Tom Tom outing in late 1945. On Saturday, November 11, 1950, a few club members hiked the Hawaiian route to the clubhouse, where they joined others for an evening of square dancing. After spending the night there, the select few climbed back up the Waimānalo *pali* to greet the regular Sunday hikers coming up Kamilonui Valley.[36] That was the last time the HTMC ever hiked the entire Tom Tom Trail.

On December 27, 1951, the HTMC unveiled a new outing, Makapu'u–Tom Tom, starting from the lookout at the gap. The precarious route headed west along the Ko'olau crest and descended the windward section of the Tom Tom Trail to Waimanalo Superette and the clubhouse. A later description in the schedule confided:

After this hike you have a good conversation piece to keep your friends in awe, about how daring you are. Secretly, you don't have to go very far before the whole hike becomes impressive. You can reverse when you have become overwhelmed with your skill and bravery.[37]

On December 11, 1955, the club first hiked another Tom Tom variation, called Marconi-Kuliouou. Led by veteran Joseph (Joe) Neilson, the group walked up Kamilonui Valley to the Koʻolau summit. Instead of descending into Waimānalo, the hikers continued along the crest past Puʻu o Kona peak and came down a steep ridge on the far side of Kuliouou Valley.[38]

In the early 1960s, the Cold War and a new housing development intruded on the Tom Tom Trail network. The U.S. Army built a Nike-Hercules battery at Bellows Air Force Base in Waimānalo. The Nike-Hercules was a surface-to-air missile designed to defend Oʻahu against a Soviet bomber attack. To track the target and fire and guide the missile, the Hawaiʻi Army National Guard manned a huge radar station on the Koʻolau crest at the head of nearby Kamiloiki Valley.[39] Around the same time, builder Henry J. Kaiser began development of the Hawaiʻi Kai subdivision near Kuapā Pond. As part of the project, workers constructed a dirt road into Kamilonui Valley, closely following the route of the leeward portion of the Tom Tom Trail.[40]

During the 1960s, the HTMC continued to hold the Makapuʻu–Tom Tom hike, presumably skirting the radar station. The club hiked Marconi-Kuliouou once more in 1962 and then dropped it from the schedule, perhaps because of access problems or the boring dirt road. In 1964, the HTMC developed Kaupō Cliffs, a steep and scary route up Waimānalo *pali* east of Tom Tom. On February 29 of that year, daredevil Fred Duerst led a select group on a short but hair-raising hike up Kaupō Cliffs, along the Koʻolau crest, and down windward Tom Tom.[41] The schedule blurb for a later but similar outing reassured prospective participants, "Kaupo Cliffs is not a cliffhanger—not quite. Rumors that you have to hang on by your teeth are unfounded."[42]

The HTMC regularly scheduled the Makapuʻu–Tom Tom hike from the 1970s on. Groups sometimes walked through the radar station, decommissioned in 1970 and largely abandoned. Near the Nike site was a launch pad first used by hang gliding enthusiasts in the 1970s. On December 4, 1982, club member Silver Piliwale resurrected the Kaupō Cliffs hike last done in 1970. He led a small group up the Waimānalo *pali* and down Kamiloiki Ridge, rather than Kamilonui Valley, where the dirt road was choked with grass and koa haole trees.[43] On October 17, 1998, the HTMC, led by

Dayle Turner, once again climbed Kaupō Cliffs as part of a super hike from Waimānalo to Niu Valley.[44]

Kūmaipō

There was also a trail which went up [from Wai'anae] and then down to Makahauka, called Kumaipo.

—Na hunahuna no ka moolelo Hawaii
Nupepa Kuokoa, January 1, 1870

In the early 1800s and before, leeward Hawaiians used the Kūmaipō Trail, a local route linking the *mauka* (inland) portions of Wai'anae and Mākaha Valleys. The steep, sometimes difficult path crossed Kamaile'unu Ridge between the peaks of Ka'ala and Kawiwi. A branch trail climbed the ridge to the Ka'ala summit plateau and then descended to Waialua.[45]

On the Wai'anae side, the main trail split about two and a half miles into the valley. The well-traveled right fork led through a gap into Lualualei Valley and over Kolekole Pass. The left fork followed Kūmaipō Stream to the back of the valley and Kamile'unu Ridge. Along the way were *lo'i* (terraces) for growing *kalo* (taro) with water diverted from the stream in *'auwai* (ditches). Adjacent to the *lo'i* were dry land agricultural fields and several houses.[46]

On the Mākaha side, the main valley trail passed sweet potato fields, a small settlement, and Kāne'ākī *heiau*, a large religious site where human sacrifice took place. Farther *mauka* were sets of *lo'i* along Mākaha Stream.[47] Eventually, the path became the Kūmaipō Trail when it swung south to climb Kamaile'unu Ridge.

Along the ridge *makai* (seaward) of the trail crossing was a pointed peak called Kawiwi. According to Hawaiian legend, an old, unhappy women lived there near the summit. When she was hungry, she cried out to passing birds, who fed her. Her mountain home became known as Pali o Keawa'awa, cliff of bitterness. Later on, *kahuna* (priests) declared Kawiwi a *pu'uhonua* (place of refuge) during times of war.[48]

In the middle 1800s, Western diseases and cultural disruption decimated the Hawaiian families living in Wai'anae and Mākaha Valleys. Ranchers moved into both valleys, and their cattle destroyed much of the lowland native cover. In 1878, lawyer and judge Hermann Widemann founded the Waianae Sugar Company, which began growing cane and later coffee in Wai'anae Valley. Under manager Julius L. Richardson, the plantation soon built a mill to process the crop and a small railroad to transport it to the mill. To obtain water for irrigation, the company initially drilled wells at Kamaile near the foot of the ridge and later dug tunnels and ditches in the back of the valley. Some of the mountain water flowed from a reservoir down a sluiceway through a small hydroelectric station, which powered the water pumps and the lights in the manager's house. During the 1890s, the plantation reforested the denuded lower slopes *mauka* and fenced out the cattle to improve the watershed.[49] Plantation laborers must have used the Kūmaipō Trail to access some of the planting areas.

In 1914, Captain Cedric E. Scheerer of the U.S. Army Fourth Cavalry asked William T. H. Ellerbrock to lead a traverse of Ka'ala from the Wai'anae to the Schofield side. Ellerbrock readily agreed, as he had reached the summit plateau from Mākaha Valley several times while managing a coffee plantation there. One morning a hand-picked group assembled at Schofield Barracks and rode on horseback over Kolekole Pass bound for Mākaha. Beside Scheerer and Ellerbrock, the party included several members of the Hawaiian Trail and Mountain Club (HTMC) as well as some trooper trail clearers led by Sergeants Yates and Serstead. The men spent the night in rest houses near a dismantled coffee mill in Mākaha Valley.

Early the next morning the party proceeded up the valley on foot through abandoned coffee trees and blackberry bushes planted years before by Ellerbrock's plantation. The men then climbed to a saddle on Kamaile'unu Ridge, probably using Kūmaipō Trail. After clambering over several large boulders along the narrow ridge and scrambling up the steep, slippery flank of Ka'ala, the group reached the leeward side of the summit plateau at 9:30 a.m. There Scheerer set his compass, and the soldiers unsheathed their bolo knives and began hacking across the boggy, featureless plateau in dense mist. After four hours of soggy tramping and several course corrections, the group finally reached the summit and the trail to Schofield. After their bushwhacking, the men appreciated the fixed ropes and well-worn path on the way down. They even passed a dozen officers and their wives on the trail. At 4 p.m. the group arrived at Captain Scheerer's quarters and dispersed, the men to the barracks and the club members to Honolulu.[50]

In 1921, the HTMC scheduled two hikes in Mākaha Valley. For the second outing, fifty-one members and guests boarded the Haleiwa Limited on the morning of July 17. By prior arrangement the train made a special stop at Mākaha to let the hikers off. The large group walked through the cane fields of Waianae Sugar Company past the *heiau* to the back of the valley. Some attempted to scale the cliff there to reach Ka'ala but had to turn back just short of the Wai'anae summit ridge. The leader may not have known about the far easier Hawaiian route up Kūmaipō and along Kamaile'unu Ridge taken by Ellerbrock. After the strenuous hike the HTMC group built a campfire on the beach while waiting for the train to pick them up at 9 p.m.[51]

On July 15, 1928, house painter Edmund J. Meadows led thirty-three hikers on a new HTMC outing called Wai'anae Kai. Starting from the hydroelectric station, the group walked a dirt road through a eucalyptus forest to an abandoned coffee plantation. In addition to coffee trees were untended plantings of avocado, mango, fig, rose apple, and plumeria. Nearby was an abandoned mountain house, the retreat of the plantation owner.[52]

On a rainy March 5, 1929, territorial forester Charles S. Judd inspected the forest in the Kūmaipō watershed. Accompanying him were O'ahu assistant forester Glenn W. Russ, ranger at large Max F. Landgraf, and Wai'anae ranger Ralph E. Turner, Jr. After noting several sections that needed replanting, the four men briefly took shelter in a small cabin, where they found a Japanese ditchman from the plantation doing the same. When the rain let up, they continued along the Kūmaipō Trail to the hydroelectric station and inspected a nearby forest reserve gate that needed repair.[53]

On December 11, 1932, the Piko Club, with twenty-six members and guests, hiked from Wai'anae to Mākaha Valleys on the Kūmaipō Trail. Along that Sunday were Charles Judd and Major General Briant H. Wells, cofounders of the club, organized to foster cooperation between the U.S. Army and the Forestry Division. The group did not reach Kamaile'unu Ridge until 12:15 p.m. as the day was very hot with little wind. Judd later joked:

> My chief job was to haul up Mrs. Wells and hold her back on the downgrades because she had no hobs [hobnails] in her shoes. She goes in shorts and is a good sport.[54]

While escorting the general's wife, Judd had plenty of time to inspect the forest reserve, which was in good shape with no sign of wild pigs. He was particularly pleased with the progress of the silk oaks planted in the Kūmaipō watershed.[55]

On Sunday, January 8, 1933, fifty club members and guests traversed from Mākaha to Wai'anae Valleys using the Kūmaipō Trail. On the Wai'anae side, twenty-five others hiked up the trail from the hydroelectric power station. The two groups rendezvoused at Kūmaipō cabin for a steak lunch and the club's annual meeting. After coffee, President Wells called the roll, and each member present stood and answered "Piko!" The members then elected the club officers and officially welcomed a number of new Pikos who had completed the required three summit hikes.[56]

During the 1930s, the Kūmaipō Trail received periodic maintenance from the Forestry Division and the U.S. Army. In October 1932, Wai'anae ranger Ralph Turner had groomed the path in preparation for the December Piko Club hike. In 1934, the U.S. Army's Third Engineers cleared and improved the route on both sides of Kamile'unu Ridge. On the 1938 *Sales Builder* map, Kūmaipō was listed as trail number 27, Makaha, and trail number 29, Waianae-kai.[57]

In the 1950s, the HTMC returned to Mākaha Valley with a new outing called Pu'u Kawiwi, usually led by mountain man Richard H. (Dick) Davis. To reach the trailhead in Makaha Ranch, club groups drove past new houses that had replaced the sugar cane of the defunct Waianae Plantation. By the *heiau* some of the hikers fed a flock of loud and iridescent peacocks cared for by Aunty Jenny Wilson.[58] Soon after starting, the members and guests split into two groups.

> Those with no fear of high places and steep narrow ridges will chase wild goats up the right side of the valley to the summit of Puu Kawiwi. Not so hardy souls can stay in the valley and end up at a cool lunch spot by a running stream.[59]

In the early 1960s, the club scheduled three hikes from Mākaha to Ka'ala. Usually led by Charles Nakamura, the hikers climbed the Kūmaipō Trail and followed Kamaile'unu Ridge to the Ka'ala summit in the footsteps of Ellerbrock.[60]

In the early 1970s, the HTMC lost access to Mākaha, so the members turned their attention to Wai'anae Valley. The club scheduled a new-old hike called Wai'anae Kai for December 2, 1973. Led by Geraldine Cline, the group walked the long dirt road from the forest reserve boundary and started up the Kūmaipō Trail. Soon they branched off on a steep but more direct route to Kamile'unu Ridge just below Ka'ala.[61] On a rainy June 9, 1974, Davis led the first Wai'anae Ka'ala hike, which extended Cline's route to the top of Ka'ala.[62] In 1976, Richard (Dick) Booth turned the Wai'anae Kai hike into a meandering loop that followed the Kūmaipō Trail on the return portion.[63] As of 2010, the club has continued to schedule those two hikes regularly. In 2007, "Wai'anae" Steve Rohrmayr developed a third valley hike called Wai'anae Waterworks, which visited the site of the plantation owner's retreat and various abandoned ditches, pipelines, and tunnels.[64]

Dupont

Nani wale kuu ike ana
I ka lua ʻo Kaala
O ka nee mai a ka ohu
I ka hene wai o uka

Beautiful to my sight,
The top of Kaala.
The creeping of the mist,
The murmuring waters of the upland.

—from *Haleiwa Hotele, Nupepa Kuokoa,*
August 11, 1899

In the early 1800s and before, Hawaiians traveled between Waiʻanae and Waialua across the summit of Kaʻala, the highest peak on Oʻahu at 4,025 feet. From Waiʻanae Valley the route followed the Kūmaipō Trail to the top of Kamaileʻunu Ridge. From there,

> a branch trail which led up Mount Kaʻala and looked down on Waialua and Mokulēʻia could be used to go down to those level lands.[65]

Upon reaching the summit, a broad plateau, the traveler had to cross a montane bog through dwarfed native trees and shrubs. The way was always wet, and it was often cold and confusing because of the mist that frequently blanketed the area. The route down followed a long side ridge past Kaupakuhale hill. The initial descent was narrow and treacherous, but lower down the going was much easier. From the foot of the ridge, the tired traveler had only a short, level walk to Waialua. Undoubtedly, the traverse was never popular because of the steep climb and descent. However, the route was more direct than either the hot, rough walk around Kaʻena Point or the roundabout way over Kolekole Pass.

In 1833, missionary John S. Emerson and his wife Ursula were stationed at Waialua to spread the gospel among the Hawaiian people living in the district. That spring two Scotsmen, one working for the Hudson Bay Company, stayed with the Emersons while on a tour of the island. As part of her journal entry for April 5, Mrs. Emerson wrote,

I have had very little sleep during their visit as they wished to ascend Mount Kaala and to make geological and botanical observations and must have early breakfast and late suppers—but we were happy to show them hospitality.[66]

On November 3, 1840, the schooner *Flying-Fish* landed two botanists, William Rich and J. D. Brackenridge, at Kawailoa. The ship was part of the United States Exploring Expedition commanded by Charles Wilkes to explore and survey the southern Pacific Ocean. The botanists spent the night at the Emersons and attempted to climb Ka'ala the following day, with the reverend as their guide. The three men reached an elevation of about 2,500 feet before turning back because of heavy rain. The expedition chronicle recorded:

This [the ridge] was in some places not more than two feet wide, almost perpendicular, and extremely dangerous from its becoming slippery with the wet. The ridge became in a short time so narrow, that they were compelled to go astride and hitch themselves along.[67]

Ursula Sophia Newell Emerson

Reverend John S. Emerson

Missionaries and trail angels Ursula and John Emerson, from a miniature painted in 1831.

On the way down the botanists collected plant specimens, including native violets and mistletoe, and noted a forest of native wiliwili at the base of the mountain. Both the botanists and the two Scotsmen seven years earlier probably used the Hawaiian route through Kaupakuhale hill.

Sometime in 1895, accountant John Effinger started a six-day tramp around Oʻahu from Waikīkī. On the third day he reached Waialua, thoroughly fed up with walking on the beach. The next morning he decided to skip Kaʻena Point by cutting across Kaʻala. The locals were happy to point out "a dim and shadowy" trail, probably the Kaupakuhale route, leading to the summit plateau. After three hours of hard climbing, Effinger reached the top and then descended through Waiʻanae Valley to Mikilua Dairy near the coast. Two days later he completed the 131-mile circuit, which he highly recommended as an uplifting and inexpensive journey.[68]

Some morning in the early 1910s, a local guide, two Honolulu men, and two boys, Joseph B. Stickney and his friend Eldridge, mounted horses and rode into Makaleha Valley. Leaving the valley behind, the group zigzagged up a side ridge toward the Waiʻanae summit. At an elevation of about 2,500 feet, the trail became too rough for the horses, so the men pitched camp on a grassy knoll. The barefoot boys and perhaps the guide continued along the ridge to the Waiʻanae summit, where they turned southeast toward Kaʻala. After surmounting a steep, narrow section, the two plowed through scratchy uluhe ferns, which tore up their feet and legs. Finally, they reached the summit plateau and found a number of confusing trails. Seeing the clouds settling, the boys raced back to camp, where Stickney built a fire and cooked dinner for the group in a light rain. He later became the assistant editor for *Mid-Pacific Magazine*.[69]

In 1912, U.S. Army engineers reopened the Kaupakuhale route up Kaʻala as part of the first topographic survey of the island. In the same year, Frank de Ponte from Waialua was a civilian blacksmith at Schofield Barracks. He might have guided the soldiers up the old Hawaiian route, which was then named after him. Perhaps the blacksmith was related to another de Ponte, whose name would grace the trail eight years later.[70]

On July 4, 1920, members of Hui Alo Pali led by Thomas P. Cadle climbed Kaʻala on the well-worn trail from Schofield Barracks. The *hui* was an informal group of hard-core hikers within the Hawaiian Trail and Mountain Club (HTMC). At the summit survey monument, the men unsheathed hatchets and knives and began chopping a trail westward across the plateau toward the ridge leading down to Kaupakuhale hill. Cadle later described the results.

> At the best we were able to construct rather a crude path, continually changing its course in order to circumvent masses of trees and bushes through which it was almost impossible to force our way.[71]

By late afternoon the group was nowhere near its goal, and they scampered back down the Schofield side of the mountain before nightfall.

On July 24, Cadle and nine others resumed work on the plateau trail. This time the group was better prepared, with a compass and food and shelter to spend a night out. Despite periodic consulting of the compass, the men at one point wandered off the rim into a small gulch with a waterfall and in another area managed to walk in a complete circle. The group finally reached the top of the Kaupakahule route well after noon on the second day. While eating a late lunch there during a torrential downpour, they decided to name the new trail. One member suggested the leader's name, but Cadle demurred and put forth the name of an acquaintance, Mary De Ponte, a nurse at Queen's Hospital. So on July 25, the trail was christened De Ponte for the first, or perhaps the second, time.

Descending the De Ponte Trail proved surprisingly easy following the ordeal across the summit plateau. After plowing through thick and scratchy uluhe ferns, the men picked up faint signs of an old trail, which became more distinct lower down the mountain. Before reaching Kaupakahule hill, the group turned right onto a side ridge ending at a small reservoir in the sugar cane fields of the Waialua Agricultural Company.[72] On October 23 and 24, another HTMC group posted directional signs along the De Ponte Trail and searched for new species of land shells (native tree snails).[73]

On August 28, 1921, Cadle and four other Hui Alo Pali members attempted to hike from Ka'ena Point to Ka'ala along the Wai'anae summit ridge. After leaving the point, the group walked through the barren, eroded Kuaokalā Forest Reserve denuded by cattle and goats. Above Mākua Valley the men entered a lovely native 'ōhi'a forest that stretched for several miles. By late afternoon the five had reached the intersection with 'Ōhikilolo Ridge after some serious up-and-down climbing. Running out of time and water, the hikers turned back and quickly descended to Mokulē'ia.

The following Saturday, September 3, the same group started from Makaleha Valley and ascended a long side ridge until after dark, when they camped just short of the Wai'anae summit. Early the next morning the men reached the 'Ōhikilolo intersection and turned left toward Ka'ala. At first the going was easy, but soon the route became choked with trees, vines, and uluhe ferns. As they neared Ka'ala, heavy rain and clouds obscured the view and slowed their progress even more. Eventually, the wet and tired hikers reached the summit plateau about 1 p.m. and met another HTMC group led by Lawrence H. Daingerfield that had come up from Schofield Barracks. Both groups then descended the De Ponte Trail to end a long but satisfying day.[74]

HTMC first scheduled the De Ponte Trail as an official club outing for August 20, 1922. On August 8, Cadle, Professor John S. Donaghho, his wife, and three others checked out the route for the upcoming hike. They found that all but one of the signs erected in 1920 had been destroyed.[75] On the hike day thirty HTMC members and guests climbed Ka'ala from Schofield Barracks. Sixteen of them, including seven women, crossed the summit plateau and descended the De Ponte Trail to Waialua. The rest of the group retraced their steps back to Schofield.[76]

On August 30, territorial forester Charles S. Judd and six others, including several botanists, inspected the forest on the Mokulē'ia side of Ka'ala. The group left Makaleha Valley at 3:30 a.m., and four reached the summit at 1 p.m. Judd noted blackberry vines escaping from Mākaha Valley and invasive Hilo grass below 2,800 feet of elevation. He decided that no trail should be built along the Wai'anae summit leading to Ka'ala because of loss of forest cover, and possible landslides and spread of Hilo grass.[77]

For January 25, 1925, the HTMC scheduled the Ka'ala hike in reverse, up the DuPonte Trail and then down to Schofield Barracks. (Note the first of several spelling changes in the trail name.) That morning, forty-two hikers, including twenty-five from California, boarded an autobus for the drive to Waialua. Club members tried to persuade the *malihini* (newcomers) to start and finish at Schofield, but they would have none of it. Suffering from the heat and the steep climbing, the mainland hikers finally reached the summit at 3 p.m., two hours after the experienced club members. Part way up a determined *malihini* puffed, "I have climbed mountains all over California, but this is what I call a virgin trail."[78] The members within hearing chuckled at the remark because DuPonte was one of the more open trails on the island. On the way down, the mainland group became more adept at hiking local style; nevertheless, the tail end struggled out well after dark.

In October 1933, Charles Judd incorporated his 1922 hike into trail project number 5, Ka'ala-Mokulē'ia, to be built by the Civilian Conservation Corps (CCC).

> Beginning at the northwest corner of the Mt. Kaala plateau at 4,000 feet elevation the route runs north-westerly along the crest of the Waianae Range on government land through a wild pig and goat infested

region to a point on the Makaleha-Kealia trail (Project 6) at 2,050 feet elevation. Total length 16,400 feet [3.10 miles], 656 man days.[79]

CCC crews may have cleared a route along the Waiʻanae summit from the Mokulēʻia Trail to Kaʻala plateau, but no record or evidence exists that they actually constructed a graded trail.

From 1935 to 1940, the HTMC scheduled Kaʻala twice a year in January and July. The hike usually started and ended at Schofield Barracks, but some intrepid members invariably descended the DuPonte Trail. After the outing of February 9, 1941, the club had to stop holding the hike because of increased training activities at Schofield. On December 7, the Japanese attacked Pearl Harbor, bringing an end to all organized hiking for the duration of the war.

After a brief postwar revival, the HTMC permanently lost access to Kaʻala from the Schofield side in 1952. In October of that year, Edward Dresner, George Whisenand, and other club members checked out and reopened the Dupont Trail in preparation for a November 9 outing, called Kaupakuhale Ridge, probably to disguise the actual hike location.[80] After meeting at Iolani Palace that morning, the group carpooled to Waialua past Andrew Cox School and turned left on a dirt road by the T. Hata store. Leaving their cars in a cane field, the hikers climbed steadily through pasture and then steeply through native forest on a narrow ridge. Below the top they ran into thorny blackberry bushes and an army sign warning about artillery duds. At the summit plateau the group spotted an old weather-beaten sign marked "DePonte Trail" with an arrow pointing back toward Waialua. The hikers crossed the plateau through thick blackberry brambles to an abandoned cable car terminal and barracks left over from World War II. After admiring the magnificent view, the group reluctantly headed back across the flat summit.

> So we started down; mist and rain began to swirl around us, to hide any view, so at times we could barely see a section of the ridge in front of us. Trail was slippery; at times we slid on our fannies. Further down, as we traversed rocky ridges approaching the place where rope was hung, we took it easy; a slip could easily have meant serious injury or death. But eventually we all got down safely.[81]

On the afternoon of August 1, 1956, John L. H. Crosson, principal of Kailua Elementary School and director of hiking at nearby YMCA Camp Erdman, slipped on a narrow section of the Dupont Trail and fell three hundred feet to his death. He and a group of twelve boys from Palama

Settlement had reached the summit earlier and were heading down when the accident happened. Two of the boys quickly descended to a small store to call the Honolulu Fire Department for help. Another boy, Stanislaus "Tandy" Akina, led the rest of the group down to safety. The McCully Rescue Squad took two hours to retrieve the body using a basket stretcher and another six hours to carry Crosson out the next day.[82]

The HTMC regularly scheduled the Dupont hike during the 1950s and 1960s. In February 1959, Richard H. (Dick) Davis led a three-day Ka'ala campout. The group ascended the Keālia Trail from Dillingham airfield and spent the night in a forestry cabin on the Mokulē'ia Trail just below the Wai'anae summit. The next day the hikers climbed to the Ka'ala plateau, camped there, and descended the Dupont Trail on the third day.[83]

In February 1964, the Federal Aviation Agency (FAA) completed a seven-and-a-half-mile paved road from Makaleha Valley to the top of Ka'ala roughly following the route taken by Stickney in the 1910s and Judd in 1922. The new road provided access to a radar station operated by the FAA for civilian air traffic control and by the Hawai'i Air National Guard for military air defense. In a March 7 article titled "Kaala Hikers Will Ignore New Road," HTMC member and *Honolulu Star-Bulletin* reporter Harry Whitten wrote,

> There is a new road to the top of Kaala, but the Hawaiian Trail and Mountain Club continues going up the old hard way on the Dupont Trail.[84]

The next day an HTMC group led by Charles Smith did just that and found that the new road had obliterated the plateau section of the Dupont Trail.[85]

In 1981, the State Division of Forestry and Wildlife established the Mount Ka'ala Natural Area Reserve to protect native vegetation, insects, and tree snails on a portion of the summit area and windward slopes. In 1989, reserve workers and volunteers built a boardwalk from the radar access road across the plateau to the top of Kamaile'unu Ridge. The walkway channeled hikers and reduced their impact on the bog, while keeping their feet reasonably dry.

The HTMC has continued to regularly schedule the Dupont Trail as of 2010. The hike still starts by the small reservoir and ends at the radar station perimeter fence overlooking the rusting cable car supports. The old Hawaiian route from Wai'anae to Waialua remains intact as one of the finest and most difficult hikes on the island. Up the Kūmaipō Trail and Kamaile'unu Ridge to the summit, across the plateau on the boardwalk, and down the Dupont Trail is still an unforgettable walk.

Mākua-Kawaihāpai

> Makole iho hewa I Mākua.
> Red-eyed one goes by mistake to Mākua.
>
> —old Hawaiian saying

In the early 1800s and before, Hawaiians traveling between Mākua and Mokulē'ia took a shortcut across the Wai'anae Range to avoid the hot, rough hike around Ka'ena Point.

> At Makua there was a trail up the mountain and down to Kawaihapai, where it met the trail from Kaena. . . . A red-eyed person who went from Mokuleia intending to go to Makaha, mistakenly went by way of Kawaihapai, thereby arriving at Makua instead.[86]

On April 27, 1823, Levi Chamberlain arrived in Honolulu with the second company of the American mission to Hawai'i. He became business manager of the Honolulu station and also taught classes in reading and writing Hawaiian to teachers who needed to improve their skills. Chamberlain made three tours around O'ahu to inspect the local schools, review the progress of the students, and give advice to the teachers.[87]

On January 29, 1828, Chamberlain, accompanied by other Hawaiian teachers and church members and several attendants and porters left Honolulu on his last tour around the island. In nine days, the group walked past Makapu'u Point, up the windward coast, and along the north shore to Waialua, stopping at schools along the way. On the morning of February 7, the party hiked to Mokulē'ia, examined several schools there, and left for the leeward coast at 11 a.m. After proceeding two miles along the coastal trail, the teachers turned inland through a marshy area toward the Wai'anae mountains to avoid Ka'ena Point.

> After ascending several hundred feet we came to a small stream of clear water conducted by spouts & gutters to the plain below affording sufficient moisture for a number of taro patches. I was told that the water never fails;–and the district into which it passes is Kawaihapai (Water lifted up).[88]

Chamberlain and his group continued to climb steadily on the rough trail along Kawaihāpai Stream. Just below the Waiʻanae crest the men stopped for a break near an abandoned cabin once used by ʻiliahi (sandalwood) cutters. The teachers admired the view, and the attendants enjoyed a smoke while waiting for the porters to bring up the baggage. At 1:30 p.m. the group reached the top and began to descend into Mākua (parents) Valley.

> Having descended the steepest part of the mountain, we came to a deep gutter worn out by the rains. Here we found cool, pure water, and we sat down by a little stream to slake our thirst & partake of some refreshment.[89]

After the late lunch the teachers descended gradually along the Kahanahāiki fork of Mākua Stream through grass, shrubs, and sweet potato patches as they neared the small settlement by the shore. There they examined another school at 3 p.m. and quickly left for Mākaha. On February 11, the group finally returned to Honolulu, having encircled the island in fourteen days.

In the 1920s, the old Hawaiian route is shown on U.S. Army map as the Kahanahāiki-Mokulēʻia Trail. The penciled-in route initially ascends the right side of Kawaihāpai Stream and crosses over to the left side halfway to the Waiʻanae crest. The trail then descends into the Kahanahāiki portion of Mākua Valley and follows the intermittent stream to the coast, much as described by Chamberlain almost a hundred years before.[90]

On January 22, 1922, the Hawaiian Trail and Mountain Club (HTMC) scheduled a new hike in the Kawaihāpai region, which was seldom visited by the club. That morning the group boarded the Haleiwa Limited, leaving at 8:36 a.m. from the Oʻahu railway station at Aʻala. The hikers left the train at Kawaihāpai station and probably climbed to the Waiʻanae summit. The group returned to Honolulu about 10 p.m. after a long but rewarding day.

The HTMC regularly hiked Kawaihāpai and several variations during the late 1920s and early 1930s. The write-up in the schedule for the February 16, 1930, outing mentioned "a gradual ascent in a deep and terraced gulch to the ridge summit overlooking Makua Valley."[91] On March 5, 1933, Myrtle King, a public school teacher in Waialua, led the Kawaihāpai-Mokulēʻia hike, which attracted twenty-two members and guests. The group climbed along Kawaihāpai Stream, turned southeast along the Waiʻanae crest, and then descended to Mokulēʻia.[92] On March 4 of the following year, the HTMC scheduled the Kawaihāpai–Kaʻena Point outing. This time the group followed the summit ridge down to Kaʻena Point and returned along the coast. The hike blurb stated, "This is a good trip even if you have to count the [railroad] ties returning to the cars."[93]

In late 1934, the Civilian Conservation Corps (CCC) completed two nearby graded trails to the Wai'anae summit. Keālia switchbacked up a steep *pali* (cliff) about a mile west of Kawaihāpai Stream. The Mokulē'ia Trail climbed to the crest about two and a half miles east of the stream and then connected with Keālia. Shortly afterward the HTMC dropped Kawaihāpai from the schedule and began hiking the two new CCC trails. With little use, the Kawaihāpai route gradually deteriorated and became overgrown.

On the Mākua side, the Territorial Forestry Division had constructed the Piko Trail, an alternate route to the Wai'anae summit, in May 1932. During World War II the army took over the valley and has used it as a firing range ever since. In 1977, Paul Rosendahl included the Mākua section of the Hawaiian route in his archaeological report on the valley for the army. He designated the Mākua Mountain Trail as site 05-80-03-9518 but found no evidence of its existence.[94] In a 1995 study, archaeologist Francis Eble and others presumed that the trail had been destroyed.[95]

Kama'āina and Club Trails
(1842–1922)

....

> [Alexander Hume Ford] . . . a fast walking, fast talking, fast thinking, fast doing chap with an eternal urge to improve the world and everybody in his vicinity.
>
> —*Honolulu Star-Bulletin,* April 13, 1943

Early Hawaiian and Kama'āina
Routes around Mānoa

Near old Honolulu and *mauka* (inland) of Waikīkī lies Mānoa, a broad and verdant valley backed by the Ko'olau Range. In the 1700s, the valley supported a large population of Hawaiians growing *kalo* (taro), sweet potatoes, bananas, and sugar cane.[1] The main route into the valley climbed past Pu'u o Mānoa (Rocky Hill) and then branched into two paths below a small knoll, known as Pu'u Pueo.[2] Native bird catchers, wood cutters, and plant gatherers developed an extensive trail network in *mauka* Mānoa, in the neighboring valleys of Pauoa and Pālolo, and in their surrounding heights. Routes led to the peaks of Pu'u 'Ōhi'a, Kōnāhuanui, and Awaawaloa and to a volcanic crater known as Ka'au.[3] During the first half of the 1800s, however, Western diseases decimated the Hawaiian families living in Mānoa (vast) Valley. Their mountain trails gradually fell into disuse and disrepair.

In 1841, Reverend Hiram Bingham donated a large tract of land in lower Mānoa for a school to educate missionary children. Oahu College (later Punahou School) held its first classes the next year and gradually expanded its enrollment to include nonmissionary children from prominent families. In those early years the students often went on weekend field trips to explore the valley and collect ferns and land shells (native tree snails). One Saturday afternoon a group of Punahou boys attempted to climb nearby Puʻu ʻŌhiʻa (ʻōhiʻa tree hill). With permission from their teacher, they scrambled to the top of ʻUalakaʻa hill and saw, to their dismay, a hidden valley separating them from their goal. Frustrated and running out of daylight, they wisely turned back and descended to campus. One of the hikers, William D. Alexander, later decided to name the peak Tantalus, after the perpetually thirsty and frustrated god in his Greek studies. The Punahou boys then proceeded to rename other peaks and hills around Mānoa. ʻUalakaʻa (rolling sweet potato) became Round Top, Puʻu Kākea (Mānoa storm wind) became Sugarloaf, and Awaawaloa (long valley) became Mount Olympus.[4] The massive mountain with twin summits at the back of the valley retained its original Hawaiian name, Kōnāhuanui (large fat testicles) probably because the students found it apt and amusing.

Punahou graduates, other leading citizens, and even early tourists soon began hiking the old Hawaiian routes in and around Mānoa. By 1873, *kamaʻāina* (island-born) hikers, such as Lorrin A. Thurston, had climbed Kōnāhuanui and Mount Olympus, and looked into Kaʻau Crater in Pālolo Valley.[5] For tourists, the *Hawaiian Guide* of 1875 recommended ascending Round Top and Tantalus and visiting the valleys of Mānoa, Nuʻuanu, Pauoa, and Pālolo.[6] In 1888, *Paradise of the Pacific* magazine advised:

> From the rear veranda of the Royal Hawaiian Hotel fine views may be had of deep, shady valleys in the mountain range behind Honolulu, and into any of these one may ride on horseback in an hour or so, and when at the end of the bridle path, may penetrate the dense woods on foot and enjoy most beautiful views of rocky glens, sparkling waterfalls and cool green grottoes, all embowered in a wealth of tropical foliage.[7]

By the late 1800s, lower Mānoa was fast becoming a prime residential area for Oʻahu's prominent families. Punahou Street near the school was lined with stately mansions, one of which was Arcadia, the two-story colonial home of Walter F. Frear, Punahou graduate, First Circuit Court judge, and avid hiker. Financier William R. Castle and his brother George erected an imposing manor house, known as Puʻuhonua, on the slope below Round Top. In 1899, Punahou School developed a large tract behind the campus, called College Hills, which attracted more wealthy *kamaʻāina* to the valley. Castle, Thurston, and Frear also built summer mountain cottages along the Tantalus carriage road completed in 1902.[8]

In September 1901, Honolulu Rapid Transit and Land Company, Ltd. began operating electric streetcars in Mānoa Valley. From Wilder Avenue the line climbed Punahou Street past the school and Rocky Hill and then followed Mānoa Road and Oʻahu Avenue through the College Hills subdivision to present-day Cooper Road. The carline opened up the valley to further development and hiking. For five cents, most Honolulu residents could now comfortably travel to Mānoa for a day's outing in the mountains. At the end of the line a steep trail climbed past Puʻuhonua to Round Top and Tantalus. Dirt roads and trails led to Mānoa Falls, Puʻu Pia, and even Mount Olympus at the back of the valley. Other streetcar lines also encouraged hiking in adjacent areas. The Nuʻuanu line provided access to Nuʻuanu Valley, the Emma Street line to Pauoa Valley and Tantalus, and the Kaimukī carline to Pālolo Valley.[9]

In 1907, President Theodore Roosevelt appointed Judge Frear governor of the Territory of Hawaiʻi. In 1907, Castle was tending to his various legal and business interests, and Thurston was publishing the *Pacific Commercial Advertiser*. In May 1907, Alexander Hume Ford, world traveler and magazine writer, arrived in Honolulu on a congressional fact-finding tour.[10] He had planned to stay for several weeks, but he stayed for the rest of his life and founded Oʻahu's first hiking club.

Hawaiian Trail and Mountain Club

Alexander Hume Ford was an energetic, even aggressive promoter with a restless, inquiring mind and an amiable disposition. His biographer, Valerie Noble, wrote,

> Everywhere welcome, he is a cyclone of a man who sweeps you away with him. He is not one to promise to do things; he just does them.[11]

Ford preferred to start up enterprises and then allow others to run them. He felt most comfortable working behind the scenes, rarely turning attention to himself or taking credit for his ideas.[12]

On his arrival in Honolulu, Ford decided to revive the ancient Hawaiian sport of surfing and turn it into a popular pastime. He learned to ride the waves at Waikīkī and even gave visiting writer Jack London and his wife a surfing lesson there. Ford also decided to foster better communication and cooperation among the far-flung Pacific nations. To that end, he traveled to Australia, New Zealand, and New Hebrides at his own expense in the summer of 1907. He carried an official letter of introduction from

Alexander Hume Ford, founder of the Hawaiian Trail and Mountain Club, 1910. (Hawai'i State Archives)

Governor Frear, who was intrigued by his idea for a pan-Pacific convention. While in New Zealand, Ford visited the fjords of the South Island and even tramped a portion of the recently established Milford Track to Sutherland Falls and Mackinnon Pass. He was impressed by the country's network of hiking trails and overnight huts. When he returned to Hawai'i, however, Ford concentrated his efforts on surfing and canoeing. On May 1, 1908, he founded the Outrigger Club to preserve and promote those two sports.[13]

In late 1907, Governor Frear appointed Ford as corresponding secretary of the Territorial Transportation Committee, formed to advance Hawai'i's interests abroad. A year later Ford left on an extended trip to the mainland to promote Hawai'i as a commercial and tourist destination. On his return he turned his attention from surfing and transportation to hiking and camping. He decided to establish a club to develop a trail and hut network similar to the one he had seen in New Zealand.[14]

The Hawaiian Trail and Mountain Club (HTMC) was founded on April 5, 1910, at the Honolulu Chamber of Commerce. Financier William R. Castle became president, and publisher Lorrin A. Thurston vice president. Although clearly the driving force behind the new club, Ford took the lesser position of corresponding secretary, as was his custom.[15]

The first HTMC bulletin, dated July 1910, listed 151 charter members, 111 men and 40 women and children. The mostly *haole* (white) membership represented a good cross section of the island's business and government elite. In addition to Castle and Thurston were Governor Frear and Ralph S. Hosmer, superintendent of forestry. Included for good measure were Prince Jonah K. Kalanianaole, delegate to congress, and several prosperous Chinese and Japanese merchants. Each adult charter member paid a hefty $5 initiation fee and $5 annual dues. New members were welcome at the same rates, but had to be approved by the Board of Directors.[16]

At the April 5 organization meeting, the charter members adopted a constitution that defined the object of the club.

> To encourage intimate acquaintance with outdoor Hawaii:
> 1) By promoting knowledge of and interest in objects of natural interest in the Territory and the ways and means of getting there;
> 2) By the construction and maintenance of trails and roads leading to the same and of rest houses incidental thereto;
> 3) Through promoting interest in travel, more particularly by foot, through the mountains of Hawaii;
> 4) Through enlisting the cooperation of the people and the Government in preserving the forests and other natural features of the Hawaiian mountains, and generally by publication and otherwise

to convey information concerning the object of the Club, both to residents of the Territory and to persons residing abroad;
5) By acting in cooperation with other Clubs or Associations having similar objects, as well as with Government and other Tourist Bureaus, and to exchange privileges therewith.[17]

Ford obviously played a key role in drafting the above statement, with its emphasis on the promotion of the sport and cooperation with government, tourist bureaus, and other hiking clubs. In fact, delegates from the Sierra Club in California and the Appalachian Mountain Club in New England attended the organization meeting to welcome the new club and to highlight their common purpose.

The HTMC immediately started to plan a network of trails and rest houses in the Koʻolau Range *mauka* of Honolulu. Since most of the uppercrust members had no inclination to perform manual labor, the club needed to hire workers to complete the various projects. The initiation fees and annual dues, however, were insufficient to finance such an ambitious undertaking. Fortunately, Ford persuaded Castle and other members to pay for some of the projects out of their own pockets by loaning or hiring laborers to build the trails. In addition, other *kamaʻāina* opened up existing trails and rest houses on their lands to club members for hiking and overnight stays. In return, the HTMC frequently named a new trail after its benefactor and agreed to maintain it.[18]

In May 1910, the HTMC began its first construction project, a nine-and-a-half-mile graded trail from Punchbowl to Kaʻau Craters. Financed by club president Castle, the route climbed the side of Pauoa Valley below Tantalus and contoured around the back of Mānoa Valley to Mount Olympus and beyond. The Castle-Olympus Trail, as it was called, linked the old Hawaiian routes to Kōnāhuanui, Awaawaloa (Olympus), and Kaʻau Crater. On July 23, the fledgling club held it first official hike, climbing over Tantalus from Makiki and returning along the Pauoa section of the new trail.[19]

At Ford's urging, two other *kamaʻāina* financed construction of routes connecting to the Castle-Olympus Trail. Anna Rice Cooke sponsored the Cooke Trail, which climbed the side of Nuʻuanu Valley from the reservoir to an overlook along the Castle-Olympus Trail. First Circuit Court judge Henry E. Cooper sponsored the Cooper Trail, linking Woodlawn in Mānoa Valley with the Hawaiian route to Mount Olympus and the Castle-Olympus Trail.[20]

Other *kamaʻāina* donated the use of existing trails and rest houses to the HTMC. James B. Castle, brother of the club president, allowed members to hike his Punaluʻu trail, originally built to investigate water sources for his sugar plantations. Renamed the Castle Trail, the magnificent route featured scenic switchbacks and a rest house by Kaluanui Stream. Others opened up trails and huts on Tantalus and in Kalihi and Nuʻuanu Valleys.[21]

In 1911, the HTMC built the Mānoa Cliff Trail, again using laborers loaned by club president Castle. The route contoured around the Mānoa side of Tantalus to Pauoa Flats and a junction with the Castle-Olympus Trail. The HTMC also partnered with Kaimuki Land Company, a developer of subdivisions in and around Pālolo Valley. The club and the company opened up routes to Kaʻau Crater and up nearby Mauʻumae Ridge toward Lanipō peak. At a meeting on July 11, the board of directors reviewed a preliminary trail map and decided to produce a comprehensive map and guide to the trails around Honolulu.[22]

The trails and rest houses constructed or improved by the HTMC and its benefactors were highly popular with the hiking public. Most of the trail users, however, were not club members and thus did not pay dues. In view of that, HTMC president Castle requested $5,000 from the City and County of Honolulu to complete an expanded trail network from Moanalua to Niu Valleys. In his letter of September 7, Castle concluded:

> The great increase in the use of the trails already available makes it apparent that the construction of mountain trails is legitimately the function of your Honorable body, as a public convenience and means of recreation for residents and tourists alike, hence this request.[23]

The response from the city Board of Supervisors was probably negative as the club never enlarged its initial trail system beyond Nuʻuanu, Mānoa, and Pālolo Valleys.

In addition to lack of funds, the HTMC faced increased restrictions from the Territorial Division of Forestry. In a letter dated September 5, 1912, Superintendent Hosmer cautioned the club not to build any new trails on government forest land without his permission. Concerning the HTMC trail network, he wrote that

> there have occurred landslips that not only render the trails dangerous but are also a menace to the welfare of the forest.[24]

In September 1913, Castle's workers repaired the landslides on the Cooke and Castle-Olympus Trails at Hosmer's request. One month later the *mauka* portion of Nuʻuanu, Mānoa, and Pālolo Valleys became part of the Honolulu Watershed Reserve to protect the city's water supply.

In many respects, the year 1915 was the heyday of early club hiking on Oʻahu. Walter Frear, the hiking former governor, became the second

HTMC president. The club published its long-awaited trail map, compiled by member John S. Donaghho, a professor at Hawaii College. Available for twenty-five cents, the three-color contour map showed all the carlines, trails, and "feasible, but dangerous" routes in back of Honolulu.[25] Ford wrote a lengthy article in his *Mid-Pacific Magazine* listing and describing club hikes.[26] Also published in 1915 was *The Aloha Guide* by Ferdinand J. H. Schnack. That comprehensive guidebook promoted the HTMC and provided descriptions of trails from Moanalua to Pālolo Valleys. The author mentioned signposts placed by the club at key junctions, such as Pauoa Flats, Mount Olympus, and Ka'au Crater.[27]

In 1916, the HTMC's organizers turned their attention to World War I and other world events with the potential to affect Hawai'i. That year saw a gradual decline in the club's trail maintenance, hiking, and social activities. By 1918 the HTMC existed on paper only with no active members and no planned events.[28]

Hawaiian Trail and Mountain Club officers, 1921. From the left, Hike Committee chairman Lawrence Daingerfield, Thomas McGuire; front from the right, John Bisho, Thomas Cadle, President E. Herrick Brown; in back, Evelyn Breckons, Alexander Ford. (Photo by R. J. Baker, HTMC Archives)

In early 1919, Ford and others decided to revive the dormant hiking club. Hearing about the "proposed resuscitation," superintendent of forestry Charles S. Judd immediately wrote Ford reminding him of the current restrictions on trail building and maintenance in the Honolulu Watershed Reserve. In a letter dated March 31, Ford requested permission to repair the Mānoa Cliff Trail and reopen a route from the end of the Mānoa carline past Frear's mountain house to the start of the cliff trail. Judd approved both requests, but turned down two other trail construction projects that Ford had in mind.[29]

The Hawaiian Trail and Mountain Club was reactivated at a meeting on May 9. Those present chose nine directors, including Ford, as provided in the original constitution. At a subsequent meeting six days later, John A. Balch, treasurer of Mutual Telephone Company, became club president and weatherman Lawrence H. Daingerfield became secretary. The board lowered the annual dues to $2.50 to quickly boost membership. By August the club had sixty members, including original members Ford, Thurston, Donaghho, and pathfinder Gilbert Brown. Many of the new members were from the middle class rather than the upper crust.[30]

In July 1919, HTMC resumed hiking and maintaining the trail network in Mānoa and Pālolo Valleys. For a time the club hired a lone laborer to repair some of the routes, but even his low wages proved too expensive. Eventually the club members began to clear the trails themselves and post directional signs at key junctions. As the only experienced guide, Brown led all the early outings until the new members became familiar with the routes. Secretary Daingerfield wrote,

> The Official Guide of the Club at the present time is Gilbert Brown. Weekends are made happy for the members by his cheerful guidance and never tiring energy as he leads the way along the mountain paths.[31]

In 1922, Charles Judd banned recreational hiking in the *mauka* portion of Mānoa and Pālolo Valleys, divorcing the club from much of its original trail network.[32] However, the HTMC had already started to range farther afield as the membership gained experience. Club explorers pioneered some new mountain routes and rediscovered others used previously by Hawaiians, *kama'āina*, hunters, surveyors, and soldiers. In addition, transportation around the island improved; instead of taking the streetcar, hiking groups rode the train, chartered an autobus, or even drove private automobiles to far-flung trailheads.

HTMC group ready to drive to the trailhead, circa 1924. Leaning against the autobus, John Bisho. (Photo by R. J. Baker, courtesy of Joyce Oka)

Since the 1920s, the HTMC has continued to schedule hikes most weekends, except for a three-year period during World War II. In 2010, its centennial, the club had almost five hundred members and conducted outings every Sunday and alternate Saturdays. The HTMC also maintains more than eighty trails on O'ahu in conjunction with Na Ala Hele, the state trail program.

....
Castle-Olympus

The Trail and Mountain Club, thanks to the generosity of its president, William R. Castle, has succeeded within the last year in making the highest mountain peaks and the entire range behind Honolulu easily accessible to anyone who makes the slightest pretensions to being a walker.

—*The Sunday Advertiser,* September 10, 1911

In May 1910, Japanese laborers began building a graded trail leading into the rugged Koʻolau mountains *mauka* (inland) of Honolulu. Starting from Tantalus Road behind Punchbowl, the planned route climbed gradually along the east side of Pauoa Valley to the flats and an overlook of Nuʻuanu Valley. The trail would then contour around the Nuʻuanu side of Kaumuhonu hill and link up with an old Hawaiian trail to the summit of Kōnāhuanui, the highest peak in the Koʻolau Range. Sponsoring this four-mile project was financier William R. Castle.[33]

Son of missionary parents, Castle was an influential lawyer, businessman, and politician. In 1876, he became attorney general in King Kalakaua's cabinet and served in the legislature from 1886 to 1899, the last two years as president. Castle was a staunch supporter of the revolution that ended the monarchy in 1893. With Benjamin F. Dillingham, he started the Oahu Land and Railway Company in 1898 and was president until 1903. Castle also helped finance the Ewa Plantation Company and the Honolulu Rapid Transit and Land Company, and he established the Honolulu Gas Company. In 1910, he became the first president of the Hawaiian Trail and Mountain Club (HTMC) and lent some of his workers to the club for trail building.[34]

By July, Castle's laborers finished the lower section from Punchbowl to Pauoa Flats. On July 23, the HTMC hiked the new "William Castle (Pauoa)" Trail as part of its first official outing. Led by charter member and attorney Charles H. Dickey, the group climbed over Tantalus from Makiki to Pauoa Flats and then returned along the new trail.[35]

During the construction of the Castle Trail, the financier and his wife left the islands on a world tour. In their absence, HTMC founder Alexander H. Ford and other members kept the project moving and even proposed an ambitious five-and-a-half-mile extension. From the ridge leading to Kōnāhuanui, the trail would continue around the back of Mānoa Valley to the Koʻolau summit and Mount Olympus. From that peak the route then switchbacked down to the rim of Kaʻau Crater to join an existing trail up from Pālolo Valley. William E. Rowell, the builder of the Castle Trail in Punaluʻu Valley, planned the extension, and HTMC member John S. Donaghho, a professor at nearby Hawaii College, helped him survey the new route, set the grade stakes, and eventually map the new trail. Castle's workers cleared and dug the path in and out of the rugged gulches in the back of Mānoa Valley. When Castle returned from overseas, he found a trail twice as long as planned, built entirely at his expense. He didn't seem to mind the cost overrun, however, even though the workers were supposed to have been renovating Kaliula, his mountain house overlooking the trail on Tantalus.[36]

Two other wealthy *kama'āina* (island-born) sponsored connecting routes to the Castle Trail. Anna Rice Cooke financed the construction of a graded path that ascended the east side of Nu'uanu Valley. The Cooke Trail started at the reservoir dam near the Cooke's country villa at Luakaha and intersected the Castle Trail at the Nu'uanu overlook. An avid art collector and patron, Mrs. Cooke later founded the Honolulu Academy of Arts. In Mānoa Valley, Judge Henry E. Cooper financed the building of a path linking Woodlawn with an old Hawaiian ridge route to Mount Olympus and the Castle Trail.[37]

Within the newly formed HTMC was a small, select group of young and adventurous hikers called the Ukulele (leaping fleas) Patrol. On June 18, 1911, the patrol planned to initiate a new member on a dangerous traverse of the Ko'olau Range. That morning pathfinder Gilbert Brown, ukulele Kenneth Reidford, victim Walter Cowes, and a visiting Swiss Army lieutenant climbed out of Mānoa Valley past the mountain home of Governor Walter F. Frear. The group picked up the Castle Trail at Pauoa Flats and ascended Kōnāhuanui through dense clouds and heavy rain. At the top they wisely decided not to attempt a precipitous windward spur, now known as Piliwale ridge. Instead the foursome backtracked to the Castle Trail and followed it over to Mount Olympus. They then descended to Woodlawn at the back of Mānoa Valley on the new Cooper Trail. The less ambitious route taken did not qualify Cowes as a Ukulele Patrol member.[38]

Sometime during the week of September 3, HTMC officers inspected the Castle Trail and formally accepted responsibility for its maintenance. Also on the trail that day were officials from the Amateur Athletic Union (AAU) and the Public Service Association, and numerous hikers investigating the new route. The official party took the Nu'uanu streetcar to its end and walked three miles up the valley to the reservoir. From the dam the group climbed the Cooke Trail past conspicuous native *Lobelia* plants to the Nu'uanu overlook. They briefly discussed building a rest house near there and then hiked the Castle Trail to Ka'au Crater and came out Pālolo Valley. The HTMC officers noted sections where additional work was required, primarily because of landslides. The AAU officials looked over the route as a possible venue for an annual mountain hiking race from the terminus of the Nu'uanu carline to the end of the Kaimukī carline.[39]

Castle's workers and HTMC members maintained the trail periodically over the next several years. They also built two rest houses, one with a water tank just below the Nu'uanu overlook and the other along the rim of Ka'au Crater. In September 1913, work parties began extensive repairs on the Cooke and Castle Trails. They cleared vegetation, dug out numerous landslides, and improved the drainage in the Mānoa Valley section. The Territorial Forestry Division under superintendent Ralph S. Hosmer closely monitored their progress as the trail now passed through the new Honolulu Watershed Reserve, established on October 13 to protect the city's water source.[40]

On October 11, 1918, Charles S. Judd, superintendent of forestry, and David T. Fullaway, an entomologist with the U.S. Agriculture Experiment Station, inspected the Castle Trail from Pauoa Flats to Mount Olympus. They found the sometimes narrow route in poor condition, primarily because of the near demise of the HTMC during World War I. The two men counted forty-six landslides, 30 percent of which they believed had been caused by trail construction. None of the slides were new, however, and most were overgrown with vegetation. Nevertheless, Judd decided to forbid further repairs on the Castle Trail and to prohibit new trail construction in the watershed reserve.[41]

On a cloudy day during the summer of 1921, Harold H. Yost, assistant secretary of the Hawaii Tourist Bureau, and a friend took the carline from Waikiki to Mānoa Valley and then climbed to Pauoa Flats following a little-used route. There they headed for Olympus on the "old," overgrown Castle Trail. The two scrambled over landslides, slipped in mud holes, and plowed through heavy patches of Hilo grass and scratchy uluhe ferns. An exhilarated Yost didn't seem to mind the conditions, later noting, "Who would care a whoop for a trail that was as easy to follow as a city sidewalk, anyhow?"[42] After slogging around the Mānoa gulches, they reached a notch in the Koʻolau summit just as the clouds lifted.

> On either side of the "window" through which we gazed the verdure-clad perpendicular cliffs stretched away for miles in a great semi-circle, forming an immense amphitheater, its roof the low-hanging clouds which mantled the mountain peaks, its stage lighted by the sun in unbelievable colors.[43]

Yost and his companion continued past other, less spectacular notches to Olympus, where they took the ridge route *makai* (seaward) down to Woodlawn. The trail petered out above a grassy slope, so the two slid the rest of the way down on *kī* (ti) leaves. They caught the Mānoa carline back home to Waikīkī and a soothing swim in the surf.

On November 4, 1921, Judd, assistant superintendent Charles J. Kraebel, and Harold L. Lyon of the Hawaiian Sugar Planters Association Experimental Station hiked the Castle Trail to investigate the spread of Hilo grass, an invasive species threatening the native forest. The three found an abundance of the alien grass along the route from Pauoa Flats to Ka'au Crater. All concluded that hikers were responsible for spreading the grass and that the Castle Trail should be closed to the public.[44]

On February 5, 1922, Judd met with the Board of Agriculture and Forestry to recommend the creation of a special zone within the Honolulu Watershed Reserve. The new Palolo-Manoa Drainage Reservation would be off-limits to hikers and livestock to protect the native vegetation and thus safeguard the city's water supply. The officers and members of the HTMC were outraged, as the proposed regulation, known as Rule V, effectively closed the Castle Trail from Nu'uanu overlook to Ka'au Crater.

As a result of the uproar, Judd scheduled a meeting at 2 p.m. on February 14 to hear the club's objections. Speaking against Rule V that afternoon were Professor Donaghho, HTMC president Thomas P. Cadle and secretary Lawrence H. Daingerfield, Herbert F. Bergman, botany professor at the University of Hawai'i, and Lorrin A. Thurston, *Honolulu Advertiser* publisher, former club vice president, and longtime *kama'āina* hiker. Most argued that the Hilo grass in the proposed reservation predated the Castle Trail and that the landslides caused by its construction were minor and quickly covered with native vegetation. To make their case, Donaghho and Daingerfield presented eighteen photographs taken on the Castle Trail the previous Sunday in the company of William R. Castle himself. Over the next several weeks the *Honolulu Advertiser* printed each set of remarks under the headline "A Plea for Mountain Trails."

Judd prevailed, however, despite the protests, and governor Wallace R. Farrington approved the establishment of the Palolo-Manoa Drainage Reservation on May 13.[45]

On May 26, Judd, Kraebel, and three forestry laborers posted three *kapu* (no trespassing) signs above the Nu'uanu overlook and erected a wooden barricade blocking the Castle Trail where it contoured around Kaumuhonu hill. Over the next few weeks workers built barbed-wire fences across the ridge route to Mount Olympus and the middle ridge and valley routes to Ka'au Crater, and they posted three signs in Mānoa Valley. On the weekends forestry personnel, including Judd, patrolled the upper Castle Trail and its connectors to enforce the ruling.[46]

Roughly two months earlier, weatherman Daingerfield, forest ranger Thomas R. L. McGuire, and ten others attempted a final climb of Kōnāhuanui before Rule V took effect. Skirting Punchbowl, the hikers climbed the Castle Trail past the mountain houses of Castle and Thurston to the Nu'uanu lookout, where they had lunch. Despite low-hanging clouds, most of the group continued around Kaumuhonu hill and then took the steep, narrow ridge trail toward the Ko'olau summit.

Toiling upward, the eight of us who had persisted, including the two ladies, soon found ourselves in that weird transition zone in the billowy border of the flying cumuli.... Ghostly knolls constantly rose before us, each promising to be the summit.... Friendly sedges rendered virile aid to our outstretched hands as we drew our bodies upward on the giant stairway.[47]

The bedraggled group finally reached the first and then the second summit of Kōnāhuanui, still shrouded in mist. All elected to descend to Nuʻuanu Pali rather than go back the way they had come. The steep descent on slippery soil and rock was exceedingly treacherous. A sixty-foot rock face almost defeated the group, but they finally worked around it to reach the safety of the Pali Lookout.

For February 3, 1924, the HTMC scheduled a work day on the lower, open section of the Castle Trail. That morning, thirty-five hikers met at the end of the Emma Street carline and cleared the route from Punchbowl to Pauoa Flats. On December 28, the club held a second trail clearing, which attracted twenty hikers. The HTMC also scheduled regular hikes along the lower Castle Trail in 1926 and 1928.[48]

In 1935, the Honolulu Unit of the Civilian Conservation Corps (CCC) regraded the Kalāwahine section of the Castle Trail below Tantalus. The project included a regrading of the Mānoa Cliff Trail and the construction of a connector between the two trails. The CCC crew also dammed Kalāwahine Spring and ran a pipe two hundred feet down to the trail to provide water for thirsty hikers.[49]

In the late 1940s, HTMC members Richard (Dick) Booth and Joseph (Joe) Neilson went up Saint Louis Heights and climbed the ridge trail to Olympus. Near its summit the men took the closed Castle Trail around the back of Mānoa Valley. The two saw no *kapu* signs along the route, which was in decent condition. (Perhaps the CCC or the Territorial Forestry Division had done some maintenance on the closed section over the years.) Approaching the Nuʻuanu overlook, Booth and Neilson were startled to see ranger McGuire emerging from the bushes along the trail. The ranger scolded both hikers for trespassing, reportedly saying "Joe, you should know better." The two men expected to hear further from the Forestry Division, but they never did. McGuire may have spotted the two wayward hikers with binoculars from Mānoa Valley and rushed up to the overlook to waylay them.[50]

Over the next fifty years, the Castle Trail received little use or maintenance. Much of the route deteriorated and then disappeared under encroaching uluhe ferns, other native vegetation, and small landslides.

In May 1996, HTMC member Wing Ng discovered a section of the lost trail just below Olympus. Other club members explored the switchbacks down to Kaʻau Crater, the contour section between the Nuʻuanu overlook and the Kōnāhuanui summit trail, and the upper section of the Cooke Trail. To aid the search for the forgotten trail, Booth provided a copy of an old map, probably hand drawn by Professor Donaghho, that showed the route of the Castle Trail and its connectors.[51]

Although much of the Castle Trail remains impassable as of 2010, several sections survive and even receive considerable use by hikers. The segment around Tantalus to the Nuʻuanu overlook is now part of the popular Kalāwahine and Pauoa Flats Trails, which are maintained by Na Ala Hele, the state trail program. The HTMC regularly schedules the Tantalus Ramble and Makiki Tantalizer hikes, which use both trails. The HTMC also uses the contour segment from the Nuʻuanu overlook around Kaumuhonu hill as part of its Kōnāhuanui climb. Although hiking restrictions in the watershed have been relaxed, a weather-beaten sign still stands guard along the Castle Trail just past the overlook, WATER RESERVE KAPU . . . 1945 BOARD OF AGRIC AND FORESTRY.

Mānoa Cliff and Kalāwahine

It's not considered good form to ask the leader if he knows where we are.

—Hawaiian Trail and Mountain Club
Schedule, December 9, 1979

During the first half of 1911, contract laborers began building a trail from the Tantalus carriage road *mauka* (inland) along the cliff above Mānoa Valley toward Pauoa Flats. William E. Rowell, the engineer who constructed the Castle Trail in Punaluʻu Valley, surveyed and financed the first mile of the new route.[52]

At a board meeting on July 11, the Hawaiian Trail and Mountain Club (HTMC) appropriated money to extend Rowell's route another mile to Pauoa Flats and appointed William A. Bryan, a professor at nearby College of Hawaii, as head of a committee to oversee the project. The board also reviewed a preliminary trail map drafted by Rowell and decided to produce a comprehensive map and guide to the trails of Honolulu.[53]

HTMC president William R. Castle lent the club four Japanese laborers for the Mānoa Cliff project. Over the next several months they constructed the one-mile extension to Pauoa Flats and the junction with the newly built Castle Trail. HTMC member and professor John S. Donaghho placed the grade stakes and flags and supervised the workers' progress.[54]

Presumably, the HTMC started using the new route immediately, but the club's first recorded use of the cliff trail was not until October 26, 1919.[55] The previous weekend, the HTMC had sponsored a race hike from the end of the Emma Street carline up the Castle Trail and then along Tantalus Road to the Halfway House, a shelter and rustic store providing ice, soda, and a few groceries during the summer months. The route then descended an old ridge trail known as Kalāwahine to the intersection of Pensacola and Wilder Streets near Lunalilo Home. On the race day all the women successfully completed the course, but a number of the men took a wrong turn. Two weeks later the club reran the event for the men, who were monitored by Boy Scouts lining the course.[56]

The HTMC next scheduled the Kalāwahine (the day of women) Trail for January 14, 1923, as a regular hike. After assembling at Pensacola and Wilder, the small group of three climbed past the Halfway House to the hogback along Tantalus Road. They then picked up the Kalāwahine section of the Castle Trail, which contoured on the Pauoa side of Tantalus peak. Before reaching Pauoa Flats, the threesome left the Castle Trail and summited Tantalus.[57]

On August 15, 1926, nine HTMC members helped clear the Mānoa Cliff Trail with tools provided by the Territorial Forestry Division.[58] In November 1932, superintendent of forestry Charles S. Judd assigned foreman Ernest W. Landgraf to clean up the cliff trail. Landgraf and his motley but first-rate crew of eighteen Puerto Ricans and unemployed relief workers spent three days clearing brush and regrading washed-out trail sections.[59] During the night of November 12, 1933, Judd rescued seven Boy Scouts who were lost on the Mānoa Cliff Trail.[60]

In his plan of June 7, 1934, Judd proposed the Kalāwahine section of the Castle Trail as project 3e in new construction for the second enrollment period (October 1, 1934, to March 31, 1935) of Emergency Conservation Work.

> The old trail on the land of Kalawahine in the Honolulu Watershed Forest Reserve needs relocating and new grading for a distance of 1.30 miles to connect with the Manoa Cliffs Trail much used by recreationists. This will require 460 man days.[61]

O'ahu assistant forester Glenn W. Russ assigned the project to the Honolulu Unit of the Civilian Conservation Corps (CCC). The unit, however, had its hands full with heavy-duty projects such as Hālawa Ridge and Waimano Trails and thus did not start the easy Kalāwahine job right away.

On December 13, a cool, clear Tuesday, Judd and several others surveyed the Kalāwahine route from the hogback ridge along Tantalus Road for about one-third of a mile *mauka* (inland). He found the grade initially level and then gradually increasing to 4 percent. On December 17, another fine winter day, Judd and others surveyed the proposed link between the Mānoa Cliff and Kalāwahine Trails. He determined that the *makai* (seaward) end of the latter trail needed to be rebuilt to connect the two trails on an easy grade.[62]

The Honolulu Unit started the Kalāwahine project on March 26, 1935, just before the end of the second CCC enrollment period. By then the project's scope had increased to include the regrading and widening of both trails as well as the construction of the connector. In addition, CCC crews would build a short secondary trail from Tantalus Road midway between the Kalāwahine and Mānoa Cliff trailheads up to the back of Tantalus and its crater. In his second-period report, Gunder E. Olson, project superintendent of the Honolulu Unit, remarked,

> Very good progress has been shown so far. Both trails were sadly in need of repair and widening and when completed will form a semicircle around Tantalus. Both ends of the trail will abut on Tantalus Road, assuring easy access.[63]

The Honolulu Unit completed the Kalāwahine project on June 14. The CCC crew had constructed 1.1 miles of new trail in 672 man-days and reconstructed 1.9 miles of old trail in 1,008 man-days. Along the route the men installed ten four-foot-wide plank bridges painted with crude oil to discourage rot and insects. The CCC gang also dammed Kalāwahine Spring and ran a pipe two hundred feet down to the trail to provide water for thirsty walkers.[64] HTMC members must have sampled the spring water on their Mānoa Cliff hike of September 29, led by Ruth Myrolie.[65]

While the CCC worked on Kalāwahine, Judd decided to turn Mānoa Cliff into a nature trail. On April 8, he identified and recorded forty native shrubs and trees along the two-mile route. Shortly afterward, he began painting a wooden sign for each plant. He finally posted twenty of the signs on April 11 of the following year. Judd and O'ahu ranger Thomas R. L. McGuire placed an additional twenty-four signs on May 1. Judd often hiked the cliff trail with Girl and Boy Scouts to teach them about native plants. He frequently quizzed the scouts on unmarked but previously seen plants.[66]

Over the years Mānoa Cliff became the common name for both portions of the circuit. On its 1947 Oʻahu map, the Territorial Forestry Division featured Mānoa Cliff as trail number 2 at three miles. The trail started at the driveway of the E. E. Black residence off Round Top Drive and finished at the hogback along Tantalus Drive. The hike description mentioned nameplates identifying various native plants on the Mānoa side.[67]

In the latter half of 1954, work crews under the Hawaii Employment Program cleared the Mānoa Cliff Trail at a cost of $3,060.87.[68] In 1961, naturalist Lorin Gill and Palama Settlement hikers put up thirty-three new botanical signs, giving the Hawaiian name, the genus and species, and a few facts about each native plant along the Mānoa portion of the trail.[69] In 1967, the State Forestry Division cleared the trail again.

The HTMC regularly scheduled the Mānoa Cliff hike from the 1950s through the 1970s. In 1979, Richard (Dick) Booth developed the Tantalus Ramble hike, which incorporated sections of the Kalāwahine, Mānoa Cliff, and an old horse trail in Pauoa Valley.[70] The blurb for the club's hike of October 27, 1990 warned,

> This hike is not necessarily the same each year. Escape routes are available for those whose sense of adventure is fulfilled prematurely.[71]

In 1981, the club developed an intricate eight-mile loop around Tantalus, called Makiki Tantalizer. First led by Jim Yuen, the tantalizer followed eight different State Forestry Division trails, including Kalāwahine and Mānoa Cliff. The club used a newly constructed bypass to skirt the private residences along Round Top Drive.[72]

In 1982, Raymond Tabata and John Moriyama of the Division of Forestry and Wildlife posted 114 wooden botanical signs along the Mānoa Cliff Trail and produced an accompanying plant identification guide.[73] In 1996, Jennie Peterson of Hawaiʻi Nature Center and others revised the 1982 guide and put up sixty plastic signs identifying various plant species.[74]

Na Ala Hele, the state trail program, sponsored a work outing on the Pauoa portion of the cliff trail on June 6, 1998, National Trails Day. Volunteers erected directional signs, built plank bridges, and rerouted a short section *mauka* near the junction with the Pauoa Flats Trail. In addition, Na Ala Hele renamed the route Kalāwahine (day of women) Trail, as suggested by Peterson. In conjunction with the Hawaiʻi Nature Center, she later produced a nature guide to the Kalāwahine Trail.[75]

In 2005, Mashuri Waite and Brandon Stone of the Botanical Society decided to reduce the number of introduced plants along the Mānoa Cliff Trail to highlight and encourage the original native vegetation. With the approval of Na Ala Hele, the two men and others began weeding selected trail sections and eventually rediscovered most of the 1996 botanical signs and even a few of the 1982 ones. Over the years their twice-a-month "linear gardening" has turned the popular cliff trail into a showcase for native plants.[76] Charles Judd would be pleased.

Ka'au Crater

A more treacherous trail I do not wish to encounter, for the first part of it went in a semi-perpendicular direction, with many a snaky twist and down it trickled a thin muddy stream of a rich red hue.

—F. Cartwright, January 1913

Ka'au is a circular crater nestled at the foot of the Ko'olau summit and the head of Pālolo Valley. The crater is a remnant of the last volcanic activity on O'ahu, known as the Honolulu Series. Ka'au was probably formed by tremendous steam explosions generated when rising molten rock encountered ground water.[77]

The creation of Ka'au Crater features prominently in an early Hawaiian legend. The demigod and trickster Māui wanted to join all the islands together. From Ka'ena Point he threw a great hook toward Kaua'i, hoping to snare the island. Initially the hook held fast, and Māui gave a mighty tug on the line. A huge boulder, known as Pōhaku o Kaua'i, dropped at his feet. The hook sailed over his head and fell in the back of Pālolo Valley, forming Ka'au Crater. The crater may have been named after Ka'auhelemoa, a supernatural chicken that lived in the valley.[78]

Prior to 1810, a well-worn path led into Pālolo Valley off the main *mauka* (inland) route through Kaimukī.[79] From the valley trail, early Hawaiian bird catchers and woodcutters probably climbed the ridge between Pūkele and Wai'ōma'o Streams and first saw the crater. By 1873, *kama'āina* (island-born) and tourists rode up the steep ridge on horseback to view the crater and picnic on its rim. A local botanist described the highlight of one such trip in 1888.

> Finally, a point is reached where the horses are tied, and on foot the visitor goes down a steep path, bordered on either hand with curious and beautiful forms of vegetation, stopping at the edge of a small stream flowing from a deep pool in the bottom of the crater.[80]

He marveled at the rich variety of plants in and around the crater and collected twenty-five different species of ferns within a circle one hundred feet in diameter.

In 1910, Kaimuki Land Company Ltd. (KLC), the developer of the nearby Palolo Hill subdivision, and the newly formed Hawaiian Trail and Mountain Club (HTMC) informally partnered to improve the access to Pālolo Crater, as it was then known. In May, KLC reopened the horse trail up the ridge and later built a thatched rest house on the crater rim.[81] On Sunday July 24, the HTMC scheduled an outing along Wai'ōma'o Stream and up the "Seven Falls of Palolo" to the crater rim. During the hike, the guide Chester E. Blacow and club founder Alexander H. Ford showed the planned route to four Japanese laborers employed by KLC. The workers then returned during the week to improve the trail and cut steps up the waterfalls.[82]

On Labor Day, September 4, 1911, twelve HTMC members attempted an ambitious and dangerous traverse of the Ko'olau Range from Pālolo Valley. Led by Albert H. Tarleton, the group included Governor Walter F. Frear, HTMC founder Alexander H. Ford, and pathfinder Gilbert Brown of the Ukulele Patrol, a select group of younger club hikers. The twelve headed into Pālolo Valley and climbed to the crater and the Ko'olau summit in short order. Because of low clouds, the leaders had trouble finding the correct ridge to descend the 1,200-foot *pali* (cliff) to the windward side. On the way down, Paul Super, general secretary of the YMCA, slipped badly but managed to save himself by grabbing a tree root. An ensuing landslide stripped the vegetation from the steep slope, which those behind him had to cross.

> The descent was necessarily slow, and it took time to place the rope in position, for it passed in front of a sheer rock pali and then down a razor back ridge with a drop of hundreds of feet on either side.[83]

Farther down, a Professor Mead slipped and rolled down the steep path after grabbing a *kī* (ti) plant that came away in his hand. But he managed to stay on the narrow ridge and so got up shaken but unhurt. During the descent the governor always brought up the rear. Perhaps the ablest climber in the bunch, he had to use all of his skills to carefully negotiate the route ruined by his companions. After completing the traverse, the

One of the Seven Falls of Pālolo Valley, 1912. (*The Mid-Pacific Magazine*, Hawai'i State Library)

twelve had a late lunch at the ranch house of William G. Irwin, where the governor was made an honorary member of the Ukulele Patrol. Nine members of the group then hiked across Nu'uanu Pali, while Super, Mead, and one other person, who had cut his hand, rode an automobile back to Honolulu.

During the summer of 1912, F. Cartwright and a photographer friend decided to take pictures of the lovely "Seven Falls of Palolo." One morning, probably in July, the two men walked the dirt road through Pālolo Valley past rice, taro, banana, and papaya patches. At the road's end three miles in, they picked up an obscure trail along Wai'ōma'o Stream. Soon the trail petered out, forcing them into the streambed. The two rock-hopped past fragrant yellow ginger, a small herd of cattle, and groves of ripe mountain apple: "of these we ate a few, for they are great thirst quenchers."[84] After over an hour of slippery, wet walking, the two men reached the bottom of the first waterfall. There the photographer unloaded his cumbersome camera and exposed his first plate.

Cartwright and his companion then scrambled past the first two cascades on a steep, muddy trail. The last five falls were closer together, separated only by narrow rock ledges.

> Though the Falls themselves were not very steep, yet the only way to reach them was by climbing close to the water. Solid slimy rock bordered the gulches, varied and beautiful plants hung over the channels, and here and there great tree ferns protruded from the banks.[85]

The men ate a late lunch at the bottom of the last fall, where they managed to drop and shatter a flask of their best cordial. After reaching the crater rim for a final picture, the two slipped and slid back down the falls. "[A]t last we arrived at the foot, lacerated and torn, but happy, and *so dirty*," exulted Cartwright.[86] Shortly afterward, his companion fell into a pool and ruined his camera and all the pictures. The two men finally made it back to town in late evening, ending their twelve-hour ordeal. Cartwright and his friend later returned to the seven falls with more success.

Pālolo rest house on the rim of Ka'au Crater, circa 1911. (*The Mid-Pacific Magazine*, Hawai'i State Library)

On October 13, 1913, Pālolo Crater and the ridge and falls trails became part of the new Honolulu Watershed Reserve, established to protect Honolulu's main water source. On March 22, 1916, superintendent of forestry Charles S. Judd and several laborers walked up the ridge trail to the crater. Along the way they saw numerous 'iliahi (sandalwood) trees and pulled up a quarter acre of thimbleberry, an exotic weed. On August 26, Judd returned to the crater and continued along the Castle-Olympus Trail to the Tantalus area. He posted signs where the trails entered the forest reserve and checked Castle for landslides caused by its construction.[87]

Although HTMC members had been hiking to Pālolo Crater for many years, the club's first recorded regular outing was not until November 22, 1919. That Saturday afternoon the group left the Kaimukī carline at 2 p.m. and climbed to the crater and back. The HTMC continued to schedule the hike for the next few years.[88]

On Sunday, December 4, 1921, Thomas P. Cadle, HTMC president Lawrence H. Daingerfield, and five others attempted to replicate the audacious Ko'olau traverse of 1911. Cadle had rediscovered and descended the perilous windward route in 1920, so the seven men were fairly confident of success. The group left the Kaimukī carline at 7:30 a.m. and proceeded up Pālolo Valley to the seven falls. The men passed the new Pālolo water tunnel and some rusted machinery at the crater rim. The machinery was all that remained of an unsuccessful venture to turn the crater into a small lake by damming the stream at its outlet.

By midmorning the hikers stood on the Ko'olau summit just below the cloud layer and took a short break. They then began the steep descent of the *pali* over loose rock and soil into Waimānalo.

> A person must at most times sit on the ground and gradually work himself down, and if he feels himself falling to throw himself full length upon the ground with arms outstretched in order to get the advantage of every obstruction.[89]

When the cliff became sheer several hundred feet down, the seven used a 150-foot rope to descend one at a time. The rope often had to be secured to small 'ō'hia trees that clung precariously to the slope. Despite the less-than-ideal rope attachments, the only accident occurred on the lower, easier section of the descent. One man grabbed a dead tree, fell off the ridge, bounced once, and luckily landed in a soft patch of uluhe ferns, unhurt. At the base of the *pali* the happy and relieved hikers congratulated themselves and walked to the Waimānalo road to await pickup by the club's autobus.

Because of problems with landslides and invasive Hilo grass along the Castle Trail, Judd recommended the creation of a special zone within the Honolulu Watershed Reserve on February 2, 1922. The new Palolo-Manoa Drainage Reservation would be off-limits to hikers and livestock to protect the native vegetation and thus safeguard the city's water supply. The officers and members of the HTMC were outraged, as the proposed regulation, known as Rule V, effectively closed much of the Castle Trail and the ridge and falls trail leading to the crater. Despite the protest, the governor, Wallace R. Farrington, approved the establishment of the drainage reservation on May 13.[90] On June 2, Judd, forest ranger Victory E. Ellis, and several laborers erected a barbed-wire fence and *kapu* (no trespassing) signs across the ridge trail near the forest reserve boundary.[91] The ban on hiking to Pālolo or Ka'au Crater remained in force for the next fifty-five years.

In 1977, the State Division of Forestry relaxed the hiking restrictions in the watershed reserve and allowed the HTMC to hold a Ka'au Crater outing. The club schedule called it a "Mysterious Kapu Hike."

> A special guest leader will guide us into a mysterious kapu area, one that we have looked into from above and few, if any, have ever sneaked into.[92]

On Sunday May 1, Jack Reeves, accompanied by a forest ranger, led a group along Wai'ōma'o Stream and up the seven falls to the twin power line towers along the crater rim. The hikers then returned down the ridge and descended steeply back to the stream to complete the loop.

The HTMC scheduled the Ka'au Crater hike regularly in the 1980s and 1990s. The main loop hike sometimes included a trail up the near rim to the Ko'olau summit or even a spectacular second loop around the entire crater rim. In 1986, club members Glenn W. Jones and Richard (Dick) Schmidt reworked the ridge trail to follow the original horse route.[93] In 1991, member Richard H. (Dick) Davis added switchbacks to the steep trail from the ridge down to the stream.[94] In 2003, the club stopped holding the crater hike because of trail deterioration, but it was resumed because of popular demand in 2009 as a members-only outing.

As of 2010, the falls trail to Ka'au Crater was well traveled by experienced hikers, despite some discouragement by the Forestry Division and the Board of Water Supply. The route remains rough, muddy, and virtually unimproved. The ascent of the seven falls is still slippery and dangerous, especially on the return. And the steep climb along the near rim to the Ko'olau summit has become badly eroded from all the foot traffic through the years.

Lanipō

> Lanipo is another one of those hikes named after a peak we never reach.
>
> —Hawaiian Trail and Mountain Club
> schedule, January 14, 1996

In 1910, Kaimuki Land Company, Ltd. (KLC) began offering house lots in an upscale subdivision on Mauʻumae Ridge between Pālolo and Waiʻalae Nui Valleys. Known as Palolo Hill, the development featured outstanding views, macadamized roads, and plentiful water.[95] An early advertisement showed a touring car parked by the twin entrance posts along Waiʻalae Road. In the background, Wilhelmina Rise climbed straight up the ridge, while Sierra Drive zigzagged leisurely through the subdivision. The ad touted Palolo Hill as "Honolulu's Homeland of Health" because of its cool, dry, and breezy location.[96]

In 1911, manager Charles A. Stanton promised the Hawaiian Trail and Mountain Club (HTMC) that KLC would construct a trail from the end of Wilhelmina Rise to the Koʻolau summit, about three and a half miles away. The company also offered to build a rest house at the top and deed it to the club. Over the next few years, KLC may have cleared the path to the summit, but the route remained largely unimproved, much as early Hawaiian bird catchers, maile collectors, and sandalwood cutters must have seen it during the previous century.[97]

An HTMC guide booklet, circa 1915, included detailed directions and mileage for trail number 52, Wilhelmina Rise. These directions (paraphrased) read: From the end of the Kaimukī carline, turn up Wilhelmina Rise and cross Sierra Drive five times. Near the top of the subdivision pass a flag pole and a large water tank marked "Palolo Hill." At the end of Sierra Drive is a small rest house. Behind the rest house pick up the trail, which soon passes the Kalepeamoa triangulation station. As the ridge narrows, descend initially and then ascend steadily to the Koʻolau summit. Total distance from the carline to the top was 4.75 miles.[98]

The HTMC's first recorded use of the rise trail took place on Saturday, December 27, 1919. At 1:30 p.m. the group met at the end of the Kaimukī carline and climbed partway up the ridge.[99] The club repeated the outing as an all-day hike called Waiʻalae Ridge on June 19 and December 19, 1920. Oʻahu forest ranger Thomas R. L. McGuire led the latter trip, whose participants picked maile shrubs for Christmas decorations.[100]

The HTMC scheduled Waiʻalae Ridge as a class A (difficult) loop hike for February 13, 1921. On that cool, clear winter day, seventeen members and guests climbed Mauʻumae Ridge to the Koʻolau summit at a peak known as Kainawaʻaunui (elevation 2,520 feet). The group then turned north along the main ridge, skirted Kaʻau Crater, and came out Pālolo Valley. The hikers found the trails in good condition, although badly overgrown in spots.[101]

The HTMC scheduled a different loop hike called Mt. Lanipo for June 19, 1921. The group again climbed Mauʻumae Ridge to the summit, but this time turned south to reach the summit of Lanipō (elevation 2,621 feet) and its triangulation station. The hikers then descended Wiliwilinui Ridge and walked back to the carline. From then on, Lanipō (dense) became the name of the out-and-back hike up Mauʻumae Ridge, whether or not the hikers actually reached the true summit.[102]

On September 21, 1925, territorial forester Charles S. Judd climbed Mauʻumae Ridge on an inspection trip. Also along that day were Bishop Estate land superintendent George M. Collins and Judd's brother Albert. Judd noted that the forest at the head of Waiʻōmaʻo Stream in Pālolo Valley needed replanting.[103] On January 27, 1927, ranger at large Max F. Landgraf and forestry workers planted one hundred Cook Pine seedlings at intervals along the Mauʻumae Ridge. The planting was part of a project to establish seed trees of that species along some of the major mountain ridges.[104]

The HTMC developed an alternate access for the Lanipō hike of October 14, 1928. Led by poet and prankster Fred E. Truman, fifteen members and guests drove partway into Pālolo Valley to a quarry and ascended steeply to Mauʻumae Ridge. The strollers then turned *makai* (seaward) down Wilhelmina Rise while the trail burners headed for the summit.[105]

After World War II, the HTMC resumed hiking Lanipō on September 23, 1945. The group took the bus to the end of Sierra Drive near the top of the Maunalani Heights subdivision. The hikers passed a water tank and the Kalepeamoa triangulation station before starting the up-and-down climb to the summit.[106] In an article written the next year, ranger McGuire described the flora and fauna along the trail:

> There are to be found prettily colored land shells [native tree snails] hidden under the leaves of ieie, maua, mehame, lehua and ti. Then the environment changes to tropical jungles with occasional cyanea and clermontia shrubs that bear flowers like mountain orchids.[107]

A beautiful day and a new year attracted more than fifty members and guests to the club's hike of January 22, 1961. Led by photographer Thelma Warner, the large group tramped up Mauʻumae Ridge to the Koʻolau summit for a view of Ka'au Crater and the windward coast. Naturalist Lorin Gill pointed out the many native plants along the way, including *Lobelia* species, maile, and 'iliahi (sandalwood). Mountain men Richard H. (Dick) Davis and Lloyd Talcott ranged ahead to clear trail and then came down Wiliwilinui Ridge. Partway down the ridge the two men may have explored the gun emplacements and underground magazines of battery William S. Kirkpatrick, constructed in 1942. The battery had twin eight-inch guns taken from the aircraft carriers Saratoga and Lexington to defend east Honolulu from Japanese attack.[108]

On May 20 of the following year, Davis led the Lanipō-Wiliwilinui hike, which the club had first done in 1921.[109] That challenging loop became an annual outing through 1978. The next year the HTMC resumed hiking Mau'umae Ridge as an out-and-back trip and has scheduled it regularly ever since.

As of 2010 Lanipō was the premier and most difficult ridge hike in east Honolulu. The up-and-down route remains rough and unimproved and is popular only with serious hikers. Although the land shells and *Lobelia* are mostly gone, the trail retains a variety of native plants and a few remnant 1927 Cook Pines. For a serious and historical workout, start at the bottom of Wilhelmina Rise and retrace the steps of the stalwart hikers of the 1910s.

Olomana

*[T]he view in all directions is splendid
even from a crouching position*

—Willis T. Pope, May 1911

Olomana (forked hill) is the craggy, commanding mountain windward of Nu'uanu Pali. The peak is a remnant of the mile-high caldera of the old Ko'olau volcano. When the volcano became dormant, streams gradually eroded the softer lava, leaving intrusions of hard, dense rock known as dikes. Olomana endures because of its complex of narrow, vertical dikes.[110]

The mountain has three distinct peaks. The elongated, razor-thin third peak is called Ahiki, and the second, central peak is called Pāku'i. Both are named after *konohiki* (overseers) of the ancient fishponds of Ka'elepulu, now called Enchanted Lake and Kawainui. The first and highest peak (elevation 1,643 feet) is named after a legendary giant.[111]

Olomana was a fearsome, evil warrior, twelve yards high, who dominated the windward side. None dared challenge him, not even the chief of O'ahu. One day the chief commanded Palila, a brash young soldier, to rid the island of the giant. Palila journeyed to Ka'elepulu where he surprised Olomana by jumping up on his shoulder. The giant haughtily asked the youngster,

> Where are you from, you most conceited boy? For my shoulder has never been stepped on by anybody, and here you have gone and done it.[112]

Palila replied that he came from a temple on Kaua'i noted for great warriors with supernatural powers. On hearing that, Olomana became afraid and begged for his life. Palila deftly struck the giant, cutting him in two. One part flew *makai* (seaward) and became Mahinui (great champion) mountain along the coast. The other part remained as the present peak of Olomana. Whether that legend and the steep climb attracted early Hawaiians to the summit or caused them to avoid it is not known.

Willis T. Pope, superintendent of public instruction and Hawaiian Trail and Mountain Club (HTMC) charter member, loved the Maunawili (twisted mountain) section of the Ko'olaupoko district. During summer vacations he often explored the rugged terrain between Olomana and the Ko'olau *pali* (cliff). Pope and a fellow hiking enthusiast finally climbed Olomana one summer day around 1910. The two found the summit so narrow that they had to admire the spectacular view from a crouched position. *Makai* (seaward) were lovely Waimānalo Bay and the lush cane fields of Waimanalo Plantation. *Mauka* (inland) were the sheer, fluted Ko'olau cliffs and fields of coffee and rice. Despite the panoramic view the two men were in for a disappointment.

> After congratulating ourselves on being the first human beings to reach this peculiar pinnacle, we were disgusted to find evidence of other braves having been there. In the crevice of the rock was a tin can with the label still displaying that it once contained Armour's Deviled Ham.[113]

The can must have been left by previous mountaineers or army surveyors mapping the island in 1909.

The HTMC first scheduled Olomana as a class A (difficult) hike for March 13, 1921. While more than a hundred members and guests walked the class B (easy) outing that Sunday around Makapuʻu Point, eight intrepid hikers, including four women, attempted to climb Olomana. Led by Thomas P. Cadle, the select group reached the summit after a harrowing ascent with the aid of ropes and alpenstocks. In some places, "it was necessary to inch across the ridge in the manner of a small boy making progress across the ridge pole of a roof." At the top they built an *ahu* (cairn) and placed a metal tube inside with the club's name, the date, and their names.[114]

A week later Cadle and club executive secretary Evelyn A. Breckons, veterans of the previous climb, and G. Hanson ascended the thin third peak of Olomana. The three started early in the morning and reached the summit at 3 p.m. The climbers used a 150-foot rope, which they left on the steepest section for other climbers. The *Honolulu Star-Bulletin* later surmised, "This is believed to be the first time that hikers have scaled the needle. It is reported that surveyors may have been there before."[115]

The HTMC held its first and last night hike of Olomana on April 17, 1924. Five members started from the end of the Nuʻuanu carline at midnight in a rainstorm, crossed Nuʻuanu Pali by moonlight, slogged through pineapple fields, and reached the summit of Olomana at sunrise. There they deservedly added their names to the log, now in a bottle: Charles Ortman, James Smith, William Bush, Rose Willison, Vernie Hansbrough.[116]

The HTMC continued to schedule Olomana during the rest of the 1920s and 1930s. The outings were usually followed by lunch at the Waimānalo clubhouse and occasionally by an afternoon lecture. After World War II the club resumed hiking the peak on August 26, 1945. The group caught a Windward Transit Company bus to Maunawili, climbed Olomana, and then met at their clubhouse in Waimānalo for a swim in the ocean.[117]

In 1954, the HTMC began scheduling Olomana around Christmas time. On December 26 of that year, the group, led by Nao Sekiguchi, walked through small banana and papaya farms and then followed a dirt road in back of Kawailoa Training School for wayward girls. As the road crossed Olomana Ridge, the hikers turned left up the ridge toward the first peak. Just below its summit, they negotiated a narrow dike and a near-vertical rock face with the aid of a rope. Most of the group were content to stop at the first peak with its panoramic view. A few adventurous souls scrambled to the second and third peaks over loose dirt and rock and razor-thin dikes.[118]

The HTMC continued to schedule Olomana annually over the ensuing years. The club abandoned the Christmas tradition in 1957, but resumed it in 1967. While the classic climbing route up the northwest ridge remained the same, the HTMC periodically had to find new access points to the ridge because of changes in land ownership and use around the mountain. In addition to the girls' school approach, club groups hiked in from Maunawili Elementary School and through farm and pasture land off Maunawili Road.

Access to Olomana finally became stable in 1989 with the completion of the Luana Hills Country Club on the Maunawili side of the mountain. The approval of the development required the owner to allow the HTMC and others to walk its paved entrance road, which connected with the dirt road crossing Olomana Ridge. With access assured, the challenging Olomana climb quickly became popular with experienced hikers. On April 26, 1995, at a short ceremony held in Maunawili Elementary School, Governor Benjamin Cayetano signed an executive order creating Olomana State Monument to preserve the mountain from future development.

HTMC hikers on the summit of Olomana, circa 1930. On the right, noted photographer R. J. Baker with hat and glasses. (HTMC Archives)

Ka'ala-Schofield

> I am the mountain Kaala. Kaala, the fragrant—Kaala, the rugged—Kaala, the magnificent. I am the Queen-Mother of the Waianae Mountains.
>
> —Fred E. Truman, March 1926

In December 1908, the U.S. Army began construction of a cantonment or temporary barracks on the Leilehua plain in the shadow of Ka'ala, the highest peak on O'ahu. In April of the following year, the cantonment was officially named Schofield Barracks, after General John M. Schofield, former U.S. Army head, who had first pointed out the strategic value of the Hawaiian Islands. The first occupants of the temporary tents and wooden barracks at Leilehua were two squadrons of the Fifth Cavalry.[119] They frequently conducted maneuvers at the foot of Ka'ala, and undoubtedly some of the officers and men scaled the steep cliffs to its summit plateau.

On June 24, 1911, Gilbert Brown, Kenneth Reidford, and Watson Ballentyne, all members of the Ukulele (jumping fleas) Patrol, attempted to climb Ka'ala. Also along were Walter Cowes and Gustav C. Ballentyne, two initiates to the patrol, a select group within the newly formed Hawaiian Trail and Mountain Club (HTMC). While approaching the mountain, the five men ran smack into an army firing exercise. The cavalry detained the hikers until noon, when the firing stopped for lunch. The officers then gave the group one and a half hours to get out of range and up the mountain. This they did with relish, reaching the top in good time. Because of the delay, the five men spent a rainy night at the summit nestled under some ferns. The next morning they descended the cliffs into the middle of another cavalry exercise but managed to evade capture. That two-day ordeal easily qualified both Cowes and G. Ballentyne as members of the patrol. Cavalry officers at Schofield later offered to guide HTMC hikers up Ka'ala on weekends when there were no scheduled maneuvers.[120]

"Ka'ala or bust." In 1915, that was the slogan of some HTMC members who tried to climb the mountain several times but never got close because their hired autobus broke down on the way to Leilehua. The next time, they tried the new jitney service, which dropped them off at Schofield Barracks after a pleasant two-hour ride. The veteran group, including one woman dressed in bloomers, climbed to the summit plateau in two hours through mist and then driving rain. At the top they ate some of their soggy food, began to shiver, and quickly descended the slippery and sloppy trail. While waiting for the jitney, the hikers found a Chinese restaurant, where they enjoyed a hot but late lunch. The owner lent the group dry clothes while their wet hiking togs dried out in his ovens. With boots in hand, the dry but dirty group piled into the jitney for the trip back to Honolulu.[121]

In 1919, five HTMC members, including Ruth E. Brown and Thomas P. Cadle, drove to Schofield Barracks, checked in with the sentry, and parked below Kolekole Pass. The group then walked through the artillery range, carefully avoiding shell holes and the duds marked by danger signs. Leaving the devastation behind, the five ascended gradually through mixed forest and crossed a stream near a small, lovely waterfall.

> Then the real climbing began. Over rocks, thru tangled ferns and vines we went, always up and up. The songs of the birds and the breaking of dry twigs beneath our feet were the only sounds.[122]

After a brief rain shower, the group began to ascend a narrow side ridge covered with giant native ʻōhiʻa trees.

> Swinging from tree to tree was our next exercise—from root to tree top. . . . Land shells [native tree snails] were found a-plenty now. We gathered a few dozens, including a number of rare specimens.[123]

In the cliff below the summit plateau, they found a small spring splashing into a miniature pool and drank its cool, crystal-clear water. Near the spring was the ʻapeʻape (*Gunnera petaloidea*), a giant native herb with thick stems and huge leaves shaped like a geranium's. After reaching the rim, the group turned right through dense native vegetation to gain the true summit, marked by a U.S. Geological Survey monument in a small clearing. From that vantage point they enjoyed a magnificent view of much of Oʻahu with its sugar and pineapple plantations, rice fields, and *kalo* (taro) patches. Before heading down, the five wrote their names in the summit register, a wad of paper in a pickle jar.

In early July 1920, Cadle and other HTMC members began cutting a trail from the summit monument west across the plateau. Their goal was a prominent side ridge leading down to Kaupakuhale hill and Waialua town. Three weeks later they found and descended that ridge, which had once been part of an old Hawaiian route across Kaʻala from Mākaha to Waialua. Experienced HTMC and other hikers quickly popularized the new traverse, up from Schofield on the Kaʻala Trail and down to Waialua on the rediscovered ridge trail, known as De Ponte (later Dupont).[124]

On March 26, 1922, Cadle, professor John S. Donaghho, and Lyndon D. Merrill reopened another old route to Ka'ala. From Kolekole Pass the three HTMC members climbed the main Wai'anae ridge across several narrow dikes to the summit of Kalena, O'ahu's second highest peak. The hikers continued along the ridge to Ka'ala where they faced a seventy-five-foot near-vertical cliff just below the rim. After some scouting, the group managed to bypass the rock face by shinnying up a crevice on the leeward side of the ridge. On the last stretch to the summit the hikers saw hundreds of 'apa'ape herbs with their gigantic leaves. In earlier years their rediscovered route was called the Sky Line Trail and may have been the original *kama'āina* (island-born) route to Ka'ala.[125]

On November 2, 1923, territorial forester Charles S. Judd inspected a new firebreak trail in the company of the fire marshal and range officer from Schofield Barracks. The army had recently constructed the rough road to protect the native watershed from periodic fires that swept up the mountainside from the artillery range. Judd suggested that the road be upgraded for easier travel and widened to thirty feet when crossing dry, exposed side ridges. In addition to containing fires, the road offered more safe and stable access to the Ka'ala Trail.[126]

The fledgling Piko Club scheduled its first Sunday outing on July 26, 1931. Led by member Major Russell A. Osmun, twenty hikers scaled Ka'ala from Schofield Barracks. Along were Judd and club president Major General Briant H. Wells, commander of the Hawaiian Division. Judd and Wells had formed the club in April to foster communication and camaraderie between army officers and forestry personnel.[127]

In October 1933, Judd and Wells included that July hike as project number 4, Schofield-Ka'ala, on the new trail construction list for the Emergency Conservation Work program.

> Beginning at the existing fire-break trail at the 2,000 feet elevation on the Schofield Barracks Military Reservation this route leads northwesterly up the slope to the summit of Mt. Kaala at 4,025 feet in the Waianae Range. The work will consist of widening the present contour trail at the lower end, establishing an easier grade up the steep spur to the 3,000 feet elevation, and cutting a trail up the 30 foot cliff on the ridge. Total length 12,000 feet [2.27 miles], 330 man days.[128]

Assistant forester Glenn W. Russ assigned the Ka'ala Trail to the Wahiawa Camp of the Civilian Conservation Corps (CCC). CCC crews completed the project in 1934 and built a small cabin at the summit for use by forestry personnel and pig hunters.[129]

The Ka'ala Trail enjoyed a brief heyday after the CCC upgrade. The HTMC scheduled the hike twice a year in January and July from 1935 through 1940. Military maneuvers rarely interfered with the club's "semi-annual pilgrimage" to O'ahu's highest peak.[130] After the outing of February 9, 1941, however, the HTMC had to stop scheduling the hike because of increased training activities at Schofield Barracks.

In September 1941, Interstate Equipment Corp. began constructing a tramway to hoist supplies and equipment to the summit for a radar station to be built there. The lower tram terminal was situated near the junction of the firebreak road with the Ka'ala Trail, and the upper terminal near the collapsed remains of the CCC cabin. The company installed the radar housing in November, but the site was not operational by the December 7 Japanese attack on Pearl Harbor. The facility was completed in July 1942 for use by the Aircraft Warning Service of the Army Signal Corps. But the long-range radar at the summit did not perform well at the higher elevation. The site eventually became a radio station for VHF control of fighter planes on O'ahu.[131]

After World War II, a makeshift but more direct trail to the summit developed along the steep route of the tramway. The Ka'ala Trail was much the better path, but was little used and became overgrown.[132] Sometime in the early 1950s, Richard H. (Dick) Davis was descending the tramway trail late in the afternoon. He had climbed Ka'ala from the Waialua side and had stopped to pick oranges below the Mokulē'ia campsite. Partway down the tramway he grabbed a rope that was not fixed and tumbled several hundred feet downslope to a dry streambed. "When I fell, I tried to relax, but it was a long way down. Those oranges in my pack cushioned the fall and may have saved my life," Davis reminisced.[133] The next morning fellow club member Joseph Neilson climbed the Ka'ala Trail to search for Davis. He spotted the fallen hiker below, cut a trail down to him, and coordinated the rescue. The trip down in a stretcher was an ordeal for Davis, who had broken his back. After a lengthy recovery he resumed hiking, much to the surprise of his doctors.[134]

In 1952, the HTMC resumed the tradition of scheduling Ka'ala as the first hike of the new year. Led by Davis, forty-six members and guests walked the firebreak road on January 6 for the first time in eleven years. Unfamiliar with the crucial and probably overgrown junction, the hikers climbed the wrong ridge and found themselves on the summit of Kalena, rather than Ka'ala. After lunch, many of the group elected to return the way they had come. Sixteen diehards, including Davis, decided to follow the old Sky Line Trail toward Ka'ala. After a grueling trek, they reached the near-vertical cliff just before sunset. Davis rigged some ropes, and the group scrambled up the rock face to the summit plateau in heavy mist and light rain. At the tramway the cold, wet hikers found an army cabin, where they called it a day. The group shared lunch leftovers and sang songs and played guessing games to get them through the long night. The next morning the sixteen descended the Ka'ala Trail to meet an army team coming up to rescue them.[135]

Unable to obtain army permission because of security concerns and/or the 1952 fiasco, the HTMC never officially hiked the Ka'ala Trail again. In late 1952, the club resumed climbing Ka'ala from the Waialua side on the Dupont Trail. In 1960, the HTMC also began ascending the mountain from Mākaha Valley and in 1974 from Wai'anae Valley.[136] As of 2010, the Ka'ala Trail remained inaccessible and is undoubtedly overgrown and deteriorated. The abandoned tramway is clearly visible below the perimeter fence of the Federal Aviation Agency radar station at the summit.

Pālehua-Palikea

> This [Pālehua] is considered an ideal trip for the nerve-racked person shut up in office or store all week.
> —Lawrence H. Daingerfield, November 1919

Kama'āina (island-born) Heinrich (Harry) M. von Holt became superintendent of ranches for Oahu Railway and Land Company in 1889. His first priority was to find additional water sources for the cattle on the company's Honouliuli Ranch in the dry foothills of the Wai'anae Range. While searching for lost or hidden springs, Holt and his *paniolo* (cowboys) often took an old Hawaiian route initially paralleling Kalo'i Gulch and eventually leading to Pālehua, an idyllic spot along the Wai'anae summit ridge.[137]

In 1896, Holt and his wife, Ida E. Knudsen, set up a tent camp at nearby Akupu and spent six weeks there during the summer. After exploring the area, the two decided to move their retreat to Pālehua because of its magnificent view. The next year the couple constructed a more permanent camp there and named it Pa Lehua (lehua flower enclosure). The retreat consisted of two large sleeping tents and a small cabin with redwood tanks to store rain water collected from the tin roof. All the building materials had to be packed on horseback or carried on foot up the narrow Kaloʻi route to the site.[138]

The von Holts spent a relaxing two months each summer at Pa Lehua. The couple took their children on short walks and picnics to their favorite spots—Inspiration Point, Elephant Rock, and Sunset View. Harry von Holt led hunting parties farther afield in search of feral goats. The men blazed routes along the summit ridge, south to Puʻu Manawahua, and north to Mauna Kapu and Palikea peaks, and Pōhākea Pass. On one of the early hunts, Harold Sewell, the American minister to the Hawaiian Kingdom, became trapped on a cliff below Mauna Kapu. He spent the better part of the night out before being found and rescued. Thereafter, the cliff became known affectionately as Sewell's Leap.[139]

Harry's master trail builder was Peter, a Portuguese black from the Cape Verde Islands. In the 1910s, he constructed a bridle path through the Waiʻanae foothills from Pa Lehua to Schofield Barracks. The von Holts, especially the two older daughters, could now visit their army officer friends and vice versa. The route was named the Schuyler Trail after Colonel Walter F. Schuyler, the commandant at Schofield.[140]

The Hawaiian Trail and Mountain Club (HTMC) first scheduled the Pālehua hike for November 2, 1919. At 7:30 that morning, twenty-two members and guests assembled at the Pan-Pacific building in downtown Honolulu. The group boarded an autobus and drove to pumping station no. 5 in the cane fields of Ewa Plantation. Led by weatherman Lawrence H. Daingerfield, the hikers climbed the Kaloʻi route past Pa Lehua to the Waiʻanae summit. From there they turned south to the survey station at Puʻu Manawahua and then looped back to the waiting autobus. In later trips during the 1920s, HTMC groups followed von Holt's hunting trail north along the summit ridge to Mauna Kapu and Palikea.[141]

On January 8, 1924, territorial forester Charles S. Judd and others began surveying the newly created Honouliuli Forest Reserve along the Waiʻanae summit ridge. They set up triangulation flags on Mauna Kapu near Sewell's Leap and on the prominent knob just south of Palikea, also known as Green Peak.[142] In 1928, Judd began a massive planting program to reforest areas of the reserve denuded by cattle. Forestry Division laborers constructed an access trail up Kaʻaikukai Gulch, built a ranger cabin just below the summit, and planted redwood trees nearby.[143] On October 3, 1929, Judd and rangers Max F. Landgraf and Tony Rocha set out an additional one hundred redwood seedlings around the cabin.[144]

On January 19, 1931, Judd first met Major General Briant H. Wells, the new commander of the Hawaiian Division at Schofield Barracks. Wells agreed to provide soldiers to help build several forestry trails. Judd agreed

Ka'aikukai cabin just below the Wai'anae crest, 1928. By the twin rain barrels, territorial forester Charles Judd. (State Division of Forestry and Wildlife)

to show some of the mountain routes to the general and his staff.[145] On February 12, Judd, Wells, and eight other officers hiked up Ka'aikukai Gulch past the cabin, crossed the Wai'anae summit, and descended into Nānākuli Valley along the route of a trail proposed by Judd.[146] Shortly afterward, the army began construction of the Nānākuli extension of the Ka'aikukai Trail and completed the project by the end of March.[147] Judd and Wells became good friends and founded the Piko Club to foster camaraderie and cooperation between forestry workers and army personnel.

For June 7, the HTMC scheduled a marathon double traverse of the Wai'anae Range incorporating the army's new trail. Led by O'ahu ranger Thomas R. L. McGuire, thirteen stalwart hikers climbed to the summit at Pōhākea Pass and descended into Lualualei Valley. At the coast they walked the Wai'anae Road to Nānākuli Valley and then hiked the army trail back across the crest all the way to Kupehau Ranch. During the early and middle 1930s, the HTMC continued to schedule the popular Pālehua hike up Kalo'i Gulch and added a new Palikea outing using the new Ka'aikukai Gulch route.[148]

On January 17, 1932, the Piko Club hiked the Ka'aikukai-Nānākuli traverse as a Sunday outing. Twenty-one members and guests climbed Ka'aikukai Gulch from Kupehau Ranch above the Kunia cane fields. Just short of the Wai'anae summit, the group stopped at the forestry cabin for lunch and coffee. There Mary Wells, wife of the general, and two others each planted a pine tree. The hikers then crossed the crest near Mauna Kapu and descended into Nānākuli Valley to their car shuttles.[149] In February, the army donated two steel barrels to store water collected on the roof of the cabin.[150]

In January 1933, Wai'anae ranger Ralph E. Turner, Jr. brushed out a trail from Nānākuli Valley to Pu'u Manawahua.[151] On April 23, forty members and guests of the Piko Club sampled that trail to the Wai'anae summit and turned north past Mauna Kapu. At the Ka'aikukai cabin they stopped for an obligatory cup of coffee before heading down to Kupehau Ranch.[152]

On April 16, 1935, Judd led seventeen Boy Scouts on a three-day outing to Pa Lehua. The group camped near the von Holt's shack and spent the afternoon planting mulberry tree slips along the Ka'aikukai Trail leading to the forestry cabin. On the layover day the scouts caught five pigs near Pa Lehua, planted yellow watermelon seeds at the Ka'aikukai cabin, and descended to an orange grove in Nānākuli Valley. The last morning Judd quizzed the scouts on ten native plants, and in the afternoon the group broke camp and headed back to town.[153]

On May 5, the Piko Club held its fourth annual meeting at Ka'aikukai cabin. To get there, fifty members and guests climbed the Wai'anae crest past the Pu'u Manawahua survey station and Sewell's Leap to the head of Ka'aikukai Gulch. At the cabin, the first order of business was lunch—broiled tenderloin steaks wrapped in bacon and popped into buttered hamburger rolls.

After coffee the group shouted the Piko Club yell, "*Pehea kou piko?*" (How's your belly button?) and sang the club song with a new fourth verse composed by Judd.

> Stout they are because their leader
> Is a strong and mighty hiker
> Over peaks, thru thorny dells
> Boldly leads our General Wells[154]

(One observer commented that maybe Judd should stick to trees.)

Finally, the elections got under way with General Wells presiding. At a crucial point in the voting, Judd and his son set off a smoke bomb to create a diversion and ensure that Wells would remain as president. Their ploy was successful. The members re-elected Wells, and "[a]fter the usual amount of bickering, accusations, threats, and insults, the meeting broke up, all a shambles."[155]

In September 1936, the Wahiawa Camp of the Civilian Conservation Corps finished the Honouliuli Trail, a graded route that stretched 16.6 miles through the Wai'anae foothills from Kalo'i Gulch to Kolekole Pass.[156] In 1937, the Army Third Engineers completed the Pa Lehua Artillery Spur, a six-mile road of crushed coral from the main Wai'anae Road to the No. 1 forestry gate near Kalo'i Gulch.[157] The soldiers linked the spur with Pu'u Manawahua, the Honouliuli Trail, and Pa Lehua. The army also upgraded von Holt's crest trail from Pu'u Manawahua to just short of Pōhākea Pass.[158] The HTMC immediately incorporated the new Honouliuli Trail and the upgraded army routes into its Pālehua and Palikea outings, turning them both into loop hikes. Those proved exceedingly popular and were often scheduled twice a year until the Japanese attacked Pearl Harbor on December 7, 1941.[159]

While bringing a halt to hiking, World War II accelerated the development of radar and communication facilities in the Pālehua area. In 1930–1931, Mutual Telephone Company had constructed the first installation there, a radio telephone station for relaying interisland calls.[160] After Pearl Harbor the military built a radar station and camp at Pu'u Manawahua and radio facilities below Mauna Kapu. A paved road linked each site with the No. 1 forestry gate at the end of the upgraded artillery spur, renamed Palehua Road.

After the war, the HTMC resumed hiking Palikea in June 1946 and Pālehua in January 1947. The paved road to Mauna Kapu shortened the Pālehua outing considerably, and the schedule noted, "It's a tougher climb for the cars than for the hikers."[161] Veteran member Joseph Neilson later commented, "It ain't like it used to be. Building the road to the Wai'anae summit ruined the best part of the hike."[162]

From the 1950s through the 1980s, the HTMC continued to schedule the six-mile Pālehua hike using the Honouliuli Trail as the return. In 1969, veteran member Richard (Dick) Booth developed a marvelous nine-mile loop that rambled through the entire Pālehua area. His extended route started at Pu'u Manawahua and followed the crest trail and road past Mauna Kapu and Sewell's Leap to Palikea peak. The hikers then backtracked along the summit and descended Ka'aikukai Gulch to the Honouliuli Trail. Groups then walked that contour trail and its extension around Pu'u Poulihale, known as the Kupehau Trail. After reaching Pālehua Road just below the lower naval communications site, the hikers climbed an obscure local trail through Akupu to complete the loop.[163] The Hawai'i Audubon Society also hiked the shorter loop. Its members frequently saw the native birds 'apapane, 'amakihi, and 'elepaio along the way.

The HTMC also regularly scheduled the Palikea (white cliff) outing until the early 1980s. The access point and the route changed frequently over the years. The club used four different side ridges to reach the Wai'anae summit and the peak itself. In 1981, the club discontinued the hike because of liability concerns of the lessee.

In May 1990, The Nature Conservancy (TNC) established the Honouliuli Preserve on 3,692 acres in the windward Wai'anae Range. The preserve stretched from Mauna Kapu to Hāpapa peaks along the summit and included most of the Honouliuli Forest Reserve and the contour trail. Under a long-term lease agreement with the landowner, the estate of James Campbell, TNC protects the habitat of more than forty-five rare native plants, birds, and tree snails.[164] The HTMC continued to offer the Pālehua hike in the preserve, with some TNC restrictions on the route, frequency, and group size because of the fragile ecosystem. Initially, the Pālehua outing became a two-mile out-and-back hike to the knob just before Palikea. In 2003, the club resumed hiking the six-mile loop using the Honouliuli Trail. In 2007, the O'ahu Natural Resource Program of the U.S. Army took over stewardship of the Honouliuli Preserve from TNC.

In September 2009, the Trust for Public Land (TPL), a nonprofit land-conservation organization, purchased the Honouliuli Preserve from the James Campbell Company using public and private funds. On March 31, 2010, the TPL transferred ownership of the preserve to the State Department of Land and Natural Resources. The Division of Forestry and Wildlife assumed management of the preserve, and it plans to incorporate some of its trails into Na Ala Hele, the state trail system.[165]

The von Holt camp is now a private retreat used by the Campbell estate. A mountain house, called Hokuloa, stands on the site of the original cabin and sleeping tents.[166] In a redwood grove below the Wai'anae crest are the remains of two cabins, one on either side of the Ka'aikukai Gulch Trail. The corrugated metal sides and roofing may have been part of an army shelter or even the original forestry cabin, which stood on the left side of the trail going down. Mauna Kapu still sports a cluster of communications towers, the latest being a Coast Guard microwave antenna to be shared with other federal and state agencies. Behind it are several commercial antenna towers for relaying wireless and cellular phone calls.

Sugar Plantation Trails
(1898–1917)

All the water
You can find, dig, direct,
Scrounge, divert, tunnel and hold.
Bring the water tribute to me, King Cane

—Beryl Blaich, *The Crop*

In the late 1800s, the sugar industry in Hawai'i was rapidly expanding for several reasons. In June 1876, King Kalakaua signed a reciprocity treaty with the United States allowing tax-free trading between the two countries. In 1890, the three McCandless brothers drilled a well on Ewa Plantation land to tap groundwater for sugar cane irrigation. In 1893, discontented *haole* (white) businessmen and public officials overthrew the Hawaiian kingdom, leading to its annexation by the United States in 1898. Sugar planters now had a ready market, a reliable source of water, and a congenial political climate.[1]

O'ahu planters founded three major companies just before the turn of the century, Oahu Sugar Company (OSC) in 1897 and Waialua Agricultural Company (WAC) and Honolulu Plantation Company (HPC) in 1899. All three plantations controlled land that gradually sloped up toward the summit ridge of the Ko'olau Range. As the companies expanded *mauka* (inland), the cost of pumping water up to the high-level fields became prohibitive. The plantation managers thus decided to investigate their mountain streams as a possible water source. Gravity could deliver water to the upper fields, instead of pumps, which used expensive imported coal and later oil.[2]

The resulting surveys revealed that Ko'olau stream flow is highly variable from month to month, depending on rainfall. Clearly, mountain water would never be a steady irrigation source, but during rainy periods it could significantly reduce the pumped water needed. Based on that conclusion, all three companies built multiple ditch and tunnel systems, as shown below.[3]

COMPANY/DITCH	COMPLETION DATE
Oahu Sugar	
Kīpapa	1898
Waikakalaua	1900
Waiawa (Ahern)	1901
Waiāhole	1916
Waialua Agricultural	
ʻŌpaeʻula	1900
Mauka (Kaukonahua)	1902
Upper Helemano	1902
Kawaiiki	1903
Kamananui (Kawainui)	1911
Honolulu Plantation	
Waimano	1913
Waimalu	1917

Each ditch system consisted of a dam, an intake, and a channel to transport the water. The dam diverted water from the stream to the intake, the gated and screened entrance to the channel. The captured water then flowed gradually downhill in an open ditch, a tunnel, and/or a flume that spanned the steep side gulches. The waterway was often lined with stone or concrete to reduce seepage. Ditch tenders controlled the volume of water using sluice gates and spillways along the route. On leaving the ditch, the water was stored in a reservoir, routed directly to the fields below, or siphoned or pumped to other upper-level fields. Each ditch had an access trail used during construction and for maintenance later on. The trail paralleled the channel when above ground but detoured around the large side ridges when the ditch went underground.

Construction of a ditch system was a major undertaking involving plantation management, civil engineers, tradesmen, and hundreds of laborers. Management conceived and approved the project, and the engineers planned and executed it. The actual ditch and trail builders were mostly Japanese workers who had immigrated to Hawaiʻi to help pay debts incurred by their families in Japan.[4] The laborers used cane knives and axes to clear the vegetation, and picks and shovels to grade the trail and dig the ditch. Some were blasting specialists who prepared and detonated the black powder or dynamite charges to bore the tunnel. Mules and horses packed in supplies and building material along the access trail to the work site.

After completion, the ditch was maintained by caretakers who lived in cabins along the trail. Because of increasing labor costs after World War II, the plantations gradually replaced their resident ditch tenders with roving maintenance crews that periodically inspected the ditch and made repairs as necessary. The homey cabins with their gardens and fruit trees were eventually abandoned or torn down.[5]

As of 2010, only four of the original Oʻahu ditches remained in operation: Waiāhole, ʻŌpaeʻula, Kawaiiki, and Kawainui. With the demise of the last sugar plantation in 1996, all four now provide water for mixed farming rather than for king cane. The ditch access trails fared better; seven are still in reasonably good condition and provide excellent hiking opportunities.

Waiawa and Waiāhole

> Bring flashlight or hard hat, or be prepared to pull in your head.
> —Hawaiian Trail and Mountain Club schedule, January 4, 1976

Soon after its founding in 1897, Oahu Sugar Company (OSC) began to incur high fuel and maintenance costs to pump artesian water to its upper-level cane fields. The company thus decided to build ditch and tunnel systems to capture water from three major streams *mauka* (inland) of its property. Under manager August Ahrens, OSC completed the Kīpapa Ditch in 1898, the Waikakalaua Ditch in 1900, and the Waiawa Ditch in 1901.[6]

The Waiawa or Ahrens Ditch (later corrupted to Ahern) was just over three miles long with six tunnels and a capacity of sixty cubic feet per second.[7] The ditch started by its intake dam across Waiawa Stream at an elevation of 700 feet and emptied into a small reservoir at 610 feet. An access trail paralleled the waterway when above ground but detoured around the large side ridges where the ditch went underground.

OSC was pleased with the performance of its three ditches. In his 1904 report, manager Ahrens wrote,

> The extraordinary expenses of irrigation have been immensely curtailed by a network of miles of large water ditches which lead mountain rainfall to our reservoirs.[8]

In October of that year the company engaged J. S. Molony, a civil engineer, to survey all the streams *mauka* of the plantation to further increase the supply of mountain water. After an eleven-month study, Molony submitted a startling and costly recommendation to gather water from windward streams and channel it to the company's leeward fields in a tunnel bored through the Koʻolau Range. Because of the expense involved, OSC got a second and favorable opinion of the project from veteran tunnel engineer Michael M. O'Shaughnessy.[9] Six years later, on August 19, 1911, company directors adopted the Waiahole Ditch Plan, a comprehensive final report authored by civil engineer J. B. Lippincott. Actual construction, however, would have to wait more than a year for the resolution of windward water rights.[10]

In 1911, OSC started to build an access trail for survey and construction crews that roughly followed the proposed underground ditch system. The leeward trail section began at the Waiawa Ditch intake and ascended gradually above Waiawa Valley to the Koʻolau summit. From there the windward section would descend the 1,200-foot *pali* (cliff) on switchbacks and then contour around the back of Waiāhole, Waikāne, and Kahana Valleys.[11]

In early 1913, OSC formed a subsidiary, Waiahole Water Company (WWC), to oversee the project and awarded the construction contract to Hubert K. Bishop, previously the supervisor of public works. In February 1913, work finally started on the main tunnel under the Koʻolau Range. Crews digging at the north or windward portal immediately encountered problems—inadequate power, equipment, and surveying; hard rock; and water gushing through the tunnel from pierced dikes. Crews on the south or leeward side faced easier working conditions but suffered a typhoid outbreak in June. On October 1, Bishop resigned, and work on the tunnel ground to a halt.[12]

Several days later veteran tunnel builder Jorgen Jorgensen took over as chief engineer and contracted to complete the entire project within thirty months. The men resumed work and made steady progress despite continual drenching with dike water. On December 13, 1915, the north and south portal crews finally met and Jorgensen reported, "Alignment and floor grade were perfect, the length, however being 124 feet more than the calculation."[13] The Waiahole Water Company officially began delivering water from the ditch to OSC under contract on May 27, 1916. Because of the problems encountered, the total cost of the tunnel system ballooned from $1.3 million to $2.3 million. In 1916, WWC also took over the water rights and the operation and maintenance of the three other OSC ditches and their access trails.[14]

When completed, the Waiāhole system consisted almost entirely of tunnels, unlike the Waiawa Ditch. The main tunnel through the Koʻolau Range measured 14,567 feet, or 2.76 miles, from north to south portal. The windward section had twenty-seven tunnels totaling 4.66 miles with thirty adits or openings to gather stream water. Linking the openings was the access trail, five to six feet wide, more than ten miles in length, and paved with stone. On the leeward side were fourteen tunnels totaling 3.64 miles. Ditch water flowed from an elevation of 790 feet in Kahana Valley to the upper boundary of the plantation at 650 feet. The capacity was 125 to 150 million gallons per day.[15]

For September 26, 1920, the Hawaiian Trail and Mountain Club (HTMC) scheduled a portion of the stone paved access trail as a class A (difficult) hike with dropoff and pickup by autobus. Led by forest ranger and club member Thomas R. L. McGuire, the group probably started at the ditch tender's cottage in Waiāhole Valley and came out Waikāne Valley. The club first hiked Waiawa Valley from the Pearl City train depot to the south portal on November 28.[16]

During the summer of 1921, George T. Armitage, secretary of the Hawaii Tourist Bureau, and several friends went out for a Sunday drive and took the winding dirt road into Waiāhole Valley.

> Coming up the valley one sees across the face of the great green cliffs what appears to be a trail zig-zagging down the mountain in great swings of uniform grade.[17]

Their interest piqued, the group continued into the valley past upland pineapple fields and the ditch tender's cottage to the road's end at a massive, wire-bound wooden pipeline. After inspecting the pipeline, which carried water pumped up from Waiāhole Stream to the ditch, they searched for the start of the switchback trail for more than an hour without success.

Several weeks later Armitage decided to find the elusive trail from the leeward side. He and his group started early from the Pearl City cannery in Waiawa Valley. After reaching the ditch tender's cottage at the south portal, they picked up an obscure trail heading along Waiawa Stream toward the Koʻolau summit. At the top the group immediately found the switchback trail and began to descend the *pali*. Except for a few small landslides, the route down was generally good, but heavily overgrown with scratchy uluhe ferns. At the base of the cliff they completely lost the trail and had to slide down a grassy slope to reach the end of the road. Their Koʻolau traverse had taken eleven hours. A few weeks later Armitage returned to Waiāhole Valley for the third time and found the trailhead up a concrete stairway near the base of a waterfall. He later wrote,

> If this trail were cleared and kept up it would provide one of the most interesting hikes in the Hawaiian Islands. As it stands to-day, however, it is too much of a guess or a gamble for the uninitiated.[18]

During the middle 1920s through the 1930s, the HTMC continued to hike the two access trails, later named the Waiawa and Waiāhole Ditch Trails. In Waiawa Valley the groups usually followed the tracks of an abandoned railroad used to deliver tunnel workers and supplies to the south portal. Down by the stream near the Waiawa Ditch intake was a caretaker's cottage with a rose garden. The hikers returned on the Waiawa Ditch Trail, sometimes walking through the tunnels, which were often dry in summer.[19] For experienced hikers the club offered a Koʻolau traverse from Wahiawā to Kahana Bay on the Schofield-Waikāne and Waiāhole Ditch Trails.

By 1925, average flow from the Waiāhole Ditch had decreased as the tapped dike water was depleted. That year WWC began development of six spur tunnels on the windward side to access additional dikes. Four of the tunnels were productive at the completion of the project in 1933. They helped maintain a good flow in the ditch when drought reduced the contribution from windward streams.[20]

In October 1933, territorial forester Charles S. Judd proposed the reconstruction of the leeward section of the Waiāhole Ditch Trail. Renamed the Waiawa Trail, the project became number 7 on the original list of Emergency Conservation Work jointly developed by Judd and U.S. Army Major General Briant H. Wells.

> Beginning in Waiawa Valley at 700 feet elevation and near the west portal of the Waiahole tunnel through the Koolau Range the route runs easterly up Waiawa Valley to the crest of the Koolau Range at 2,050 feet elevation. This is on private land but the trail is essential in order to connect up with the Waiahole trail on government land coming up the cliffs on the windward side of the island. Total length is 16,000 feet [3.03 miles], 640 man days.[21]

Sometime before work started, Judd changed the project route to follow the ridge north of Waiawa Stream. He must have decided that the connection with the windward Waiāhole Ditch Trail was not essential and/or too difficult to rebuild and maintain. The ridge offered a more direct and easily constructed route to the summit for forestry activities such as tree planting and pig control. In February 1935, a Civilian Conservation Corps (CCC) crew finished the ridge route, later known as the Kīpapa Trail.[22]

Also on Judd's list at number 8 was the Kahana Trail.

> Beginning at the north end of the Waiahole ditch trail in Kahana valley at 800 feet elevation the route runs north-easterly through forest jungle down the valley to connect with the valley trail at approximately the 200 foot elevation. This is on private land but this small section of trail is of the greatest importance in order to afford a quick route from the north end of the Waiahole ditch trail system to the sea. Total length 6,880 feet, 340 man days.[23]

CCC crews probably completed that extension in 1934.

On April 15, 1942, Oahu Sugar Company organized a battalion of Hawaii Scouts, a volunteer force to help defend the islands against a Japanese invasion. The Third, or Waipahu, Battalion included more than 350 OSC employees, who received equipment and training from the U.S. Army. They periodically held maneuvers on the Waiawa Ditch Trail.[24]

After World War II, the HTMC resumed regular scheduling of the Waiawa Ditch Trail as an out-and-back trip. Well into the hike, group members faced a choice: continue on the trail up and over a side ridge or tunnel one-third of a mile through the ridge. For those going underground, the blurb for the September 1970 hike advised,

> Bring your flashlight to see you through the black, wet, creepy tunnel. Eerie and squealing noises from the chicken-hearted bounce off the rocky walls.[25]

In 1981, the HTMC lost access to the Waiawa Ditch Trail because of liability concerns of the OSC.

On April 29, 1960, Richard (Dick) Booth led Waianu, an HTMC hike that used a portion of the Waiāhole Ditch Trail on the windward side. Over the years the route gradually evolved into the current version, Kuolani-Waianu, which was first led by Booth's son Phil on August 31, 1980. That loop hike followed the ditch trail north through eight gulches from

Waianu to Uwau Streams. Along the way were several openings into the main tunnel, and at Uwau was the access to the most productive spur tunnel.[26]

In 1994, the same year the OSC shut down, HTMC members John Hall and Gerald Leao developed a new but arduous access to the Waiawa Ditch Trail. Starting *mauka* of Pacific Palisades subdivision, the up-and-down route crossed both Mānana and Waiawa Streams before finally reaching the trail about a half-mile along its length. On February 25, 1995, Hall led the first HTMC hike since 1980 along the now-abandoned ditch. The group proceeded as far as a saddle overlooking the final descent to the intake and then turned around. The club continued to schedule the ditch hike through 2005, after which it was deemed too difficult. The next year Hall and Leao developed an easier replacement hike that crossed Mānana Stream, climbed the next ridge through stands of ʻiliahi (sandalwood) trees, and returned to Pacific Palisades on the Mānana Trail. Known as ʻIliahi Ridge, the new loop proved very popular with club hikers.[27]

On the rainy morning of April 8, 2000, HTMC members Dayle Turner, Patrick Rorie, and two others hiked up Waikāne Valley Road to the Waiāhole Ditch and Trail. There the four headed north past the saddle junction with the Schofield-Waikāne Trail into Kahana Valley. After contouring through a seemingly endless number of gulches, they reached the site of a camp and the rusted remains of a caretaker's cabin. Just beyond was a green stream gaging station with an antenna, solar panels, and a nearby elevated helipad. After crossing a side ridge, the group finally reached the end of the ditch trail at the first intake. After a short rest they came out the valley on the old CCC trail, rebuilt singlehandedly by club member Richard H. (Dick) Davis in 1982. Wet, muddy, and tired, but happy, the four reached their cars at 7 p.m. just after sunset.[28]

Although hard to access, the Waiawa Ditch Trail still receives some use from hunters and hikers. The route is in surprisingly good condition because the nearby abandoned ditch catches much of the upslope rubble, leaving the path intact. The leeward Waiāhole Ditch Trail and the windward switchback section are mostly covered by small landslides and uluhe fern tangles. Small portions of the long windward contour trail are still used for ditch maintenance, but most of the route is gradually succumbing to downed trees, landslides, and encroaching vegetation. The HTMC currently hikes the lower section of the CCC trail in Kahana Valley, but the upper portion to the first intake is heavily overgrown. The State of Hawaiʻi now owns and operates the Waiāhole Ditch, which delivers water to leeward vegetable farms rather than to OSC cane fields.

ʻŌpaeʻula and Kawaiiki

The kids walk in the water through the trestle and the brave balance their way over the planks above the water, and the fearful sneak down below in the gulch.

—Hawaiian Trail and Mountain Club
schedule, July 2, 1972

Shortly after its founding in 1899, the Waialua Agricultural Company (WAC) decided to investigate using stream water instead of expensive pumped water to irrigate its planned high-level cane fields above Haleʻiwa town. Later that year engineers under manager William W. Goodale surveyed ʻŌpaeʻula, Kawaiiki, and Kawainui, three of the major streams *mauka* (inland) of the plantation. Acting on the favorable results, the WAC decided to build ʻŌpaeʻula and Kawaiiki Ditches first, followed by Kamananui (later Kawainui) Ditch.[29]

Construction of the ʻŌpaeʻula Ditch and its access trail started in early 1900 and finished before the year's end. The system was 2.75 miles long, half underground and half open ditch, with a capacity of forty million gallons per day. Stream water diverted by a concrete dam at an elevation of 1,101 feet emerged at the top of the cane fields at an elevation of 932 feet just above ʻŌpaeʻula Camp. A 1,400-foot siphon delivered the water across Kawailoa Gulch to additional upper-level fields above Kawailoa Camp. The 2.5-mile access trail roughly followed the *mauka* section of the ditch and ended at the intake. The total cost of the project was about $64,000.[30]

In 1902, the WAC began building the Kawaiiki Ditch and its access trail and completed both the following year. The 1.2-mile system with a capacity of forty million gallons per day was mostly underground, except for two flumes spanning steep side gulches. Water gathered from the stream at an elevation of 1,100 feet emptied into ʻŌpaeʻula Ditch. The Kawaiiki access trail branched off the ʻŌpaeʻula Trail, descended into the valley, and contoured along the ditch route for a little over two miles to the intake. The total cost of the Kawaiiki project was about $34,000.[31]

In 1903 the WAC also completed the ʻŌpaeʻula reservoir to store the runoff collected by the two ditches. Backing up the water was an earthen dam seventy feet high. In May 1911, sections of two ʻŌpaeʻula Ditch tunnels collapsed, cutting off water for forty-six days. Workers bypassed the blockages with a single tunnel bored through more solid ground.[32] In December 1911, the company completed the third ditch project, Kamananui.[33]

In 1919 a long drought allowed the WAC to embark on a two-year project to upgrade the original two ditches. The company almost doubled the capacity of the 'Ōpae'ula Ditch below its junction with the Kawaiiki Ditch to take full advantage of increased flows during heavy storms. To reduce seepage, workers lined both ditches with stone or concrete. The WAC also built a second 'Ōpae'ula reservoir below the first one.[34]

The Hawaiian Trail and Mountain Club (HTMC) first scheduled a hike along the 'Ōpae'ula Ditch access trail for December 12, 1920. That morning the group met at the Pan-Pacific building in downtown Honolulu and took the club's new autobus to Haleiwa Hotel. From there they drove to the end of the main cane road paralleling 'Ōpae'ula (red shrimp) Gulch. On foot the hikers descended into the gulch on the switchbacks of the upper section of the access trail. They crossed 'Ōpae'ula Ditch at its junction with Kawaiiki Ditch and followed the contour trail to the intake. Undoubtedly, the group explored farther upstream looking for swimming holes.[35]

The initial trip must have been a success because the club repeated the 'Ōpae'ula outing on April 11, 1921. A group of seventy-five members and guests in three autobuses drove to the top of the WAC cane fields and walked the short access trail. Several hikers crossed a broad ridge covered with 'iliahi (sandalwood) and descended into Kawaiiki Gulch. Just above the stream they picked up the ditch access trail and followed it back to the buses.[36] On July 19, 1925, the HTMC returned to 'Ōpae'ula, this time with fifty-seven hikers led by John R. Bisho and Otto H. Swezey, an entomologist with the Hawaiian Sugar Planters Association.[37]

On October 20, 1932, territorial forester Charles S. Judd led an overnight trip to search for a herd of wild cattle in a seldom-visited section of the Kawailoa Forest Reserve. Along were special hunter Nicholas Mendes, ranger at large Max F. Landgraf, and two Piko Club members, Lieutenant Thomas J. Wells, the son and aide of Major General Briant H. Wells, and Frederick D. Lowrey, vice president of Lewers and Cooke, Ltd. The group quickly hiked the Kawaiiki Ditch access trail to the intake. There the five men crossed the ridge to Kawainui Stream and worked upstream to the first major fork, where they spent a comfortable night. The next day the group followed the north fork, climbed up a spur ridge to Pu'u Ka'inapua'a, and came out the Mālaekahana Trail.[38]

In 1937, the U.S. Army Third Engineers and Civilian Conservation Corps crews completed the Wahiawa-Pupukea Trail, later known as Drum Drive, and Pa'ala'a Uka Pūpūkea Road. Built of crushed coral, the one-lane route wound through the leeward Ko'olau foothills linking various army training areas. Drum Drive provided alternate access to the 'Ōpae'ula/Kawaiiki trailhead from Helemano.[39]

During the late 1920s and 1930s the HTMC did not schedule either 'Ōpae'ula or Kawaiiki, probably because there were good swimming hikes closer to Honolulu. However, after World War II the club began hiking Kawaiiki in 1946 and resumed hiking 'Ōpae'ula in 1953.[40] On the 'Ōpae'ula outing of October 17, 1954, the group drove through Wahiawā, turned *mauka* past the pineapple stand, and followed Drum Drive to the trailhead. Led by Adeline Whisenand, the hikers walked the access trail and continued upstream to a long and lovely pool four or five feet deep. The group passed pump 17, which the WAC had installed the previous year, along the stream less than a half-mile above the intake. The electric pump delivered water to upslope storage tanks near Bryan's mountain house and the Pe'ahinai'a trailhead.[41]

Whisenand also led the Kawaiiki hike on July 8, 1956. That beautiful Sunday, the group descended to the stream and sauntered along the access trail to the two elevated concrete flumes. There each hiker made a choice,

> The kids walk in the water through the trestle and the brave balance their way over the planks above the water, and the fearful sneak down below in the gulch.[42]

After negotiating the flumes, the group passed the dam and intake and continued upstream about half a mile to several enticing pools.[43]

In 1964, HTMC member Lloyd Talcott and others investigated the lower section of the 'Ōpae'ula Ditch access trail from Drum Drive down to the upper-level cane fields. The pleasant, well-graded route contoured above the stream past avocado trees and large 'iliahi. The club incorporated the lower section into the 'Ōpae'ula hike of August 2 led by Talcott and in subsequent hikes over the next few years.[44]

The HTMC continued to schedule 'Ōpae'ula and Kawaiiki regularly through 1995. But the club lost access to both hikes the next year because of the closing of Waialua Sugar Company and the liability concerns of the new tenant farmers. Over the weekend of November 5–7, 1998, a small, informal group of HTMC members camped at Palama Uka, a rustic retreat along Drum Drive. On Saturday morning they hiked 'Ōpae'ula in the morning and Kawaiiki in the afternoon, with a swim in the twin pools beyond the intake. On Sunday morning the group followed the Kawainui Trail to

Walking the plank on the Kawaiiki Trail, August 16, 1970. In front, Charles Smith (Photo by Thelma Smith, HTMC Archives)

the large, circular pool. There they enjoyed a refreshing dip and a back massage at a mini-waterfall just upstream.[45]

As of 2010, the Kawaiiki Trail and the upper section of the 'Ōpae'ula Trail are partially overgrown, but both remain passable to their intakes and swimming holes because of regular use by the Sierra Club, Hawai'i Chapter. The lower 'Ōpae'ula section has deteriorated significantly because of little use and no maintenance. Both ditches still channel water to the 'Ōpae'ula reservoirs to irrigate mixed crops, rather than sugar cane.

Kawainui

> Kamananui [Kawainui] will be an expensive ditch, a large part of it will be in tunnels through hard rock along the side of the deepest ravine on the plantation.
>
> —William W. Goodale, December 31, 1909

Shortly after its incorporation in 1899, the Waialua Agricultural Company (WAC) decided to investigate using stream water instead of expensive pumped water to irrigate its planned high-level cane fields above Hale'iwa town. Later that year engineers under manager William W. Goodale surveyed 'Ōpae'ula, Kawai Iki, and Kawainui, three of the major streams *mauka* (inland) of the plantation. Acting on the favorable results of the investigation, the WAC built 'Ōpae'ula Ditch in 1900 and Kawaiiki Ditch in 1903.[46]

After a detailed investigation of Kawainui Stream in 1902, the company started building Kamananui Ditch the next year, only to abandon the project in 1904, probably because of low sugar prices.[47] In 1909, WAC engineers developed revised specifications and estimated costs for a tunnel and ditch system with an access trail. In his report for the year, Goodale wrote,

> Kamananui will be an expensive ditch, a large part of it will be in tunnels through hard rock along the side of the deepest ravine on the plantation. When finished, the ditch will make available 1,000 acres for cultivation.[48]

Construction of the Kamananui Ditch started on June 10, 1910, and finished on December 7, 1911, about a year and a half later. The ditch channeled water 3.7 miles from the concrete dam across Kawainui Stream at an elevation of 713 feet to the cane fields above Kawailoa Camp at 669 feet. The three-and-a-half-mile access trail roughly paralleled the ditch for half its length. The total cost of the Kamananui project was $79,963.81.

During its first few months of operation the ditch captured an average of 2,188,471 gallons per day.[49] The flow, however, dropped dramatically for much of 1912, an unusually dry year in the Ko'olau Range. The WAC used the drought as an opportunity to line the tunnels with concrete to reduce seepage and to redesign the intake to better divert water when the rain resumed.[50] In 1918 the company again rebuilt the intake and lined the lower ditch section with stone.[51]

On January 21, 1934, the Piko Club first hiked the ditch access trail, then known as the Kawailoa Gulch Trail. The group of mostly army officers and their guests hiked to the dam and back in four and a half hours. Along that Sunday was Major General Briant H. Wells, commander of the Hawaiian Department and cofounder of the club.[52]

In 1937, U.S. Army Third Engineers and Civilian Conservation Corps crews completed the Wahiawa-Pupukea Trail, later known as Drum Drive, and Paʻalaʻa Uka Pūpūkea Road. Built of crushed coral, the one-lane route wound through the leeward Koʻolau foothills linking various trailheads and army training areas. Near the junction of Kawaiiki and Kawainui Streams, the road crossed the Kawailoa Gulch Trail, providing easier access to it.[53]

The Hawaiian Trail and Mountain Club (HTMC) first scheduled the Kawailoa Gulch Trail for October 31, 1937. Led by First Circuit Court judge John A. Matthewman, the group hiked to the intake and probably beyond. If some went far enough, they may have found one of the best swimming holes on the island.[54]

In the early 1950s, the HTMC resumed scheduling the ditch route, renamed the Kawainui Trail. Getting there from Haleʻiwa involved a long drive through the WAC cane fields on dirt ʻŌpaeʻula Road. At ʻŌpaeʻula reservoir the car caravan took Drum Drive to a small parking lot just past Palama Uka, a rustic retreat built by naturalist Lorin Gill and the Palama Settlement in 1957. On foot the groups continued down Drum Drive to its intersection with the Kawainui Trail. The hikers followed the contour route to the ditch intake and then worked upstream for less than a mile to a spacious swimming hole ringed with kukui trees. On the weekend of June 21, 1969, the club held the first of many campouts by the lovely pool.[55]

In the middle 1960s, Lloyd Talcott and other HTMC members reopened the lower section of the ditch trail below Drum Drive. Called Kawailoa Gulch, the pleasant hike contoured above the stream through mango and sisal groves past Hawaiian terraces and inviting pools. The groups sometimes searched for antique bottles along the route.[56]

The HTMC continued to schedule Kawainui regularly as a day hike and a campout through 1995, but the club lost access to the ʻŌpaeʻula area the next year because of the closing of Waialua Sugar Company and the liability concerns of the new tenant farmers. Over the weekend of November 5–7, 1998, a small, informal group of HTMC members camped at Palama Uka along Drum Drive. On Saturday morning they hiked the ʻŌpaeʻula Trail in the morning and the Kawaiiki Trail in the afternoon, with a swim in the twin pools beyond the intake. On Sunday morning the group followed the

Kawainui Trail to the large, circular pool. There they enjoyed a refreshing dip and a back massage at a mini-waterfall just upstream.[57]

As of 2010, the Kawainui Trail was moderately overgrown but remains passable to the intake and the swimming hole because of regular use by the Sierra Club, Hawai'i Chapter. The Kawailoa Gulch Trail below Drum Drive receives little use and no maintenance and is heavily overgrown. The Kawainui Ditch still provides water, but for mixed farming rather than for king cane.

Castle (Pig God)

[A] trail that sometimes slips and always compels you to pack your mule on one side only and even then there is danger of his dropping down over the edge of the scenery.

—Hugh M. Polworth, July 1911

In 1906, Punalu'u Valley was home to a small Chinese community of rice growers. They lived in gray, weather-beaten houses toward the front of the valley and tended their rice paddies irrigated by Punalu'u Stream. *Mauka* (inland) was the rice mill with a waterwheel and red roof. Behind the mill were newly planted cane fields controlled by sugar baron James B. Castle.[58]

An energetic entrepreneur, Castle envisioned sugar and other plantations lining the windward coast from Kahuku to Kailua. As a first step, he had started the Kahuku Plantation Company (KPC) in 1890. Later the Mormons organized their lands into Laie Plantation and began shipping cane to the Kahuku mill. In 1907, Castle founded the Koolau Agricultural Company (KAC) to consolidate his agricultural properties between Hau'ula and Kahana, including a portion of Punalu'u Valley leased from B. P. Bishop Estate in 1906. That same year Castle began construction of Punalu'u Ditch to irrigate the cane fields there, and the Koolau Railway to link the windward plantations with the Kahuku mill.[59]

Castle also decided to investigate the potential of Kaluanui and Kaipapa'u Streams to supply water to his Hau'ula acreage. In early 1906, he contracted the stream measurement project to engineer William E. Rowell, former assistant superintendent in the Department of Public Works. Rowell soon determined that a direct approach upstream to the two watersheds was not feasible because of numerous narrows and waterfalls. He then developed a flanking route, rugged but suitable for mules carrying material and measuring equipment. The trail would climb the west side of Punalu'u Valley on eight switchbacks, cross Kaluanui Stream above the last major waterfall, and contour around Ma'akua Gulch to Kaipapa'u Stream.

Later in 1906, a crew, probably from the KPC, began building the trail, soon to be named after its founder. After reaching the Kaluanui crossing, the laborers constructed a twelve-person wood cabin to provide overnight shelter while they completed the contour section. By October, Rowell installed four weirs with measuring devices on Kaluanui Stream, one at an elevation of 1,900 feet near the cabin and one on each of the three upper forks at 2,500 feet. He also built a fifth weir at 1,900 feet on Kaipapa'u Stream. The engineer then recorded monthly stream flow from October 1906 through October 1907.[60]

In 1910, James Castle made an informal agreement with the newly founded Hawaiian Trail and Mountain Club (HTMC) and its first president, his brother William R. Castle. The club would have use of the trail and the cabin in return for maintaining the route. However, no records exist of the HTMC using or maintaining the Castle Trail in the 1910s.[61]

In 1915, the KAC helped install stream gaging station number 3040 on the right bank of Kaluanui Stream just above the cabin. A continuous recording device measured water flow for the next two years to determine if Kaluanui Stream could provide hydroelectric power to run the pumps at Kahuku Plantation. The KAC had already constructed a ditch below the first waterfall, known as Kaliuwa'a, or Sacred Falls, to irrigate its cane fields at the front of the valley.[62]

For February 20, 1921, the HTMC scheduled two hikes, Sacred Falls (class B, moderate) and the Castle Trail (class A, difficult). That morning four autobuses with 110 hikers aboard left the Pan-Pacific building in downtown Honolulu. Because of a delay in Kāne'ohe, the caravan did not reach Punalu'u Valley until 11 a.m. Thirty intrepid hikers got off the buses there, and the rest continued to Kaliuwa'a Valley bound for Sacred Falls. Led by forestry ranger and HTMC member Thomas R. L. McGuire, the smaller group climbed the overgrown but passable switchbacks, crossed Kaluanui Stream, and ascended to a saddle on the ridge separating Kaluanui and Ma'akua Streams. There the hikers were supposed to descend the ridge *makai* (seaward) back to their waiting bus. But the group either missed the turn at the saddle or at another junction farther down the ridge and ended up bushwhacking by moonlight. The "dirty thirty" finally reached Hau'ula well after midnight and Honolulu just before dawn. Part Hawaiian,

McGuire blamed it all on the resident pig demigod Kamapua'a for obliterating the trail and leading them down the wrong ridge. The group later decided the outing was one of the best trips ever. Participant, weatherman, and sometime poet Lawrence H. Daingerfield captured the hardships and rewards of hiking *Mauka Sacred Falls*.

> Upward where the mud is king,
> And the birds in rain tree sing-
> That's the place to go on the wing,
> Mauka Sacred Falls.
>
> Iridescent tree shells stray
> A yard a year in search of prey,
> And wild bananas, wind swept, sway
> Mauka Sacred Falls.
>
> This is Kamapuaa's place-
> Pig God of the crooked face-
> where the trail is but a trace
> Mauka Sacred Falls.[63]

In 1923, the Bishop Estate requested assistance from the Territorial Forestry Division in reducing the destructive pig population *mauka* Sacred Falls. On September 9, head forester Charles S. Judd introduced two estate hunters to the Castle or Pig God Trail and the upper Kaluanui drainage in the Hau'ula Forest Reserve. After the hike, Judd reported,

> Forest is suffering considerably from ravages of these wild animals and in effort to clear them out Bishop Estate has authorized me to pay bounty of $1 for each wild pig killed.[64]

Later that year the estate also closed the Castle Trail to recreational hikers, fearing their impact on the native vegetation.[65] Over the next several years Judd made periodic visits to the upper Kaluanui region to monitor the native forest. On September 17, 1925, he found the vegetation much recovered as a result of estate and public hunting efforts.[66]

On June 28, 1928, he climbed the Castle Trail to the saddle above Kaluanui Stream and then bushwhacked up the ridge to the Ko'olau summit. Also along on the inspection were O'ahu ranger McGuire, ranger at large Max F. Landgraf, and two hunters with dogs. Near the summit Judd found extensive pig damage, which he immediately reported to the

Bishop Estate.[67] In November, Kahuku ranger Robert Plunkett and his trail crew packed pig traps up the Castle Trail for use by estate hunters.[68]

On May 22, 1930, Judd hired special hunters John Pahamoa and Nicholas Mendes to kill pigs along the summit in the Kaipapaʻu and Hauʻula Forest Reserves for $75 per month.[69] The two men and their dogs frequently used the Castle Trail to access the summit area. For one week in July, Plunkett and his gang worked up the trail to the saddle and then improved the route to the Koʻolau crest.[70]

After an eight-year hiatus, the HTMC returned to the Pig God Trail on November 24, 1929. Led by house painter Edmund J. Meadows, the group ascended the Castle Trail and returned the same way before dark. On September 28, 1930, McGuire and William Bush guided an HTMC group to Kaluanui Stream and probably beyond toward the summit.[71]

On February 17, 1931, Judd led nine army officers, Mendes, and Bishop Estate forester George R. Ewart III on a reconnaissance hike above Punaluʻu Valley. The group climbed the Castle Trail to the saddle and followed the improved route to the top. They then turned south along the summit and descended a spur ridge back into Punaluʻu Valley. During that grueling loop, the men first discussed forming a hiking club with members drawn from the army and the Division of Forestry. After finishing the hike well after dark, the group enjoyed a swim in the ocean and continued the discussion over a late dinner at Cooper Ranch Inn in Hauʻula. Several months later Judd and Major General Briant H. Wells formed the Piko Club.[72]

The Piko Club engendered cooperation between the U.S. Army and the Division of Forestry. Rangers developed trail maps for army division officers and included them on inspection hikes in the forest reserves. In turn, the army cleared a trail at the back of Punaluʻu Valley among others, and even helped build a cabin near the Koʻolau summit.[73]

On November 14, 1932, Forestry Division workers delivered three bundles wrapped in burlap to the army bomber hangar at Luke Field on Ford Island. Inside the bundles were redwood frames and tin roof and siding for a ten-by-ten-foot cabin to be dropped at the head of Kaipapaʻu Stream near the Koʻolau summit. On November 16, Judd, Oʻahu assistant forester Glenn W. Russ, and Landgraf hiked up the Castle Trail to the cabin site, cleared it, and set up a six-by-twenty-foot white cloth as target for the bombers. That evening a severe Kona storm came in and dumped eight inches of rain on the summit. Despite the storm the group spent a "fairly comfortable" night in their tent. The next morning heavy clouds draped the summit, keeping the bombers on the ground.

On November 21, the clouds lifted briefly, allowing a single bomber to drop one bundle. It landed within seventy-five feet of the target, but unfortunately hit a rock bank. The tin sections survived the impact, but the redwood beams shattered. On the afternoon of November 29, bombers from the 19th Pursuit Squadron dropped the remaining two bundles on target and in good condition. On December 23, a forestry crew finished building the cabin, to be used by pig hunters. The army assistance had saved the crews many hours packing the material up the Castle Trail.[74]

The Piko Club first scheduled the Castle Trail as a Sunday outing on November 19, 1933. That warm day forty-seven hikers ascended the switchbacks to Kaluanui Stream. Most then headed downstream to the top of a waterfall above Kaliuwaʻa (Sacred) Falls for lunch. A few continued up the trail to the saddle, informally known as the pig wire, and then climbed the ridge to the Kaipapaʻu cabin near the Koʻolau summit. The HTMC also conducted hikes on the Castle Trail in March of 1933 and 1934.[75]

In August 1934, the Honolulu Unit of the Civilian Conservation Corps (CCC) began to reconstruct the Castle Trail and its extension to the Koʻolau summit. The veteran crew assigned to the project had already built the Summit Trail from Black Junction to Puʻu Kainapuaʻa. On an August 30 inspection, Judd and Landgraf found the gang, led by foreman Ernest W. Landgraf, working halfway up the switchback section.[76]

On October 18, Judd and Max Landgraf climbed the rebuilt Castle Trail past the shipshape CCC camp by Kaluanui Stream to the pig wire. There Ernest Landgraf joined them, and the three men began scouting along the contour section of the trail for a feasible route to the summit. After floundering around Kaipapaʻu Gulch, all three decided the area was too rough for the new route. Judd then told Ernest Landgraf to extend the Castle Trail from the pig wire up the ridge to the Koʻolau summit near the Kaipapaʻu cabin at a 12 percent grade.[77] Landgraf and his first-rate crew built the Castle extension as instructed, completing it before year's end, and then resumed work on the Summit Trail. Vegetation and landslides gradually reclaimed the bypassed Castle contour section.

On Sunday July 14, 1935, the Piko Club completed a magnificent Koʻolau summit traverse on three new CCC trails. Thirty Pikos took the Poamoho Trail to the top, where they bushwhacked north briefly to the current end of the Summit Trail. After strolling along the wide-open path, the group descended the rebuilt Castle Trail. Halfway down, chief scout Joseph B. Sweet served coffee at the CCC camp near Kaluanui Stream. The club repeated the hike on November 1, 1936, shortly before its demise. The HTMC also scheduled the Castle Trail on May 6, 1935.[78]

During World War II, the army built cabins at the Kaluanui Stream crossing and just below the Koʻolau crest. Soldiers also dug a network of foxholes around the Castle and Summit Trail junction.[79] In 1943, the army established the Unit Jungle Training Center to better prepare its soldiers for combat in the Pacific Islands. The center had three layouts or courses of instruction, red and blue in Kahana Valley, and green in Punaluʻu Valley. The green course was the most demanding as it taught instructors for the other two courses. Both the Castle and the Koʻolau Summit Trails formed a part of the green course for field exercises and edible plant identification classes.[80] After training all day, the troops stopped for refreshments at the Punaluʻu Store, established by Yan Quong Ching in 1935.[81]

After the war, the HTMC resumed hiking the Castle Trail on December 22, 1946. The hike blurb in the schedule read,

> Although the trail is not nearly as clear as it was in the good old days, it's still the good old Pig God Trail. The finest view on the island if it doesn't rain, only it always rains.[82]

The club also conducted a Castle campout on Labor Day weekend 1947. That year the Territorial Forestry Division included Castle as trail number 16 at five miles on its Oʻahu map. In the early 1950s at the saddle, a wooden sign painted white with black lettering "Hauʻula pig wyre" (corrupted Welsh for trail) pointed down the ridge, according to naturalist Lorin T. Gill.[83]

The HTMC continued to schedule Castle regularly from the 1950s through 1973. For the next seven years the club was unable to get permission from the Bishop Estate to hike the trail because of liability concerns. As a result, the route began to deteriorate; downed trees and landslides blocked the switchbacks, and uluhe ferns and *Clidemia* shrubs clogged the upper section.

In 1980, HTMC members Zon Owen and Lorna Turner obtained permission from the Bishop Estate for the club to hike the Castle Trail once again. Owen organized three trail clearing outings to reopen the route up the switchbacks to the Kaluanui Stream crossing. He then led the Castle hike for HTMC on January 25, 1981.[84] In her poem *Confrontation*, Beryl Sawyer recalled the excitement of the crowd's meeting at Iolani Palace that Sunday morning.

> Ninety-two, at the palace, at eight.
> For Castly Trail, closed of late.
> Lorna Turner, leader-learner-
> Chat, chat, chat, of this and that.

All signed on? The crowd was wide.
Don't get lost! Who needs a ride?

A member of the HPD,
On motor-cycle came to see.
Demonstration? Confrontation?
Accident? Or fender bent?

Assured we were HTMC,
He wished us well from HPD.[85]

The club continued to hike the Castle Trail annually through 1985. On August 11 of that year, seventy-four members and guests led by Stuart Ball ascended the switchbacks to the Kaluanui crossing. Twelve stalwarts pushed on to the misty, still Koʻolau summit and a fleeting view of Kaʻala in the Waiʻanae Range. The last hikers finally emerged from the forest at 6:15 p.m. after a long but satisfying day. The next year the club lost access once again because of liability concerns of the lessee in Punaluʻu Valley.[86]

In late 2007, Kamehameha Schools–Bishop Estate granted the club entry to Punaluʻu Valley to reopen and hike the Castle Trail. An exploratory outing revealed that the switchback section to Kaluanui Stream was actually passable despite decades of neglect. On November 11, the club's trail maintenance crew led by Michael (Mike) Algiers cleared and repaired the trail to the stream. The HTMC returned to hike the trail on December 2, a cloudy, rainy Sunday with Kona (southerly) winds. Led by Stuart Ball, thirty-two members crossed Punaluʻu Stream and began climbing the muddy switchbacks. Some of the group stopped at the stream; others continued to a waterfall overlook past the pig wire. Twelve hard-core hikers reached the Koʻolau summit as the sky cleared briefly during midday. In the late afternoon the "dirty thirty-two" straggled back to the trailhead as cloud and drizzle descended *mauka* Sacred Falls.[87]

In 2008, the HTMC scheduled the Castle hike twice, each time opening up more of the trail. As of 2010, the route was reasonably clear to the waterfall overlook. The final stretch to the summit is passable but overgrown. The original contour section from the pig wire to Kaipapaʻu Stream is lost under thick vegetation and numerous landslides. The cabin site and camping spot by Kaluanui Stream is muddy and partially covered by dark strawberry guava trees, but it remains a wild, lovely spot to pitch a tent or hang a hammock. Punaluʻu Valley is often called green valley after the name of the training course there. Ching's store still offers refreshments—to locals and tourists instead of to GIs.

Waimano

> Fresh water obtained from the [Waimano] ditch has been a great help to the sections on which it was run. Yields have increased materially.
>
> —Honolulu Plantation Company
> Annual Report, 1916

In 1902, the Honolulu Plantation Company (HPC) wanted to expand its sugar cane fields upslope but was concerned about the high cost of irrigating them with water pumped from wells at a lower elevation. The company thus decided to investigate the potential of the three major streams *mauka* (inland) of the plantation as a possible high-level water source. In December, HPC engineers built small weirs and installed water flow and rain gauges on Hālawa, Waimalu, and Waimano Streams.[88]

The automatic devices measured wide variations in flow for all three streams during the first two years of the investigation. Waimano Stream, for example, produced 352.8 million gallons across the weir in 1903 and 873.3 million gallons in 1904.[89] Clearly, the stream would never be a steady source of water, but it could supplement pumped water for the higher-level fields. For the next eight years the HPC continued to monitor the data but declined to develop the streams because of more important projects, such as its 'Aiea refinery.

In the fall of 1912, the HPC, under manager James Gibb, finally built a ditch system with an access trail in Waimano Valley at a cost of about $21,000. The ditch was three miles long and had fifteen tunnels. The intake dam was constructed across the stream at an elevation of 636 feet on the site of the original weir. The ditch ended at an elevation of 580 feet on the ridge at the Waiau side of the valley.[90] In 1913, its first full year of operation, the Waimano Ditch delivered 469.5 million gallons of water to newly planted *mauka* fields.[91]

In 1914, the HPC built a small reservoir at the ditch end to store some of the overflow. From there a riveted steel siphon, twenty inches wide, spanned Waimano Valley to deliver water to new plantings above Pearl City.[92] In 1916, the HPC annual report remarked,

> Fresh water obtained from the ditch has been a great help to the sections on which it was run. Yields have increased materially.[93]

Under contract with the Territory of Hawaiʻi, HPC began providing water from the reservoir to the newly built Home for the Feeble-Minded and Epileptic in 1920. Better known as Waimano Home, the institution occupied a 617-acre site *mauka* of the reservoir at the end of a narrow dirt road. The inmates there worked seven days a week, the boys at farming and raising livestock, the girls at cooking and cleaning.[94]

Also in 1920, the Hawaiian Trail and Mountain Club (HTMC) scheduled a new outing called Waiau Ridge for March 28. That morning thirty-one members and guests arrived in Pearl City by train and automobile. Led by forestry ranger and HTMC member Thomas R. L. McGuire, the group walked the ditch trail to the dam, passing several large groves of ʻōhiʻa ʻai (mountain apple). The hikers then climbed the ridge on the Waiau side to look for land shells (native tree snails). The group retraced their steps to the train station, where they drove home or caught the 5:30 p.m. Haleiwa Limited for Honolulu. Although tired by the fourteen-mile round trip, the group was well-pleased with the new hike and vowed to return during mountain apple season in summer.[95]

The HTMC next scheduled Waimano (many waters) Valley as a class B (moderate) outing for May 15, 1921. From the reservoir the group followed the access trail as it paralleled the open ditch or its tunnels. At one point the hikers had to walk above the ditch on a narrow plank fastened to the cliff. About two miles in they passed a ditchman's cabin situated as the ditch crossed a side stream on a flume. The group then climbed a low side ridge and descended through mountain apple trees to the dam and intake just below a fork in the stream. Beyond the dam was a cascade where the adventurous could slide down a slippery groove into a deep pool. The outing was undoubtedly a success, as the club repeated it twice during 1922.[96]

On April 17, 1929, territorial forester Charles S. Judd and Oʻahu assistant forester Glenn W. Russ led a small group into Waimano Valley to look for wild cattle and pigs in the ʻEwa Forest Reserve. The five men and their five dogs took an old ranch route *mauka* of Waimano Home down to the cabin and picked up the ditch trail there. About a quarter-mile upstream of the dam they found five cows, a bull, and a calf. Shortly afterward, Judd and one other turned around, while the remaining three, including ranger at large Max F. Landgraf, continued up the south fork on a three-day exploratory hike. After reaching the summit of the Koʻolau Range, the men descended the north fork, flushing two pigs and killing one of them.[97]

On June 7, 1934, Judd included a two-part extension of the ditch trail as an Emergency Conservation Work project for the second enrollment period (October 1, 1934, to March 31, 1935). Called the Waimano Trail, the proposed project started at the ʻEwa Forest Reserve boundary *mauka* of

Waimano Home. The route would descend gradually to the cabin, roughly following the ranch route. The ditch trail would then be extended from the dam up the ridge between the north and south forks to the Koʻolau summit. The total estimated distance of the extension was four and a half miles, requiring 2,584 man-days. After its approval, Russ assigned the Waimano project to the Honolulu Unit of the Civilian Conservation Corps (CCC).[98]

On September 25, Judd, Landgraf, and four CCC men from Kalihi scouted and flagged the initial section from a mango tree back of Waimano Home down to the ditchman's cabin.[99] On October 9, a Honolulu Unit trail crew began grading the marked route, which gently descended into the valley on three switchbacks. The work was easy at first but became more difficult later on because of rainy weather and rough terrain along the ridge leading to the Koʻolau summit. Honolulu Unit project superintendent Gunder E. Olson later remarked, "Progress on this trail has been considerably impeded by rocky cliffs on which much blasting has been necessary."[100]

On the afternoon of February 27, 1935, an intense winter storm developed at the head of Waimano and Waimalu Valleys. Heavy runoff filled the ditch with sediment and severely damaged sections of newly built trail. The next day Olson switched the crew to the drier ʻAiea Loop Trail project, while waiting for the summit weather to improve. Despite the hardships the gang had managed to complete 3.4 miles of the Waimano Trail before the transfer.

The same crew finished the ʻAiea Loop Trail on June 12 and resumed work on the ravaged Waimano Trail the next morning. After clearing the landslides left by the February cloudburst, the men pushed doggedly for the summit. On July 17, they moved into a comfortable side camp at the two-mile mark, probably on a bench above the stream near the dam. The summer weather was generally good, but the grading still proved slow and difficult. Olson commented,

> Rough, heavily wooded country and many cliffs of hard, decomposed basalt, have impeded progress on this trail to a great extent the past two months.[101]

The CCC crew finally reached the Koʻolau summit in November 1935. The completed Waimano Trail stretched 5.7 miles and required 5,552 man-days. Average construction per man-day was a low 5.4 feet because of the terrain and weather. After finishing the project, the Honolulu Unit dismantled the side camp and used the material from the kitchen to build a small overnight cabin farther up the trail for hunters and forestry personnel.[102]

A CCC crew digs out the Waimano Trail, 1935. Before. (Charles Judd papers, Hawai'i State Archives)

After.

On January 26, 1936, the HTMC first hiked the CCC extension to the summit. The group may have passed plantings done by Colin Potter, superintendent of Foster Park (later Foster Botanical Gardens), soon after the trail was completed. He planted orchids, ornamental kī (ti), and king palms from Australia along the switchback section just after the ditch intake.[103]

Before and during World War II, the Honolulu Plantation Company lost more than two thousand acres, fully one-third of its prime fields, to the military for various installations. Although compensated by the government, HPC was unable to grow enough sugar cane to keep its refinery running profitably after the war. On January 1, 1947, the company sold all its property to the Oahu Sugar Company (OSC) for $3,750,000. The Waiahole Water Company, a subsidiary of the OSC, took over operation of Waimano Ditch, but soon abandoned it because of high maintenance costs.[104]

The HTMC scheduled the Waimano Trail regularly during the 1950s and 1960s. The groups enjoyed mountain apples in season, although vandals had chopped down many of the trees near the intake. Some of the hikers stopped at a pool in front of the dam, while others continued to the summit, a round trip distance of fourteen miles. In 1959 and 1962, Richard H. (Dick) Davis led camping trips to a cabin by Waimano Stream about a mile below the summit. Probably built by the army during World War II, the rustic shelter served as a base camp for the group, who explored along the summit ridge toward the Kīpapa Trail.[105]

The HTMC continued to hike the Waimano Trail from the 1970s through the early 2000s. On the outing of February 1, 1970, James Malcolm reportedly saw a black bear about five and a half feet tall.

> The hair on the back of my head stood straight up. We just looked at each other. Then he went up the mountain, and I went straight down the trail![106]

In 1971, Norman Roberts and his two sons hiked to the dam for a picnic and a swim. At a small sand beach by the *mauka* end of the pool, Roberts found what appeared to be bear tracks. Nearby was a rotted log torn apart and claw-like marks on a kukui tree trunk. Those two instances were the last reports about Butch, the legendary Koʻolau bear.

Back in March 1956, a black bear cub named Butch escaped from Heeia Kea Animal Farm, a private zoo in back of Kāneʻohe. He left trailing a six-foot iron chain attached to his collar, so the zoo owner, Al Jensen, didn't think the cub would travel far. Butch, however, eluded capture around the farm and somehow detached his collar. He then roamed the Koʻolau Range from Pūpūkea to ʻAiea for the next fifteen years, based on repeated, sometimes questionable sightings. With a twenty-year life span, Butch would have died happy sometime around 1976, assuming he had not succumbed much earlier.[107]

The HTMC hike of November 15, 1981, featured the wedding of members Jim Yuen and Beverley Haylett. The ceremony took place at a lovely ridge-top clearing above the site of the ditchman's cabin just over two miles in. Judge and HTMC member Gay Conklin married the couple, who both wore hiking outfits and muddy jungle boots.

> After the exchange of vows and Hawaiian style rings, the gang drank a toast of passion-fruit-orange juice from plastic wine glasses and the newly-weds sliced into the double Chinese wedding cookie with, what else?, Jim's trusty machete.[108]

After the reception the bride and groom resumed hiking the Waimano Trail toward the summit.

Newlyweds Jim and Beverley Yuen by the Waimano Trail, November 15, 1981. (Courtesy of Jim Yuen)

As of 2010, the Waimano Trail was the best preserved of the long Koʻolau ridge trails of the CCC era. The route is open to the public without permission, and is usually clear to the intake and passable to the summit. Although frequently clogged with earth and vegetation, the abandoned ditch is still much in evidence along the initial portion of the trail. The site of the Yuens' wedding is marked by a covered picnic table built by the Boy Scouts. The dam and pool are gone, but the nearby mountain apple grove remains. Potter's palms and ornamental *kī* still line the switchbacks beyond the intake. The forest has virtually reclaimed the army cabin, but inscriptions dating from the war are visible on a partially collapsed wall. And finally, the HPC upper-level cane fields irrigated by the ditch are now the subdivisions of Pacific Palisades and Momilani, and the reservoir is the site of a State Department of Land and Natural Resources baseyard.

Waimalu

Go along the ditch trail on the side of the hill—it is very pleasant walking and winds in and out of the hills.

—Edmund J. Meadows, Oahu Trail
pamphlet, circa 1930

In 1902, the Honolulu Plantation Company (HPC) wanted to expand its sugar cane fields upslope but was concerned about the high cost of irrigating them with water pumped from wells at a lower elevation. The company thus decided to investigate the potential of the three major streams *mauka* (inland) of the plantation as a possible high-level water source. In December, HPC engineers built small weirs and installed water flow and rain gauges on Hālawa, Waimalu, and Waimano Streams.[109]

The automatic devices measured wide variations in flow for all three streams during the first two years of the investigation. Waimalu Stream, for example, produced 386.8 million gallons across the weir in 1903 and 1,031.8 million gallons in 1904.[110] Clearly, the stream would never be a steady source of water, but it could supplement pumped water for the higher-level fields. For the next eight years the HPC continued to monitor the data but declined to develop the streams because of more important projects, such as its ʻAiea refinery.

On the afternoon of November 26, 1915, HPC manager James Gibb and superintendent of forestry Charles S. Judd rode into Waimalu (sheltered water) Valley on an inspection tour. Just past the ʻEwa Forest Reserve boundary, they found a small house, a kiln for making charcoal, and several acres of bananas. The men talked briefly with the two Japanese tenants, who rented the land from Lincoln L. McCandless. Gibb had earlier mentioned that he was negotiating with McCandless for a right of way to build a ditch and tunnel system in the valley.[111]

Gibb envisioned a four-mile-long ditch, of which three miles would be underground because of the steep side slopes in the valley. The intake dam would be built at an elevation of 560 feet on the site of the original weir. The ditch would end at an elevation of 530 feet on the ridge above the Kalauao side of the valley. The estimated capacity was thirty million gallons daily with an expected flow of 500 to 600 million gallons per year. The project would take three to four months to complete and cost $45,000.[112]

The HPC began construction on the ditch and access trail in December 1915. The tunnel crews encountered hard rock for more than half the distance, slowing progress considerably. The company finally completed the project in April 1917 at a cost of $95,664.10. The three-and-a-half-mile ditch was entirely underground except for periodic openings for access.[113] Despite the cost overrun, Gibb was pleased with the project. "It will be a good investment as has been proven in the case of Waimano Tunnel."[114] In 1918, its first full year in commission, Waimalu or McCandless Ditch, as it was sometimes called, delivered 506 million gallons to a recently built reservoir that fed the upper-level Kalauao fields. Gibb reported, "Fresh water from the mountains is a great help as it washed salt out of land deposited by artesian water from the pumps."[115]

The ditch trail provided access to the tunnel during construction and for maintenance. The route initially paralleled the tunnel and then forked about a mile and a half in. The right fork continued to follow the tunnel up a side gulch and ended where the ditch crossed a small stream just below ground. The left fork descended to the same stream, crossed it, and contoured along the side of the main valley to eventually rejoin the tunnel and end at the ditch intake.

The Hawaiian Trail and Mountain Club (HTMC) first scheduled a hike in Waimalu Valley for July 10, 1921. That morning fifty-two members and guests took the Haleiwa Limited train to Kalauao depot. Led by club member Otto H. Swezey of the Hawaiian Sugar Planters Association, the group climbed through the cane fields to the ditch tender's cottage at the trailhead. From there the hikers followed the access trail to the ditch intake and returned by the stream. Along the way they picked ripe mangoes and mountain apples and enjoyed a swim in several of the inviting pools. The HTMC repeated that very successful hike in 1924 and 1927.[116]

Before and during World War II, the Honolulu Plantation Company lost more than two thousand acres, fully one-third of its prime fields, to the military for various installations. Although compensated by the government, HPC was unable to grow enough sugar cane to keep its refinery running profitably after the war. On January 1, 1947, the company sold all its property to the Oahu Sugar Company (OSC) for $3,750,000. The Waiahole Water Company, a subsidiary of the OSC, took over operation of Waimalu Ditch.[117] In 1950, the ditch delivered 478.93 million gallons for the OSC.[118]

After hiking Waimalu in 1947, the HTMC did not return to the valley until April 30, 1961, probably because of access problems. That morning the group drove past 'Aiea town and turned *mauka* on a dirt road through OSC cane fields to the trailhead. Led by Richard H. (Dick) Davis, the hikers followed the main access trail to a grassy, open area near the stream. From there the group crossed the stream six times to reach a large swimming hole at the ditch intake. The original route contoured above the stream from the grassy area to the intake but had become overgrown through lack of use.[119]

In the middle 1960s, the HTMC developed an alternate route to the ditch trail because of housing construction in the Kalauao cane fields. The club took an overgrown road into Waimalu Valley past various rusted remains of HPC activities. At the old house site and charcoal kiln the hikers climbed through hala trees to reach the ditch trail.[120] Sometime in the late 1960s or early 1970s, the OSC abandoned the Waimalu Ditch because the upper-level cane fields were earmarked for development.

Housing construction on the Kalauao ridge finished in 1987 with the completion of Nahalekaha, a gated community near the end of Kaonohi Street. A short, steep route by the gate provided access to the ditch trail at about the half-mile mark. The HTMC regularly used that access route for its scheduled Waimalu hikes from 1989 on.[121]

On June 2, 1991, club members Gerald Leao and Stuart Ball hiked to the ditch intake, crossed Waimalu Stream three more times, and began to explore a middle ridge between the north and south forks. Over the next two years Leao and Ball, sometimes joined by others, gradually worked their way up the ridge toward the Ko'olau summit. During the sixteenth outing on September 4, 1993, Ball finally reached the top at a high, grassy knoll with a 360-degree view. On the way back he jumped into a deep swimming hole at the second stream crossing for a cooling, soothing dip. Ball hiked the middle ridge two more times to introduce the route to club friends.[122] On July 24, 1999, Dayle Turner and Patrick Rorie led the Waimalu

Summit super hike for the HTMC. The elite group climbed the middle ridge, turned north along the summit, and descended the Waiau Trail and a side ridge back into Waimalu Valley.[123]

In 1999, Leao and John Hall developed a loop hike incorporating the right fork of the ditch trail. From the trail's end where the ditch tunnels under the side stream, the two men blazed a route up and along the ridge to the north. They then descended a spur ridge to rejoin the main ditch trail by the first stream crossing near an open, grassy area still recovering from a fire in 1992.[124]

As of 2010, the ditch trail was still used frequently by hunters and occasionally by hikers. The main route from the front of the gated community to the intake via the stream is usually passable, although uneven and narrow in spots because of slippage through the years. The right fork is usually open to the side stream crossing, but the loop trail may be clogged with scratchy uluhe ferns along the ridge section. The first half-mile of the original route is severely overgrown because access was blocked by houses in the Pearl Ridge Estates subdivision. The last section, contouring from the grassy area to the intake, is also heavily overgrown because of the popularity of the stream route. The ditch itself is visible at the periodic access openings and at the intake just before the seventh stream crossing. To take a look at the charcoal kiln and house site by Waimalu Stream, drop down the hala slopes just past the side stream crossing.

Army and Territorial Forestry Division Trails
(1909–1933)

"Pehea kou piko?" How's your belly button?
"Maika'i no!" Fine!

—Piko Club yell, 1931

Army Training Routes

By January 1909, the U.S. Army had infantry stationed at Fort Shafter, cavalry at Schofield Barracks, and engineers at Kalia Military Reservation (later Fort DeRussy). That year Company A, First Battalion, Second Volunteer Engineers began a survey of the entire island of O'ahu. During the four-year project, Company A and its successors, Companies G and I, determined the boundaries of the new military reservations, looked for possible defensive sites, and produced a topographic map. In the mountains the engineers cut trails along many of the ridges to reach vantage points for triangulation surveying. The engineers were particularly interested in routes traversing the Ko'olau Range from the Wahiawā area to the windward side. If passable, those trails could provide access for a Japanese attack on Schofield Barracks.[1]

In July 1910, Company H, 20th Infantry based at Fort Shafter successfully traversed the Ko'olau Range from Wahiawā to Kahana Bay. They hiked a sugar plantation trail to its end and then followed a rough track, possibly Hawaiian, across the mountains. The next year army engineers improved the plantation trail and extended it along the ridge to the Ko'olau summit.

Initially called the Kahana Bay Trail, the new route eventually became the Schofield-Waikāne Trail.[2]

In June and July of 1918 the regular army troops stationed at Fort Shafter left for the mainland to support the World War I effort. Replacing them were two regiments of the Hawai'i National Guard, the First and Second Hawaiian Infantry. While first regiment commander and post commandant at Fort Shafter in 1919, Lieutenant Colonel Donald S. Bowman and his troops cleared the ridge route named after him. Unlike Schofield-Waikāne, the Bowman Trail had little tactical value, but it provided nearby training and recreational opportunities for the guard.[3]

On August 5, 1921, Major General Charles P. Summerall became commander of the Hawaiian Department at Fort Shafter. He was a decorated war hero, nearing the height of his military career. Graduating from West Point in 1892, Summerall took part in the Philippines campaign and the Peking relief expedition and then taught artillery tactics at West Point and lectured at the army's War College. During World War I he commanded a First Artillery brigade, the First Infantry, and finally the Fifth Army Corps during the Meuse-Argonne offensive of 1918.

While stationed in Hawai'i, Summerall developed a comprehensive defense plan against an attack by the Japanese, code-named "Orange." To provide troop access to the windward side from Schofield Barracks, he ordered the rebuilding of the deteriorated Schofield-Waikāne Trail in 1923. The next year he authorized construction of the Pūpūkea-Kahuku Trail to accommodate increased training exercises in the mountains.[4]

The Forestry Division's War on Pigs

In 1915 the Board of Agriculture and Forestry appointed Charles S. Judd as superintendent of forestry. Born and raised in Hawai'i, he attended Yale University, receiving a BA degree in 1905 and a master of forestry degree in 1907. Judd began his career with the United States Forest Service in the northwest region. In 1910, he was promoted to assistant district forester based in Portland, Oregon. Five years later Judd returned to Hawai'i to take the top Forestry Division job.

Judd proved to be a talented, dedicated public servant with a passion for saving and planting trees. As superintendent (later territorial forester), he managed and expanded the forest reserve system, consisting of *mauka* (inland) land set aside to protect the water supply for the populace and the sugar plantations. Initially, cattle from nearby ranches were the foremost threat to the forest watershed. Judd's rangers and work crews built and maintained boundary fences and planted trees in the areas denuded by cutting and grazing. With cattle largely fenced out of the Oʻahu reserves by the late 1920s, Judd turned his attention to the wild pigs inside. On inspection trips into the Koʻolau Range, he and his rangers found an extensive network of pig trails and diggings in the native vegetation, especially in the summit area.

Judd began by enlisting the support of companies and landowners with a stake in preserving the central Koʻolau watershed. In March 1927, the Division of Forestry built a cabin for pig hunters partway up the Kīpapa-Waiawa ridge in the heart of the ʻEwa Forest Reserve. The Bishop Estate provided the funds and Oahu Sugar Company provided the labor for construction.[5] In late 1927 the Division of Forestry and the Hawaiian Sugar Planters Association (HSPA) jointly cleared the new Peʻahināiʻa Trail on the ridge south of ʻŌpaeʻula Stream. Ranger at large Max F. Landgraf and Oʻahu ranger Thomas R. L. McGuire directed a trail crew of plantation laborers. When the trail was finished, the HSPA established two rain gauges along the route and allowed access to the summit for pig hunters and surveyors.[6] In November 1928, Kahuku ranger Robert Plunkett and his crew packed pig traps up the Castle Trail to upper Kaluanui Valley for use by hunters hired by the Bishop Estate.[7]

On May 22, 1930, Judd hired special hunters Nicholas Mendes and John K. Pahamoa to clear trail and hunt pigs along the summit in the Kaipapaʻu and Hauʻula Forest Reserves for $75 per month. Despite heavy rains, the two men killed thirteen pigs in the first week on the job. To find their quarry, the special hunters blazed routes above the Castle Trail in both directions along the Koʻolau summit ridge.[8]

Later that year Judd wrote,

> It is felt that the solution to the pig problem on Oʻahu may be attained through the construction of trails and consequently opening up of the mountain country to voluntary hunters.[9]

During March and April 1931, Ranger Plunkett and his crew brushed out the new Mālaekahana Trail in the Kahuku Forest Reserve. In July, they built a cabin near the trail end at the summit. The small shelter was a frequent overnight stop for Mendes, now working alone. He and his dogs killed 320 pigs during the last nine months of 1931.[10] The efforts of Mendes and other special hunters gradually pushed the pigs off the summit ridge into the lower, more accessible valleys for easier taking. In addition, the number

Along the Piko Trail, May 5, 1932. Territorial forester Charles Judd with his white dog, Panache. (General Wells collection, U.S. Army Museum of Hawai'i)

of pig hunters had increased as the Great Depression deepened. Unemployed men turned to hunting to help put food on the table. The result was 3,834 pigs reported killed during the two-year period ending December 31, 1932. Judd's pig control efforts were providing the native forest with some respite.[11]

Army and Forestry Division Cooperation: The Piko Club

In October 1930, Major General Briant H. Wells arrived on O'ahu to take command of the Hawaiian Division at Schofield Barracks. He was an exuberant, hard-charging soldier nearing the end of a long, illustrious career in the army. After graduating from West Point in 1894, Wells served in the Spanish American War, the Philippine insurrection, the Pancho Villa campaign, and the First World War. By 1928, Major General Wells was deputy chief of staff, the second highest position in the U.S. Army.

As the new Hawaiian Division commander, Wells was largely responsible for the land defense of O'ahu. The current defense plan viewed the two mountain ranges on the island as formidable barriers to an invading force. In the most likely scenario, the Japanese, code-named "Orange," would land along the north shore and then push inland between the two ranges toward Schofield Barracks and Pearl Harbor. After seeing the terrain, Wells believed that the mountains were less of a barrier than previously envisioned. He decided, therefore, to explore the various routes over and along the Ko'olau and Wai'anae Ranges on foot.[12]

Charles Judd and General Wells first met at Schofield Barracks on January 19, 1931, to discuss tree removal and planting for the post. Wells agreed to provide soldiers to help reopen several forestry trails. Judd agreed to show some of the mountain routes to the general and his staff.[13] In subsequent meetings, usually on foot or on horseback, the *kama'āina* (island-born) forester and the *malihini* (newcomer) general developed a close working relationship and became good friends.

On February 17, Judd led Major Charles W. Thomas, Jr., Captain Raymond G. Sherman, and seven other army officers on a reconnaissance hike above Punalu'u Valley. The group climbed the old Castle Trail, bushwhacked to and along the Ko'olau summit, and then descended a spur ridge back into Punalu'u Valley. During that grueling loop, the men first discussed forming a hiking club with members drawn from the army and

Army and Territorial Forestry Division Trails 107

The Piko Club hikes the Mālaekahana Trail, June 25, 1933. On the right, General Briant Wells wearing his trademark canary kerchief. (General Wells collection, U.S. Army Museum of Hawai'i)

the Division of Forestry. After finishing the hike well after dark, the group enjoyed a swim in the ocean and continued the discussion over a late dinner at Cooper Ranch Inn in Hau'ula.[14]

General Wells heartily approved of the new hiking club and agreed to become its first president. He and Judd chose *piko* (summit) for the club's name and motto because the group would emphasize hikes traversing the

Koʻolau and Waiʻanae Ranges. A facetious Hawaiian greeting using another meaning of *piko* became the club's yell. *Pehea kou piko?* How's your belly button?[15]

On March 1, Judd, Wells, his wife Mary, and Major Thomas further discussed the club while riding along Kaukonahua Gulch Trail, recently built by the army. After that outing Judd designed the membership certificate and wrote the Piko Club song. Set to an old tune called *Ahi Wela* (Love Hot as Fire), the lyrics featured the club yell as a chorus. The membership certificate showed an army hiker, a small white dog, an apple pie, and the club tree, kopiko, of course. Apple pie was Judd's favorite dessert, and the dog was his constant trail companion.[16]

On April 25, 1931, the Piko Club organization banquet took place at Haleiwa Beach Club. Invited for an evening of dining and dancing were twenty charter members and their wives. The informal meeting after dinner included remarks by each of the three initial club officers, President Wells, Chief Guide Judd, and Chief Scout Thomas. The members discussed and approved the articles of organization, and Wells presented each Piko with his membership certificate and a bandanna. Livening the program were several rounds of the club's yell and song led by the chief guide and Captain Sherman. The latter received an apple pie for his slip-sliding descent into Punaluʻu Valley on the club's founding hike.[17]

Written somewhat tongue-in-cheek, the articles of organization established the Piko Club as "an association of men who enjoyed hiking and the exploration of the out-of-the-way places on Oahu."[18] The purpose of the club was to encourage friendships among its members and to acquaint them with the mountain trails. Membership requirements included crossing the Koʻolau and/or Waiʻanae Ranges three times on foot.

The twenty original members were largely drawn from the army and the Division of Forestry. Over half were army officers stationed at Schofield Barracks or Fort Shafter. Forestry Division members were Judd, Oʻahu assistant forester Glenn W. Russ, and rangers Max F. Landgraf and Robert R. L. McGuire. The club extended charter membership to other key civilians, notably George R. Ewart III, Bishop Estate forester, and Lawrence M. Judd, Territory of Hawaiʻi governor and now Piko Club honorary president.[19] The group would have few problems crossing private or government land to reach the mountains.

The club members had started hiking together before the organization banquet. Judd and/or Wells usually led midweek reconnaissance trips to investigate established trails and obscure routes across the mountains. Groups of officers traversed the Waiʻanae Range at Maunakapu, Pōhākea Pass, and Keawaʻula. In the Koʻolau Range members hiked the old Poamoho,

Pūpūkea-Kahuku, and Schofield-Waikāne Trails, and the new Mālaekahana Trail. The men frequently took rifles and dogs to hunt pigs along the way. After each hike, General Wells penciled in the route on a map in his office.[20]

In *Excelsior!* Piko poet Captain Arnold W. Shutter captures the spirit of those reconnaissance hikes.

> . . . The algeroba tore his shirt,
> The thick lantan done him dirt,
> The cactus stung, as cactus will.
> The rain clouds washed him off a hill.
> KU' PIKO!
>
> Until at last he said: "Hell's Bells!
> I must report to Gen'ral Wells
> Each mountain and each trail I've clumb,
> And thus some day, I may become
> A PIKO![21]

On July 26, the Piko Club scheduled its first Sunday outing, guided by member Major Russell A. Osmun. Twenty hikers, including Judd, Wells, and Thomas climbed Ka'ala, the highest peak on O'ahu at 4,025 feet, from the Schofield side.[22] Although often challenging, the club's subsequent Sunday hikes emphasized fun and camaraderie rather than reconnaissance. The relaxed, informal atmosphere soon attracted large groups, including prospective members, women, and children. On the trail the leaders would periodically yell *"Pehea kou piko?"* How's your belly button? The rear guard would respond with a rousing *"Maika'i no!"* Fine! After lunch or during coffee and smoke breaks, the group would sometimes sing the Piko Club song.

Judd always hiked in shorts and smeared his legs with Vaseline to ward off scratchy lantana shrubs and uluhe ferns. Accompanying him was his small but stalwart dog Panache, or Pan for short, who had to be carried over difficult trail sections. Wells often wore riding britches, leggings, a blue jumper, and a canary yellow silk kerchief with a kukui nut fastener. Both men sometimes carried machetes for spot trail clearing; others brought cane knives or bolos with both saw and knife blades.[23]

The Piko Club fostered close cooperation between the army and the Forestry Division, to the benefit of both. On the Sunday and reconnaissance hikes General Wells and his division officers gradually learned the routes across the Ko'olau and Wai'anae Ranges. In turn, Judd and his rangers received army assistance in clearing trails and erecting cabins in the fight against wild pigs. Wells even had bombers drop material for a new cabin above the Castle Trail.

In April 1932, ranger Max Landgraf, Waiʻanae ranger Ralph E. Turner, Jr., and foreman Ernest W. Landgraf with his Puerto Rican crew cleared a new trail in the back of Mākua Valley. Named after the Piko Club, the route climbed the steep cliff to the Waiʻanae summit, where it connected with two trails leading down to Mokulēʻia. On May 5, Judd introduced the Piko Club to the Piko Trail. On October 30, General and Mrs. Wells each planted a Norfolk Island (Cook) Pine on the Waiʻanae crest to mark the end of the trail.[24]

Forestry Division Trails

In August 1932, the Forestry Division received eighteen laborers from the Unemployed Workers Relief Commission, recently established by Governor Judd. Formerly with the Hawaiian Pineapple Company, the new men were paid $1.00 per day from relief funds. Foreman Ernest Landgraf quickly incorporated some of them into his regular trail crew of six Puerto Rican workers.[25]

With the additional manpower, the Forestry Division built three new trails, Punaiki (later Maʻakua Ridge), Hauʻula, and Kaunala, during the ten-month period from August 1932 to May 1933. The trails provided easier access to the forest reserves for tree planting, fence building, fire protection, and wild pig control. As each trail was completed, Judd proudly showed it off to the Piko Club members.

In December 1932, Plunkett and Ernest Landgraf and their crews completed construction of the Punaiki Trail, a loop starting above Hauʻula behind the Cooper Ranch Inn. In April 1933, the crews finished the Hauʻula Trail, a second, nearby loop. On April 9, Judd led the Piko Club on the Punaiki Trail, where the group conducted its annual meeting.[26] In May 1933, Forestry Division crews completed the Kaunala Trail. The new route left the Pūpūkea-Kahuku Trail at Owl Flat and rejoined the army trail at Chicken Hill. On May 7, Judd introduced the Piko Club to the Kaunala Trail, with its hand-painted labels identifying native trees and shrubs. The group received a botany lesson and quiz from Judd and enjoyed steaks, chops, and beer at an idyllic lunch spot known as Camp Wells.[27]

Later that month Judd received devastating news at work. Because of poor economic conditions, the Territorial Legislature reduced Forestry

Division appropriations by 75 percent. For the coming biennial period beginning July 1, the division would receive only $65,800, compared with $260,165 for the previous two years. Judd let go seventy-four of his eighty-seven employees on that day. Gone were all the field crews, most of the nursery workers, and thirteen of the eighteen rangers. On Oʻahu, only rangers Robert R. L. McGuire and Max F. Landgraf survived the cut. Judd spent two days writing letters of recommendation for the dismissed men.[28] He also must have spent some time pondering the future of forestry in Hawaiʻi.

Schofield-Waikāne

> *If there is a lovelier, finer trail in all Oahu, lead us to it so that we fall down and worship it.*
> —Lawrence H. Daingerfield, July 1920

In June 1900, laborers under contractor Albert A. Wilson began building a six-mile trail *mauka* (inland) of the Wahiawā colony along the ridge south of the north fork of Kaukonahua Stream. After reaching a small saddle at 1,600 feet of elevation, the men cleared down to the stream, finishing sometime in July. The workers then started construction of a twelve-mile contour trail, roughly paralleling the *mauka* route, but in the gulch, following the meandering north fork.

The two trails were the preliminary phase of a ditch project to divert water from the north fork of Kaukonahua Stream for use by the Wahiawā colony and Waialua Agricultural Company (WAC). The *mauka* trail provided quick access to the planned intake area, while the contour trail approximated the proposed route of the entire ditch. When completed in May 1902, the Mauka Ditch consisted of thirty-seven tunnels totaling 16,794 feet in length with 6,519 feet of open ditch. The total project cost was $71,607.81 paid by Wahiawa Water Company, a WAC affiliate. A small portion of those funds went to build Headgate cabin, a one-room wooden shack along the stream near the junction of the *mauka* and contour trails.[29]

On January 28, 1910, Vaughn MacCaughey and John S. Donaghho, professors at the College of Hawaii, and Dexter Fraser, a student there, embarked on a three-day traverse of the Koʻolau Range. The three men caught the afternoon train of the Oahu Railway and Land Company (OR&L) from Honolulu to Wahiawā (fare 80 cents), arriving at 6:30 p.m. By lantern light they proceeded *mauka* on the government road past the Consolidated Pineapple Company cannery and its extensive pineapple fields. After entering the forest, the men turned off the road by a *kapu* sign onto the *mauka* trail and reached Headgate cabin at 10:30 p.m.

Early the next morning the men hiked the contour trail a short distance to its end at the ditch intake and then took the right fork of Kaukonahua Stream. For the next three hours they bushwhacked, rock-hopped, and waded upstream to the next major fork. There the men spotted a blazed tree marking the start of the ridge trail to the Koʻolau summit.

> The blazing is three feet long. On this same tree various travelers have hung old articles of clothing—khaki coat, a white handkerchief, and a discarded cap.[30]

After two hours of hard climbing, the threesome reached the summit overlooking wild Kahana Valley.

After lunch the men hiked southeast along the summit for about a half-mile and then descended a prominent side ridge, an old Hawaiian route into the valley. With darkness fast approaching, the three followed Kahana Stream to a deserted grass house where they spent a fairly comfortable night. The next morning the men hiked a well-used trail to Kahana village and took the noon train of the Koolau Railway to Kahuku and then on to Honolulu via the OR&L.[31]

In July, Company H of the 20th Infantry based at Fort Shafter received orders to march over the Koʻolau Range *mauka* of Wahiawā. The mission was an endurance test to determine if a traverse was possible by soldiers carrying full gear weighing more than sixty pounds. If so, then Japanese soldiers could attack Schofield Barracks from the windward side.

Leaving Fort Shafter on July 29, Company H, commanded by Lieutenant Austin M. Pardee, marched to Pearl Harbor that day and to Wahiawā the next. At noon on July 31, the soldiers met their guide, Professor MacCaughey, and Alexander H. Ford, the recent founder of the Hawaiian Trail and Mountain Club, and one other, who had all come up from Honolulu by train that morning. In the afternoon the group hiked to Headgate cabin along the deserted *mauka* trail, now in need of repair. The company commander and the three civilians took over the cabin, while the soldiers put up their dog tents in the pouring rain.

At 5:45 a.m., after a breakfast of hardtack and bacon, the group began wading up Kaukonahua Stream, cold and swollen from the recent rain.

Fording the stream lengthwise. A waterlogged Company H of the Twentieth Infantry traverses the Koʻolau Range, July 31–August 2, 1910. (*The Mid-Pacific Magazine*, Hawaiʻi State Library)

> It was certainly a picturesque sight to watch fifty men in khaki, fully armed, marching up a stream, sometimes but their head and shoulders above water,[32]

wrote Ford in his soggy notebook. He snapped a few pictures of the sodden soldiers until his expensive German camera became waterlogged.

After three and a half hours of fording the stream "lengthwise," the soldiers started up the steep, slippery ridge to the Koʻolau summit. Eight men with bolo knives took the lead to hack the trail open. At 12:30 p.m. the company stood at the top, looking at lush Kahana Valley and the smoke from their commissary fires, a reminder of the hot dinner awaiting them on the beach just five miles away.

Anxious to get down, Pardee decided to take the side ridge directly in front of the lookout, which was reportedly passable. Unfortunately the route chosen had several fresh landslides and ended abruptly at a precipice. Running out of time, food, and water, the men clambered back up the cliff and bivouacked right on the narrow summit.

> Many men admitted in the morning that they had spent much of the night in fear, for the little fringe of rolling moss on the ridge trembled violently in the rain and windstorm that arose after dark; but none complained when daylight came.[33]

With the bolo men in front, the tired, hungry soldiers proceeded gingerly along the summit the next morning. The group found and descended a prominent side ridge to Kahana Stream, where everyone drank heartily from the muddy pools. Farther down the valley they slogged past the grass houses of startled native Hawaiians. Upon reaching the beach, the men headed for the mess tent to devour hot dogs and, later that evening, a huge dinner. Thanks to Company H and Professor MacCaughey, the army now had a cleared route across the Ko'olau Range.[34]

Sometime during the next twelve months army engineers significantly improved the new Wahiawā-Kahana route. They widened the *mauka* trail and extended it four miles along the ridge to the Ko'olau crest (elevation 2,450 feet). The soldiers then cleared the rough trail up the side ridge from the Kahana side and cut a quarter-mile path along the summit to connect the leeward and windward sections. Although involving some up-and-down hiking along the ridge line, the improved route eliminated the cold Kaukonahua wade and the steep ascent to the summit.[35]

On December 16, 1912, Professor MacCaughey and two colleagues, professor William A. Bryan and instructor Jessie Shaw, embarked on a biological reconnaissance of the country between Wahiawā and Kahana. The three men followed the *mauka* trail to a signed junction at the small saddle. Instead of turning left down to Headgate cabin, they continued straight on the new army route.

> The main criticism of this ridge trail is the numerous elevations and depressions, that soon prove tedious. Otherwise, the trail is well cut, and affords many magnificent views.[36]

The route was also well marked with wooden signs pointing "To Kahana." Short of the summit at 5 p.m., the three descended a spur ridge to Kaukonahua Stream and camped there near a lovely loulu palm. The next day the men reached the Ko'olau crest at lunch time and then easily descended into Kahana Valley in the afternoon.

Throughout the expedition the three biologists took measurements, collected specimens, and made observations. MacCaughey recorded barometric pressure and wind speed and direction, and gathered algae and liverworts. Bryan measured temperature and collected tree snails. Shaw concentrated on plants, especially those in the *Lobeliad* family.[37]

The Hawaiian Trail and Mountain Club (HTMC) first scheduled the Wahiawā-Kahana traverse for July 4, 1920. That morning at 7 a.m., twenty-five members and guests boarded trucks for the one-hour ride to Wahiawā. Led by Lawrence H. Daingerfield, meteorologist and club president, the group slogged up the muddy, overgrown ridge trail past landslides and through downed trees. "If the trail is ever to be used for military purposes, some work will have to be done on it,"[38] Daingerfield later commented. At about 12:30 p.m. the hikers finally reached the Koʻolau summit and turned right (southeast) to climb Puʻu Kaʻaumakua (elevation 2,681 feet). At the top the group waxed eloquent about the grand view of Oʻahu and the neighbor islands on that exceptionally clear Independence Day.

At 1:45 p.m. the HTMC members and guests began a hair-raising descent of the ridge separating Waikāne and Kahana Valleys. Partway down, the steep, makeshift trail became a narrow ledge with uncertain hand holds. At a saddle the group turned left (northwest) on the wide, graded Waiāhole Ditch Trail, built about five years before. The hikers gradually worked around the back of Kahana Valley, passing numerous intakes and two Japanese ditch tender's cottages with terraced gardens. At the ditch trail's end the group headed out Kahana Valley on an access route overgrown with grass and uluhe ferns. The hikers reached Kahana Bay at dusk for a well-earned supper of sandwiches and hot coffee. The group returned to Honolulu via Nuʻuanu Pali at 11 p.m. after a long but satisfying day.[39]

For 1923, U.S. Army Major General Charles P. Summerall, commander of the Hawaiian Department, ordered a complete overhaul of the Wahiawā-Kahana route, known as the Kahana Bay Trail. On the Wahiawā side the Third Engineers built contour sections around the major humps in the ridge, thus eliminating much of the up-and-down hiking. On the windward side the soldiers reconstructed a steep zigzag trail following the north side of the ridge between Waikāne and Kahana Valleys. Wire railing provided security at several steep, narrow spots. At the saddle the new route connected with the Waiāhole Ditch Trail, giving access to both valleys.[40]

On a lovely Palm Sunday, April 13, 1924, thirty-two HTMC members and guests gathered at the Armed Forces YMCA in Honolulu to hike the renovated Kahana Bay Trail. At 7:30 a.m. the autobus left for Wahiawā where they picked up an army guide, Lieutenant M. D. Taylor of the Third Engineers. Along the contoured route Oʻahu forester and HTMC leader Robert R. L. McGuire pointed out several land shells (native tree snails), which were promptly pocketed, and entomologist Otto Swezey collected insects with a white scoop net. At the summit the hikers marveled at the stunning windward view, and McGuire murmured a short prayer of thanks for the beauty surrounding them. After lunch the HTMC members and guests easily descended the rebuilt windward section into Waikāne Valley. The group arrived back in Honolulu at twilight "after a most enchanting Palm Sunday sermon with 100 per cent increase in energy, a clarified mind, a visioned soul, and a robust appetite."[41]

On June 9, 1931, Major General Briant H. Wells, commander of the Hawaiian Division, inspected the Kahana Bay Trail, officially known as the

Schofield-Waikāne Trail. Accompanying him on the reconnaissance hike were his staff and other army officers, all members of the recently formed Piko Club. The trail must have been in reasonably good condition because the group completed the eleven-mile traverse in six and a half hours. On May 23, 1934, General Wells and others hiked the Schofield-Waikāne Trail again, probably after the Wahiawa Camp of the Civilian Conservation Corps had cleared the trail and regraded some of the steeper sections.

During World War II the army built a dirt road over the first two and a half miles of the Schofield-Waikāne Trail. Soldiers also constructed a cabin, elevated on wooden posts on the leeward side of the summit.[42]

In the early 1950s the HTMC began to regularly schedule the Wahiawā Trail, the new name for the Schofield section. Usually led by army telephone engineer Richard (Dick) Booth, the hike started near the end of California Avenue and then followed the army dirt road through the East Range training area to the trailhead. From there the group either hiked to the Koʻolau summit and back or descended the old *mauka* trail to Kaukonahua Stream for a refreshing swim. In 1984 the club started calling the summit hike by its official army name, Schofield-Waikāne.[43]

While hiking the Schofield section in May 1996, wildlife biologist Eric Vandervoort spotted several red birds with black wings and curved bills. He identified them as native ʻiʻiwi, an extremely rare and endangered species on Oʻahu. They were feeding on nectar from ʻōhiʻa tree blossoms along the ridge and down in Kaukonahua Gulch.[44]

For May 8, 1999, the HTMC scheduled a new hike called Puʻu Kaʻaumakua. Led by Patrick Rorie and Dayle Turner, fourteen members took the Waiāhole Ditch Trail to the saddle between Waikāne and Kahana Valleys and then pushed up the Waikāne section to the Koʻolau summit. After a short walk on the Summit Trail, the hikers ascended Puʻu Kaʻaumakua and reveled in the superb but fleeting view. At the top was a benchmark erected in 1927 by surveyors updating the Oʻahu topographic maps.[45]

Since 1999, the HTMC has continued to hike the Schofield-Waikāne Trail to the summit from both ends. The route remains passable although sometimes overgrown with scratchy uluhe ferns and shrubs. In spots the path is uneven and narrow from slippage and erosion through the years. Near the summit on the leeward side is a piece of corrugated metal roofing, all that remains of the cabin, which was blown over by heavy wind in 1963. A short section of the *mauka* trail still leads down to Kaukonahua Stream past the site of Headgate cabin to the blocked intake of the Mauka Ditch, now abandoned. Permission to hike the Schofield-Waikāne Trail is required from the U.S. Army.

Bowman

> Not a CCC sidewalk trail, but a good,
> old-fashioned class A [difficult] hike.
>
> —Hawaiian Trail and Mountain Club
> schedule, November 27, 1937

In 1907, the U.S. Army established Fort Shafter Military Reservation, the first permanent garrison in Hawai'i. To support the defense of both Honolulu and Pearl Harbor, the new post was strategically located in the *ahupua'a* (land division) of Kahauiki, just north of Kalihi Valley. The southern boundary of the reservation and the *ahupua'a* was a prominent ridge separating Kalihi and Kahauiki Valleys. At some point army engineers traipsed up and down that ridge to survey the perimeter of the post.[46]

In early 1915, army engineers resurveyed the boundaries of Fort Shafter. They marked the perimeter with monuments made of galvanized pipe filled with concrete. On top of each was a numbered brass plate, 2.5 inches square, with an imbedded bullet casing. Monument number 23 marked the southern boundary at a distinct knob called Kapuakau, the site of Kāholoakekua triangulation station. From there the engineers placed markers 22 through 17 at intervals along the Kalihi-Kahauiki ridge toward the summit. Standing at the head of Kahauiki Valley and the *ahupua'a*, monument 16 marked the farthest extent *mauka* (inland) of the reservation. From there the boundary line turned west down the Kahauiki-Moanalua ridge.[47]

In June and July 1918, army regiments stationed at Fort Shafter transferred to the mainland to support the World War I effort. To replace the regulars, the army mobilized the National Guard of Hawai'i on June 1. The guard fielded two regiments, the First and Second Hawaiian Infantry, which were stationed at Schofield Barracks and Fort Shafter. As commander of the first regiment, Colonel William R. Riley automatically became post commandant at Fort Shafter.[48]

Serving under Riley was Lieutenant Colonel Donald S. Bowman. An expert in public health, Bowman had been the chief sanitary inspector on the Big Island since 1901. After the guard demobilized in July 1919, he retired from the army as commander of the first regiment and commandant at Fort Shafter. Bowman then took a position with the Hawaiian Sugar Planters Association. As director of the Industrial Service Bureau, he was responsible for improving the living conditions at the plantation worker camps.[49]

While at Fort Shafter in 1919, Bowman and his soldiers opened up the ridge route named after him.[50] From the post the route climbed the Kalihi-Kahauiki ridge past monuments 23 through 16. Leaving the boundary at marker 16, the trail followed the main ridge to the summit of the Koʻolau Range at Puʻu Kahauali (elevation 2,740 feet). Bowman quickly became "one of the better known trails adjacent to Honolulu."[51]

The Hawaiian Trail and Mountain Club (HTMC) first scheduled the Bowman Trail as a Saturday afternoon hike for January 31, 1920. At 1:30 p.m. members and guests gathered at the intersection of King Street and Kamehameha IV Road. To get there, most of the hikers had taken the streetcars of the Honolulu Rapid Transit and Land Company at a fare of five cents. After a short briefing, the group probably entered Fort Shafter at the Kalihi (now Patch) Gate and began climbing the Kalihi-Kahauiki ridge on the Bowman Trail. Given the late start on a short winter day, the hikers undoubtedly turned around well before monument 16. The outing must have been enjoyable because the club hiked Bowman again on Saturday afternoon, October 16.[52]

The next year the HTMC scheduled Bowman as a full-day trip. The hike writeup suggested seriously, "Wear hiking clothes, and bring lunch and a canteen."[53] At 8:30 a.m. on September 11, 1921, the group assembled at the end of the King Street carline. There the leaders split the members and guests into two groups, class A (advanced) and class B (novice). The class A hikers probably had a long, rough day as the round-trip distance from King Street and Kamehameha IV Road to Puʻu Kahauali at the Koʻolau summit is about fifteen miles.

The HTMC scheduled Bowman annually or semiannually through 1929. The hike usually attracted a small, select group of hard-core walkers. Because of the long distance, the hike starting time advanced from 8:30 a.m. to 8 to 7:30. In 1927, the club developed a shorter, eight-mile version called Puʻu Kahauali. The group met at the end of the Kalihi Valley bus line near the Catholic orphanage. From there the hikers climbed a steep side ridge to reach the Bowman Trail about three miles from the summit.[54]

Bowman was not included in the Civilian Conservation Corps (CCC) trail projects of the middle 1930s, but crews reforested the eroded slopes behind Fort Shafter in 1935 and 1936. For easier access to the planting areas, the CCC constructed a mile-and-a-half-long dirt road, which joined the Bowman Trail at the Kāholokeakua triangulation station.[55] Although dazzled by the new, graded CCC trails, the HTMC managed to schedule the Bowman hike from Fort Shafter in 1934 and 1937. The up-and-down route was "not a CCC sidewalk trail, but a good, old-fashioned class A hike."[56]

After World War II the HTMC resumed regular hiking on Bowman, affectionately known as "the Old Kimono Trail." In the mid-1950s the club developed another approach from upper Kalihi Valley. The five-mile route reached the Bowman Trail at monument 17 about a mile and a half from the summit. The HTMC used that shorter version for the rest of the 1950s and the 1960s. In the early 1970s, the Forestry Division included that route as Bowman, trail number 81 on its comprehensive O'ahu trail listing and map.[57]

 On September 9, 1973, the HTMC returned to the original route of Bowman. "Let's start as we did in the 30's making the long rugged scramble along Kalihi Valley ridge from just above Fort Shafter."[58] Led by veteran hiker Joseph Neilson, the members and guests climbed the Kalihi-Kahauiki ridge from behind Kalihi Elementary School. At the top the group turned *mauka* on the Bowman Trail, now a dirt road past the site of the Kāholokeakua triangulation station. At the road's end the hikers started the difficult trek to Pu'u Kahauali "for a small chance at a large view."[59] The round-trip distance was twelve miles, shorter than the original 1920s route but still a solid class A hike.

In 1980, the Sierra Club, Hawai'i Chapter began scheduling short morning outings known as wallaby watches. From a lookout just off the lower Bowman Trail, club members and guests watched Australian brush-tailed rock wallabies on the cliffs across Kalihi Valley. The marsupials were the descendants of a pair that escaped from a small, private zoo on 'Ālewa Heights in 1916. Since then, the colony has grown to between forty and one hundred individuals, which have quickly evolved to survive in their new habitat. The local wallabies are smaller and have shorter fur and longer ears than their Australian counterparts.[60]

The HTMC has continued to schedule Bowman almost annually using the school approach, except for a short period in the 1980s. Because of a parking problem at the school, the 1985 hike started from Richardson Theater in Fort Shafter. The new route climbed Radar Hill Road to join the Bowman Trail near the site of the Kāholokeakua triangulation station. While the road offered a more gradual approach, it added almost three miles to an already long hike. With the parking problem resolved, the club resumed using the elementary school access in 1990.[61]

As of 2010, Bowman remained open to hard-core hikers, but some sections may be overgrown with uluhe ferns and *Clidemia* shrubs. The elementary school approach does not require a permit. To hike Radar Hill Road or Simpson Street (the original route) in Fort Shafter requires permission from the U.S. Army. The Kalihi Valley routes are little used and mostly overgrown because of the awkward access from Likelike Highway. Pipe monuments 22, 20, 18, and 17 still stand along the boundary ridge, although the bullet casings are missing.

Pūpūkea-Kahuku

A cool and shady hike through tropical forest with practically no climbing.
—Hawaiian Trail and Mountain Club
schedule, March 3, 1929

On the morning of April 9, 1924, U.S. Army Major General Charles P. Summerall, commander of the Hawaiian Department, arrived at the temporary camp of the Third Engineers at Mālaekahana. Waiting there was Charles S. Judd, superintendent of forestry, George A. McEldowney, Oʻahu forest supervisor at the Hawaiian Sugar Planters Association (HSPA) Experiment Station, and several other army officers. After a slow, muddy drive through the cane fields, the group mounted horses to inspect the completed portion of a trail that the engineers were building from Kahuku to Pūpūkea.

Upon reaching the trail crew, the general complimented the men on their fine work. Judd, however, was not as pleased. He disliked the route because it cut through prime ʻōhiʻa forest in the proposed Kahuku Forest Reserve. He explained to the army officials that the native vegetation would suffer from cattle grazing and aggressive, alien plants introduced by trail users. Since the route was justified only for military reasons, Judd requested that the army barricade the trail and restrict its use to military exercises only. He even sent a letter outlining the discussion to Governor Farrington.[62]

The Third Engineers, nicknamed "the beavers," finished the six-mile Pūpūkea-Kahuku Trail later that year. The five-foot-wide, graded route started at the Pūpūkea Forest Reserve boundary by the end of the dirt homestead road at an elevation of 983 feet. The trail climbed gradually along the Koʻolau summit ridge, skirting Kaleleiki and Paumalū drainages. Past Chicken Hill (Puʻu Moa), the route left the main ridge and crossed Kaunala and ʻŌʻio Streams below their sources. The trail then climbed steadily to a side ridge with a broad windward overlook.

From the lookout the route turned left down the side ridge and forded 'Ōhiʻa ʻAi Stream. The trail then descended the side ridge on the right of the stream to the proposed Kahuku Forest Reserve boundary at an elevation of 840 feet. There the route connected with a dirt road leading to Kahuku town through pineapple fields and the sugar cane fields of Kahuku Plantation Company.[63]

On November 11, 1924, the Hawaiian Trail and Mountain Club (HTMC) hiked the Pūpūkea-Kahuku Trail for the first time. Early that morning thirty-four members and guests, including eighteen women, met at the Army-Navy YMCA and boarded an autobus for the around-the-island trip. After passing Waimea Bay, the autobus turned right by the train depot and labored up the dirt homestead road through pineapple fields surrounded by windbreaks. At the end of the road by a water tank was the start of the new trail.

Guiding the hike were H. L. Thompson and Fred E. Truman, sometime poet and humorist. Truman loved to tell tall stories and play pranks on novice hikers. He joked that a first-class guide must have nerve and pep to gain the confidence of the group and keep it amused. Also along that day were Thomas R. L. McGuire, Oʻahu forest ranger, and R. J. Baker, noted photographer, world traveler, and future president of the club.

After filling canteens at the water tank, the HTMC group strolled excitedly along the wide and easy contour trail. Open sections on the summit ridge provided sweeping views of the north shore. From the windward overlook the hikers saw Kahuku town and mill, the wireless station, and the Mormon Temple, white against the surrounding cane fields. The way down was cool and shady under tall ʻōhiʻa trees, kukui with bird's nest fern, and groves of mountain apple. After a road walk through the plantation, the hikers boarded the autobus in Kahuku for the return trip along the windward coast and over Nuʻuanu Pali to downtown Honolulu. The trip was undoubtedly a success, as the club hiked the Pūpūkea-Kahuku Trail annually during the middle and late 1920s.[64]

Despite Judd's initial displeasure, the Forestry Division used the trail periodically to access the Pūpūkea (white shell) Reserve and the newly created Kahuku (the projection) Reserve for tree planting and fence repair. On January 16, 1925, Judd hiked the entire trail with Hamilton P. Agee, director of the HSPA Experiment Station, Harold L. Lyon, in charge of botany and forestry at the station, and George A. McEldowney, forest supervisor there. They noted and photographed encroaching pineapples, cattle damage, and the native tree kaulu. On November 17, 1926, Judd inspected the two reserves while his crew planted fifty Cook Pines in the open areas along the Pūpūkea section of the trail. Judd found pig tracks on the summit and signs of cattle grazing near the Kahuku section of the trail. He also gathered the boat-shaped kaulu seed for a trial planting.[65]

On October 24, 1930, Major General Briant H. Wells arrived on Oʻahu to take command of the Hawaiian Division at Schofield Barracks. Shortly afterward he began to review the army training areas. On January 11, 1931, he and his staff hiked the Pūpūkea-Kahuku Trail, now overgrown and blocked by fallen trees. Wells immediately ordered the trail reopened as part of a tactical exercise. In March the Twenty-seventh Infantry cleared the entire trail wide enough for a mule pulling a machine-gun cart.[66]

After the clearing the trail received considerable use by the army, the Forestry Division, and hiking clubs. On April 23, Wells and others inspected the Pūpūkea section as part of a Koʻolau traverse from Kawailoa. In 1931 and 1932, the Piko Club conducted reconnaissance hikes to familiarize army officers with the terrain. During the early 1930s, the HTMC hiked the Pūpūkea-Kahuku Trail annually. In 1933, the Forestry Division built the Kaunala Trail, which left and then rejoined the Pūpūkea section. Crews planted paperbark trees at Owl Flat near the start of the new trail.[67]

In early May 1934, the Honolulu Unit of the Civilian Conservation Corps (CCC) began building the Koʻolau Summit Trail. Foreman Ernest W. Landgraf and his thirty-man trail crew climbed the Pūpūkea-Kahuku Trail

The Twenty-seventh Infantry strides along the recently cleared Pūpūkea-Kahuku Trail, March 1931. (General Wells collection, U.S. Army Museum of Hawaiʻi)

to a marked point just beyond the broad windward overlook. There the crew began clearing due south along a side ridge leading to the Koʻolau summit. The army later named the new intersection Black Junction.

On May 18, Judd and ranger at large Max F. Landgraf joined a CCC crew and helped set charges to blast rock in ʻŌhiʻa ʻAi Gulch. The two then hiked to Black Junction and walked about a third of a mile to the current end of the Summit Trail. There they found Ernest Landgraf and his crew pushing southeast around the head of ʻŌhiʻa ʻAi Gulch. Judd and Max Landgraf scouted ahead to mark a route for the new trail.[68]

In June 1934, Judd included the Pūpūkea-Kahuku Trail as a CCC project for the period October 1, 1934, to March 31, 1935. The work involved realignment of the upper Kahuku section to reduce the grade from 25 percent to 15 percent, the CCC standard. An estimated two hundred man-days would be needed to complete the 0.7-mile project. The Pūpūkea section was also included as a maintenance project for the same period.[69]

On August 30, Judd and Max Landgraf inspected the CCC work on the Castle Trail. On the way down at 2 p.m. they received word of a fire in the Pūpūkea Forest Reserve. The two immediately rounded up thirty CCC workers and drove to Pūpūkea. After hiking along the Pūpūkea-Kahuku Trail for about a mile and a half, the group cleared a fire line across the path of the fire and then successfully set a backfire to halt the advance. After dark, one hundred soldiers from the Eleventh Field Artillery arrived to relieve the tired CCC workers. Later that night steady rain dampened the fire considerably. Mop-up crews, using fire pumps and hoses, however, did not put out the last stumps until September 9. The fire burned 132 acres, much of it prime koa and ʻiliahi (sandalwood) forest.[70]

By March 1935, CCC crews from the Wahiawa Camp completed the realignment of the Pūpūkea-Kahuku Trail from the ʻŌhiʻa ʻAi Stream crossing to Black Junction. On June 10, Judd inspected the lower Kahuku section and decided it needed some regrading. Later that month a Wahiawa Camp crew spent eighty-five man-days smoothing out the old army alignment. The CCC had now reworked the entire Kahuku section of the trail from the stream crossing to the trailhead in a silk oak grove.[71]

With Judd's permission, the Thirteenth Artillery brigade camped at the Kahuku trailhead in mid-July and used the regraded route for maneuvers. While inspecting the trail on July 24, Judd found the upper section completely chewed up between the ʻŌhiʻa ʻAi Stream crossing and Black Junction. In places the mules and artillery had sunk six to eight inches in the soft dirt. The next day Judd fired off a letter to the commanding general of Schofield Barracks requesting that the army repair the damage.[72]

Also in July, Wahiawa Camp workers began widening the Pūpūkea-Kahuku Trail from the end of the homestead road to just short of Owl Flat. That quarter-mile section was to become part of the Wahiawa-Pupukea Trail, an army dirt road through the leeward Koʻolau foothills. In August an army excavator joined the CCC trail crew to help with earth moving. The twenty-mile road was finished in 1937 and renamed Drum Drive after Major General Hugh A. Drum, commander of the Hawaiian Department.[73]

The HTMC scheduled a new hike called Pūpūkea-Lāʻie for November 17, 1935. That morning the group drove to the homestead road's end past the orchards of the Hawaiian Avocado Company. The hikers quickly walked the short road section and then kept left on the Pūpūkea-Kahuku Trail as Drum Drive descended to ʻElehāhā Stream. Past Owl Flat and the Kaunala Trail junction, they entered the 1934 burn area, now partially covered with six-foot-tall koa saplings. At Black Junction the group turned right on the wide-open Koʻolau Summit Trail. Probably some of the fast hikers made it to the top of the newly constructed Wailele (later Lāʻie) Trail. In 1939, the club extended the route down the Lāʻie Trail with a stop at a pool along Kahaiwainui Stream. Leading the hike of April 2 was a young, upcoming guide named Joseph (Joe) Neilson.[74]

Sometime before 1943, the army built a dirt road over most of the Pūpūkea section of the Pūpūkea-Kahuku Trail. The road extended from the Drum Drive intersection to within a quarter-mile of Black Junction. Soldiers now had faster and easier access to the Kawailoa training area for maneuvers. During the war the army also opened up the nearby Kahuku Trail, which climbed the ridge south of Hina Gulch to the Koʻolau summit.[75]

On March 9, 1947, the HTMC held its Pūpūkea hike for the first time after the war. The group walked the three-mile army road and then hiked a short way along the overgrown Summit Trail. On March 2, 1952, Harry Whitten, a reporter for the *Honolulu Star-Bulletin,* led the Pūpūkea Summit hike. In his weekly column "Trail Ways," Whitten mentioned the new Boy Scout Camp at the end of Pūpūkea Homestead Road and Black Junction, with its cluster of trail signs giving the mileage to Lāʻie, Kawailoa, and points south. To this day the club has continued to schedule the out-and-back Pūpūkea Summit hike, which now ends at the Hina lookout near the top of the Kahuku Trail.[76]

For a time after the war the Kahuku section of the Pūpūkea-Kahuku received sporadic use by the army. However, the dirt road from Pūpūkea provided easier access to the summit area for both soldiers and hikers. The 1947 Oʻahu trail map did not even show the Kahuku section. Little-used and unmaintained, the route gradually overgrew with strawberry guava trees and uluhe ferns.[77]

On May 26, 2001, Stuart Ball and Thomas Yoza walked the dirt road from Pūpūkea in the company of nine other HTMC members just starting a summit camping trip. At Black Junction the backpackers turned right on the Koʻolau Summit Trail, while Ball and Yoza turned left to search for the Kahuku section of the Pūpūkea-Kahuku Trail. All morning the two crisscrossed the area below the broad windward overlook without success. In the afternoon they finally found an overgrown switchback trail near a small observation post.

The next Sunday, Ball, Yoza, and eight other HTMC members returned to the overlook to explore the rediscovered trail. Eventually, the group reached an apparent dead end at a training area scattered with foxholes. Yoza and Dayle Turner descended a steep gully and found a more promising trail just above ʻŌhiʻa ʻAi Stream. The group then split up and began following the new trail up- and downstream. The route downstream was reasonably obvious at first, but then became confusing as the ground leveled off in a *kī* (ti) grove. On the way out several members found the start of the new trail between Black Junction and the overlook. After some discussion, Ball, Yoza, and Turner decided that the second trail must be the CCC realignment of 1935, and the first might be the original army route of 1924.

Ball and Yoza coordinated three more outings to explore and reopen the CCC trail. On July 7, five HTMC members partially cleared the trail to the *kī* grove and picked up the route from there. Past the grove the group saw a boulder with a carved arrow pointing the way through rose apple trees to the ʻŌhiʻa ʻAi Stream crossing. On September 29, a group of nine continued clearing through scratchy lantana shrubs and uluhe ferns on the side ridge above the stream. Two of the group found a lovely swimming hole upstream of the crossing. On November 12, Ball, Yoza and eight others finally reached the end of the trail in a stand of Cook Pines. The group continued down an overgrown dirt road until it joined another road leading to the abandoned sugar cane fields below.[78]

Patrick Rorie coordinated the HTMC Pūpūkea Summit hike on September 28, 2003, a beautiful trade wind day. Forty-one members and guests walked the army road and then hiked the Summit Trail to Hina lookout. On the way back some of the group turned right at Black Junction and descended the Pūpūkea-Kahuku Trail to ʻŌhiʻa ʻAi Stream. They then bushwhacked briefly upstream to the swimming hole, which was filled with cool, shoulder-deep water. The club had last hiked that section seventy years earlier in 1933.[79]

Permission to hike the Pūpūkea-Kahuku Trail is required from the lessee, the U.S. Army. In 2009, the army paved most of the Pūpūkea section to accommodate the heavy vehicles of their new Stryker brigade. A short stretch remains as a dirt road that narrows to a trail shortly before Black Junction. The reclaimed Kahuku section receives little use and is gradually becoming overgrown once again.

Pe'ahināi'a Trail

Perhaps someone may reach the summit this time.
—Hawaiian Trail and Mountain Club schedule, May 3, 1964

On February 27, 1927, territorial forester Charles S. Judd inspected the ridge south of 'Ōpae'ula Stream with George A. McEldowney, forest supervisor for the Hawaiian Sugar Planters Association (HSPA), and James B. Mann, an engineer from the Bishop Estate. On the lower section the men found 'ōhi'a trees colonizing abandoned pineapple fields. Farther *mauka* (inland), they noted uluhe (false staghorn fern) spreading through the forest understory.

In September 1927, Judd received verbal permission from George M. Collins, land department superintendent for the Bishop Estate, to clear a multi-use trail along the same ridge. The new route would allow access to an unexplored, remote section of the Kawailoa Forest Reserve for inspection and wild pig control. Experimental planting of fire-resistant trees along the trail would create a firebreak between patches of flammable uluhe. The HSPA planned to set up several gauges along the route to measure rainfall *mauka* of the 'Ōpae'ula ditch system. Surveyors would also use the trail to map the region for a new series of U.S. Geological Survey topographic maps.[80]

On September 26, ranger at large Max F. Landgraf and O'ahu ranger Thomas R. L. McGuire drove to Waialua and turned off Kamehameha Highway onto a dirt road paralleling 'Ōpae'ula Gulch. Their vehicle ascended gradually through the sugar cane and pineapple fields of the Waialua Agricultural Company (WAC) past several camps of workers' cottages. The road ended at Bryan's mountain house, a retreat for plantation managers, probably named after Kenneth C. Bryan, head carpenter at the WAC. The two men hiked to Quadruped triangulation station (elevation 1,642 feet) on Pu'u Pe'ahināi'a (beckoning porpoise hill) and then began surveying and clearing the new trail *mauka* along the ridgeline.[81]

The planned route followed the ridge separating 'Ōpae'ula and Helemano Streams all the way to the summit of the Ko'olau Range (elevation 2,750 feet), a distance of about six and a half miles. Construction of the Pe'ahināi'a Trail was a joint venture of the Territorial Forestry Division and the HSPA. The Forestry Division provided trail surveying and building expertise, and the HSPA contributed the labor. The arrangement must have worked reasonably well because the trail was completely cleared to the summit by December.[82]

The Hawaiian Trail and Mountain Club (HTMC) attempted to hike the new route on December 18. The group, however, didn't even reach the trailhead because heavy rain had washed out sections of the approach road. The club quickly rescheduled the hike for January 29, 1928. That morning at 7:15 a.m. thirty-eight members and guests met at the Armed Forces YMCA in downtown Honolulu and then drove to the mountain house. Leading the group was Ranger McGuire, who was also an HTMC member.[83] Rear guide was Edmund J. Meadows, a house painter, who later described the route.

> Travel along a ridge of light forest trees, Lehua and ohia and the native olive, past a rain gauge–The way is now through heavy virgin forest, huge massive trees and thick vines.[84]

Despite its long length, the hike must have been a success because the club continued to schedule it, once in 1929 and twice in 1930.

On September 14, 1928, Judd, Landgraf, and McGuire hiked the entire Pe'ahināi'a Trail to check on the condition of the native forest. The men started at 6 a.m. from the mountain house and reached the Ko'olau summit seven hours later. Along the way they passed two HSPA rain gauges and shot two wild pigs at close range with their pistols. Judd noted that most of the pig damage to the forest occurred in the upper half of the trail, the hardest part for hunters to reach.

At the summit the three men spent two hours constructing a hut of loulu palm fronds for hunters to use. Leaving the top at 3 p.m., the men pushed rapidly down the trail but were eventually overtaken by darkness. Judd's small white dog, Panache, led the men back to their vehicle at 8 p.m.[85] Judd later remarked, "Hamburgers and hot coffee at Kemoo Farm café afterwards at 9 p.m. tasted mighty good."[86]

On January 19, 1931, Judd met Major General Briant H. Wells, the new commander of the Hawaiian Division at Schofield Barracks. The two men initially discussed tree removal and planting for the post. Judd agreed to show some of the mountain routes to the general and his staff. Wells agreed to provide soldiers to help open up several forestry trails, including Pe'ahināi'a. Since its initial clearing in 1927, the trail had received little maintenance and was overgrown with uluhe.[87]

On July 29, 1932, two army officers and five enlisted men from the Nineteenth Infantry embarked on an ambitious, thirteen-mile traverse of the Ko'olau Range. Led by Piko Club member Major Joseph P. Vachon, the group climbed the Pe'ahināi'a Trail but became disoriented and then separated along the cloud-draped Ko'olau crest. Over the next two days search parties failed to locate three of the soldiers, so the army asked Judd for assistance.

Early on the morning of August 1, Judd and Glenn W. Russ, O'ahu assistant forester, left Cooper Ranch Inn in Hau'ula to follow the army group's planned exit route, the ridge separating Ma'akua and Papali Gulches. After about three hours of climbing, Judd and Russ found the three men, alive but exhausted.

> They had passed the stage of eating ordinary food, and the soles of their feet, which had borne wet shoes for four days, looked like deeply wrinkled prunes and were very tender.[88]

Judd gave the rescued men some soup warmed up over a small fire. The smoke from the fire attracted an army search plane from the Eighteenth Pursuit Group. The pilot deftly dropped a message, "Take off blue shirt if lost party," which Judd promptly did. The tired but relieved group slowly descended the ridge, reaching Cooper's in about five hours. Colonel Adolphe Huguet, commander of the Nineteenth Infantry, later commended Judd and Russ for their help in rescuing the three soldiers. One of them, Captain George S. Pierce, later became chief scout for the Piko Club.[89]

The Wahiawa Camp of the Civilian Conservation Corps (CCC) recleared the Pe'ahināi'a Trail in 1934, and the army Third Engineers upgraded the approach road in 1936. Known as the Opaeula Artillery Spur, the improved road extended from the new Wahiawa-Pupukea Trail (later Drum Drive) past Bryan's mountain house to the Quadruped triangulation station. Workers paid under the Emergency Relief Appropriations Road and Trail Project built the road of crushed coral to withstand use by heavy artillery. Pu'u Pe'ahināi'a was an ideal position to defend the north shore against an invading force.[90]

In 1936, Judd wrote a long article for the *Honolulu Star-Bulletin* describing the trails on O'ahu to encourage their use for recreation. Pe'ahināi'a was the toughest hike mentioned, "a hard seven hour grind on a brushed-out ridge top which has numerous, short ups and downs."[91] The May 1938 *Sales Builder* featured a similar article that warns Pe'ahināi'a hikers, "Too much loitering brings darkness, a lost trail, searching parties. Better take a guide."[92] Despite (or because of) the publicity the route continued to receive only light use, mostly by plantation hunters.

During and after World War II the army used the trail for exercises in the Kawailoa Training Area. In the late 1940s and 1950s, the HTMC scheduled the Pe'ahināi'a hike six times, often taking advantage of periodic army trail clearings. Leading two of those outings was Richard (Dick) Booth, army telephone engineer, who had first hiked the trail in 1939. Twenty years later he couldn't remember a club hike where anyone had reached the Ko'olau summit and returned on the same day. Frequently hikers would descend to a lovely swimming hole along 'Ōpae'ula Stream, rather than go the distance.[93]

After a two-year hiatus the HTMC scheduled the Pe'ahināi'a Trail for May 3, 1964. The writeup in the schedule suggested wistfully, "Perhaps someone may reach the summit this time."[94] The leader, John Hall, assistant professor of biochemistry at University of Hawai'i, and Fred Duerst decided to check out the trail about two weeks before the actual hike. Just after dawn, Hall's wife Gaylien drove them up Twin Bridge Road to the trailhead past the site of Bryan's mountain house, which had collapsed during a windstorm the year before. On the trail the two men slogged for hours through shin-deep mud churned up by soldiers on training exercises. They finally reached the Ko'olau summit at 1 p.m. and came out at dusk. On the way home Hall was so exhausted that his wife had to stop the car while he got out and threw up. On the day of the outing, Hall completed about half the trail, as did most of the others. That was the last time the HTMC ever hiked the Pe'ahināi'a Trail.[95]

On June 13, 1989, sixteen Boy Scouts from Kahuku Troop 199 assembled at Helemano Military Reservation for a five-day trip to earn their backpacking badges. Leading the expedition to Kahuku was Randall Au, Army National Guard helicopter pilot, and two others. The group walked the dirt Pa'ala'a Uka Pūpūkea Road (formerly Drum Drive) and then turned *mauka* on Twin Bridge Road past the mountain house site to the road's end at Pu'u Pe'ahināi'a. The boys pushed up the muddy, overgrown Pe'ahināi'a Trail and then turned north along the Ko'olau Summit Trail toward Kahuku. On the fourth day, with water running low, the group left the Summit Trail to search for water in the leeward gulches. In the afternoon Lawrence Kahalepuna radioed the Coast Guard for assistance. That night the boys huddled under ponchos and tarps as heavy rain drenched the area, making the trail virtually impassable. The next morning a Honolulu Fire Department rescue

Biologist Joby Rohrer inspects wild pig damage near the Pe'ahināi'a Trail, 2000. (Photo by Kapua Kawelo, O'ahu Army Natural Resource Program)

helicopter found the tired, wet group near the Summit Trail above Hau'ula and ferried them to Wheeler Air Force Base.[96]

In August 1995, the U.S. Army established the O'ahu Natural Resource Program (ONRP) to find, monitor, and protect endangered species in its training areas. Shortly afterward, ONRP personnel began to explore along the Pe'ahināi'a Trail. Over the next few months they discovered several rare native plants and fenced in one species to protect it from wild pigs.

In February 1996, a group of ONRP employees hiked the Pe'ahināi'a Trail for about four hours and set up camp along the ridge. The next morning ONRP manager Steve Kim, natural resource management specialist Vince Costello, and biologist Joby Rohrer continued along the trail, which became increasingly difficult to follow. At one point the two men had to tunnel under a ten-foot high bank of uluhe. Before turning around, they climbed a tree and saw a flat hill nearby that could be used as a helicopter landing pad for easier access to the area. The next year Costello, Rohrer, and others returned to clear the hill, now informally known as Puʻu Roberto after the first helicopter pilot to land there.

During 1996 and 1997, ONRP personnel had also been exploring the upper section of the Peʻahināiʻa Trail. From a small tent camp near the Koʻolau summit, biologists and management specialists combed the area and found a number of endangered plants and tree snails. No one, however, had searched the middle section of the Peʻahināiʻa Trail.

On May 28, 1998, Costello, management specialist Matt Burt, and two volunteers began an adventurous overnight hike from the summit camp down the Peʻahināiʻa Trail to Puʻu Roberto. About an hour out the group passed a tree stump with an old machete cut. Costello later commented,

> We never again saw any sign whatsoever that a trail had ever existed along this ridge. For all we could tell this was all virgin uluhe.[97]

The four men bushwhacked down the ridge until dusk when they found a flat area large enough to pitch their two tents.

The next day the group continued to wade through patches of waist-deep uluhe. At each hill someone would climb a tree to determine where the main ridge went next. Once, they all descended into a gulch by mistake and had to backtrack out. The four tired hikers finally reached Puʻu Roberto thirty minutes before their scheduled 2 p.m. pickup by helicopter. Costello later remarked, "On the map it looked like we would have a lot of time to search for plants and snails but that was wishful thinking."[98]

On January 16, 1999, Patrick Rorie, Dayle Turner, and several other HTMC members left Camp Palama Uka, hiked a portion of the ʻŌpaeʻula Trail, and then climbed out of the gulch to Twin Bridge Road. At a junction they saw a weathered sign "Bryan's Mountain," but no evidence of the mountain house site. Farther along the road was a concrete bunker and clusters of portable toilets for use during army training exercises. On reaching the overgrown Peʻahināiʻa Trail, most of the group turned back, leaving Rorie, Turner, and one other to continue. With machetes out the three men made slow but steady progress along the up-and-down route through frequent patches of scratchy uluhe ferns and *Clidemia* shrubs. As planned, they turned around at 1:30 p.m. and on the way back discussed hiking the entire trail in the future. Turner later estimated that they had covered about two of the six and a half miles to the Koʻolau summit.[99]

In May 2001, the Oʻahu Natural Resource Program coordinated the building of an exclosure fence, a section of which followed the last six hundred feet of the Pe'ahināi'a Trail. Enclosing about two hundred acres at the head of 'Ōpae'ula Stream, the boundary fence protected nine endangered species of native plants and two endangered species of O'ahu tree snails. The exclosure was sponsored by the 'Ōpae'ula Watershed Protection Partnership, a joint effort of the Kamehameha Schools–Bishop Estate, the U.S. Army, the state Department of Land and Natural Resources, and the U.S. Fish and Wildlife Service. Biologists Kapua Kawelo and Joby Rohrer led the effort for ONRP.[100]

Permission to hike the Pe'ahināi'a Trail is required from the landowner, Kamehameha Schools–Bishop Estate, and the lessee, the U.S. Army. The trail remains passable at both ends. Soldiers, hunters, and occasional hikers keep the lower section partially open. The wind keeps the vegetation down on the upper section. In between, however, the trail is lost in a tangle of uluhe and *Clidemia* shrubs.

Mālaekahana

*[Special Hunter] Mendes has done a good
job of clearing out the wild pigs.*

—Charles S. Judd, September 1932

For several years prior to 1931, territorial forester Charles S. Judd had received reports of extensive pig damage to the native forest along a stretch of the Ko'olau summit above Koloa Gulch informally known as "Waimea Flats." Hunters, however, could not easily reach the flats from the existing trails, Pūpūkea-Kahuku to the north and Castle to the south. In early 1931, Judd decided to clear a route up the ridge between Mālaekahana and Kahawainui Streams to the Ko'olau summit, just north of Pu'u Ka'inapua'a (pig procession hill). Near the trail's end he planned to build a small cabin for overnight use by rangers and hunters.[101]

Sometime in March, Kahuku ranger Robert Plunkett and his trail crew drove to the outskirts of Kahuku town and turned off Kamehameha Highway on a dirt road through the sugar cane fields of Kahuku Plantation Company. The road initially paralleled Mālaekahana Stream and a spur line of the Koolau Railway. At the rail's end their vehicle turned left, crossed the stream, and labored up the ridge for just over a mile. At the road's end the men shouldered their tools and quickly hiked to the Morgan triangulation station (elevation 723 feet) at the boundary of the Kahuku Forest Reserve. From there the crew began surveying and clearing *mauka* (inland) along the ridgeline toward the top of the Koʻolau Range.[102]

By early April, Plunkett and his crew reached the Koʻolau summit (elevation 2,120 feet), although much work remained to be done on the lower sections of the trail. On April 8, Judd, his two children, and special hunter Nicholas (Nick) Mendes hiked the entire 2.7-mile route.[103] It became known as the Mālaekahana Trail after the nearby stream and the *ahupuaʻa* (land division) through which it passed. In the epic Hawaiian romance *Ka Moʻolelo O Lāʻiekawai*, Mālaekahana was also the wife of an Oʻahu chief and the mother of the heroine, Lāʻiekawai.[104]

On April 29, Judd led a marathon reconnaissance hike for the Piko Club, an association of forestry rangers and army officers. Along were Oʻahu assistant forester Glenn W. Russ, Bishop Estate forester George R. Ewart III, and four army officers. The group probably started on the Kawaiiki Trail, crossed over to Kawainui Stream and then bushwhacked up a spur ridge to Puʻu Kaʻinapuaʻa. There the men turned north along the summit through Waimea Flats. Two of the army officers became exhausted and slowed the group down. The men descended the Mālaekahana Trail in the dark and in the rain. After the fourteen-hour hike, the weary group enjoyed a late-night dinner at Cooper Ranch Inn in Hauʻula.[105]

During the next three months Plunkett and his crew widened and reworked the Mālaekahana Trail. His men dug several contour sections to bypass knobs in the ridge. In July, as planned, the crew built the hunters' cabin near the trail's end at the summit. The ten-by-ten-foot hut had a redwood frame, galvanized iron roof and walls, and a small kitchen. The total construction cost was $41.36.[106]

The cabin was a frequent overnight stop for Nick Mendes from Hauʻula. On April 1, Judd had rehired him as a special hunter to reduce the pig population along the Koʻolau summit. His salary was $75 per month plus all the 30-30 ammunition he could use. During the next nine months Mendes and his dogs killed 320 pigs, the last one on New Year's Eve.[107] That day Judd climbed the Mālaekahana Trail to inspect the cabin. Along the way he met Mendes clearing trail, and the two men killed a 150-lb. boar in the late afternoon.[108]

On September 13, 1932, Judd led an overnight trip to inspect the native forest along the northern Koʻolau summit. Also along were Mendes, Russ, ranger at large Max F. Landgraf, and U.S. Army Captain William M. Weiner. The group climbed the Mālaekahana Trail in two hours, left their camping gear at the cabin, and turned south along the summit ridge to Waimea Flats. Judd later reported,

> This is heavy jungle country through which one cannot travel faster than two miles per hour. The forest is generally in good condition and functioning well as a conserver of water. At Waimea Flats opposite Koloa Valley Mendes has done a good job of clearing out the wild pigs.[109]

After returning to the cabin for the night, the men put up a Mālaekahana Trail sign at the summit.

Leaving at 8:15 the next morning, the group bushwhacked north along the summit ridge to the Pūpūkea-Kahuku Trail in about six hours. En route they shot two pigs and found yellow land shells (native tree snails). The five men then quickly descended the Pūpūkea-Kahuku Trail, reaching the cars about 3 p.m.[110]

On October 20, 1932, Judd led another Koʻolau overnight trip to search for a herd of wild cattle. Along this time were Mendes, Landgraf, Lieutenant Thomas J. Wells, the son and aide of General Briant H. Wells, and Frederick D. Lowrey, vice president of Lewers and Cooke, Ltd. The group started hiking the Kawaiiki Trail, built by the Waialua Agricultural Company in 1902. At the ditch intake the five men crossed the ridge to Kawainui Stream and worked upstream to the first major fork, where they spent a comfortable night. The next day the group followed the north fork for a while, and then climbed up a spur ridge to Puʻu Kaʻinapuaʻa. They came out the Mālaekahana Trail, reaching their cars at 3:30 p.m. During their trip the men saw no cattle and shot only two wild pigs. Judd was pleased with the excellent condition of the native forest, which was due primarily to Mendes' pig hunting.[111]

The Piko Club hiked the Mālaekahana Trail on June 25, 1933, a fine Sunday. At the cabin the members presented General Wells with an old ʻumeke (calabash) made of milo. Judd had purchased the bowl from Coconut Hut on King Street for $28. Each Piko contributed fifty cents for the gift. After the hike the group went for a swim in the ocean off Lāʻie.[112]

On July 30, 1934, Judd and Russ climbed the Pūpūkea-Kahuku Trail and turned south along the initial section of the new Koʻolau Summit Trail, being built by the Honolulu Unit of the Civilian Conservation Corps (CCC). Accompanying them was Ernest W. Landgraf, the foreman of the thirty-man summit trail crew. Half a mile past the junction with the Mālaekahana Trail, the three men reached the crew slowly working south along the Koʻolau crest. Judd pronounced the newly graded trail "well built, but muddy."[113] They then descended the Mālaekahana Trail, also muddy from traffic to and from the hunters' cabin, now a CCC side camp housing Landgraf's crew during the week.

On the morning of March 12, 1935, Judd and Lieutenant Wells climbed the reconstructed Castle Trail. Also along was Gunder E. Olson, project superintendent of the CCC Honolulu Unit. They first inspected the side camp just below the Koʻolau summit and then headed north along the Summit Trail. At Waimea Flats the men passed Landgraf's crew working steadily toward Puʻu Kaʻinapuaʻa and a junction with the new Kawailoa Trail. The three pushed through a short, unfinished section along the summit and then descended the Mālaekahana Trail, reaching their cars at 9:15 p.m. Judd later noted, "Stormy day but fine trip. Walked 11 hours and pooped Pan [Panache, his small, white dog]."[114]

Four months later a crew from the CCC Wahiawa Camp completed the Wailele (later Lāʻie) Trail. The new route roughly paralleled the Mālaekahana Trail, less than a mile away.[115] Hunters, hikers, and rangers began using the Wailele Trail because it offered a shorter and easier trip to the summit. As a result, the Mālaekahana Trail gradually fell into disuse and disrepair.

While exploring *mauka* of Lāʻie in 1947, Richard H. (Dick) Davis of the Hawaiian Trail and Mountain Club (HTMC) found the lost Mālaekahana Trail. He began clearing it by himself and finally reached the Koʻolau summit after a number of outings. Just below the top he found a dilapidated, three-sided shelter in a grove of loulu palms. Despite Davis' work, the HTMC declined to schedule the Mālaekahana Trail as a regular hike.[116]

In late 1994, Jesse Palmer of Lāʻie heard about a nearby *mauka* trail leading to a waterfall with a thirty-foot jump into a pool. He and a few friends explored possible approach routes several times after school. Finally, in December they found the much-overgrown trail to the awesome swimming hole. The route initially climbed the ridge west of the Lāʻie Trail and then joined the original Mālaekahana Trail about a half mile *mauka* of the Morgan triangulation station.

As member of Kahuku Boy Scout troop 226, Palmer decided to reopen the trail for an Eagle Scout project. In mid-January 1995, Palmer and friends spent four days and more than three hundred man-hours clearing the trail to the waterfall and a well-earned swim. Where possible, the boys followed the original graded sections of the trail that contoured around humps in the ridge.[117]

HTMC member Charlotte Yamane had heard about Palmer's efforts from her sister, who lived in Lāʻie. Yamane and Mabel Kekina, head of the club's trail maintenance crew, decided to investigate the new approach route and possibly reopen the Mālaekahana Trail all the way to the Koʻolau summit. On December 5, the two women and six others checked out the route to the waterfalls and pools. All agreed that the Mālaekahana Trail would make an excellent club hike.

Over the next six months Kekina led seven maintenance outings on the Mālaekahana Trail. The HTMC crew rerouted the graded sections to the ridgeline for easier maintenance and gradually extended the cleared trail toward the summit. The last outing was on June 3, National Trails Day, and included twenty-five volunteers from the Hawaiian Electric Company.[118]

The next day Kekina led the first official HTMC hike on the Mālaekahana Trail. Most of the fifty-seven hikers descended to the pools for a refreshing swim on that warm trade wind day. A few ventured up the ridge to an overlook less than a mile from the Ko'olau summit. Everyone was pleased with the new hike.[119]

At 7 a.m. on June 12, 1995, seven HTMC members left Lā'ie and quickly climbed the Mālaekahana Trail to the end of the clearing at the overlook. They then bushwhacked about 0.7 miles to the summit, arriving at noon. Along the way the group found more evidence of the old trail, but none of the cabin near the top. After lunch they headed north along the Ko'olau Summit Trail and then descended the Lā'ie Trail. At 5 p.m. Kekina greeted the returning group with drinks and snacks. She later wrote in her journal, "A job well done."[120]

Since 1995 the HTMC has continued to hike the Mālaekahana Trail to the pools once a year. The club made occasional forays to or from the summit as part of loop hikes involving the Ko'olau Summit Trail, and the Kahuku or Lā'ie Trails. As of 2010, the Mālaekahana Trail was open to the pools and passable to the summit. Permission is required from the landowner, Hawai'i Reserves.

Piko

In time they [Piko pines] should grow to great height and become conspicuous landmarks in that wild country.
—Charles S. Judd, October 31, 1932

On March 23, 1932, territorial forester Charles S. Judd drove into Mākua (parents) Valley with Wai'anae ranger Ralph E. Turner, Jr., and foreman

Ernest W. Landgraf. For about a mile and a half they followed a rough dirt road *mauka* (inland) past small vegetable farms and through a cattle ranch owned by the McCandless family. From the road's end the three men probably hiked along a pipeline to a tunnel that tapped a spring, which supplied the ranch with water. Just past the tunnel, they entered the forest reserve and carefully scanned the thousand-foot cliff at the back of the valley. Eventually, the three found what they were looking for, a possible route for a trail up the *pali* (cliff) to the crest of the Waiʻanae range.[121]

Earlier in the year Judd had decided that the Forestry Division needed a trail in the back of Mākua Valley. The new route would provide easier access to much of the Mākua-Keʻeau Forest Reserve for inspection, fire protection, and wild pig control. In addition, a route up the cliff would connect with two existing routes leading down to Mokulēʻia, one known as the Mendonca contour trail along the ridge west of Makaleha Valley and the other through Peacock Flat to Dillingham Ranch.[122]

On April 13, Judd and Turner returned to Mākua Valley and laid out the new route one-third of the way up the *pali*. One week later Glenn W. Russ, assistant Oʻahu forester and Max F. Landgraf, ranger at large, reached the Waiʻanae summit (elevation 2,250 feet) to complete the survey. Max Landgraf, Ernest Landgraf, and a six-man Puerto Rican crew cleared the entire 1.2-mile route in two days, April 28 and 29. On the afternoon of the second day, Judd and Russ inspected the new trail. They descended from the Waiʻanae crest to the road in one hour and ten minutes.[123]

On May 5, Judd introduced the Piko Club, an association of forestry rangers and army officers, to the Piko Trail, as the new route came to be known. Twenty-five members and guests easily scaled the Mākua cliff to the Waiʻanae summit ridge. On the way down they stopped briefly at Kukuiala cabin, a new six-bunk forestry shelter built near Peacock Flat. The group then continued the descent to their cars at Dillingham Ranch. The traverse, Mākua to Mokulēʻia, took just four hours.[124]

At 7 a.m. on Sunday, October 30, thirty-three Pikos and guests assembled at the Fort Shafter quarters of Major General Briant H. Wells for a club hike and tree planting organized and led by Judd. From the road's end in Mākua Valley, the group climbed the Piko Trail to the Waiʻanae crest. There General and Mrs. Wells each planted a one-foot-tall Norfolk Island (Cook) Pine to mark the end of the trail. Others attending were Judd's wife Louise, their two children, and Lieutenant Thomas J. Wells, the general's son and aide. After the planting the group descended through Peacock Flat and reached Dillingham Ranch about five hours after they had started.[125]

The next day Judd wrote to Wells thanking him and his wife for planting the twin pines.

> In time they should grow to great height and become conspicuous landmarks in that wild country. They will always be to us a pleasant reminder of two personalities whom we have come to love.[126]

Several days later Turner returned to the site, cleared around the pines and set up a small sign describing the event.

During the early summer of 1935, the Wahiawa Camp of the Civilian Conservation Corps (CCC) extended the Mākua Valley road to the forest reserve boundary to provide easier access for tree planting. Requiring about 1,800 man-days, the 0.8-mile extension was well built for a truck road, with a twelve-foot culvert and three stone crossings of Mākua Stream. The road crew routinely worked ten-hour days because of the long forty-mile drive from Wahiawā.[127]

While finishing the road in July, the Wahiawa Camp also rebuilt the Piko Trail from the forest reserve boundary to the Wai'anae crest. In ninety-eight man-days the crew rerouted the lower section onto a ridge with a better grade and cleared and widened the upper section on the cliff. In his monthly report camp superintendent Robert C. Bayless noted, "Nothing was done where ladders are used to get over rocky ledges as the ladders were in good condition and apparently new."[128]

At 9 a.m. on December 15, forty-one Pikos and guests gathered at Mākua. The group drove to the road's end at the forest reserve boundary and ascended the Piko Trail. On the way up they saw cowboys working for Lincoln (Link) L. McCandless attempting to drive wild cattle out of the forest reserve and into the ranch where they belonged. After passing the twin pines, the Pikos had lunch and coffee near Pahole spring along the new Makaleha (later Mokulē'ia) Trail. The group then descended that trail and reached their cars four hours and twenty minutes after starting. Judd later complained about the weak coffee on the hike. He suggested measuring the water before putting in the coffee grounds in the container. His recipe called for one-half pound of coffee for each gallon of water.[129]

The Hawaiian Trail and Mountain Club (HTMC) first hiked the Piko Trail on August 9, 1936. The club schedule called it the Mākua Cliff Trail, also known as the Piko Club Trail. "We are assured it is so well improved it presents no difficulty to the ordinary hiker."[130] The hike started at 8 a.m. from the Armed Forces YMCA in downtown Honolulu and was led by John A. Matthewman, a judge at the First Circuit Court. Along the trail the hikers undoubtedly noticed a large reforestation project undertaken by the CCC in early 1936. Crews from the Wahiawa Camp had planted thousands of koa and silk oak and more than six hundred ʻiliahi (sandalwood) in the back of Mākua Valley.[131]

The 1936 hike must have been a success because the HTMC scheduled the Piko Trail annually through 1940. Led by Judge Matthewman, the outing on May 17, 1937, attracted eighteen hikers, including R. J. Baker, noted photographer and world traveler. His diary entry for the day succinctly read "fine view, plenty of breeze, a little rain."[132]

In 1941, HTMC scheduled another nearby hike, Mākua-Kaʻena Point, instead of the Piko Trail. As the group gathered at the YMCA on the morning of December 7, the Japanese attacked Pearl Harbor. Initial comments were "very realistic war games" and "must be having maneuvers of some sort." As planned, the hikers left for Mākua, but their cars were turned around at a roadblock near Oʻahu prison. Back at the YMCA, old-timer Joseph Whittle was heard to say, "Let's take a trail in the other direction from Pearl Harbor. Since war's come, we may not be able to do much hiking for a while." No one else, however, wanted to miss the excitement, so he headed out alone in the direction of Koko Head.[133]

The day after Pearl Harbor the U.S. Army placed the Territory of Hawaiʻi under martial law. All of Mākua Valley became an army training area, where soldiers may have used the Piko Trail for exercises. After the war the army retained Mākua for use as a firing range, primarily for artillery. Much of the valley floor became pockmarked with shell holes and littered with duds. The Piko Trail, little used and unmaintained, began to deteriorate.

On June 1, 1952, Richard H. (Dick) Davis and a companion hiked from Keālia cabin along the rim of Mākua Valley. They reported,

> Near Makaleha we found two Norfolk pines with signs saying they were set out by Gen. and Mrs. B. H. Wells. This marked start of Piko Trail into Mākua Valley, but now kapu because of firing in valley. Near trail holes where machine gun nests probably were once.[134]

The two then descended briefly to the Kukuiala cabin below the pines. They then returned to the Keālia cabin where they and other HTMC members had camped for two nights.

In the early 1950s, the HTMC resumed scheduling the Mākua-Kaʻena hike. Because of the restricted access to Mākua Valley, the route actually started from Keawaula (Yokohama) Bay, farther down the coast. The hikers climbed either the Kaluakauila Trail, an old Hawaiian route, or perhaps a ranch wagon road to the Wai'anae summit. They then descended along the crest to Ka'ena Point and returned along the coast, following the railbed of the Oahu Railway and Land Company.[135]

In the mid-1960s, the HTMC resurrected the Piko name for an entirely different hike developed and led by Dick Davis. The route initially climbed the ridge between Mākua Valley and Kaluakauila Stream, reaching the Wai'anae summit at a distinctive hole in the rock informally known as "puka" or "piko" rock. From there the group descended an old ranch route into a narrow side canyon filled with kukui trees and huge bird's nest ferns. At the mouth of the canyon the hikers followed intermittent Punapōhaku Stream out the Kahanahāiki side of Mākua Valley.[136]

Today little or no evidence remains of the Piko Trail. The twin pines at the end of the trail, however, are tall and conspicuous, just as Charles Judd predicted. To see them, take the Mokulē'ia Trail through Peacock Flat campground and enter Pahole Natural Area Reserve. At a small shelter near the cabin site, turn right and climb briefly to the Wai'anae crest. Turn right again on the Mākua Rim Trail along the fence and walk five minutes to the pines.

No historical signs mark the site. The plaques from the 1950s have disappeared. In 1999 each tree had a small metal tag affixed to the trunk stating the type of tree and the date of planting. Those tags have since been removed by forestry workers for safekeeping.

Ma'akua Ridge and Hau'ula

Hiking clothes are not really necessary, but a pair of comfortable shoes are to be recommended, and ladies with new silk stockings had best remove them before starting.

—E. H. Bryan, Jr., August 1933

By 1927, territorial forester Charles S. Judd was very familiar with the region *mauka* (inland) of Hau'ula town. For ten days in 1917 he had surveyed the proposed Hau'ula Forest Reserve, which was finally established on December 31, 1918. In the middle 1920s, he periodically inspected sections of the reserve boundary fence and explored deep into the gulches looking for wayward cattle.[137]

After working in the Hauʻula area, Judd frequently stopped for dinner at the recently opened Cooper Ranch Inn. Fronting Hauʻula Homestead Road, the inn was a small resort hotel owned by Will J. and Lucy V. Cooper. The two-story colonial house had a dining room overlooking the ocean and five rooms for overnight guests. On the ten-acre grounds were several cottages and eventually a hibiscus garden with three thousand varieties, and avocado and mango orchards. Cooper's letterhead featured a classic quote from Samuel Johnson, "The greatest joy in life, sir, is a good dinner at a good inn."[138]

On January 7, 1927, Judd, ranger at large Max F. Landgraf, and eight others, including Will Cooper, hiked partway into Maʻakua Gulch and then climbed the ridge to the east to a junction with the Castle Trail at a small saddle. Along the way Judd looked for a suitable site for a pig hunters' cabin.[139] He later reported, "The difficult going and steep topography were most discouraging and frequent signs of rampant wild pigs were observed."[140] After the cold, rainy hike the men enjoyed a hot dinner at the inn.

Judd introduced Major General Briant H. Wells to Hauʻula hiking and hospitality on March 12, 1931. The two men, accompanied by nine other army officers, climbed the Maʻakua-Papali ridge behind Cooper Ranch Inn toward the Koʻolau summit. At the saddle, informally known as the "pig wire" (corrupted Welsh for trail), the group turned down the Castle Trail, crossed Kaluanui Stream, and descended into Punaluʻu Valley. After that nine-hour hike the men stopped at Cooper's for a relaxing swim and dinner.[141]

The Hawaiian Trail and Mountain Club (HTMC) scheduled a similar hike for June 21, 1931. Seventeen members and guests followed a local guide up the ridge in back of the inn and then returned the same way. After the hike the group stopped at Cooper's for refreshments and toured the "groves of hibiscus, winter pears [avocado], and other rare and peculiar fruit."[142]

In 1932, Judd wanted to improve access to the Hauʻula Forest Reserve for tree planters, pig hunters, firefighters, and fence builders. After scouting the terrain for three days in May and June, he decided to construct two loop trails starting in back of Cooper's. On August 9, Judd set grade stakes for the initial switchback section of the first loop.[143]

At 7 a.m. the next day, Judd, Kahuku ranger Robert Plunkett, and his crew began building the Punaiki (later Maʻakua Ridge) loop. After completing the switchbacks by early September, the trail crew worked steadily through heavy guava and hala to Papali Gulch. Plunkett and his men then pushed up the side of Punaiki Gulch over the next two months.[144]

On December 13, Judd brought in a second, larger crew to help finish the project. Led by foreman Ernest W. Landgraf, the eighteen-man crew consisted of Puerto Rican laborers and unemployed men hired by the governor's Unemployment Relief Commission. Working together, the two crews quickly graded the unfinished sections in Punaiki and Ma'akua Gulches to complete the loop on December 29, 1932. Judd and Max Landgraf measured the loop and set out sign and mileposts on March 9, 1933. The total round trip distance was 2.95 miles from the south corner of the Cooper Ranch Inn property.[145]

Judd introduced the Piko Club, an association of forestry rangers and army officers, to the new Punaiki Trail on Sunday, April 9, 1933. At 10 a.m. seventy-five members and guests gathered at the Cooper Ranch Inn for the short hike and their second annual meeting. The large group climbed the switchbacks and admired the fine view *makai* (seaward), from the Kahuku mill and the Mormon temple on the left to the beach cottages at Punalu'u on the right. The Pikos then turned right at the signed junction and ascended steadily out of Ma'akua Gulch through hala trees and *kī* (ti) plants. Along the crest of the ridge they passed more than six hundred tree seedlings planted the week before by Plunkett's crew. Metal tags on brightly colored stakes identified the species by common and scientific name, Formosa koa on the left, naio on the right and even a few kauila and iliau.

As the trail left the ridge to descend into Papali Gulch, the group saw a small sign pointing up the ridge "To Kawailoa." Half in jest, Judd had erected the sign to mark the rough cross-country route leading to the Castle Trail, the Ko'olau summit, and eventually the Pe'ahināi'a Trail. Judd had hiked portions of the route in 1927 and 1931, and in 1932 to rescue Captain Pierce and other lost army hikers.

In Papali Gulch the group stopped for lunch beneath an 'ōhi'a 'ai (mountain apple) grove. At the ensuing annual meeting the Pikos elected Judd as president and retained Pierce as chief scout. After the meeting the group quickly descended along the side of Punaiki Gulch and then contoured around the bluff overlooking Manuel B. Silva's dairy. After completing the loop, they met at the Cooper bath house for a swim in the ocean.[146]

In January 1933, surveying and grading had started for the second loop, known as the Hau'ula (red hau tree) Trail. Over the next four months foreman Ernest Landgraf and his crew worked up Hānaimoa Gulch, into Waipilopilo Gulch, and then back along the ridge above Kaipapa'u Gulch. In April two men from Plunkett's crew blasted rock and built a bridge across Hānaimoa Stream to complete the loop. On May 16, Judd measured the Hauʻula Trail at 2.23 miles and set out sign- and mileposts. He sent several copies of his new Hauʻula trails map to Will Cooper for use at the inn.[147]

When not grading trail, Landgraf's crew planted tree seedlings in eroded areas adjacent to the loop and on the ridge between Kawaipapa and Hānaimoa Gulches. From March through April the men dug holes for and set out 4,377 Cook Pines (locally known as Norfolk Island Pines) and 3,817 ironwoods. Judd helped the crew plant ironwoods in Waipilopilo Gulch on May 26.[148]

Judd and Oʻahu ranger Thomas R. L. McGuire inspected the two loops and the tree planting on May 11, 1934, a cloudy, rainy day. The two men found the Hauʻula loop badly in need of clearing. The Cook Pines and ironwoods were growing slowly with about a 50 percent survival rate. The Formosa koa, naio, and iliau on the Punaiki loop were doing well.[149]

In June 1934, Judd included the Punaiki and Hauʻula Trails as a Civilian Conservation Corps (CCC) maintenance project for the period from October 31, 1934, to March 31, 1935. The work involved clearing both loops and smoothing their grade. It was estimated that five hundred man-days would be needed to complete the project, which included the maintenance of other nearby trails.[150]

On January 8, 1935, Judd, Max Landgraf, and Gunder E. Olson, project superintendent of the CCC Honolulu Unit, walked the loops through two heavy rain showers. Judd showed Olson where the two trails needed clearing and grading. Judd also gave the project superintendent a map detailing the species and location for additional tree planting during the next six months.[151]

Judd inspected recent CCC work in the Hauʻula area on February 7. Crews led by foremen J. Kekahuna and Thomas Frazier were planting silk oak seedlings in Hānaimoa Gulch. Down in Waipilopilo Gulch, Ernest Landgraf, now a CCC foreman, and his crew were weeding the Cook Pines planted in 1933 and digging replacement holes. Landgraf's men had been building the Koʻolau Summit Trail above Kaipapaʻu Gulch, but extremely wet weather had forced their temporary reassignment to Hauʻula.[152]

In March, Judd visited the Hauʻula area twice to inspect the trails and the reforestation efforts. On the first outing he and two others planted twenty-one sandalwood trees in Hānaimoa and Waipilopilo Gulches. They also fertilized a test plot of 1933 Cook Pines. Six months later Judd returned to measure the growth of the test trees and to check on the sandalwoods, which were doing fine.[153]

On July 9, 1935, Olson submitted his project report to Judd for the period from April 1, 1934, to June 30, 1935. His Honolulu Unit had spent 379 man-days renovating the two loops at a payroll cost of $776.95. CCC trail crews returned to the two trails for routine maintenance in May 1936.[154]

The HTMC scheduled the Punaiki Trail for the first time on September 12, 1937. Some hikers took the three-mile loop, which they found to be easy and in good condition. Others meandered up narrow Maʻakua Gulch to the waterfalls.[155]

The Territorial Forestry Division included both loops on its 1947 Oʻahu trail map. Punaiki, renamed Maʻakua, was trail number 13 at 2.6 miles, and Hauʻula was trail number 14 at 2.5 miles. The map also showed a half-mile extension of trail number 13 into Maʻakua Gulch. Both trails now started directly from Hauʻula Homestead Road, rather than in back of the Cooper Ranch Inn.[156]

The HTMC scheduled one or both loops periodically during the 1950s. The hike on May 11, 1952, was a doubleheader, Sacred Falls in the morning and Maʻakua in the afternoon. In the summer of 1954 work crews hired under the Hawaii Employment Program completely recleared the two trails at a cost of $8,279.12. The men also improved the makeshift trail up Maʻakua Gulch.[157]

The 1979 State Forestry Division recreation map changed the name of the Maʻakua loop to Papali, probably to avoid confusion with the Maʻakua Gulch Trail.[158] In the 1980s the HTMC began calling its double-loop hike Hauʻula-Papali. "These two short loop trails sprout out like the wings of a butterfly from a valley above Hauʻula Beach Park."[159] The description for the hike on March 17, 1990, noted that in 1970 Papali was the only Oʻahu trail where you could still see the white two-by-four markers put up every half mile by the CCC.[160]

On June 23, 2002, HTMC members Art Isbell and Inger Lidman found a narrow metal strip on the ground just off the Hauʻula Trail on the ridge between Hānaimoa and Waipilopilo Gulches. Three embedded nail heads indicated that the strip had been affixed to a tree or a stake. Inscribed on the tag were the words "PAPERBARK 4–1935 J.KEKAHUNA—T. FRAZIER," indicating the tree type, planting date, and the names of the two CCC foremen.[161]

The Hauʻula Trail and the Maʻakua Ridge (formerly Papali) Trail are currently administered by the State Forestry and Wildlife Division under the Na Ala Hele Trail and Access System Program. Both loops are usually clear and open to hikers without permission. Many of the Cook Pines and ironwoods are still standing, as are some of the Formosa koa and a few sandalwood. A Mormon church and offices occupy the site of the Cooper Ranch Inn.

Kaunala

> If we're lucky, neither the Boy Scouts, Girl Scouts, nor the U.S. Army will ambush us along the way.
>
> —Hawaiian Trail and Mountain Club schedule, February 10, 1991

On February 1, 1933, territorial forester Charles S. Judd and ranger at large Max F. Landgraf drove to the end of the homestead road above Waimea Bay and took the Pūpūkea-Kahuku Trail. About a half-mile in they stopped at Owl Flat, where a planting crew was packing in paperbark seedlings. At the flat the two men turned left through scratchy uluhe ferns and descended into the Paumalū Stream drainage to scout a route for a new trail.[162]

Judd, Landgraf, and Oʻahu assistant forester Glenn W. Russ marked the proposed route from Owl Flat to the first switchback in Kawaipi Gulch on February 10. From there the planned trail would cross Kawaipi and Paumalū Gulches at about the one-thousand-foot contour. The route would then climb the ridge separating Paumalū and Kaunala Gulches to Puʻu Moa and a junction with the Pūpūkea-Kahuku Trail. With a maximum grade of 12 percent, the three-foot-wide trail would provide easy access for tree planters to the Paumalū section of the Pūpūkea Forest Reserve.[163]

Construction of the new Kaunala (the plaiting) Trail started from Owl Flat in February. Led by foreman Ernest W. Landgraf, the crew assigned consisted of six Puerto Rican forestry laborers and eight Japanese and Korean workers formerly with the Hawaiian Pineapple Company. The latter continued to live in plantation housing but were paid $1.00 per day from the governor's Unemployment Relief Commission. By late March, the gang reached the ridge between Kawaipi and Paumalū Gulches. On March 21, Judd inspected the trail and measured its completed length at 1.25 miles.[164]

On April 27, Judd, Max Landgraf, and Oʻahu ranger Thomas R. L. McGuire set out quarter-mile posts for one and a half miles, the current end of the improved trail. Judd listed the native trees and shrubs along the way for future labeling. After lunch at Paumalū Stream, Judd and Landgraf went over the rest of the planned route and came back over Puʻu Moa and out the Pūpūkea-Kahuku Trail.[165]

In late April, Landgraf's gang started working on the section past Paumalū Stream. The crew managed to finish the Kaunala Trail in early May just before the inaugural hike by the Piko Club, an association of forestry rangers and army officers. In preparation for that hike, Judd placed hand-painted wooden labels identifying twenty-three native trees and shrubs along the trail on May 3. He also built a small stone bridge across Paumalū Stream.[166]

On Sunday, May 7, sixty Piko Club members and guests took the Pūpūkea-Kahuku Trail to Puʻu Moa, descended the Paumalū-Kaunala ridge, and then returned on the new Kaunala Trail. Some of the Pikos undoubtedly received a botany lesson and quiz from Judd, who loved to share his knowledge of native plants. At Paumalū Stream the group enjoyed steaks and chops cooked over an ʻiliahi (sandalwood) fire. During the meal a bag of beer dropped unannounced from a kukui tree to everyone's delight. The well-watered group named the lunch spot Camp Wells in honor of the "Grand Piko," Major General Briant H. Wells.[167]

Later that month Judd learned that a severe budget cutback would force the dismissal of all his field crews on June 30. He quickly decided to extend the Kaunala Trail three-quarters of a mile eastward into Kahuku Forest Reserve during the time remaining. For the next month and a half Ernest Landgraf and his gang worked steadily into Kaunala Gulch, over Kaunala Ridge, and into ʻŌʻio Gulch. By the end of June the men reached ʻŌʻio Stream.[168]

In October, Judd included a second extension of the Kaunala Trail as a Civilian Conservation Corps (CCC) project for the period from October 1, 1933, to March 31, 1934.

> 10. KAUNALA-KAHUKU. Beginning at 1,200 feet elevation at the end of the present new trail at Oio stream in the Kahuku Forest Reserve the route runs northeasterly on private land surrendered to the government to the reserve boundary at 900 feet elevation south-west of Kahuku 6 Trig. [triangulation] Station.[169]

At the reserve boundary the trail would connect with a dirt road coming up from Kamehameha Highway at pump 5, one mile north of Kahuku.

Estimated trail length was eight thousand feet, or 1.51 miles, and the estimated man-days were four hundred. CCC specifications called for a four-foot-wide path with a grade not to exceed 15 percent. Judd, Russ, and Max Landgraf hiked the proposed route on November 23 and December 27 and found it satisfactory.[170]

In late March 1934, the CCC Honolulu Unit began building the Kahuku extension of the Kaunala Trail. Assigned to the project was Ernest Landgraf, now a CCC foreman. During April his thirty-man crew averaged four hundred to six hundred feet of new trail per day depending on the terrain and vegetation.

On April 27 Judd and Max Landgraf drove up the dirt road from pump 5 through the sugar cane fields of the Kahuku Plantation Company. After leaving the vehicle at the reserve boundary, they hiked up the newly graded extension. The two eventually ran into Ernest Landgraf and his crew working downslope into ʻŌʻio Gulch to link up with the previous extension. Judd later commented,

> Grade is good and trail nicely cleaned up—no lunch papers. Trail wet and muddy from recent rains. A few slides have occurred and there will be more.[171]

One week later Judd and Max Landgraf climbed the Paumalū-Kaunala ridge from ʻAimuʻu Gulch. They turned east on the Kaunala Trail and found the Kahuku extension finished. The two men hiked past holes dug for a paperbark planting at ʻŌʻio Flat and then met a gang cleaning up the new trail. Judd put the crew to work building three wood bridges in ʻŌʻio Gulch.[172]

Project superintendent Gunder E. Olson later reported that his CCC Honolulu Unit had spent 610 man-days to construct or improve 2.1 miles of the Kaunala Trail. The payroll cost was $1,367, and other cost was $48.19.[173]

On August 21, Judd and his daughter Emma climbed to the Kaunala Trail from ʻAimuʻu Gulch. Judd mapped the route westward to Camp Wells and then eastward to the ridge between Kaunala and ʻŌʻio Gulches. He observed that the trail was overgrowing with grass and weeds but had few landslides. Judd completed the mapping on August 28, a dry, hot day. He and McGuire hiked the Kahuku extension to the Kaunala-ʻŌʻio ridge. The two noted that the paperbark seedlings at ʻŌʻio Flat were doing well, with about a 75 percent survival rate.[174]

Judd took several students from Kamehameha School on a botany field trip over the Kaunala Trail on September 28. The group hiked the original section from Owl Flat and had lunch at Camp Wells. With the forester's help, the students listed forty-two native trees and shrubs along the way. Returning on the Pūpūkea-Kahuku Trail, the group passed through the area burned by the fire of August 30. Judd later commented, "Wherever there are old koa trees growing, young koa are coming up thickly and are now three inches tall."[175]

The Hawaiian Trail and Mountain Club (HTMC) first scheduled the Kaunala-Kahuku hike for April 14, 1935. The group completed the original section from Owl Flat and returned on the Pūpūkea-Kahuku Trail.

The hike description mentioned the labeled native plants and good water at Camp Wells.[176]

During or just after World War II the army built a dirt road over the Kahuku extension of the Kaunala Trail. After crossing ʻŌʻio Stream, the new road continued up Kaunala Ridge to join the dirt road already constructed over the Pūpūkea section of the Pūpūkea-Kahuku Trail. On its 1947 Oʻahu hiking map the Territorial Forestry Division featured Pūpūkea-Kaunala as trail number 10 at 4.0 miles. The route description included the original section, the first extension almost to ʻŌʻio Stream, and the new dirt road down to the plantation fields.[177]

The HTMC scheduled the Kaunala Trail regularly from the late 1940s through the late 1960s. The hike of June 16, 1957, was a typical outing. From the Armed Forces YMCA in downtown Honolulu, the group drove to the north shore and turned right on Pūpūkea Homestead road by Niimi Store. After passing the Boy Scout Camp Pūpūkea, the hikers took the recently improved army dirt road to the paperbark grove at Owl Flat. The group hiked the original route past Camp Wells and then the first extension to Kaunala Ridge. The hikers then turned right on the army road and followed it back to their cars. Along the way the botanically inclined observed remnant ʻōhiʻa and sandalwood trees and ʻawa shrubs.[178]

HTMC member Richard H. Booth developed a different route for the hike of May 12, 1968. Starting from the Girl Scout Camp Paumalū, the new loop meandered into Kaunala Gulch and then climbed Kaunala Ridge. The return incorporated the Kaunala Trail extension to ʻŌʻio Stream and a dirt road descending the Paumalū-Kaunala ridge back to the Girl Scout camp.[179]

The HTMC later named Booth's new hike Kaunala East to distinguish it from the original hike, called Kaunala West. The club scheduled the two hikes in alternate years through the late 1980s. Since then the HTMC has only hiked the original route because of its easier access on the homestead road.[180]

The Kaunala Trail is currently administered by State Forestry and Wildlife Division under the Na Ala Hele Trail and Access System Program. The original section is usually clear and is open to the public on weekends and holidays. Permission to hike the ʻŌʻio extension is required from the lessee, the U.S. Army. The paperbark grove still stands at Owl Flat, and Camp Wells remains a pleasant stop for lunch.

Civilian Conservation Corps Trails (1933–1942)

[the cane knife] a heavy, wide knife, 18 inches in length, shaped like a butcher's cleaver.

—Honolulu Unit Superintendent Gunder E. Olson,
September 30, 1935

Emergency Conservation Work

Because of poor economic conditions, the Hawai'i legislature reduced forestry appropriations by 75 percent in late May 1933. With money so tight, territorial forester Charles S. Judd and his younger brother, Governor Lawrence M. Judd, decided to apply for federal funds to continue forestry operations. On July 3, the governor sent a radiogram to Harold L. Ickes, secretary of the interior, requesting that Hawai'i be included in the Emergency Conservation Work program (ECW).[1] The U.S. Congress had enacted ECW on March 31, 1933, ten days after President Franklin D. Roosevelt proposed it. The act called for 250,000 unemployed men to join the Civilian Conservation Corps (CCC) to work in national forests and parks on the mainland. As a territory, Hawai'i had been overlooked in the initial distribution of ECW funds in April.

Charles Judd quickly marshaled support for the territory's ECW application. On July 7 and 17, he met with Major General Briant H. Wells, commander of the Hawaiian Department at Fort Shafter. After the second meeting Wells sent a strongly worded letter to the army adjutant general requesting the War Department to support Hawai'i's application for ECW funds. He stated that a protected watershed and a network of trails were essential to the army's defense of the islands.[2] On July 19, Judd described the ECW application and the forestry situation in a letter to Lincoln L. McCandless, Hawai'i's lone delegate to Congress. On July 29, Judd sailed for the mainland on a well-deserved vacation. He also planned to spend several days in Washington, D.C., lobbying for ECW money.[3]

Secretary Ickes disapproved Hawai'i's application in a letter to Governor Judd, dated August 2. However, the secretary stated that he would consider a future request if ECW continued into 1934.[4] In late August, ECW projects were approved for Puerto Rico, another U.S. territory. On September 11, the governor wrote Ickes mentioning Puerto Rico and stressing the forestry and military importance of Hawai'i's application.[5] During the middle of September, Charles Judd arrived in Washington, D.C., and began visiting his contacts in the U.S. Forest Service. He also inspected an ECW camp run by the army in Connecticut. The head of the camp was Captain Raymond G. Sherman, a former member of the Piko Club, an association of forestry rangers and army officers in Hawai'i. On September 27, Ickes wired the governor to have Judd prepare a detailed plan of conservation projects for the consideration of ECW director Robert Fechner.[6]

On October 23, Judd returned to Honolulu on board the S.S. *Monterey*. The next day he met with the governor and General Wells all morning and started working on the plan that afternoon with O'ahu assistant forester Glenn W. Russ.[7] Four days later the two men finished the report, titled "Program for Emergency Conservation Work—Territory of Hawaii" and submitted it to the governor. The thirty-two-page document first covered the economic conditions and forestry situation in Hawai'i. The report then described the proposed trail-building and tree-planting projects that would put 777 unemployed men back to work at an estimated cost of $441,460 for the first six-month period. O'ahu would receive the lion's share at $200,632 for 400 men.[8]

On November 14, Governor Judd approved the project plan and forwarded it in triplicate to Secretary Ickes for the consideration of ECW director Robert Fechner.[9] On December 21, 1933, Judd received the following radiogram from Ickes.

> Director Fechner approves Emergency Conservation Project for Hawaii STOP Allotment of $299,885 exclusive of amount for Hawaii National Park. For Hawaii National Park $121,373. Total allotment $421,258 STOP Army participation limited to disbursing and accounting for all funds.[10]

The allotted money covered the third ECW six-month period (April 1, 1934, to September 30, 1934), as the territory had missed the first two periods.

CCC Setup

On December 28, 1933, Governor Judd met with the heads of the organizations involved to discuss responsibilities and procedures for the ECW project. Charles Judd and George Ii Brown, president, represented the Board of Commissioners of Agriculture and Forestry, which would manage the project. Director Harold A. Mountain attended for the Unemployment Work Relief Commission, which would select the workers. Superintendent E. C. Wingate represented Hawaiʻi (later Volcanoes) National Park. Army Colonel E. D. Powers, finance officer, and his assistant Captain Herbert Baldwin attended for the Hawaiian Department. At the meeting's conclusion Judd and Wingate drafted a radiogram summarizing the discussion for Secretary Ickes.[11]

In early 1934, Judd assigned Russ to direct the ECW projects on Oʻahu. Realizing that his small staff could only manage the forestry aspects of ECW, Judd asked the governor to transfer the business functions to another department. On January 10, Governor Judd designated his budget director, James W. Lloyd, as ECW business administrator, and contracting and purchasing officer.[12]

Lloyd faced several immediate problems, including a critical shortage of trucks on Oʻahu to transport workers to the job sites. He quickly ordered nineteen 1.5-ton stake body trucks from the mainland for $1,037.86 each. They did not arrive, however, until March 14, delaying the start of the actual work until late that month.[13] There was, of course, no shortage of enthusiastic but inexperienced young men willing to build trail and plant trees.

The unemployed men hired to work on ECW projects became members of the Civilian Conservation Corps (CCC). On Oʻahu the CCC was organized into two separate divisions, the Wahiawa Camp and the Honolulu Unit. Both divisions had about two hundred men and twelve foremen, but each was operated differently. The Wahiawa Camp resembled a mainland CCC camp, where the men lived in barracks, were provided with food and clothing, and were paid $30 per month. The camp was located at the National Guard camp in Schofield Barracks, courtesy of General Wells. In charge was camp superintendent Robert C. Bayless.[14]

The Honolulu Unit was a local adaptation of the Puerto Rican model. The men lived at home, provided their own food and clothing, and were paid $2.00 a day. During the workweek they assembled at staging areas for transportation to the job site. The unit had a small field office in back of the Board of Agriculture and Forestry building at Young and Ke'eaumoku Streets. Heading the Honolulu Unit was project superintendent Gunder E. Olson.[15]

First Hawai'i ECW Period
(April 1, 1934, to September 30, 1934)

The initial proposal of October 1933 had included ten O'ahu trail construction projects jointly developed by Charles Judd and General Wells. Assistant forester Glenn W. Russ assigned the trails to the Honolulu Unit and the Wahiawa Camp as follows.

PRIORITY TRAIL	MILES	MAN-DAYS	ASSIGNED
1. Poamoho	4.16	880	Wahiawa
2. Kawailoa	3.37	920	Wahiawa
3. Ko'olau Summit	12.31	6,500	Honolulu
4. Schofield-Ka'ala	2.27	330	Wahiawa
5. Ka'ala-Mokulē'ia	3.10	656	Wahiawa
6. Makaleha-Keālia	6.57	1,146	Wahiawa
7. Waiawa	3.03	640	Honolulu
8. Kahana	1.29	340	Honolulu
9. Keālia	0.46	240	Wahiawa
10. Kaunala-Kahuku	1.51	400	Honolulu

The total estimated trail length was 38.07 miles, requiring 12,052 man-days. To allow for pack animal use, the plan specified a four-foot-wide path with grades not to exceed 15 percent when feasible.[16]

The Honolulu Unit began construction of the Kahuku extension of the Kaunala Trail in late March 1934. The thirty-man crew from the windward side completed the extension in May and immediately switched to the long and difficult Ko'olau Summit Trail. Another Honolulu Unit crew started work on the Waiawa (later Kīpapa) Trail in early April. In late March the Wahiawa Camp began building the Kawailoa, Makaleha-Keālia (later Mokulē'ia), and Keālia Trails using double forty-man crews. A regular twenty-man crew started grading the Poamoho Trail by the middle of April. No information was available on the start (or completion) of the Schofield-Ka'ala, Ka'ala-Mokulē'ia, or Kahana Trails.[17]

Both divisions built trail using a twenty- to thirty-man crew, divided into three groups. First on the trail were several surveyors, who ranged ahead to determine and mark the proposed route. Next came the clearers, who cut brush and trees with cane knives and saws. Last were the pickmen, the bulk of the crew, who dug and graded the new trail. The rate of construction varied with the terrain, vegetation, weather, and quality of the crew. Progress was slow at first because of inexperienced workers and a shortage of qualified foremen. The Forestry Division had to teach basic trail-building techniques and supervisory skills to many of the new foremen. As the crews became better led and more experienced, their work rate, measured in feet of trail constructed per man-day, improved significantly.[18]

By September 30, the end of the first period, CCC crews had made good progress on the original trail construction projects. The Honolulu

CCC surveyors determining the trail route, 1935. (Charles Judd papers, Hawai'i State Archives)

Unit built more than half of the Kīpapa Trail and 5.2 miles of the Summit Trail from Black Junction south to the end of the Kawailoa Trail at Pu'u Ka'inapua'a. The Wahiawa Camp finished Poamoho in August and Keālia, Mokulē'ia, and Kawailoa in September. Invariably, the completed trails were significantly longer and required more man-days than originally estimated.

Second Hawai'i ECW Period
(October 1, 1934, to March 31, 1935)

During the first two weeks of June 1934, Judd and Russ had prepared a program report with cost estimates for the second six-month ECW period ending March 31, 1935. The report included the Ko'olau Summit and Kīpapa Trails still outstanding from the first period. Added were six new trail construction projects for O'ahu.

TRAIL	MILES	MAN-DAYS	ASSIGNED
Wailele	3.0	1,056	Wahiawa
'Ōhi'a Ai	0.7	200	Wahiawa
'Aiea	4.5	792	Honolulu
South Hālawa	4.0	2,400	Honolulu
Kalāwahine	1.3	460	Honolulu
Waimano	4.5	2,584	Honolulu

The total estimated trail length was 18.0 miles, requiring 7,492 man-days. The maintenance section included upkeep of the new CCC trails and clearing and regrading the Punaiki (later Ma'akua Ridge), Hau'ula, and Mālaekahana Trails built by the Forestry Division in the early 1930s.[19]

On June 16, new governor Joseph B. Poindexter reviewed the projects and their total cost of $234,000, of which $148,920 was for O'ahu. He approved the request and sent it to Secretary Ickes. Later in the month ECW director Robert Fechner approved the projects with little modification.[20]

In October, the Honolulu Unit started building the South Hālawa (later Hālawa) Trail and the extension of the Waimano Trail to the Ko'olau Summit. In December, a crew from the Wahiawa Camp began constructing the Wailele (later Lā'ie) Trail. Work didn't start on the Kalawahine, 'Aiea (later 'Aiea Loop) Trail and the regrading of the 'Ōhi'a Ai (Pūpūkea-Kahuku) Trail until March, near the end of the period.

While building trail, the CCC men worked a five-day week and an eight-hour day, starting at 7 a.m. and ending at 3 p.m. The eight hours included the drive to and from the trailhead and the hike in and out to the job site. Lunch was half an hour and consisted of four kinds of sandwiches, and fruit for dessert. That left about six hours at most for actual trail construction. On the long projects, such as Koʻolau Summit, Kīpapa, and Kawailoa, the men spent Monday through Thursday nights at a side camp along the trail to be closer to the work area.[21]

Heavy winter rain in the Koʻolau Range slowed progress considerably during the second period. Conditions were so bad in the first quarter that the Honolulu Unit switched the Summit and Hālawa gangs to tree planting and the Waimano gang to the ʻAiea Loop Trail for a time. Nevertheless, the Summit crew extended the Castle Trail to the Koʻolau crest and then turned north, almost reaching the Kawailoa Trail junction, a distance of 4.6 miles. The Hālawa crew built 2.75 miles before reassignment on January 1, and the Waimano crew constructed 3.4 miles before transferring on February 28. The tough Kīpapa crew finally finished its project in February despite the wet weather. On the windward side, the Wahiawa Camp constructed 1.75 miles of the Lāʻie Trail.

Third Hawaiʻi ECW Period
(April 1, 1935, to September 30, 1935)

During the first quarter of 1935, Judd and Russ worked on the program plan for the third ECW period ending September 30, 1935. The final report requested funds for the completion of the seven trails still outstanding, Koʻolau Summit from the first period, and Hālawa, Waimano, Lāʻie, ʻAiea Loop, Kalāwahine, and Pūpūkea-Kahuku from the second period. The estimated length was 10.0 miles, requiring 10,600 man-days. Additional projects included trail maintenance to repair the damage from the winter storms and a relocation of the Wahiawa Camp from Schofield Barracks to Wahiawā, as the army needed the barracks for use as a summer camp for the Hawaiʻi National Guard. Governor Poindexter and the ECW director approved the requested expenditure of $193,008 for Oʻahu.[22]

During the current and previous period, the Honolulu Unit did most of the heavy trail construction. Because of the constant cutting and digging at close quarters, Superintendent Olson frequently reminded his foremen about safety on the job. In the third period the Honolulu Unit reported thirty injuries, twenty-five of which required a doctor and stitches. The primary cause was carelessness and fatigue, and the primary instrument was the cane knife, "a heavy, wide knife, 18 inches in length, shaped like a butcher's cleaver."[23] Since its inception, the unit had suffered only two serious injuries. A falling rock broke one man's leg, and a truck colliding with a stone bridge fractured another man's thigh.

Hot, dry summer weather allowed the CCC crews to make excellent progress during the third period. Both divisions experienced fewer rain layoffs and sick absences, and less wet, muddy clothing and tools than in the previous period. Under new field supervisor Everett E. Tillett, the Honolulu Unit completed the 'Aiea Loop, Kalāwahine, and Pūpūkea-Kahuku projects in June and Hālawa with a double crew in July. After finishing 'Aiea Loop, the gang resumed work on the Waimano Trail and built 1.6 miles. The Summit crew constructed an additional 5.4 miles from the Castle Trail junction toward the Schofield-Waikāne Trail junction. The Wahiawa Camp completed the Lāi'e Trail in July.

Fourth Hawai'i ECW Period
(October 1, 1935, to March 31, 1936)

On September 13, Judd finished the program plan for the fourth ECW period ending March 31, 1936. He listed six construction projects, of which only two, Honouliuli and Waimea, were brand-new trails.

TRAIL	MILES	MAN-DAYS	ASSIGNED
Waimano	0.5	600	Honolulu
Summit Trail	4.0	3,960	Honolulu
'Aiea Trail	4.75	4,400	Honolulu
Kuli'ou'ou	0.1	80	Honolulu
Honouliuli	7.5	5,400	Wahiawa
Waimea	3.0	3,000	Wahiawa

The total estimated trail length was 19.85 miles, requiring 17,440 man-days. In addition, the plan included reforestation and trail maintenance work by both CCC divisions. The total cost for O'ahu was $161,252, which was approved by the ECW director.[24]

Shortly after the start of the period Judd heard about a probable reduction in the workforce of the Honolulu Unit for the next ECW period beginning April 1.[25] He immediately made route and specification changes in some of the unit's projects to ensure their completion by March 31. The Honolulu Unit finished the Waimano Trail in November 1935 and the Summit Trail in January 1936. The Summit crew again struggled with wet winter weather but finally reached Kīpapa Trail junction, the end of their twenty-month project, well within the deadline. Construction started on the extension of the ʻAiea Loop Trail to the Koʻolau Summit in January and finished in February. In December 1935, the Wahiawa Camp began work on the Honouliuli Trail, a long contour route in the Waiʻanae Range. Because of objections from the army, the camp never built the Waimea Trail, connecting the Kawailoa and Summit Trails.

Subsequent ECW Periods

As expected, reduced ECW funding for the coming period forced the closure of the Honolulu Unit in April 1936. Project superintendent Gunder Olson transferred to Hawaiʻi National Park. The foremen and their crews were discharged over a three-month period ending in June. The Wahiawa Camp survived but with a reduced complement of 166 men and seven foremen.[26] The camp took over maintenance of all CCC trails and finished the Honouliuli Trail, the last construction project, in July.

In March, Charles Judd had been diagnosed with high blood pressure and told to take it easy. He submitted the project plans for the seventh and eighth ECW periods, but soon had to take a medical leave of absence from his job. After a long illness, he died at noon in Queen's Hospital on June 29, 1939.[27]

Charley Judd's obituary reads in part,

> Modest and not inclined to demonstration, he had a rare zeal for his work. He loved to see the greening of reforested areas, the reclamation of desert spots into areas of beauty.[28]

Well known for his tree planting, Judd also proved a staunch defender of the existing native forest. His pig control efforts provided the forest with some respite and ultimately resulted in a magnificent trail network. To see Judd's monument, hike the CCC trails and look around you.

The Wahiawā Camp continued to plant trees and keep the trails open until December 7, 1941. After the Pearl Harbor attack, the army immediately

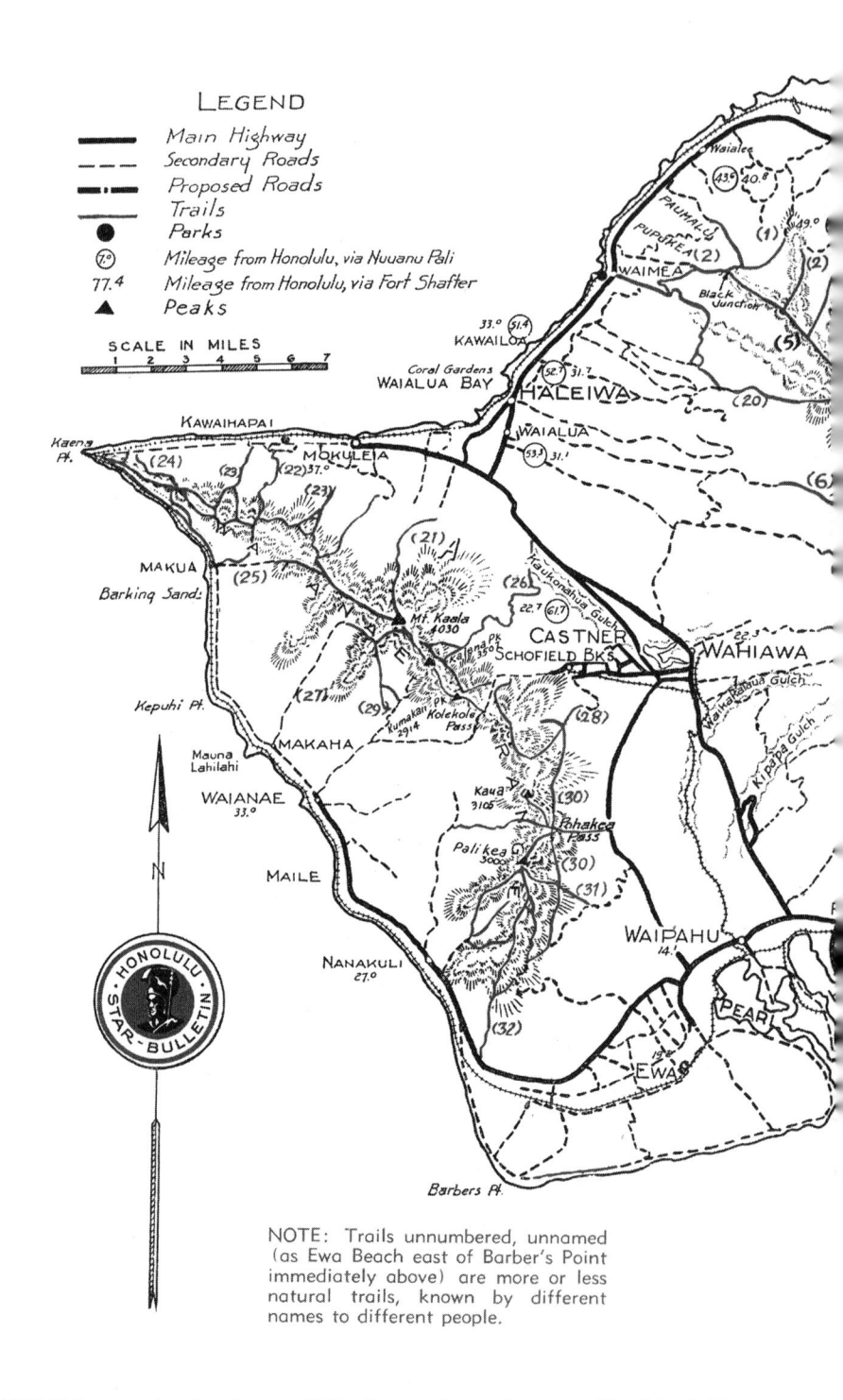

1938 O'ahu map showing the new CCC trails, as well as earlier routes. (*The Sales Builder*, Star Bulletin Printing House)

TRAILS
on the Island of OAHU

1 Kaunala
2-2 Pupukea-Kahuku
3 Malae-Kahana
4 Wailele (Laie)
5-5-5 Summit
6 Peahinaia
7 Pig God (Castle)
8 Poamoho
9-9 Schofield-Waikane
9-a Waiahole Intake
10 Waiawa (Kipapa)
11 Waiahole
12 Waimano
13 Aiea Heights
14 Aiea Summit
15 North Halawa
16 South Halawa
17 Red Hill
18 Tom Tom (Marconi)
19 Wilhelmina Rise-Lanipo
20 Kawailoa
21 Dupont
22 Kealia
23 Mokuleia
24 Pringle
25 Makua Valley
26 Firebreak
27 Makaha
28 Kanehoa-Hapapa
29 Waianae-kai
30 Honouliuli (Gowan)
31 Kaaikukai
32 Pa Lehua

took over maintenance and use of Oʻahu's trail system. The CCC men were transferred to high-priority military projects. On September 17, 1942, the entire ECW program in Hawaiʻi was disbanded and the workers transferred to the army. The Emergency Conservation Work program had lasted more than eight years and employed 7,195 men at a cost of about $5,845,000.[29]

Poamoho

> Trail is well built and has settled well. Upper part of trail is muddy and streams full of water.
>
> —Charles S. Judd, July 6, 1934

According to Hawaiian lore, early travelers on the remote ridge between Poamoho and Helemano Streams had to contend with a band of cannibals ostracized from Waialua. Led by chief KaloʻAi Kanaka, the man-eaters built a *heiau* (religious site) and dwellings at an idyllic, secluded, and strategic spot. *Makai* (seaward) the ridge narrowed considerably, forcing wood cutters and windward wayfarers to pass close to the chief's house. The band nabbed the unfortunate ones, roasted them in an *imu* (underground oven), and carved them on a large flat stone or *ipu kai* (meat platter). Their abhorrent practice ended when Kaʻanokeʻewe, the main procurer of victims, fell to his death while fighting his brother-in-law.[30]

On February 20, 1931, territorial forester Charles S. Judd, Oʻahu assistant forester Glenn W. Russ, ranger at large Max F. Landgraf, and army officers from the staff of Major General Briant H. Wells drove through Wahiawā and then turned *mauka* (inland) into the pineapple fields past Helemano Camp. At the road's end near the ʻEwa Forest Reserve boundary, the group parked their vehicles and began hiking along the Poamoho-Helemano ridge. The path, informally known as the marsh trail, was little used and overgrown, but the men reached the Koʻolau summit in about four hours. At the top the group enjoyed the superb windward view on that cool, clear winter day. Undoubtedly, they talked about the Piko Club, an army-forestry hiking association first proposed three days previously on another reconnaissance outing up the Castle Trail and down into Punaluʻu Valley.[31]

After the Poamoho hike, Judd stopped at Schofield Barracks to meet with General Wells. The two discussed opening up the route from Poamoho to Punalu'u and forming the hiking club. In March, soldiers cleared the marsh trail to the summit and then a spur ridge into Punalu'u Valley.[32]

On January 20, 1932, Judd led another reconnaissance hike on the marsh trail with Russ, Landgraf, special hunter Nicholas Mendes, Lieutenant Thomas J. Wells, son of General Wells, and other army officers. The hike was messy: "Pouring rain all day. Trail in rotten shape. Nick got two boars. Shells [native tree snails] abundant."[33] Judd decided that a cabin near the summit would encourage local hunters to use the trail and keep the pig population down.

The HTMC hiked the marsh trail to the summit for the first time on May 22. Called Helemano by the club, the route was described as an old Hawaiian trail, recently cleared. The outing was led by Edmund J. Meadows, house painter and author of a pamphlet describing hike routes of the 1930s.[34]

In early October, Ernest Landgraf and his six-man Puerto Rican crew spent six days clearing the marsh route. On October 5, Judd hiked the trail to select a site for a pig hunters' cabin near the summit. Also along were Russ, Tom Wells, and Albert A. Wilson of Wahiawa Water Company. The men found a protected site for the cabin near a small stream just below the summit. Wilson inspected a purported lake at the headwaters of Poamoho Stream, but the "lake" was just a widening of the streambed and not useful as a water source. On the way back the group met Landgraf and his gang packing up lumber for the cabin. The crew completed the ten-by-ten-foot cabin on October 11.[35]

After an early breakfast at Kemoo Farm, Judd, Landgraf, Tom Wells, and others hiked up the marsh trail on July 11, 1933, a clear, dry Tuesday. Along the route they found a few signs of pigs and several land shells. After lunch at the cabin, the group climbed to the summit and descended into Punalu'u Valley to complete a Ko'olau traverse.[36]

In late October, a reconstruction of the marsh or Poamoho Trail became the number one project on the original list of Emergency Conservation Work jointly developed by Judd and General Wells.

> Beginning at the end of the present automobile road at approximately 1,300 feet elevation on the ridge bounding the lands of Wahiawa and Paalaa this route runs easterly and generally along the ridge between these two lands and will be confined so far as possible to the government land of Wahiawa. It will terminate at the crest of the Koolau Range at approximately 2,600 feet elevation and connect up with the Koolau

Summit Trail (Project 3). The work will consist of widening and relocating for easier grades in part the present route to facilitate quicker travel. Total length 22,000 feet [4.16 miles], 880 man days.[37]

O'ahu assistant forester Glenn W. Russ assigned the Poamoho Trail project to the Wahiawa Camp of the Civilian Conservation Corps (CCC). By the middle of April 1934, a twenty-one-man crew under foreman Buster H. Quinn was rebuilding the old marsh trail. Judd and Max Landgraf inspected the work on April 24, a rainy Tuesday. The two men walked halfway to the summit with Quinn, instructing him to construct the new route using as much of the old trail as possible.[38]

On a hot, muggy July 6, Judd and Russ hiked the regraded Poamoho Trail for more than two miles before meeting a CCC trail crew under foreman Arthur W. McKenzie. The three men discussed the progress so far and the potential problems as the work approached the summit. Judd later remarked, "Trail is well built and has settled well. Upper part of trail is muddy and streams full of water."[39]

Judd and Russ inspected the entire Poamoho Trail on August 17. They passed four gangs working within a quarter-mile of the cabin. With that much manpower the reconstruction was probably completed by the end of the month. The new contoured route measured 5.36 miles, longer than the old marsh trail. As part of the project, CCC workers equipped the cabin with a wood floor.[40]

On April 24, 1935, Judd, Max Landgraf, and two others climbed the Poamoho Trail to map the upper section. They found numerous small landslides across the path and many land shells in the trees. After lunch at the cabin, the group crossed the Ko'olau summit and descended into Punalu'u Valley. Judd tried fishing the stream for trout without success. (The Forestry Division had stocked Punalu'u Stream with trout eggs several years earlier.)[41]

On July 14, the Piko Club completed a nine-hour Ko'olau traverse from Poamoho to Punalu'u. Thirty members and guests took the Poamoho Trail to the top, where they bushwhacked north briefly to what was then the end of the Summit Trail. After strolling along the wide-open path, the group descended the rebuilt Castle Trail. Halfway down, Captain Joseph B. Sweet, chief scout, served coffee at the CCC camp near Kaluanui Stream. On the same day, the HTMC hiked the Poamoho Trail, perhaps meeting the Pikos on the way up.[42]

On November 3, Judd led the Piko Club on another Ko'olau traverse, this time from Poamoho to Waikāne. Fifty-three members and guests climbed the muddy Poamoho Trail. At the top the group headed south along a spectacular windward section of the Summit Trail below Puʻu Pauao. The Pikos then descended the Waikāne Trail past the ditchman's house to their waiting cars.[43]

The Wahiawa Camp periodically maintained the Poamoho Trail during 1935 and 1936. The CCC crews dug out landslides, regraded the path, and cleared blowdowns. Judd inspected the trail twice in 1936. On his second visit in May, he brought back flowers of the rare native shrub *Hesperomannia arborescens*. On November 1, the Piko Club held a reprise of the Poamoho–Summit–Castle Trail hike done in 1935. It was one of the club's last outings before disbanding in early 1937.[44]

In June 1941, the army proposed paving the entire Poamoho Trail and a connecting portion of the Koʻolau Summit Trail to allow vehicle access to and along the summit. In a letter dated July 5, the Board of Agriculture and Forestry agreed to the request, initiated by Lieutenant General Walter C. Short, commander of the Hawaiian Department. However, the army never started the project, probably because of other priorities or the Pearl Harbor attack. Later during the war, the army did extend the dirt road into the forest reserve for about two miles. The road building destroyed much of the lower section of the Poamoho Trail, reducing its length to 3.4 miles. The army also rebuilt the CCC cabin just below the summit.[45]

After the war, the Territorial Forestry Division included Poamoho as trail number 7 on its 1947 Oʻahu map. The HTMC resumed hiking the trail on September 26, 1948. During the 1950s and 1960s, Poamoho Trail received steady use from the army for training and from outdoor clubs for hiking, bird watching, and botanizing.[46]

On May 8, 1955, seven members of the Hawaiʻi Audubon Society turned *mauka* past the Dole pineapple stand just outside Wahiawā. After skirting Helemano radio station, the group parked at the forest reserve boundary and began walking up the badly eroded road at 6 a.m. At the trailhead the birders saw a pair of iʻiwi in an ʻōhiʻa tree. Farther in they spotted ʻapapane, red-billed leiothrix, and a pair of hwamei, or Chinese thrush with its flute-like song. With such an early start, the group even had time to hike to the summit. They found the trail well cleared by the army with corduroy or logs laid crosswise over the wet spots.[47]

In late 1973, the State Forestry Division built a new Poamoho cabin nestled on the leeward side of the Koʻolau summit about one-half mile past the Poamoho Trail junction. The cabin slept eight to ten persons and featured a water tank with rain catchment, a pit toilet, and a wood-burning stove. On February 2 and 3, 1974, Geraldine Cline, an enthusiastic and dedicated HTMC and Sierra Club member, led a backpacking trip to check out the new Poamoho cabin.[48]

On January 22, 1978, seventy-six friends and relatives of Geraldine Cline hiked up the Poamoho Trail toward the summit. Each carried a small lava rock to build a memorial to Cline, who had died in a car accident in 1975. Two weeks later ten people erected a rock obelisk at the windswept junction of the Poamoho and Summit Trails, one of Cline's favorite spots. Affixed to the monument was a plaque, listing mileages north and south to the connector trails.[49]

More than eighty people attended the dedication of the Geraldine Cline Memorial on April 9, 1978, a typical windy, rainy day at the summit. HTMC member Silver Piliwale gave the blessing in Hawaiian and in English. Participants draped *lei* (flower garlands) on the monument and then trudged back down the Poamoho Trail.[50]

The HTMC hiked the Poamoho Trail regularly in the 1980s through the early 1990s but had to stop in 1993 because of access problems. In 1998 the Forestry Division tore down the vandalized 1973 cabin and built a new one with four bunks but no water source or toilet.

On September 24, 2000, a group of HTMC members climbed the Poamoho Trail to reinstall the brass mileage plaque on the Cline Memorial.

Silver Piliwale blesses the Geraldine Cline Memorial on April 9, 1978, a rainy Sunday at the Poamoho summit. (HTMC Archives)

At the top Jim Yuen and Ralph Valentino completed the job, while others explored along the Summit Trail in both directions. In 1987 the club had replaced the original laminate marker with a sturdy brass plaque giving revised mileages. About ten years later the plaque had fallen off the monument, to be rescued by a passing fire department helicopter and returned to Yuen.[51]

In recent years, hiking the Poamoho Trail has become increasingly difficult because of the rough, unimproved approach road and the liability requirements of the lessee, Dole Foods Hawaiʻi. In 2007, Na Ala Hele (NAH), the state trail program, finally secured public access to the trailhead after three years of negotiation with Dole. At a cost of $75,000, NAH improved and fenced a two-mile section of the dirt road through former pineapple fields. As of 2010, NAH required a permit and a four-wheel drive vehicle to gain access to the road and the trailhead. Once there, look for an abandoned section of the original trail below a grove of eucalyptus. The site of the 1932 cabin is now a sheltered camping spot for hikers attempting the Koʻolau Summit Trail.

Mokulēʻia

Although it [the coffee] was nice and hot,
it did not seem to have much kick in it.

—Charles S. Judd, December 23, 1935

In the early 1930s, a well-trodden cattle path led up the ridge west of Makaleha Valley to the Mokulēʻia Forest Reserve. From the boundary fence an old cowboy route known as the Mendonca contour trail climbed to the top of the Waiʻanae Range and then meandered below the crest toward Keālia. To provide shelter for forestry crews and pig and goat hunters, the Territorial Forestry Division constructed Kukuiala cabin above Peacock Flat in April 1932. Built of sheet metal, the shelter contained six bunks and was conveniently located near a spring.[52]

On May 8, the Hawaiian Trail and Mountain Club (HTMC) scheduled a new hike, called Mokulēʻia. Led by Myrtle King, the group started near Dillingham Ranch and climbed through Peacock Flat to the summit. After lunch there and a look at Mākua Valley, the hikers descended the contour trail and the cattle path to the main highway.[53]

On June 2, 1933, territorial forester Charles S. Judd and two others ascended the *pali* (cliff) behind Kawaihāpai to Hakakoa and Keālia triangulation stations. From there the men roughly paralleled the Wai'anae crest on a contour trail built to service the reserve boundary fence. After reaching Kukuiala cabin at 1:30 p.m., they retraced their steps back to their car parked below the cliff, informally known as General Wells bluff.[54]

In October, Judd and Major General Briant H. Wells incorporated much of that June hike into two trail construction projects on the list of Emergency Conservation Work. The route up the *pali* became project number 9, Keālia Trail. The contour section from Keālia station through Peacock Flat and the Mendonca route down the ridge to the reserve boundary became project number 6, Makaleha-Keālia (later Mokulē'ia) Trail.

> Beginning on the ridge near the boundary of Makaleha and Mokuleia, Waianae Range at 1,500 feet elevation and running south up the ridge and westerly across two gulches to the junction of the Kaala-Mokuleia trail (Project 5), then north and west along old contour trail keeping on government land in the Mokuleia Forest Reserve and ending at the crest of the range at 1,900 feet elevation south of Kealia Trig. Station. This trail will assist in the administration of this reserve which is infested with wild goats, pigs, and cattle. The total length 34,700 feet [6.57 miles], 1,146 man days.[55]

O'ahu assistant forester Glenn W. Russ assigned the Makaleha Trail to the Wahiawa Camp of the Civilian Conservation Corps (CCC). In late March 1934, work started on an approach road from the main highway up the ridge to the forest reserve boundary. By April 14, two trail crews under foremen L. W. Coflin and Robert McCluskey completed the dirt road and began building the trail itself.[56]

On May 1, Judd and Russ met Wahiawa Camp superintendent Robert C. Bayless well above the forest reserve boundary, where the trail crew was working that morning. As they proceeded along the Mendonca contour trail, Judd showed Bayless how to change its grade to meet CCC standards. The men ate lunch on the Wai'anae summit at the head of the Piko Trail by the twin pines, planted in 1932 by General and Mrs. Wells. Judd and Russ then descended through Peacock Flat to Dillingham Ranch.[57]

On September 8, Judd posted the entire Makaleha Trail on a map in his office, so the CCC crews must have completed the 5.12-mile route just before then. Makaleha was easier to build than most of the other CCC trails. The project benefited from a double crew, dry weather, and a route that often followed existing trails over relatively gentle terrain.[58]

Led by Judd, forty-one members and guests of the Piko Club, an association of forestry rangers and army officers, ascended the Piko Trail from Mākua Valley on December 15. On the way up they saw cowboys working for Lincoln L. (Link) McCandless attempting to drive their cattle out of the forest reserve and into the ranch where they belonged. After passing the Piko pines, the group had lunch and coffee near a small stream along the Makaleha Trail.[59] Judd later commented, "Although it [the coffee] was nice and hot, it did not seem to have much kick in it."[60] He suggested an improved recipe for future Piko hikes.

On February 17, 1935, the HTMC scheduled a new hike, which incorporated the Keālia and Makaleha Trails. The group climbed the switchbacks and the ridge to the Keālia fence and Hakakoa triangulation station. From there they strolled along the lovely Makaleha Trail through groves of native 'ōhi'a and kokio ke'oke'o (white hibiscus) covered with land shells (native tree snails). After stopping briefly at Kukuiala cabin with its nearby water supply, the group continued along the Makaleha Trail to the forest reserve boundary and then out to the main highway. On May 7 and 8, Judd, Russ, and several others completed a similar trip as an overnighter to check Mokulē'ia Forest Reserve for wild pigs and cattle.[61]

On June 3, 1936, Judd inspected the Makaleha Trail with Lieutenant Colonel George S. Patton, Jr., the new intelligence officer of the Army Hawaiian Department and a prospective Piko. At the Mākua Valley overlook the two turned south along the Wai'anae crest past 'Ōhikilolo Ridge. The men then descended into Mākaha Valley and followed the stream past a spring to their waiting cars.[62]

During World War II the army constructed a dirt road from the highway near Dillingham Ranch to Hakakoa station. The road climbed to Peacock Flat and then roughly paralleled the Makaleha Trail and the Wai'anae crest to Hakakoa above the current end of the Keālia Trail. The army also built a cabin near Hakakoa station and a second one just below the Piko pines along the Makaleha Trail.[63]

After the war the Territorial Forestry Division included Mokulē'ia (formerly Makaleha) as trail number 20 at 5.2 miles on its 1947 O'ahu map. The description reads,

> Trail starts from [forest reserve] gate and runs up ridge to top of divide above Makua Valley, then down through Peacock Flat to border fence and around contour to west end of Reserve. Remnants of lehua, Koa, Wiliwili, etc.[64]

During the late 1940s and 1950s, the HTMC regularly scheduled the Mokulēʻia Trail up the ridge to the Mākua Valley overlook. The hike write-ups mentioned an orange grove, a lone peach tree, wild peacocks, and a rustic cabin in a grassy meadow below the Piko pines. However, the contour section received little use or maintenance because of the paralleling army dirt road and gradually deteriorated.[65]

On Washington's Birthday weekend, February 20–22, 1965, the HTMC held its first Mokulēʻia campout. Led by Richard H. (Dick) Davis, the group turned off Farrington Highway onto Mount Kaʻala Road, built by the Federal Aviation Administration to the summit of Kaʻala in 1961. They parked by a locked gate and began climbing through pasture belonging to Mokuleia Ranch and Land Company. At the reserve boundary the hikers followed the Mokulēʻia Trail up the ridge to the cabin. Most chose to tent in the meadow or at the Mākua overlook rather than sleep in the dilapidated cabin. On the layover day some of the campers explored along the Waiʻanae crest. Those heading west toward the Keālia Trail passed near a Nike-Hercules missile radar station built in 1961. The campers must have had fun because the club has scheduled the trip regularly to this day, frequently combining it with a day hike.[66]

In 1981, the state legislature established Pahole Natural Area Reserve (PNAR) to protect rare native plants and animals in a portion of the Mokulēʻia Forest Reserve. PNAR encompassed 658 acres roughly bounded by the Mokulēʻia Trail, the Waiʻanae crest, the Nike station, and Peacock Flat. After an initial period of underfunding, the Forestry and Wildlife Division finally began to actively manage the reserve. Their workers and volunteers controlled invasive weeds and planted native species suited to the dry land forest habitat. They also built protective fences around native tree snail colonies and plants, such as ʻōhā wai, an endangered *Lobeliad*.[67]

As of 2010, the Mokulēʻia Trail was in decent shape from the reserve boundary up to the cabin site and down to Peacock Flat. The contour section to the Keālia Trail has virtually disappeared, a victim of the paralleling army road, subsequently improved and named Mokulēʻia firebreak road, and later called Kuaokalā Access Road. Hikers can reach the open trail section by walking the Mokulēʻia Forest Reserve access road from Farrington Highway to Peacock Flat campground. At the end of that road is the Nike station, decommissioned in 1970 and now used as nursery for growing native plants. The army cabin below the Waiʻanae crest collapsed many years ago and was replaced by an open-sided picnic shelter, which is deteriorating in turn. Nearby Pahole spring still provides water for campers, although it runs dry during long periods of drought. Farther down the trail the orange grove continues to produce fruit, most of it quite sour.

Keālia

This is an extremely rocky and precipitous trail.
—A. S. Newman, April 14, 1934

During the summer of 1913, U.S. Army engineers erected the Hakakoa triangulation station in the *ahupua'a* (land division) of Keālia (crusted salt). Located on a prominent knob (elevation 1,908 feet), the station was an important survey point in the Mokulē'ia area for the early topographic mapping of O'ahu. To get to the site, the engineers had to scramble up a thousand-foot *pali* (cliff) and then climb the ridge next to Haili Gulch almost to the crest of the Wai'anae Range.[68]

On March 19, 1931, territorial forester Charles S. Judd led Major General Briant H. Wells and more than 250 other army officers on a reconnaissance traverse of the Wai'anae Range. From Keawa'ula Bay the large group probably climbed the Kaluakauila Trail, an old Hawaiian route, to Kuaokalā Forest Reserve. The men then skirted the rim of Mākua Valley and descended the side ridge past Hakakoa station and along the Keālia fence to the top of the *pali*. Undoubtedly, the officers joked or grumbled about the hot, steep scramble down to the shoreline. Nevertheless, all clambered down the crumbly cliff, which they informally and affectionately named General Wells bluff.[69]

In October 1933, Judd and Wells included a switchback trail up the bluff as trail construction project number 9 on the list of Emergency Conservation Work.

> Beginning at the south boundary of the cultivated fields at 100 feet elevation on the coastal plain on the private land of Kealia, the route runs up the steep escarpment on a maximum grade of 15 per cent to the 1,000 feet elevation to connect with the open government land of Kuaokala. There is now no passable trail up this escarpment and a trail up this steep slope will greatly facilitate the administration of government forest lands in the upper region. Total length 2,400 feet, 240 man days.[70]

At the top of the *pali* the switchback trail would connect with a cattle and hiker trail that had gradually developed along the ridge. At Hakakoa triangulation station the makeshift route would join the graded Makaleha (later Mokulēʻia) Trail to be constructed along the Waiʻanae crest.

Oʻahu assistant forester Glenn W. Russ assigned the Keālia Trail to the Wahiawa Camp of the Civilian Conservation Corps (CCC). In late March 1934, several CCC trucks drove through Mokulēʻia on Farrington Highway past Dillingham Ranch and fields of sugar cane and rice. Just after Kawaihāpai the trucks turned *mauka* (inland) for about a half-mile to reach the trailhead at the base of the cliff. The forty-two-man crew unloaded their tools and began digging out the route to the first switchback.

By April 14, the trail crew, under foremen David Freeman and Roland O. Wilson, completed the first two thousand feet of the route. "This is an extremely rocky and precipitous trail.... Considerable blasting must be done by experts in that phase of work,"[71] wrote A. S. Newman, a reporter for the *Honolulu Star-Bulletin*. On August 14, one of the CCC men carved his initials, O. K. L., into the rock after the eleventh switchback. In September the crew reached the top of the *pali*. The completed trail measured 1.4 miles with nineteen switchbacks.[72]

On February 17, 1935, the HTMC scheduled a new hike, which incorporated the Keālia and Makaleha Trails. The group started near a rock crusher and hiked to the base of the cliff past wauke trees and maʻo hau hele (native yellow hibiscus). The hikers then climbed the nineteen zigzags and the ridge to the Keālia fence and Hakakoa station. From there they followed the lovely Makaleha Trail, which contoured below the Waiʻanae crest through groves of native ʻōhiʻa and kokio keʻokeʻo (white hibiscus) covered with land shells (native tree snails). After stopping briefly at Kukuiala cabin above Peacock Flat, the group continued along the Makaleha Trail to the forest reserve boundary and then out to the main highway. On May 7 and 8, Judd, Russ, and several others completed a similar trip as an overnighter to check the Mokulēʻia Forest Reserve for wild pigs and cattle.[73]

During World War II the U.S. Army upgraded a short sand and grass airstrip near the Keālia trailhead. Engineers filled in the adjacent rice fields with crushed rock from a nearby quarry. By April 1942, the Mokulēʻia (later Dillingham) Airfield had a paved runway eight thousand feet long and a network of revetments to protect aircraft from strafing and bombing attacks.[74]

During the war the army also built a dirt road from the highway near Dillingham Ranch to Peacock Flat. From there the road roughly paralleled the Mokulēʻia Trail to Hakakoa. Nearby was a cabin, probably built to house observers at the triangulation station.[75]

In 1947, Keālia became trail number 20b at 1.4 miles on the Territorial Forestry Division's Oʻahu map. The description read,

> Trail starts Waialua side of quarry crusher behind Redwood water tank to climb pali and run through Ranch land to Reserve boundary and junction with Mokuleia Contour Trail.[76]

Along the route were open pasture, and scattered native alahe'e and wiliwili trees, as well as planted silk oak.

During the 1950s, the HTMC periodically scheduled Keālia as an overnight trip on a long weekend. Serving as base camp was the army cabin, recently refurbished by the Territorial Forestry Division. The rustic shelter had roof water catchment and was shaded by ironwood trees. Those camping outside enjoyed a soft bed of needles and the trade winds soughing through the branches. During the day some hikers explored down Ke'eke'e Gulch with its peacocks or Manini Gulch with its cool spring. Others ambled along the Wai'anae crest to the army cabin below the twin pines planted by General and Mrs. Wells in 1932.[77]

In 1961, the U.S. Army completed construction of a Nike-Hercules battery *mauka* (inland) of the airfield. The Nike-Hercules was a surface-to-air missile to defend O'ahu against a Soviet bomber attack. On November 8, a missile launched from the battery successfully destroyed a jet drone. The Hawai'i Army National Guard tracked the target, then fired and guided the missile from a radar station on the Wai'anae crest above Peacock Flat.[78]

Since the 1960s, the HTMC has conducted Keālia as a day hike. On the outing of May 14, 1961, the group drove past the Hawaiian Rock and Supply Company quarry and parked near a revetment in back of the airfield. Led by Thelma Warner (later Greig), twenty-two hikers followed a water line to a tank and the first switchback up the cliff. At the top they found large strips of ground bulldozed for planting Norfolk Island (Cook) Pines. They then took a dirt road graded over the old trail to the cabin, where they picked up the Mokulē'ia Firebreak (later Kuaokalā Access) Road to an overlook of Mākua Valley.[79]

In early 1993, Na Ala Hele, the new state trail program, completely renovated the switchback section, which had gradually deteriorated over the years. On June 6, renowned trail builder Richard H. (Dick) Davis led an evening procession up the refurbished route to celebrate National Trails Day. About 240 people climbed to the top of the *pali* by flashlight.[80]

As of 2010, the Keālia Trail was open to the public and in good condition. Look for the CCC inscription after the eleventh switchback. The nearby holes in the lava rock are not left over from CCC blasting, but were drilled more recently by geologists studying changes in the earth's magnetic field. The collapsed remains of the cabin are hidden by vegetation at the junction of the trail and Kuaokalā Access Road. Dillingham Airfield provides facilities for private aircraft and fixed wing glider rides and sky diving for tourists. The abandoned quarry has filled with brackish water and is home to farmed tilapia destined for Honolulu restaurants.

Kawailoa

> Expect a workout unless you'd rather idle along and
> wait for the trail burners to come back.
> —Hawaiian Trail and Mountain Club
> schedule, March 11, 1950

On October 20, 1932, territorial forester Charles S. Judd led an overnight trip to search for a herd of wild cattle in a seldom-visited section of the Kawailoa Forest Reserve. Along were special hunter Nicholas Mendes, ranger at large Max F. Landgraf, and two Piko Club members, Lieutenant Thomas J. Wells, the son and aide of Major General Briant H. Wells, and Frederick D. Lowrey, vice president of Lewers and Cooke, Ltd. The group started hiking the Kawaiiki Ditch access trail, built by the Waialua Agricultural Company in 1902. At the ditch intake the five men crossed the ridge to Kawainui Stream and worked upstream to the first major fork, where they spent a comfortable night. The next day the group followed the north fork, climbed up a spur ridge to Puʻu Kaʻinapuaʻa, and came out the Mālaekahana Trail. Almost one year later Judd proposed building a trail that would follow portions of that trip's route.[81]

The Kawailoa Trail became number 2 on the original list of Emergency Conservation Work (EWC) trail construction projects jointly developed by Judd and General Wells in late October 1933.

> Beginning at the end of the present ditch intake trail on the Kawaiiki Stream on the land of Kawailoa at approximately 1,050 feet elevation this route runs northeasterly crossing over the steep ridge and dropping down into Kawainui Stream valley then runs up and along a side spur to the ridge on the boundary of Waimea then to the crest of the Koolau Range at Puu Kainapuaa at 2,250 feet elevation. This project will be entirely new construction. Total length 17,800 feet [3.37 miles], 920 man days.[82]

Before construction started, Judd revised the proposed route, probably to avoid crossing Kawainui Stream. The Kawailoa (long water) Trail would instead start at the Anahulu triangulation station (elevation 1,269 feet) and follow the ridge between Kawainui and Kaiwikoʻele Streams to Puʻu Kaʻinapuaʻa on the Koʻolau summit. Although longer at 5.7 miles, the revised route would be easier to build and maintain.

Oʻahu assistant forester Glenn W. Russ assigned the Kawailoa Trail project to the Wahiawa Camp of the Civilian Conservation Corps (CCC). Sometime in late March 1934, a trail crew drove through Haleʻiwa and turned *mauka* (inland) past Kawailoa Camp. For several miles the trucks labored up the dirt road through the sugar cane and pineapple fields of the Waialua Agricultural Company. At the road's end near the triangulation station, the men stretched their legs, picked up their tools, and began clearing east toward the Koʻolau summit.

On April 16, Judd and Russ briefly inspected the Kawailoa or Anahulu Trail, as it was sometimes called. They found two twenty-one-man crews at work under the direction of foremen Wallace S. Kiyota and Arthur W. McKenzie. Their progress was good through the relatively gentle terrain of the lower ridge section.[83]

On Sunday, May 27, the Piko Club, an association of forestry rangers and army officers, held an ambitious Koʻolau cross-country hike and its third annual meeting. The group walked the unfinished Kawailoa Trail, bushwhacked past Puʻu Kaʻinapuaʻa to the recently started Koʻolau Summit Trail, and then descended the Kaunala Trail. At the annual meeting, perhaps at Mālaekahana cabin, the members present elected General Wells president, his son Tom chief scout, and local attorney Clifton H. Tracy chief guide. The group also amended the articles of organization to allow women to join the club. Several months later, Judd's wife Louise and daughter Emma became the first female Pikos.[84]

Judd and Russ inspected the Kawailoa Trail again on August 15, a cloudy, sultry day. About two miles in, they passed a side camp where the CCC crew spent the night during the week. At four miles they reached the trail gang working toward the summit. Judd later commented, "Trail and woods fairly dry and trail well made. Camp comfortable and in good shape."[85]

The Wahiawa Camp completed the Kawailoa Trail sometime in late September or early October. Its measured length was 6.1 miles from the triangulation station to Puʻu Kaʻinapuaʻa on the Koʻolau summit. The Kawailoa crew working east reached Puʻu Kaʻinapuaʻa at about the same time as the Summit Trail crew working south.[86]

The Hawaiian Trail and Mountain Club (HTMC) first hiked the Kawailoa

Trail on May 12, 1935. Part of the group camped on a nearby beach the night before, while others took the train to Kawailoa Station that morning. Leading the outing was First Circuit Court judge John A. Matthewman.[87]

In July 1935, Judd proposed building a link between the Kawailoa and Koʻolau Summit Trails. Located in the Waimea *ahupuaʻa* (land division), the rugged route would cross both Kaiwikoʻele and Kamananui Streams. With the verbal approval of army Major General Hugh A. Drum, commander of the Hawaiian Department, Judd included the new trail in the project plan for fourth ECW enrollment period (October 1, 1935, to March 31, 1936). Foot trail construction project number 3b for the Wahiawa Camp was the Waimea Trail.

> This trail will connect the two mile post on the Summit Trail with the 3 mile post on the Anahulu [Kawailoa] Trail. It crosses some of the most inaccessible country on the island and will be of great use in eradicating wild pigs as well as for military and recreational uses. Its length is estimated at 3 miles and approximately 3,000 man days will be used.[88]

On November 1, Judd met with CCC field supervisor Everett E. Tillett, army engineer Colonel Peterson, and other officers to discuss the routes of the Honouliuli and Waimea Trails. Peterson was against the latter because it provided another approach for an invading force attacking across the Koʻolau Range. He planned to confer with Drum about the Waimea Trail and declined to provide an officer to accompany Judd on an upcoming checkout hike because "none is in fit condition."[89]

Early in the morning of November 6, Judd, Tillett, Kiyota, rangers Max F. Landgraf and Manuel Rodrigues, and army Captain Joseph B. Sweet, chief scout of the Piko Club, hiked up the Kawailoa Trail. Just past the old CCC side camp, they left the ridge and headed cross-country for the Summit Trail. After floundering around the Waimea gulches for about seven hours, the men finally gave up and returned to the Kawailoa Trail at the four-mile mark.[90] Judd later remarked,

> The going in these headwater valleys was found to be very difficult. Streams in box canyons had to be waded thigh high and 100 foot cliffs covered with staghorn ferns and small shrubs had to be scaled.[91]

On November 18, Drum wrote Tillett requesting that the Waimea cross-country route be abandoned for the same reason offered earlier by Peterson, his engineer. Judd took the matter to Governor Joseph B. Poindexter, who sided with the army.[92] A disappointed Judd later commented,

"This trail would have been of great assistance in the important work of destructive animal eradication."[93]

From 1935 through 1941 the Wahiawa Camp periodically maintained the Kawailoa Trail. In February 1936, the Nineteenth Infantry regraded sections of the trail torn up by mules during army maneuvers. In 1937, army Third Engineers and CCC crews completed the Wahiawa-Pupukea Trail (later Drum Drive), which provided additional access to the Kawailoa trailhead for training exercises.[94]

During World War II, the army built a dirt road along the first two miles of the Kawailoa Trail, destroying most of the original path. The rough road followed the up-and-down ridge line, whereas the trail had contoured below it. The army also constructed a cabin windward of the Kawailoa-Summit Trail junction at Pu'u Ka'inapua'a. The cabin had sheet metal siding covered with camouflage paint. In 1943, live ammunition exercises in the Kawailoa Training Area started fires that burned five thousand acres near the start of the trail.[95]

After the war, the Territorial Forestry Division included Kawailoa as trail number 8 at 6.2 miles on its 1947 O'ahu map. The HTMC scheduled the Kawailoa hike regularly through the mid-1960s, although the trail was often overgrown between periodic army clearings. In early December 1962, army live fire exercises in dry conditions resulted in three thousand acres burned near the trailhead. Hikers on the HTMC outing of March 29, 1964, reported koa seedlings growing in the burned area along the trail.[96]

After sporadic scheduling of Kawailoa in the 1970s, the HTMC hiked the trail four times in the 1980s. The outing of January 23, 1983, was a particularly memorable one. While on the army road, the group had to scramble over and under huge trees felled by hurricane 'Iwa. Farther in a hiker spotted a pair of 'i'iwi, a rare and endangered native bird on O'ahu. After plowing through miles of scratchy uluhe ferns and *Clidemia* shrubs, the remaining stalwarts enjoyed the wide-open upper section, which had been recently cleared by the army at the club's request. At the top, leader Jim Yuen allowed a small group to follow the Summit Trail north and then descend the Lā'ie Trail to complete a Ko'olau traverse.[97]

The HTMC dropped Kawailoa from its schedule after a disappointing hike on August 7, 1994. Two weeks earlier the club's maintenance crew was able to clear only the lower third of the route because of a late start and a stuck vehicle. Led by Stuart Ball, twenty-four members and guests covered the cleared portion all too quickly and then ran into a wall of vegetation. The more determined hikers pushed through for a while, but by the halfway point all had turned around.[98]

Except for its use by a few pig hunters, the Kawailoa Trail remained largely abandoned for about fifteen years until March 8, 2009. On that Sunday a group of Sierra Club and HTMC members led by Ed Mersino cleared the lower section in preparation for a Sierra Club hike on April 19.[99] The middle section, however, is still partially overgrown, even after subsequent clearings in 2010. All that remains of the cabin at Puʻu Kaʻinapuaʻa is the wooden stubs of the corner posts. The site has become a camping spot for groups hiking the Koʻolau Summit Trail.

Kīpapa

*The hike seemed to have given them
all the exercise they desired.*

—Charles S. Judd, December 23, 1935

On a rainy October 6, 1926, territorial forester Charles S. Judd, ranger at large Max F. Landgraf, and five others hiked a recently cleared surveyor's trail on the ridge between Waiawa and Kīpapa Streams in the ʻEwa Forest Reserve. The group planted one hundred Cook Pines at intervals along the path. Each seedling was marked by a redwood stake painted white with a number and the date.[100] Near the Koʻolau summit Judd found an extensive network of pig trails and diggings. The feral swine had destroyed much of the native cover, causing small landslides. A dismayed Judd later commented, "The ground looked as if someone had a pig farm up there."[101]

To encourage local hunters to visit the summit area, the Forestry Division built a cabin near the top of the Waiawa-Kīpapa ridge in March 1927. The landowner, the Bishop Estate, provided the funds and the Oahu Sugar Company (OSC) provided the labor for construction. The material for the small cabin cost $55.08 and included two barrels to collect drinking water.[102]

The Hawaiian Trail and Mountain Club (HTMC) scheduled a new hike called Waipiʻo for August 28. On that morning the group took Kamehameha Highway past Waipahu and turned *mauka* (inland) on a plantation road just before Kīpapa Gulch. The road ascended gradually through OSC sugar cane and pineapple fields past Waipio Camp B. The group parked their vehicles at the road's end near the forest reserve boundary (elevation 1,140 feet). On the trail the hikers passed the marked and numbered Cook Pines. Those reaching the summit enjoyed lunch at the cabin and replenished their water from the barrels before heading down. The HTMC repeated the hike, renamed Waipi'o Ridge, on July 29, 1928.[103]

Judd inspected the Waiawa-Kīpapa ridge annually from 1931 to 1933. He found no pig diggings along the trail and later reported, "The cabin has demonstrated the advisability of making animal infested areas open to the public."[104] Judd also monitored the progress of the Cook Pines. Many of the seedlings had died, but the strongest survivors were six to ten feet tall in 1932.[105]

In October 1933, Judd proposed the reconstruction of the nearby leeward section of the Waiāhole Ditch Trail. Renamed the Waiawa Trail, the project became number 7 on the original list of Emergency Conservation Work jointly developed by Judd and army Major General Briant H. Wells.

> Beginning in Waiawa Valley at 700 feet elevation and near the west portal of the Waiahole tunnel through the Koolau Range the route runs easterly up Waiawa Valley to the crest of the Koolau Range at 2,050 feet elevation. This is on private land but the trail is essential in order to connect up with the Waiahole trail on government land coming up the cliffs on the windward side of the island. Total length is 16,000 feet [3.03 miles], 640 man days.[106]

Sometime before work started, Judd changed the project route to follow the Waiawa-Kīpapa ridge. He must have decided that the connection with the Waiāhole Ditch Trail was not essential and/or too difficult to rebuild and maintain. The ridge offered a more direct and easily constructed route to the summit for forestry activities, such as tree planting and pig control.

O'ahu assistant forester Glenn W. Russ assigned the Waiawa (later Kīpapa) Trail to the Honolulu Unit of the Civilian Conservation Corps (CCC), which began work in early April 1934. Averaging seven feet per man-day, the crews built four miles of tread by mid-July. About three and a half miles in, the unit established a side camp where the CCC men spent the night during the week.

On July 13, Judd and Landgraf checked out the trail and found the crew working about a quarter-mile *mauka* of the camp. The two then followed the original trail for less than a mile to the pig hunters' cabin, where they had lunch. Judd later remarked, "It [the trail] is well built. Inspected camp which is rather sloppy and wet. Cookshed is comfortable."[107]

By December, the CCC crews were nearing the Koʻolau summit, but the last section was particularly difficult to build. The route left the Waiawa-Kīpapa ridge, descended to the head of Kīpapa Stream, and then climbed to the top on five switchbacks. The men struggled with mud and landslides as heavy winter rain regularly drenched the summit area. Their progress slowed to five feet per man-day.

The Honolulu Unit finally completed the Waiawa project in February 1935. The four-foot-wide trail was 6.57 miles long with a maximum 12 percent grade. Total man-days were 5,468 for new construction and 1,016 for maintenance, at a payroll cost of $15,610.62.[108]

On February 20, 1935, Judd, Landgraf, ranger Thomas R. L. McGuire, and Gunder E. Olson, project superintendent of the Honolulu Unit, inspected the completed Waiawa Trail. Judd mapped the route from the old pig hunters' cabin to the Koʻolau summit. He noted that the trail was poorly built near the head of Kīpapa Stream and would soon wash out. After admiring the panoramic view from the top, the men selected a site for a new cabin.[109]

Judd returned to the Waiawa Trail with Landgraf, Olson, and his nurseryman Walter W. Holt on March 20. Judd, Holt, and a forestry laborer planted 203 Japanese sugi cedars in a denuded area below the switchback section of the trail. Landgraf and Olson helped build the new cabin, which was completed the next day.[110]

The shelter stood at the end of the trail right on the Koʻolau summit (elevation 2,786 feet). Most of the building material came from the cook shed of the dismantled side camp. The twelve-by-sixteen-foot cabin featured sheet iron siding and roof, a wooden floor, and a lean-to kitchen. The roof gathered rain water into a three-by-three-foot redwood tank.[111]

Uncle Tom's cabin, shrouded in mist at the top of Kīpapa Trail, March 1935. (Talbert Takahama papers)

On Sunday, March 24, Judd introduced the Piko Club, an association of forestry rangers and army officers, to the Waiawa Trail, popularly known as the Kīpapa Trail. Thirty-six members and guests covered the six-and-a-half-mile "sidewalk" route in just over two hours. At the top the group had lunch outside the shelter, which they christened Uncle Tom's cabin, probably after Ranger Tom McGuire.[112]

The HTMC first scheduled the entire Kīpapa Trail for September 15. The club had already hiked part of the route in January before it was finished.[113] Other groups and individuals flocked to this long but easy path into the central Ko'olau wilderness with its unusual native plants and birds.

> The trail is already gaining popularity with hunters and hikers and, no doubt in the future, it will prove a valuable asset to this Island especially in case of military emergency.[114]

On December 19, Judd inspected the Kīpapa Trail with army Lieutenant Colonel (later General) George S. Patton, Jr., the new intelligence officer of the Hawaiian Department and a prospective Piko. Around noon the two men and several others reached the Ko'olau summit, where the view from Uncle Tom's cabin was spectacular on that cool, clear winter day. They then bushwhacked north along the ridge, passing foreman Ernest W. Landgraf's CCC crew working south on the Summit Trail. The group followed the newly built path to Waikāne junction and then descended the army trail.[115] The men completed the twelve-mile walk in six hours. Judd later remarked, "The hike seemed to have given them all the exercise they desired."[116] Judd repeated the outing for fifty-seven members and guests of the Piko Club on March 15, 1936, a "peppy" day.[117]

In the late afternoon of September 27, Judd walked up the Kīpapa Trail to meet thirty-three army personnel and civilians finishing the Piko Marathon, an all day, twenty-six-mile trek along the Ko'olau Summit Trail.[118] Judd later recounted his experience with the tired tail end of the group.

> At the last stream crossing near the zigzags where there is water, Capt. Wilson, Tom [McGuire], some wahines, and several men and I had a little party in the dark, and I invented the PIKO cocktail on the spot, and 6 cupfuls were passed around among the crowd which made the walk down by moonlight very pleasant.[119]

During World War II, the army used the Kīpapa Trail for training exercises and the summit area as an observation post. Soldiers built a shelter on the leeward side near the Summit-Kīpapa Trail junction to replace the dilapidated and exposed Uncle Tom's cabin. Occupants could open a window from the inside and fill their canteens from a water trough.[120]

After the war, the Territorial Forestry Division included Waiawa (Kīpapa) as trail number 6 at six miles on its 1947 Oʻahu map. The route description advised turning right along the rim of Kīpapa Gulch and then following a dirt road for four and a half miles past pineapple fields and through an abandoned artillery range to the forest reserve boundary. "The Board [of Forestry] has attempted to mark areas that may still contain dangerous duds. Keep to the road or trail."[121] At the start of the hike was a grove of cashew nut trees planted in 1936.

In 1957, the Kīpapa Trail became the site of a rainfall and runoff study by the State of Hawaiʻi to determine the amount of ground water available for development of central Oʻahu. Under the direction of John F. Mink, a team erected fourteen rain gauges at intervals along the trail and three stream gauges along nearby Kīpapa Stream. After recording water levels for three years, Mink determined that 50 percent of rainfall recharged ground water, 25 percent ran off down the stream, and 25 percent evaporated.[122]

The HTMC hiked the Kīpapa Trail sporadically during the 1950s through the 1970s. The route was often overgrown, and Koa Ridge Farm frequently did not permit access across its pastures to the trailhead. For the hike of November 23, 1980, the club developed a new approach from Mililani Memorial Park road. The group left their cars at an abandoned military communication site and then crossed Pānakauahi Gulch to reach the Kīpapa Trail well *mauka* of the farm. In 1987, the HTMC revised the approach to avoid Waiawa prison, which had been built on the communication site. Both approaches added more than four miles to an already long hike that was difficult to keep open. After the outing of June 9, 1991, the club stopped scheduling Kīpapa entirely because of access and trail maintenance problems.[123]

On December 21, 2000, the U.S. Fish and Wildlife Service (FWS) established the Oʻahu Forest National Wildlife Refuge on 4,775 acres in the northern Koʻolau Range. Purchased from Castle and Cooke, Inc. with help from The Nature Conservancy, the parcel extended leeward from the summit between the Kīpapa and Schofield-Waikāne Trails. The refuge protected and conserved the native forest ecosystem there with emphasis on the recovery of threatened or endangered plants and animals, such as tree snails.[124]

On March 3, 2001, the FWS and the HTMC began a joint project to reopen the clogged Kīpapa Trail. On that sunny, breezy morning, nineteen volunteers accompanied by two FWS biologists drove to the trailhead through Koa Ridge Ranch. The group quickly hiked the first mile of trail, which had been cleared by Hui O Mālama I Ka 'Āina, a pig hunters' organization. At the refuge boundary, the biologists then took the lead to mark rare native plants. The rest pulled out their tools, including a chain saw and a hedge trimmer, and began opening up the route. In some areas the crew had a hard time even finding the original trail because of downed trees or a blanket of uluhe ferns and *Clidemia* shrubs across the path.[125]

Over the next two years HTMC volunteers and FWS personnel devoted many hours toward the Kīpapa clearing project. On the outing of March 24, 2002, most of the crew, including assistant refuge manager Nancy Hoffman, finally pushed through to the Ko'olau summit. To show appreciation for the club's hard work, the FWS allowed the HTMC to schedule Kīpapa for members only on October 18, 2003. Led by Jay Feldman, forty club members enjoyed the revived "sidewalk" route, much as hikers had enjoyed it in the 1930s.[126]

As of 2010, the lower and upper trail sections remained passable, but the middle section was overgrown. The FWS currently permits access only for conservation efforts. Just past the ranch house, a Forestry Division sign put up in the 1960s marks the start of "32. Kipapa Ridge Trail, 6 miles." A few of the Cook Pines planted in 1926 still stand along the route. At the junction with the Summit Trail is a rusty metal stake marked "TH" for Territory of Hawai'i. A few minutes along the Summit Trail is the ruin of the army cabin near some remnant sugi cedars. Nothing remains of Uncle Tom's cabin on the Ko'olau summit.

'Aiea Loop and Ridge

> It will also be a popular trail with hikers, picnicers etc
> because of its close proximity to Honolulu.
> —Gunder E. Olson, March 31, 1935

According to Hawaiian legend, the *kama'āina* (island-born) rats of He'eia, with red feet, constantly feuded with the *malihini* (newcomer) rats of Honolulu, 'Ewa, and Waialua, with black or white feet. The leeward rats frequently climbed the ridge between Kalauao and Hālawa Streams to the Ko'olau summit. There they met the He'eia rats, who graciously offered to help them descend the treacherous *pali* (cliff) to the windward side.

Halfway down was a rock, slippery with moss, but always pronounced safe by the Heʻeia rats. After stepping on the rock, the lead *kamaʻāina* rat deftly jumped to a narrow side ledge. The following *malihini* rats slipped and fell into a small pool at the back of ʻIolekaʻa (rolling rat) Valley.[127]

During the time of Kākuhihewa, a renowned sixteenth-century chief, Hawaiians built a *heiau hoʻole,* or medicinal center, partway up the Kalauao-Hālawa ridge. The structure was 168 feet long and 94 feet wide with nine-foot walls, several platforms, and an inner floor paved with flat stones. There *kāhuna lapaʻau* (healers) treated patients with herbs from the surrounding gardens. Commoners considered their practices *keaīwa* (mysterious), which became the name of the *heiau*. Undoubtedly the healers ranged farther along the ridge looking for medicinal plants.[128]

For February 6, 1921, the Hawaiian Trail and Mountain Club (HTMC) scheduled a new class A (hard) hike called Puʻu Uau. Early that morning, thirty-eight members and guests assembled at the Oʻahu railway station in Aʻala. They caught the Haleiwa Limited to ʻAiea and then walked up the homestead road past the sugar mill. At the road's end the leader, Oʻahu ranger Thomas R. L. McGuire, probably pointed out the abandoned *heiau*, much diminished because of rock removal for building in the nearby house lots. The group then continued up the ridge on a faint, overgrown trail, but had to turn around well short of their goal, the Koʻolau summit. The trip must have been popular as the club scheduled it regularly during the 1920s. In 1928, McGuire and his forestry crew planted Norfolk Island (Cook) Pines on the eroded slope behind the *heiau*.[129]

In the early 1930s, the HTMC began scheduling a loop variation of the original ridge route. From the homestead road club members and guests climbed the Kalauao-Hālawa ridge and at some point descended into Kalauao Valley. They then returned along the stream past a swimming hole and ascended back to their cars parked along the road. House painter Edmund J. Meadows led the inaugural outing on September 21, 1930.[130]

On June 7, 1934, territorial forester Charles S. Judd included the ʻAiea Trail (later ʻAiea Loop Trail) as project 3c in new trail construction for the second enrollment period (October 1, 1934, to March 31, 1935) of Emergency Conservation Work (ECW).

> This will be along boundary of the land of Aiea in the Ewa Forest Reserve, going up one ridge to the north end of the land and down the other and crossing Aiea Gulch to starting point. Total distance 4.50 miles, 792 man days.[131]

CCC workers grading the 'Aiea Loop Trail, 1935. (Charles Judd papers, Hawai'i State Archives)

O'ahu assistant forester Glenn W. Russ assigned the 'Aiea Trail project to the Honolulu Unit of the Civilian Conservation Corps (CCC).

On March 1, 1935, construction started on the 'Aiea Loop Trail using a crew transferred from the Waimano Trail because of bad weather. By the end of the month, the gang built 1.7 miles to Pu'u Uau using 558 mandays. The gentle, open terrain made for fast construction—sixteen feet of new trail per man-day.[132]

The Honolulu Unit completed the loop on June 12. The last three miles required 1,340 man-days for an average of twelve feet per man-day. Project superintendent Gunder E. Olson commented,

> Very little rock encountered. With the help of favorable weather conditions and moderately sloping ground, better progress was made on this trail than any other heretofore built.[133]

The finished trail measured 4.7 miles long and four feet wide with a maximum 12 percent grade. The CCC crew also improved a 0.9-mile dirt access road from the homestead road's end to the trailhead. The payroll cost of the trail construction and the road maintenance was $4,659.33. Because it was easy and close to town, the loop trail quickly became popular with the hiking public.[134]

For the fourth ECW enrollment period (October 1, 1935, to March 31, 1936) Judd included an extension of the loop trail as project 3c under foot trail construction.

> It is proposed to extend the Aiea Trail, Fifth [Hawai'i third] Enrollment Project No. 2, to the summit of the Koolau Range and then along the crest eastward to connect with the Halawa Trail. Total distance is 4¾ miles. A side camp will be established here. Man days: 4,400.[135]

On October 2, Judd, ranger at large Max F. Landgraf, Everett E. Tillett, field supervisor of the Honolulu Unit, and two others took the 'Aiea Loop Trail to Pu'u Uau. There each planted an 'iliahi (sandalwood) seedling at the head of 'Aiea Gulch. The group then hiked about one mile along the proposed route of the extension. After some discussion, the men decided to build a secondary trail only two feet wide to the summit and the Hālawa Trail junction. The treadway would follow the ridge line where level and contour around any major humps. To create a firebreak, the uluhe ferns would be cut back fifteen feet on either side of the trail.[136]

The Honolulu Unit started clearing the extension in January 1936 and completed it the following month. The two-foot-wide route was 5.3 miles long and required 682 man-days.[137] On April 1, Judd, Tillett, and one other person hiked the Hālawa Trail to the summit and returned on the extended 'Aiea Trail (later 'Aiea Ridge Trail). The men saw hundreds of koa tree seedlings emerging from the wide swath cut on either side of the path. They noted that the route did not contour around the humps as it approached the summit. Tillett remarked,

> I was greatly disappointed in the new section connecting the old Aiea Trail with the Halawa Trail. It is a lowering of CCC's reputation to turn out such a trail.[138]

Judd agreed and requested that the missing contour sections be included in trail maintenance projects for the next ECW enrollment period.[139]

The HTMC first hiked the 'Aiea Ridge Trail on May 24, 1936. The club had already walked the loop trail on November 24, 1935, a few months after its completion. The HTMC scheduled a Hālawa-'Aiea hike for November 15. Led by Anton Postl, club members and guests climbed 'Aiea extended to the Ko'olau summit and then descended the Hālawa Trail.[140]

Shortly before 5 a.m. on May 5, 1944, a new Consolidated B-24J army bomber departed Hickam Field bound for Australia. After takeoff, the aircraft failed to make the right turn toward the ocean and plowed into the wooded ridge above 'Aiea Gulch. Most of the plane ended up on the Hālawa side of the ridge near the return leg of the loop trail. Fuel in the tanks soon ignited the wreckage, its occupants, and the surrounding trees, creating a blazing inferno. The cause of the crash, whether pilot error or mechanical failure, was never determined.[141]

After World War II, the loop trail gradually regained its popularity with hikers, birders, and picnickers. Personnel stationed at nearby 'Aiea Naval Hospital rode horseback along the Hālawa section. In 1947, the Territorial Forestry Division included 'Aiea Loop as trail number 4 at five miles on its O'ahu map. In the late 1940s, the HTMC regularly scheduled the 'Aiea Heights hike, which followed the loop trail and its extension to the summit.[142]

On the afternoon of November 15, 1951, more than a thousand people attended a rededication of the Keaīwa *heiau*. Participants in the ceremony included a Hawaiian chief and chanter, doctors from forty different states and six Pacific countries, and an honor guard of twenty Hawaiian warriors. *Kāhuna lapa'au* Kamakaokalanikapiliokomoku (eyes of heaven guide your boat straight) dipped olena leaves in a calabash of ocean water and sprinkled each dignitary entering the *heiau* as a purification. The healer was better known as retired ranger Thomas R. L. McGuire, a direct descendent of an ancient *kahuna lapa'au*. After the actual rededication, three speakers talked about the history of the *heiau*, the training of a *kāhuna lapa'au*, and the development of Hawaiian medicine.[143]

During the fiscal year ending June 30, 1952, the Territory of Hawai'i included Keaīwa *heiau* in its new park system. Welfare workers cleared the *heiau* and the surrounding area of brush and established a garden of medicinal plants. They also developed a picnic area with tables and fireplaces. The Keaīwa Heiau Park officially opened in late 1952.[144]

In the 1950s and 1960s, the HTMC continued to schedule the loop and its extension. In 1954, unemployed and welfare workers under the Hawaii Employment Program completely cleared the loop trail at a payroll cost of $2,733.85.[145] In 1965, HTMC member Richard (Dick) Booth scouted a nearby stream hike called Kalauao, similar to the one scheduled in the early 1930s. His variation left the loop trail before Pu'u Uau and descended a side ridge into Kalauao Valley. The route then followed the stream past a small pool and waterfall and eventually rejoined the 'Aiea loop below the trailhead.[146]

Since the middle 1960s, the HTMC has regularly hiked the 'Aiea Ridge Trail to the summit. Because so many people were already familiar with the loop trail, the club rarely scheduled it, except as a shorter option on the ridge hike. Over the years the Kalauao route has undergone several changes. It now leaves the loop near the trailhead and returns near Pu'u Uau by the junction with the ridge trail.

As of 2010, the 'Aiea Loop Trail remained popular with hikers, birders, and school groups. Military personnel from Camp Smith (formerly 'Aiea Naval Hospital) run the loop instead of riding horseback. A section of the wing and the rear gun turret of the army bomber lie in 'Aiea Gulch just off the path. The 'Aiea Ridge Trail is passable to the Ko'olau summit, although it may be overgrown with scratchy uluhe ferns and *Clidemia* shrubs. The *heiau* is still the centerpiece of lovely Keaīwa Heiau State Park with picnic and camping areas under the tall Cook Pines. At dusk you may be able to spot *malihini* rats hustling through the park and up the ridge to the Ko'olau summit.

Lā'ie

A side trail leading to a lovely pool ends many an ambitious trek.
—Hawaiian Trail and Mountain Club
schedule, August 4, 1991

On June 7, 1934, territorial forester Charles S. Judd finished the program plan for the second enrollment period (October 1, 1934, to March 31, 1935) of Emergency Conservation Work (ECW). Heading the list of new trail construction projects was the Wailele (later Lā'ie) Trail.

> Starting from near the boundary of the Kahuku Forest Reserve on the land of Laie this trail will go up the ridge between Wailele and Ihiihi gulches to the summit of the Koolau Range to connect with the Koolau Summit Trail. It will tap a country now quite inaccessible. Total Distance approximately 3.00 miles, 1,056 man days.[147]

Apparently Judd was not entirely satisfied with his proposed route. On August 8, he and fellow Piko Club member Frederick D. Lowrey explored halfway up the next ridge over, between ʻIhiʻihi and Kahawainui Gulches. Both men liked that ridge better because they did not have to cross ʻIhiʻihi Gulch from the planned starting point in Lāʻie. In spite of the route change, the project continued to be called the Wailele (waterfall) Trail.[148]

The Forestry Division assigned the Wailele Trail construction to the Wahiawa Camp of the Civilian Conservation Corps (CCC), headed by superintendent Robert C. Bayless. Sometime in early December, a CCC trail crew left their camp at Kahuku and drove to Lāʻie on Kamehameha Highway. Before reaching the turnoff to the Mormon temple, the trucks headed *mauka* (inland) on a dirt road paralleling a spur of the Koolau Railway through the sugar cane fields of the Kahuku Plantation Company. At the end of the line the crew followed a rough dirt road up the ʻIhiʻihi-Kahawainui ridge to a newly planted grove of Norfolk Island (Cook) Pines near the Kahuku Forest Reserve boundary. There the crew began working south along the ridge toward the Koʻolau summit. While clearing, the men carefully transplanted the pine seedlings in the way of the new trail.

On a rainy December 28, Judd put chains on his vehicle and drove up the slippery dirt road to the trailhead. After hiking in for about a quarter-mile, he found the trail crew working up an easy grade.[149] About two months later, on March 8, 1935, Judd and ranger at large Max F. Landgraf inspected the completed portion of the Wailele Trail and were not pleased with the progress. "Work is going too slowly and some of the grade is too steep,"[150] Judd commented. He returned to the trail on March 30 and found the construction satisfactory with 1.75 miles completed.[151]

During April and May the trail crew advanced only a quarter of a mile, primarily because of wet weather. The men had to make a two-hundred-foot-long and sixty-foot-high cut to get the trail safely around a very steep hump in the ridge. The crew also dug a rough side trail down to a swimming hole in Kahawainui Stream.

Because of the slow progress, Bayless assigned a second crew to the Wailele project. In June, the two gangs completed 0.6 miles of new trail in 768 man-days. In July, the men worked 299 man-days to build the last 0.2 miles to the Koʻolau crest (elevation 2,240 feet). At 2.8 miles in length, the Wailele Trail was the shortest CCC route to the Summit Trail.[152]

On a wet September 1, 1935, Judd introduced the Piko Club, an association of forestry rangers and army officers, to the new Wailele Trail. After meeting at Paumalū Station, thirty-five members and guests climbed Kaunala Ridge to Puʻu Moa and then headed south on the Pūpūkea-Kahuku and Koʻolau Summit Trails. Past Mālaekahana cabin they descended the Wailele Trail and stopped for a swim at a pool along Kahawainui Stream.[153]

The Hawaiian Trail and Mountain Club (HTMC) first scheduled the Wailele Trail for October 6. The hike blurb suggests, "Come out and see if it meets your approval."[154] Led by First Circuit Court judge John A. Matthewman, some of the group hiked to the summit, while others were diverted by the lovely pool and double waterfall along the stream. The members must have approved of the trail, because the club scheduled it several more times during the 1930s.

The waterfalls may have inspired the love poem "Wailele," published in January 1936 in *Paradise of the Pacific*. The author describes a meeting, real or imagined, by the falls one afternoon. The third verse goes,

> The gentle patter of the water's fall,
> Like loving laughter over all.
> Shall be a treasured memory
> Of an afternoon by Wailele.[155]

On January 3, 1936, Judd led selected Pikos on another summit hike incorporating the Wailele Trail. The small group climbed Wailele, which Judd found to be in good shape with some signs of pigs near the top. The Pikos then turned south on the Summit Trail and descended the Castle Trail for a 12.5-mile hike in eight hours. With Judd were his wife Louise, their son Charles, Jr., and Lieutenant Colonel (later General) George S. Patton, his wife Beatrice, their daughter Ruth Ellen, and several others.[156]

During World War II the army feared that an invading Japanese force would use the Wailele Trail to cross the Koʻolau Range. At three narrow points along the route, soldiers dug trenches to be filled with explosives to block the trail in the event of a Japanese attack. The first trench was located at the *mauka* end of the sixty-foot vertical cliff. The other two were dug before and after a small saddle where the trail crossed over the ridge from left to right. During the war the army also used the grassy areas below the trailhead as an impact zone for artillery practice.[157]

After the war the Wailele Trail became known as the Lāʻie Trail. The HTMC hike of March 10, 1946, was called Lāʻie, although the pool continued to be called Wailele, probably because of the twin waterfalls. The Territorial Forestry Division included Lāʻie, trail number 12 at 2.5 miles in its 1947 Oʻahu map. The route description warned,

> Storm erosion of road may block passage of cars before reaching forest line. Wartime use of this area may have left dud shells but roadway is clear.[158]

The HTMC scheduled the Lā'ie Trail regularly during the 1950s and subsequent decades. On February 22–23, 1953, Richard H. (Dick) Davis led a campout to rebuild the steep stream trail, which had been damaged by a landslide in 1950. The dirt road up the ridge was regraded in 1960 allowing hikers to drive their vehicles all the way to the trailhead.[159] By the 1970s, however, groups had to start from the ball field on Po'haili Street because the road was deeply rutted in spots. The round trip hike to the summit doubled to twelve miles with the addition of the road walk. Over the years, the pool and waterfalls assumed the name of the trail, although students at nearby Brigham Young University–Hawai'i nicknamed the falls *pa'ipa'i* for the slapping of the water against the rock.[160]

In early 1986, a landslide blocked a section of the trail between the vertical cliff and the saddle crossover. HTMC trail clearers led by Jim Yuen developed a short but steep bypass route through a side gulch. Almost twenty years later, on February 5, 2006, a small HTMC group restored the original contoured path during the Lā'ie hike led by Michael (Mike) Algiers.[161]

As of 2010, the Lā'ie Trail was in reasonably good condition, although the upper section has some rough spots and may be overgrown. The stately Cook Pines stand tall at the trailhead. The pool and waterfalls remain popular and still divert hikers planning to go the summit. On the way to the summit watch for the three deep trenches dug during World War II. Permission to hike the Lā'ie Trail is required from the landowner, Hawai'i Reserves, Inc.

Hālawa

Well, you just ruined one of our better hikes.

—Joseph B. Neilson, 1943

In 1933, a rough dirt road climbed partway along the ridge between North and South Hālawa Streams. At the road's end a short trail led to Barrel triangulation station, so named because it originally sported a barrel on top of a long pole. Army engineers had hoisted the barrel sometime after 1908 during the first topographic survey of O'ahu. Situated on a prominent knoll (elevation 1,157 feet), the station was clearly visible from Fort Shafter, the starting point of the mapping project.[162]

On June 7, 1934, territorial forester Charles S. Judd proposed six new trails for the second enrollment period (October 1, 1934, to March 31, 1935) of Emergency Conservation Work (ECW). Fourth on the list was the South Hālawa (later Hālawa) Trail.

> This [trail] will run up the ridge between North and South Halawa in the Ewa Forest Reserve to the summit of the Koolau Range. Total distance approximately 4.00 miles, 2,400 man days.[163]

O'ahu assistant forester Glenn W. Russ assigned the South Hālawa Trail construction to the Honolulu Unit of the Civilian Conservation Corps (CCC) headed by project superintendent Gunder E. Olson. In early October a forty-man crew drove up the dirt road to its end and then hiked to the Barrel triangulation station, where they began clearing *mauka* (inland) toward the Ko'olau summit. On October 11, 1934, Judd and ranger at large Max F. Landgraf inspected the gang's progress and explored farther along the ridge.

> After a week trail almost a mile from Barrel Trig Sta and going fast. Easy going so far through open country, but now hitting staghorn fern.[164]

Judd lamented that the crew had to cut several 'iliahi (sandalwood) trees, but he made sure the wood was put to good use.

Judd and Russ checked out the South Hālawa Trail on December 20, 1934, a cool, clear day. The two men reached the end of the improved trail at about two and a half miles and then bushwhacked to "pyramid hill" about three-quarters of a mile from the summit. Heavy vegetation and a two-hundred-yard section of rock had slowed the crew down considerably. Judd noted that the remaining two miles to be built would also be slow going because of the rough terrain near the top.[165]

Beginning in late December, heavy rains swept the Ko'olau Range day after day. The Hālawa crew could not even drive up the dirt road, much less work on the wet, muddy trail. On January 3, 1935, Olson reassigned the gang to tree planting in drier Kuliouou Valley.[166]

Despite the wet conditions, Judd led the Piko Club, an association of forestry rangers and army officers, up the unfinished Hālawa (curve) Trail on February 24. Fifty-three members and guests walked two and a half miles over the improved route and then pushed several hundred yards farther along the ridge.[167]

On May 1, work resumed on the trail, but progress was slow because of the rough terrain. Olson remarked,

> Toward the upper end of the trail much steep country was encountered necessitating deep cuts and considerable blasting of rock. Mud also slowed up the work to some extent though this condition cleared up when proper drainage ditches were put in.[168]

In addition, the CCC crew was exhausted by the difficult work and the long hike in and out each day. As productivity plummeted, Olson quickly assigned another forty-man crew to the Hālawa project. The combined eighty-man gang completed the trail in record time on July 24. As a reward, the men were given an easy project near Honolulu, where most of them lived.

At completion, the Hālawa Trail stretched 4.6 miles from the Barrel triangulation station to the Ko'olau summit (elevation 2,200 feet) overlooking Ha'ikū Valley. The four-foot-wide path with a maximum grade of 12 percent required 4,457 man-days for an average of 5.4 feet per man-day. In addition, the crew spent 258 man-days regrading the dirt road and extending it 0.6 miles to the triangulation station.[169]

A CCC crew ready for a hard day's work on the Hālawa Trail, 1935. (Charles Judd papers, Hawai'i State Archives)

During the next twelve months, crews from the Honolulu Unit revisited the Hālawa Trail periodically to clear downed trees and landslides. The Hawaiian Trail and Mountain Club (HTMC) took advantage of the new trail, hiking it on November 10.[170] The club scheduled Hālawa again on May 10, 1936, because "this new trail on the ridge between North and South Hālawa Gulches received the hearty approval of all who made the first trip."[171] On November 15, an HTMC group club hiked up the new ʻAiea Loop Trail and its summit extension and then descended the Hālawa Trail.[172]

During World War II, the U.S. Navy decided to build a radio station on Oʻahu to communicate with its far-flung commands in the Pacific. In 1942, the navy selected a site in secluded Haʻikū Valley on the windward side. The U-shaped, two-thousand-foot-high cliff there provided ideal anchor points for a long-range antenna stretched across the valley.

At the start of the project the navy hired professional climbers to pioneer a route up the near-vertical cliff to the peak of Puʻu Keahi a Kahoe on the south side of the valley. Two "high-scalers" finally reached the top after thirteen days of climbing using ropes and spikes. Workers installed ladders along the route, then a wooden stairway, and finally an aerial tramway to haul up supplies for the antenna and its concrete anchors. The station sent its first message in August 1943.[173]

The project was supposed to be a secret, but astonished HTMC hikers avidly watched the work in progress from the end of the Hālawa Trail. Some wondered why the climbers hadn't just walked up the trail to the summit. Probably because of security concerns, the navy had not communicated with the Territorial Forestry Division, the army, or the HTMC to determine an easier route to the summit. A naval officer finally visited future HTMC president Joseph B. Neilson and was shocked to learn about the Hālawa Trail. He asked Neilson where to put a no-trespassing sign to discourage use of the route. Neilson told him and then remarked, "Well, you just ruined one of our better hikes." The officer replied, "You're not supporting the war effort."[174]

The Territorial Forestry Division included Hālawa as trail number 3 on its 1947 Oʻahu map. Reaching the trailhead required driving past a rock quarry, then up the rough dirt road to the triangulation station. The HTMC used that access regularly during the 1950s and early 1960s. For the hike of July 31, 1966, the club developed a new route, bypassing the quarry. The group drove into North Hālawa Valley past the animal quarantine station to a Board of Water Supply pumping station. From there the hikers briefly followed a trail along the stream and then climbed the ridge on the right to reach the dirt road leading to the trailhead.[175]

The HTMC Hālawa outing of March 19, 1972, featured a new leader, Richard G. (Dick) Schmidt. He liked the route so much that he frequently led the club hike during the rest of the 1970s and the 1980s. Each year Schmidt would spend several days clearing and marking the trail in preparation for the upcoming outing. In 1987, the State Department of Transportation built a service road for the H-3 freeway into North Hālawa Valley. After the freeway was finished, the HTMC resumed hiking the Hālawa Ridge Trail using the service road or a trail around a xeriscape garden and the pumping station *mauka* (inland) of Hālawa Industrial Park.[176]

As of 2010, the Hālawa Trail was passable, although overgrown in spots. At the trailhead are the concrete support and pole of the triangulation station, but no barrel. The radio antennas are gone from Ha'ikū Valley, but a magnificent metal staircase, known as the Ha'ikū Stairs, climbs precipitously from the valley to the summit of Pu'u Keahi a Kahoe. Unfortunately, both the Hālawa Trail and the Ha'ikū Stairs remain officially closed to hikers—the trail because of security concerns stemming from the September 11, 2001, terrorist attack, and the stairs because of parking problems and wrangling between the City and County of Honolulu and the State Department of Hawaiian Home Lands over jurisdiction.

Ko'olau Summit

*For those daring adventurers who love to push
through brush and slop through mud for 26 miles
and still keep a good disposition.*
—Hawaiian Trail and Mountain Club
schedule, July 3, 1970

By 1933, the Territorial Forestry Division, the U.S. Army, and the sugar plantations had built five trails to the crest of the Ko'olau (windward) Range. In addition, early Hawaiians, forest rangers, pig hunters, surveyors, soldiers, and adventurous hikers had blazed other, makeshift routes to and across the top. With so many access points in use, a rough and rudimentary route had gradually developed along the Ko'olau summit ridge joining the Pūpūkea-Kahuku Trail in the north with the Schofield-Waikāne Trail in the south.

In late 1933, territorial forester Charles S. Judd and army Major General Briant H. Wells jointly developed a list of Emergency Conservation Work (ECW) trail construction projects. Both men agreed on the need for an improved trail along the summit to connect existing and proposed Koʻolau routes. The Summit Trail thus became number 3 on their list, after Poamoho and Kawailoa.

> Beginning at the point where the existing Schofield-Waikane Trail crosses the crest of the Koolau Range at 2,400 feet elevation, this route runs in a general north-westerly direction along or near the crest of the Koolau Range to a point on the range at 1,700 feet elevation where it will join the present Pupukea-Kahuku Trail.[177]

The estimated trail length was 65,000 feet, or 12.31 miles, and estimated man-days were 6,500. To allow for pack animal use, specifications called for a four-foot-wide path with grades not to exceed 15 percent. The project also included a short connector to the Castle Trail.

Oʻahu assistant forester Glenn W. Russ assigned the summit trail project to the Honolulu Unit of the Civilian Conservation Corps (CCC). On March 26, 1934, trucks from the unit fanned out over Oʻahu to pick up workers at staging areas and transport them to the job sites. Some of the Lāʻie men found themselves in a trail crew headed by Ernest W. Landgraf. He was one of the most experienced CCC foremen, having helped build the Punaiki (later Maʻakua Ridge) and Hauʻula Trails for the Forestry Division just over a year before. In April, his new gang extended Kaunala Trail across ʻŌʻio Stream and down toward Kahuku.[178]

In early May, Landgraf and his thirty-man trail crew climbed the Pūpūkea-Kahuku Trail to a marked point just beyond a broad windward overlook. There the crew began clearing due south along a side ridge leading to the Koʻolau summit. The army later named the new intersection Black Junction. On the ECW monthly work progress report it was called Mile 0.0 of Project T3, the Koʻolau Summit Trail.

On May 18, Charles Judd ignored the paperwork on his desk and joined a CCC crew realigning the Pūpūkea-Kahuku Trail. He and ranger at large Max F. Landgraf helped set charges to blast rock in ʻŌhiʻa ʻAi Gulch. The two then hiked to Black Junction and walked about a third of a mile to the end of the Summit Trail. There they found Ernest Landgraf and his crew pushing southeast around the head of ʻŌhiʻa ʻAi Gulch. Judd and Ernest Landgraf scouted ahead to mark a route for the new trail.[179]

On July 30, Judd, Oʻahu assistant forester Glenn W. Russ, and Ernest Landgraf climbed the Pūpūkea-Kahuku Trail and started hiking along the

Summit Trail. They finally reached the crew working a half-mile south of the Mālaekahana junction. Judd commented, "The new trail is well built, but muddy and will require going over in a few places after it dries up somewhat."[180] The three then descended the Mālaekahana Trail past the pig hunters' cabin, now turned into a CCC side camp to house the trail crew during the week. By September 30, the end of the first six-month ECW period, the Koʻolau Summit Trail stretched from Black Junction to Puʻu Kaʻinapuaʻa, a distance of about 5.2 miles.

October 1934 found Ernest Landgraf and his CCC crew improving Castle Trail as part of the Summit Trail project. Their side camp stood on a small but fairly dry site where the Castle Trail crossed Kaluanui Stream. During the week the men lived on wild pig killed in the vicinity of camp. Gunder E. Olson, project superintendent of the Honolulu Unit, tastefully remarked, "Although strong and gamey-flavored, the pork, when properly prepared, is quite edible."[181]

On October 18, Judd and Max Landgraf climbed the reconstructed Castle Trail past the tidy, well-run CCC camp to the saddle in the next ridge, informally known as "the pig wire." Ernest Landgraf joined them there, and the three began scouting along the contour section of the trail for a feasible route to the summit. After floundering around Kaipapaʻu Gulch, all three decided the area was too rough for the new route. Judd then told Ernest Landgraf to extend the Castle Trail from "the pig wire" up the ridge to the summit at a 12 percent grade.[182]

As instructed, Landgraf built the Castle extension to reach the Koʻolau summit near the Kaipapaʻu cabin. There his gang turned northwest and resumed construction of the Summit Trail. During the fall and early winter the weather was decent, allowing steady progress through this wet and muddy section. The crew averaged sixteen feet of new trail built per man-day.

In January 1935, the wet season arrived with a vengeance. Cold, soaking rain swept the summit day after day. Work slowed and then stopped as men and tools became mired in the mud. Landslides obliterated whole sections of newly built trail. On January 18, Landgraf and his wet, weary crew retreated down the mountain. While waiting for better conditions, the summit gang planted Norfolk Island (Cook) Pines in back of Hauʻula.

Work on the Summit Trail resumed on March 1 as the weather improved marginally. The Honolulu Unit had previously relocated the side camp to a site farther up the Castle Trail just below the summit. After repairing the storm damage, Landgraf's trail crew pushed steadily northwest. By March 31, the end of the second six-month ECW period, the men were within a half-mile of the junction with the new Kawailoa Trail at Puʻu Kaʻinapuaʻa.

Honolulu Unit records for the Summit Trail project during that period show 4.6 miles of new trail constructed (including the Castle Trail extension) in 1,514 man-days, and 8.1 miles maintained in 223 man-days. Camp duties, such as ferrying supplies and hunting and cooking wild pigs, took an additional 991 man-days for a total of 2,731 man-days.[183]

After finishing the short segment to Kawailoa Trail, Ernest Landgraf and his crew pushed southeast from the Castle Trail junction toward the Poamoho Trail. The relatively gentle terrain along that summit section made for fast construction. Through June 1935, the crew averaged a blistering twenty-one feet of new trail per man-day. Project superintendent Gunder Olson remarked,

> The country boys that compose this 30 man [summit] crew have steadily done more and better work than any 40 man crew on our other projects composed of city boys.[184]

After Landgraf's crew passed Pe'ahināi'a Trail in early July, the Honolulu Unit moved the side camp from the top of Castle Trail to Poamoho.

The stalwart summit CCC crew pushes southeast along the Ko'olau crest toward Poamoho, 1935. (Charles Judd papers, Hawai'i State Archives)

The muddy, cramped Poamoho side camp along the Koʻolau Summit Trail, 1935. (Charles Judd papers, Hawaiʻi State Archives)

The new camp was situated along the Poamoho Trail in a narrow gulch just below the summit. Olson later commented,

> At this side camp, the sun does not shine for weeks at a time because of low hanging clouds and almost incessant rains. These conditions cause bedclothes, tents, wearing apparel etc. to be continually damp; the trail and campsites are perpetually muddy and, with the strong trade winds that blow here, conditions are very disagreeable.[185]

On July 14, Charles Judd led a summit hike for the Piko Club, an association of forestry rangers and army officers. Thirty members and guests climbed the new Poamoho Trail past the muddy, cramped side camp. From the top they bushwhacked north a third of a mile to the end of the Summit Trail. After strolling along the wide-open path, the group stopped for coffee at the Kaluanui side camp around 2 p.m. The Pikos then finished descending the rebuilt Castle Trail and reached their cars in Punalu'u Valley at 6 p.m.[186]

On that hike, Lieutenant Thomas J. Wells, the son of General Wells, discovered dark blue and cream-colored clay along the Summit Trail near its junction with Castle. He brought back a sample to Nancy Andrews, his pottery class instructor at the Honolulu Academy of Arts. She determined that the summit clay was actually of better quality than the imported mainland variety. The class, which included Judd, later found several more patches, much to the consternation of local geologists, who thought clay not possible on volcanic O'ahu.[187]

Approaching Poamoho from the windward side, Landgraf's men encountered steep cliffs, which dropped almost two thousand feet into Punalu'u Valley. The crew began using dynamite to blast deep cuts in the rocky slope. After a brief respite past the Poamoho Trail and cabin, the men faced a long, tough windward section below Pu'u Pauao, a massive hump on the summit ridge. As the crew blasted and chipped away at the stubborn rock, their progress slowed to eight feet per man-day in August and ten in September. Assistant forester Glenn W. Russ took it all in stride, reporting,

> 8/35—Summit Trail being worked on without notable incident.
>
> 9/35—Summit Trail being worked on, and fair weather has given the men a chance to make progress.[188]

At the close of the third six-month period on September 30, 1935, Ernest Landgraf and his men were still in the shadow of Pu'u Pauao, but well on their way to a junction with the Schofield-Waikāne Trail. Honolulu Unit records for the Summit Trail project during that period show 5.4 miles of new trail constructed in 1,991 man-days and 14.6 miles maintained in 223 man-days.[189]

On September 13, Judd finished the program plan for the fourth six-month ECW period ending March 31, 1936. Requested under Project 3, Foot Trail Construction, was an extension of the Ko'olau Summit Trail to connect the Schofield-Waikāne Trail with the new Waiawa (later Kīpapa) Trail. The estimated length was four miles, and the estimated man-days were 3,960. For the first time, the plan mentioned recreation, in addition to animal eradication and forestry management, as a justification for the trail projects requested.[190]

In the middle of November 1935, Ernest Landgraf and his men reached the army's Schofield-Waikāne Trail, the original terminus of the Ko'olau summit project. As the ECW director had approved the Waiawa extension, the crew continued southeast, rebuilding the army trail along the summit. Meanwhile the Honolulu Unit moved the side camp from Poamoho to a protected leeward site near the top of the Waikāne Trail.

Earlier, Judd had heard about a probable reduction in the CCC workforce for the next six-month period beginning April 1936. Fearing a cutback in the Honolulu Unit, he told Ernest Landgraf to stay on the leeward

CCC supervisors inspect recent work on the wide Ko'olau Summit Trail, 1935. (Charles Judd papers, Hawai'i State Archives)

side of the summit ridge around Puʻu Kaʻaumakua and the rest of the way to the Waiawa Trail.[191] Although longer and less scenic, the leeward route offered faster construction over more gentle terrain.

On December 19, 1935, Judd inspected the Waiawa Trail with Lieutenant Colonel (later General) George S. Patton, Jr., the intelligence officer of the army's Hawaiian Department. Around noon the two and several others reached Uncle Tom's cabin, perched on the Koʻolau summit. The view from the cabin was spectacular on this clear, cool winter day. They then hiked north along the summit ridge, passing Landgraf's crew working south. The group followed the newly built path to Waikāne junction and then descended the army trail past the ditchman's house. The men completed the twelve-mile walk in six hours. Judd later remarked, "The hike seemed to have given them all the exercise they desired."[192]

In late January 1936, Ernest Landgraf and his crew reached the Waiawa Trail and Uncle Tom's cabin. To complete the last summit section, the men had constructed 2.3 miles of new trail at fifteen feet per man-day during a wet December and January. Project Superintendent Olson later wrote,

> Because of severe weather in this section of the Koolau Range, and the uncomfortable living conditions which the men had to endure, they are to be praised highly for their fortitude and excellent work on this trail. The group is composed mostly of Mormons and live in the vicinity of Laie.[193]

The completed Koʻolau Summit Trail now stretched eighteen and a half miles from Black Junction on the Pūpūkea-Kahuku Trail to Uncle Tom's cabin at the end of the Waiawa Trail. The twenty-two-month summit project was the longest and most difficult CCC undertaking in Hawaiʻi. In his January routine report, assistant forester Glenn W. Russ wrapped up the project succinctly: "Summit Trail completed to Kipapa Trail this month, and now nothing but maintenance remains to be done in that region."[194]

During the fourth six-month period ending March 31, 1936, the Honolulu Unit constructed 4.4 miles of new Summit Trail in 1,578 man-days and maintained 16.0 miles in 496 man-days. Camp duties took an additional 608 man-days for a total of 2,186 man-days.[195]

In February 1936, the Honolulu Unit dismantled the last side camp on the Koʻolau Summit Trail. As Charles Judd had feared, reduced ECW funding forced the closing of that unit. Project superintendent Gunder Olson transferred to Hawaiʻi National Park. The foremen and their crews were discharged over a three-month period ending in June. In July, Ernest Landgraf became a foreman at the CCC Wahiawa Camp, which took over maintenance of the Summit Trail.[196]

In early September, Piko president Charles Judd, chief guide Thomas McGuire, and chief scout Leroy C. Wilson began planning an ambitious one-day summit hike. The route would follow the Pūpūkea-Kahuku Trail, the Summit Trail, and the Kīpapa Trail, a distance of about twenty-eight miles. The plan called for a 5:00 a.m. rendezvous at Waimea Station and a 5:30 start at the Pūpūkea Forest Reserve gate above the orchards of the Hawaiian Avocado Company. The hikers would reach Uncle Tom's cabin at 6:00 p.m. just before sunset. There, a second party coming up Kīpapa Trail would provide the marathoners with supper and coffee. Both groups would then descend by moonlight and be home by midnight. In an emergency, pigeons carried by the hikers would deliver a message to Schofield Barracks to summon cars to Kawailoa, Lā'ie, Castle, Poamoho, or Waikāne trailheads. In the hike flyer, Captain Wilson warns,

> This hike is 28 miles and is not intended for infants. . . . It is mainly a question of feet. Shoes and socks must be perfect. Hobnails are indispensable.[197]

The Piko marathon took place on Sunday, September 27, and was a rousing success. Ten army officers, seven enlisted men, and sixteen civilians, including four women, went the distance without injury. Most of the army personnel were well down the Kīpapa Trail by 5:30 p.m. and reached the cars before dark. Judd later recounted his experience that day.

> I went up the Waiawa [Kīpapa] Trail in the late afternoon and came out with the cowtailers. At the last stream crossing near the zigzags where there is water, Capt. Wilson, Tom [Ranger McGuire], some wahines, and several men and I had a little party in the dark, and I invented the PIKO cocktail on the spot, and 6 cupfuls were passed around among the crowd which made the walk down by moonlight very pleasant.[198]

From 1936 through 1941 the CCC Wahiawa Camp and the army periodically maintained the Ko'olau Summit Trail. The men cleared blowdowns, dug out landslides, and stabilized the pathway. Vegetation gradually covered up the construction scars and reclaimed the side camps.

After the attack on Pearl Harbor, the army took over maintenance of the Summit Trail and its feeders, as the CCC men at the Wahiawa Camp were transferred to high-priority military projects. Along the summit near each connecting trail, soldiers built a network of trenches and foxholes for defense and training. The army also erected at least three new cabins. The first stood just windward of the Kawailoa Trail junction and had sheet metal siding covered with camouflage paint. A second cabin was elevated on four-by-four posts leeward of the Schofield-Waikāne junction. The third army cabin was situated just before the Kīpapa Trail junction. Mules of the army's Hawaiian pack train delivered supplies to those remote cabins and fortified areas.[199]

In July 1942, the army and navy staged a mock invasion of Oʻahu. The invaders established beachheads along the south and north shores of the island. The northern force attacked across the Koʻolau Range, much as envisioned by General Wells ten years earlier.[200] The Summit Trail and its windward connectors, Pūpūkea-Kahuku and Lāʻie, must have been the scene of some fierce skirmishing.

On V-J Day, September 1, 1945, the Japanese surrendered aboard the battleship U.S.S. *Missouri* in Tokyo Bay. The next morning several HTMC members began a two-day traverse of the Koʻolau Range. Their route led through ravaged Kahana Valley, up the well-worn Waikāne Trail, along the Koʻolau Summit Trail, and down Kīpapa. In the monthly schedule the trip blurb had urged the club members to "get out your pack sacks and pup tents for the first overnite hike since the Blitz."[201]

On June 10 and 11, 1951, nine HTMC members hiked the Summit and Kīpapa Trails, a distance of twenty-six miles, in two days. Past the Waikāne Trail junction the group surprised a herd of fifteen wild pigs, which dashed madly along the trail until they could find a spot wide enough to get off. Harry Whitten, *Honolulu Star-Bulletin* reporter and club member, wrote that all the hikers had an enjoyable time without too much rain, but "some were rather weary by the time they came out of the mountains."[202]

The HTMC again scheduled the entire Summit Trail as a two-day backpack on July 3 and 4, 1955. Eleven stalwarts made the trip including Richard H. (Dick) Davis, the leader, David Sanford, Robert (Bob) Wenkam, and Beryl Sawyer. After dropping off a car at Kīpapa, the group all piled into Davis' car and drove to the Pūpūkea trailhead near the end of the dirt army road. The group finally started hiking at 11 a.m. and quickly reached Black Junction, where a sign listed the length of the Summit Trail as 18.75 miles. Nearby stood a refurbished army cabin.

From Black Junction the group headed out along the Summit Trail to the Mālaekahana Trail junction. The skies were sunny, and the trail was wide open, having recently been cleared by the army. Just before the Lāʻie junction the clouds settled, obscuring all views. After passing Kawailoa cabin in the mist, the hikers negotiated the rugged terrain in back of Maʻakua and

Summit Trail sign at Black Junction, circa 1955. (HTMC Archives)

Kaipapaʻu Gulches to reach Castle Trail junction. Here Davis led his group a short distance down Castle to a dilapidated shelter near a stream.

The small, three-sided shelter was not ideal for such a large group. No one could stand upright without bumping his head. Despite the cramped conditions the group managed to cook dinner on stoves, burning sterno or heat tablets. All spent a wet, uncomfortable night as the roof leaked in several places.

Not surprisingly, the group got up at 5:30 the next morning and were back on the trail before seven. Just past Poamoho Trail junction the clouds lifted to reveal a spectacular view of the Summit Trail ahead and Punaluʻu and Kahana Valleys below. After Waikāne Trail junction the route became overgrown, and the clouds settled down once more. Just before reaching Kīpapa junction the group passed an army cabin used as storage for coils of barbed wire. Nearby on the summit was a second cabin with a dirt floor and a water trough to collect rainwater from the roof. The group then descended the Kīpapa Trail back into the sunshine. The hikers finally reached their cars just after 6 p.m. Sawyer later wrote, "We were weary and footsore, but it had been a memorable trip."[203]

Weston (Wes) Williams, a computer programmer at Castle and Cooke, heard about the Summit Trail while hiking with the HTMC. Fascinated by the trail, he was determined to hike the entire route from Black to Kīpapa junctions. After two failed backpacking attempts in 1968, Williams decided to travel light and walk the Summit Trail in one day.

About 2 a.m. on July 4, 1969, Williams parked his car below the entrance to Koa Ridge Ranch, then hitchhiked to Niimi Store at Pūpūkea and began walking up the homestead road by moonlight. He carried just two-quart canteens of water on a web belt and several candy bars in his pocket.

Williams reached the Boy Scout camp at 4:30 a.m. and was on the Summit Trail by sunup, which revealed a fine trade wind day. The route was generally clear on either side of the connector trails, but the muddy, overgrown sections in between slowed him down and gradually wore him out. By noon Williams was well behind schedule; at Poamoho junction he ran out of food and water.

Williams had never hiked the Summit Trail beyond Poamoho. Nevertheless, that afternoon he gamely covered the remaining two sections, the glorious windward stretch from Poamoho to Waikāne and the clogged leeward contour to Kīpapa. With sunset fast approaching, Williams began to jog down the wide-open Kīpapa Trail. Shaking with exhaustion, he finally reached his car just after dark. Williams had hiked more than thirty miles in about sixteen hours without once losing the trail. On the drive home he saw the Fourth of July fireworks display over Honolulu.[204]

In April 1973, HTMC member Silver Piliwale embarked on a solo summit adventure to celebrate his seventy-second birthday. Starting at the Boy Scout camp in the rain, Piliwale hiked to the dilapidated Kawailoa cabin where he spent the night. Over the next two days he completed the official trail to Kīpapa junction despite a broken pack frame and a leaky tent.

Instead of turning down the Kīpapa Trail, Piliwale continued along the narrow, windswept summit ridge. With no graded trail, the going was rough, slow, and treacherous. Past Mānana junction he inadvertently left the main ridge in the fog and had to wait half a day for the clouds to lift and reveal the correct route. On the fifth day Piliwale finally emerged from Moanalua Valley, happy to reach his car. He later remarked, "My feet were sore, and I was so tired, but I wouldn't give up." Before his retirement, Piliwale was a heavy crane operator, seaman, and musician, playing the ukulele. A full-blooded Hawaiian, he often gave poi-pounding demonstrations at Bishop Museum and Lyon Arboretum.[205]

On their summit trips, Piliwale, Davis, and Williams had all passed the remains of the cabins built by the CCC in the 1930s and the army in the 1940s. Few were usable, and most had collapsed as their wood framework succumbed to wind and rain. In late 1973, the State Forestry Division built two new cabins along the Summit Trail to encourage continued hiking and hunting there. The Kahuku cabin stood windward of the trail about one mile past Kawailoa junction. The Poamoho cabin was nestled on the leeward side about one-half mile south of Poamoho junction. Each slept eight to ten persons and featured a water tank with rain catchment, a pit toilet, and a wood-burning stove. On February 2 and 3, 1974, Geraldine Cline led an HTMC backpack to check out the new Poamoho cabin.[206]

For Memorial Day weekend 1976, the HTMC scheduled a double traverse of the summit. Simon Sanidad led a group up the Lāʻie Trail, along the Koʻolau Summit, and down the Poamoho Trail, with overnights at both cabins. A second contingent, including Jim Yuen and Beverley Haylett, hiked the reverse route. The two groups exchanged greetings and car keys as they passed each other on the second day.[207]

In April 1979, Silver Piliwale, now seventy-eight years old, attempted to repeat his summit hike of six years before. He and Jo Anne Brown started from Pūpūkea and spent the first two nights at the Kahuku and Poamoho cabins. Past Kīpapa junction the going was very slow because of rough terrain and afternoon fogs. The two, exhausted, out of water, and a day late, came down the Aiea Ridge Trail instead of Moanalua Valley as planned.

Brown, an experienced hiker, later recollected that she did not realize what she was in for when agreeing to join Piliwale. Despite the hardships, she had pleasant memories of the trip: dining on steak the first night out; playing her nose flute in the evening; watching down feathers from Silver's old sleeping bag drift into their morning tea.[208]

After a seven-year hiatus, the HTMC scheduled a Summit Trail backpack on May 26–28, 1984. Led by Stuart Ball, the trip attracted eight others, including Jo Anne Brown, the only one with previous summit experience. Off to a late start from Pūpūkea, the group struggled through narrow guava corridors and waist-high uluhe ferns. Past Lāʻie junction, descending clouds brought heavy fog and light rain. The stragglers finally reached Kahuku cabin well after dark. The group spent a wet, sleepless night, as part of the cabin roof and floor were missing.

The next morning three people, hurting and ill-equipped, left down the Lāʻie Trail. The remaining six continued along the summit and reached Poamoho cabin in the late afternoon. The route was muddy and overgrown, but the spectacular views more than made up for the constant slogging.

On the last morning the group hiked together to Schofield-Waikāne junction under clear skies. Here four members took the army trail down to Wahiawā. Ball and Paul Strona decided to continue along the summit and exit via the Kīpapa Trail. Past Waikāne junction the clouds lowered, and visibility dropped to near zero. The two pushed blindly on, losing the trail several times in the heavy undergrowth. About an hour before sunset, Ball and Strona, tired and wet but happy, reached an abandoned naval communications site and a ride home.[209]

Ball returned to the Summit Trail twice in 1989. The first trip took place on May 27–29 with Chuck Godek, Carole Moon, and Jason Sunada. Starting from Pūpūkea, the group camped at Lā'ie Trail junction, Poamoho, and then came down the Schofield-Waikāne Trail. The trip featured a treacherous crossing of a fresh landslide near Poamoho and an incredibly windy, rainy night spent near the Cline Memorial.

On August 19–21, Ball, Moon, and Sunada completed the Summit Trail section left unfinished in May. The group hiked to the back of Kahana Valley and then followed the Waiāhole Ditch Trail to Waikāne saddle. The next day the three climbed to the Summit Trail in the mist and camped near the collapsed cabin with the rolls of rusted barbed wire. Past Pu'u Ka'aumakua the group had run into Godek and Albert Miller up for a day hike along the summit. The last day the three descended the Kīpapa Trail to Mililani Memorial Park, where Godek picked them up.[210]

For May 28–30, 1994, the HTMC scheduled another Ko'olau Summit backpack, a trip with a skill level of "masochist." Ball led nine intrepid club members up the Lā'ie Trail, along the summit, and down the Poamoho Trail. On the first day the group hiked through a heavy rainstorm to reach the campsite by the helipad at the top of the Kawailoa Trail.

The next morning the group moved out slowly under low clouds. Summit veteran Kost Pankiwskyj botanized briefly with Ken Suzuki, and then took the lead. The route was wet, rough, and overgrown; hikers fell off the trail or skidded into mud holes. Ball stopped at the Castle Trail junction to wait for stragglers and ended up camping there with Carole Moon and Deborah Uchida. Low on water, he spooned two quarts from the footprints of the lead group, which he hoped was at the Poamoho campsite by then.

The last morning, under clear skies, the three continued along the Summit Trail to an enthusiastic welcome from the forward contingent waiting near the Cline Memorial. Given the hour, the reunited group elected to descend the Poamoho Trail rather than the Schofield-Waikāne Trail as planned. Near the trailhead, HTMC trail maintenance boss Mabel Kekina met the tired summit hikers with drinks and snacks.[211]

On May 23–25, 1998, HTMC members Patrick Rorie and Gene Robinson attempted to repeat Silver Piliwale's summit trek of twenty-five years before. On a lovely trade wind morning the two quickly climbed the Lā'ie Trail and began slogging south along the summit toward Poamoho Trail junction. In the afternoon, under heavy clouds, Rorie and Robinson passed the neatly stacked remains of the Kahuku cabin, a victim of vandals and the elements. In the early evening the two reached the streamside Poamoho campsite and a welcome cache of food and water. Without sleeping bags both spent a cold, restless night as intermittent wind and rain pummeled their tents.

The next morning found Rorie and Robinson reveling in the panoramic windward views as they proceeded along the flank of Puʻu Pauao. Just after starting, they had passed the site of the Poamoho cabin, dismantled by the Forestry Division because of deterioration. At the top of Puʻu Kaʻamakua several friends joined them for lunch, bringing fresh oranges and needed supplies. The group happily toasted Piliwale and his achievements with red wine in plastic glasses. But the euphoria did not last long. In the afternoon, clouds engulfed the summit, and the "trail from hell" to Kīpapa junction was often overgrown, washed out, and hard to follow. As night fell, the two made a hurried camp on the Kīpapa Trail by the small stream below the summit.

On the third day Rorie and Robinson negotiated the narrow, roller coaster summit route from Kīpapa to Waimano junctions mostly in dense fog. After losing the trail briefly, they reached Waimano in the late afternoon. Here Robinson decided enough was enough, and he left down the Waimano Trail. Using his headlamp, he hiked several hours in the dark and reached home safely that night. On the way down, Robinson passed several friends hiking up to spend the night at the top of the Waimano Trail with the two. Having decided not to continue to Moanalua Valley, Rorie reluctantly headed down the Waimano Trail with his friends the next morning.[212]

In November 1998, the Oʻahu Natural Resource Program (ONRP) of the U.S. Army erected an exclosure fence leeward of the Summit Trail north of Peʻahināiʻa Trail junction. Enclosing about seven-eighths of an acre, the fence protects the only true montane bog on Oʻahu from damage by wild pigs. Sponsoring the project were Kamehameha Schools–Bishop Estate (the landowner) and the U.S. Army (the lessee). Biologists Kapua Kawelo and Joby Rohrer led the ONRP effort.[213]

In 1999, the HTMC continued the tradition, begun in 1984, of conducting a summit backpack once every five years. The dates scheduled for this trip were July 30 to August 1 with Patrick Rorie and Dayle Turner as coleaders. Signing up were ten other members, a good mix of summit veterans and neophytes.

On the first day the group started early from the end of Pūpūkea Road under partly cloudy skies. Although a portion of the route had been recently cleared, the hikers still had to deal with the summit mud all the way to their camp at Kawailoa Trail junction. Here several members pitched their tents on the site of the Kawailoa cabin windward of the helipad.

The next morning a light fog gradually dissipated, promising a fine day for summit hiking. On the trail early, the group quickly strung out, with Turner near the front and Rorie bringing up the rear. The two leaders communicated hourly, using walkie-talkies to monitor the group's progress. After a muddy but satisfying day, the last contingent reached the Cline Memorial in the early evening. About half the group camped by the small stream just down the Poamoho Trail, while the others opted for the new Poamoho cabin recently built by the Forestry Division.

On the final day the group enjoyed continued fine weather for the spectacular windward stretch beyond Poamoho. Leaving the summit as planned, the hikers turned down the Schofield-Waikāne Trail and headed for home. In the early evening the hot and tired rear echelon emerged onto California Avenue, Wahiawā, to warm greetings and cold drinks.[214]

For May 27–29, 2000, the HTMC again scheduled a summit backpack for those members who had been unable to make the trip the previous year. Leading the group of nine was Dayle Turner assisted by Thomas Yoza. Because of an extended drought the Summit Trail was relatively dry, allowing steady progress from Pūpūkea Road to Kawailoa Trail junction. Here the group camped at the cabin site and managed to find water in a small windward ravine nearby. In the late afternoon the wind picked up, flapping tents and making sleep difficult that night.

The next morning the group started early as gusty trade winds pushed clouds across the summit. With less mud underfoot, the hikers maintained a sure, steady pace except through several clogged leeward sections. As the clouds lifted in mid-afternoon, the rear guard under Yoza was nearing the Cline Memorial. At the streamside camp Yoza, Stuart Ball, and Lynne Masuyama joined Roger Breton, who had hiked up from Hauʻula that day. The rest of the group spent the night in the Poamoho cabin.

The third day dawned clear but extremely windy. After reassembling at the cabin, the group began the narrow, exposed traverse under Puʻu Pauao. Strong gusts slammed into the summit ridge, stopping the hikers in their tracks and throwing them off balance. Eventually, the group left the summit down the Waikāne Trail as planned. After a long road walk and a short shuttle, the windblown hikers enjoyed refreshments at Kay Lynch's house before heading for home.[215]

On December 21, 2000, the U.S. Fish and Wildlife Service purchased 4,525 acres in the northern Koʻolau Range from Castle and Cooke, Inc. Named the Oʻahu Forest National Wildlife Refuge, the parcel extends leeward from the summit between the Kīpapa and Schofield-Waikāne Trails. The refuge protects critical habitat for seventeen endangered species of native plants and four species of tree snails.

In May 2001, the ʻŌpaeʻula Watershed Protection Partnership (OWPP) completed a pig exclosure at the Koʻolau summit by Peʻahināiʻa Trail junction. Enclosing about two hundred acres at the head of ʻŌpaeʻula Stream, the boundary fence protects nine endangered species of native plants and two endangered species of Oʻahu tree snails. The OWPP is a joint effort of the Kamehameha Schools–Bishop Estate (the landowner), the U.S. Army (the lessee), the State Department of Land and Natural Resurces, and the U.S. Fish and Wildlife Service.

Coordinating the project were biologists Kapua Kawelo and Joby Rohrer of the army's Oʻahu Natural Resource Program (ONRP). In July 2000, the ONRP crew began carefully clearing the fence line with the assistance of HTMC member Charlotte Yamane and other volunteers. Helicopters ferried all workers and materials, including a prefabricated rain shelter, to the site. To reduce the cutting of native vegetation, a one-third-mile section of the fence line closely followed the Summit Trail. Rohrer and HTMC president Patrick Rorie worked together to minimize the impact of the fence on the original trail route. The ONRP installed step stiles to allow hikers to easily follow the Summit Trail in and out of the exclosure. After completion of the boundary fence, an ONRP crew began to rid the exclosure of strawberry guava, an aggressive, alien weed.[216]

As of 2010, the Koʻolau Summit Trail remained barely passable from Black Junction to Schofield-Waikāne junction. The leeward section to the Kīpapa Trail junction is clogged with *Clidemia* shrubs and uluhe ferns. The entire route is rough, muddy, overgrown, and obscure, although rarely all at the same time.

....

Honouliuli

Along the flanks of the hills his eye picked out the thin tracery of a line that faded to the South. That was the Honouliuli Trail . . .

—James Jones, *From Here to Eternity*

On January 27, 1924, twenty-two members and guests of the Hawaiian Trail and Mountain Club (HTMC) met at the Oahu Railway Station and boarded the 7:30 a.m. train for Leilehua. After disembarking, the group walked through Schofield Barracks and turned north on the Firebreak Trail just below Kolekole Pass. The ten-mile route contoured through the foothills of the Wai'anae Range below the summit of Ka'ala to Mā'ili hill and triangulation station. The U.S. Army had earlier built the Firebreak Trail as a buffer between the artillery range below and the forest reserve above. In 1925–1926, the Third Engineers smoothed and widened the path to better control the brush fires started by exploding artillery rounds.[217]

On February 9, 1931, territorial forester Charles S. Judd and Major General Briant H. Wells, commander of the Hawaiian Division at Schofield, inspected the Firebreak Trail on horseback. During the three-and-a-half-hour ride the two men discussed firefighting and reforestation along the path. They also planned several reconnaissance hikes to familiarize army officers with the routes over the Wai'anae and Ko'olau Ranges. Fast becoming friends, Judd and Wells repeated the ride on April 22. They inspected recent planting above the Firebreak Trail and discussed the upcoming organization banquet of the Piko Club, an association of forestry rangers and army officers.[218]

On July 29, 1935, Judd proposed a contour trail through the Wai'anae foothills on the opposite or south side of Kolekole Pass. As envisioned, the route would start at No. 5 forestry gate above Kupehau Ranch and roughly follow an old cowboy trail to the boundary between Honouliuli Forest Reserve and Schofield Barracks in Kānehoa Gulch. He included the Honouliuli Trail for the fourth enrollment period (October 1, 1935, to March 31, 1936) of Emergency Conservation Work.

> This proposed trail traverses most of the length of the Honouliuli Forest Reserve and will be of great use in tree planting, animal eradication and for recreational purposes. The country is half forested, dry and construction will be fairly easy. The estimated length is seven and one-half miles and 5,400 man days will be required. Estimated material costs are $500.00.[219]

O'ahu assistant forester Glenn W. Russ assigned the Honouliuli (dark bay) Trail to the Wahiawa Camp of the Civilian Conservation Corps (CCC).

On November 12, Judd, Russ, Robert C. Bayless, superintendent of Wahiawa Camp, Everett E. Tillett, field supervisor of the Honolulu Unit, and three army officers roughly determined the route of the new trail. They climbed to an elevation of 1,750 feet from No. 5 gate, the starting point, and again near Pohakea Pass at about the midpoint. They decided to build the path between the 1,500- and 1,800-feet contours to avoid the cliffs *mauka* (inland). Trail width would be two and a half feet, widening to four feet on steep slopes.[220]

On November 20, Judd and Bayless went back to the trailhead and began marking the proposed route. Also along were ranger at large Max F. Landgraf and O'ahu ranger Thomas R. L. McGuire. The group placed control flags from Nāmo'opuna (later Pu'u Mo'opuna) gap to the second side ridge northward. The old cowboy trail was so overgrown with lantana that the men frequently had to crawl on their hands and knees.[221]

Sometime in December 1935, a CCC crew from Wahiawa Camp drove down Kunia Road through pineapple fields and then the cane fields of Oahu Sugar Company. After crossing Waiāhole Ditch, the trucks turned right onto a dirt road leading past Kupehau Ranch to No. 5 gate. There the crew unloaded their tools and began clearing toward Nāmo'opuna gap.

Judd inspected the Honouliuli Trail several times in January 1936. He, Bayless, and Tillett hiked 1.75 miles from No. 5 gate to the end of the improved trail on January 15. They passed a CCC crew digging planting holes along the route and saw one thousand silk oak seedlings planted the week before. On January 23, Judd and Landgraf planted one hundred native hau hele 'ula (*Kokia cookei*), a rare Moloka'i hibiscus, on the side ridge before Ka'aikukai Gulch with the help of four CCC workers. Joined by Bayless, the two then checked out the trail location below Pōhākea Pass and also a nearby spring with several native ma'o hau hele (*Hibiscus brackenridgei*) planted by Judd about nine years before.[222]

On February 16, the Piko Club sampled the completed portion of the Honouliuli Trail. Led by Judd, fifty-eight members and guests met at Kunia Road near Waiāhole Ditch at 9 a.m. The group climbed to the summit of Palikea and then turned south along the Wai'anae crest. For lunch the Pikos enjoyed broiled steak in hamburger buns with hot coffee at the Forestry Division's Ka'aikukai cabin. Naturalist Kenneth Emory humorously explained the different meanings of the word "piko." After lunch the hikers descended to the Honouliuli Trail and followed it to their car shuttles waiting at No. 5 gate.[223]

In July, a CCC crew reached the Schofield Barracks boundary in Kānehoa Gulch, thus completing the construction project. The Honouliuli Trail measured 15.0 miles in length, twice the distance of the original estimate. Judd decided to extend the trail southward around Pu'u Poulihale to the Kalo'i Gulch Trail. The Wahiawa Camp finished that 1.6-mile extension in September 1936.[224]

The Honouliuli Trail was the scene of the last official hike of the Piko Club on December 6, a cool, rainy day. To retain army support for the club, Captain Leroy C. Wilson, Piko chief scout, had invited Brigadier General James C. Gowen, commander of the Hawaiian Division at Schofield Barracks. The general did not enjoy the hike, even though the club renamed the trail after him. For a time the contour route had two names, Honouliuli and Gowen, but the latter disappeared from general use after World War II.[225]

On December 14, Major General Hugh A. Drum, commander of the Hawaiian Department at Fort Shafter, requested permission from the Territorial Forestry Division to build a network of trails in the Wai'anae Range for the defense of O'ahu. Frank H. Locey, president of the Board of Agriculture and Forestry, approved the request on December 16. The Third Engineers were assigned to survey and coordinate the trail project, to be built with troop labor.[226]

Beginning in January 1937, soldiers extended the Honouliuli Trail from Kānehoa Gulch to Kolekole Pass. They built three connector routes from the contour trail to the Wai'anae crest at Kānehoa, Pōhākea Pass, and Pālehua. They also upgraded an old *kama'āina* (island-born) trail along the crest from Pōhākea Pass, over the summits of Palikea, Mauna Kapu, and Pālehua to Pu'u Manawahua. Lastly, the soldiers linked the Honouliuli Trail at Nāmo'opuna gap with the Pa Lehua Artillery Spur (later Pālehua Road) at No. 1 forestry gate near Kalo'i Gulch. Started in November 1936, the spur left the Wai'anae Road two miles past the Kunia junction and climbed six miles to the No. 1 gate. Workers paid under the Emergency Relief Appropriations Road and Trail Project built the road of crushed coral to withstand use by heavy artillery.[227]

In the novel *From Here to Eternity*, the Honouliuli Trail played a small, unheralded role in island defense during the months before the Pearl Harbor attack.

> Along the flanks of the hills his eye picked out the thin tracery of a line that faded to the South. That was the Honouliuli Trail, the officers went riding there, with their women. You could always find innumerable condoms along the trail, and trees where idle horses had chewed off bark.[228]

During World War II the army built a paved road from No. 1 gate to a radar installation at Pu'u Manawahua and to radio facilities at Mauna Kapu. The army also widened the connector from the new road down to Nāmo'opuna gap, and the Honouliuli Trail from the gap to below Pōhākea Pass for use by jeeps.[229]

After the war the Territorial Forestry Division included the Honouliuli Contour as trail number 18 at seventeen miles in the 1947 O'ahu map. The route description advised driving through cane fields and pasture to No. 5 gate and then hiking on the contour trail until turnaround time. In 1950, the Forestry Division cleared and widened the jeep portion of the trail to better serve as a firebreak.[230]

Starting in the late 1940s, the HTMC began to incorporate the Honouliuli Trail into four loop hikes, Pālehua, Palikea, Kaua, and Kānehoa-Hāpapa. The Pālehua route started at Mauna Kapu and climbed the Waiʻanae crest to Palikea peak. The hikers then backtracked to Kaʻaikukai cabin for lunch and descended to the Honouliuli Trail. From there, they contoured to Nāmoʻopuna gap and turned up the army cutoff to the paved road back to their cars. Over the years veteran member Richard (Dick) Booth lengthened the loop, adding the Puʻu Poulihale extension, known as the Kupehau Trail, and the summit section from Puʻu Manawahua to Mauna Kapu.[231]

Booth also scouted out the Palikea hike. The route first climbed a steep side ridge to the Waiʻanae crest near Pōhākea Pass. The hikers then walked the summit ridge south past Palikea to the cabin. From there they descended to the contour trail and followed it north to complete the loop.[232]

Richard H. (Dick) Davis developed the Kaua hike for the HTMC. The route initially climbed to an old army cabin at Pōhākea Pass. From there the hikers scrambled up a narrow stretch of the Waiʻanae crest to reach the summit of Kaua, the third highest peak on Oʻahu. They then descended a side ridge and returned along the Honouliuli Trail. Later versions reversed the hike direction and descended another side ridge short of the pass.[233]

Kānehoa-Hāpapa, the fourth loop hike, started in the Kunia pineapple fields and ascended Maunauna ridge past a triangulation station to the peak of Kānehoa. The route next followed the Waiʻanae crest past Hāpapa peak and descended a side ridge just before Kolekole Pass. The hikers then walked a seemingly endless section of the contour trail back to Maunauna ridge.[234]

The HTMC continued to schedule the four loops regularly during the 1960s through 1980s. In November 1982, wind from hurricane ʻIwa swept over the Waiʻanae crest and knocked down hundreds of trees across the trail. The club cleared some of the blowdowns but had to reroute or even abandon several sections of the loop hikes.

In May 1990, The Nature Conservancy (TNC) established the Honouliuli Preserve on 3,692 acres in the windward Waiʻanae Range. The preserve stretched from Mauna Kapu to Hāpapa along the summit and included most of the Honouliuli Forest Reserve and the contour trail. Under a long-term lease agreement with the landowner, the estate of James Campbell, TNC protected the habitat of more than forty-five rare native plants, birds, and tree snails. From September 1992 through May 1993, the conservancy completely rebuilt a section of the Honouliuli Trail south of Maunauna ridge and began conducting monthly loop hikes there. The HTMC continued to offer the Pālehua, Kaua, and Kānehoa-Hāpapa hikes in the preserve with some TNC restrictions on the route, frequency, and group size because of the fragile ecosystem. In 2007, the Oʻahu Natural Resource Program (ONRP) of the U.S. Army shouldered some of the preserve maintenance as a result of staff cutbacks at TNC.[235]

In September 2009, the Trust for Public Land (TPL), a nonprofit land conservation organization, purchased the Honouliuli Preserve from the James Campbell Company using public and private funds. On March 31, 2010, the TPL transferred ownership of the preserve to the State Department of Land and Natural Resources. The Division of Forestry and Wildlife assumed management of the preserve and plans to incorporate some of its trails into Na Ala Hele, the state trail system.[236]

As of 2010, the condition of the Honouliuli Trail varied considerably depending on the use received. Those sections regularly traveled by the ONRP or the HTMC remain open. Unused sections range from barely passable to totally overgrown.

Volunteer Trails
(1945–1998)

....

Mālama I Ka Honua (cherish the earth)

—title of the Sierra Club, Hawai'i Chapter
newsletter, May 1969

Sierra Club, Hawai'i Chapter

On May 9, 1968, more than fifty persons attended a meeting to establish a chapter of the Sierra Club in Hawai'i. The group elected an executive committee chaired by photographer and author Robert (Bob) Wenkam, who was instrumental in the chapter's founding. In April 1969, the club held its first outing, the Alewa-Kapalama loop, led by Peter Escherich, member of the executive committee and science teacher at Kamehameha School for Boys. One month later the chapter began publishing a monthly newsletter, *Mālama I Ka Honua*. In October, the club organized a group at the University of Hawai'i to get the students there involved in conservation issues. Their first hike was Mānoa Falls on November 1.[1]

By early 1971, the chapter had about four hundred members, but the hike offerings were sporadic at best. In April, Lorin T. Gill became head of the outings committee. He instituted a regular hiking schedule and developed two new programs, High School Hikers (HSH) and Trail Maintenance Projects (TMP). HSH featured day hikes and camping trips on O'ahu to foster student interest in the outdoors and in environmental careers. Farrington and Kailua were the first two high schools to sign up, followed by McKinley and Castle.[2]

The TMP program emerged from a discussion in 1970 between Gill and Hiroshi Motomura, a mainland high school student. Gill, Harry

Whitten, Silver Piliwale, Robert Mizuno, and several others had met Motomura during the summer of 1969 while backpacking in the High Sierra. Gill invited Motomura to go camping on the neighbor islands the next summer. While in Kalalau Valley on Kaua'i, Motomura came up with the idea of holding a TMP event on the run-down trail there for volunteer local and mainland upper high school and college students. The first project thus became the restoration of a washed-out section of the Kalalau Trail in August 1971, with Motomura as assistant leader. The next summer, volunteer TMP crews rebuilt trails in Wailau Valley on Moloka'i. Subsequent trips led by Ron Nagata involved fence building in Haleakalā National Park to keep out feral goats. In 1974, TMP became known as HSTP, the Hawai'i Service Trip Program. During the summer of 1976, Gill received a Special Appreciation Award from the mainland Sierra Club for developing HSTP and High School Hikers.[3]

In 1978, the Sierra Club, Hawai'i Chapter began a rewarding partnership with the State Department of Land and Natural Resources (DLNR) to construct trails on O'ahu. In the middle 1970s, during an oil crisis, the DLNR had decided to expand the trail system in the newly created Makiki-Tantalus Recreation Area close to town. Planned were five new trails to provide easier access to the network, especially by bus, and to better connect the existing routes. Sponsored and financed by the DLNR, the HSTP built the 'Aihualama Trail in 1978, Nahuina and Moleka in 1979, 'Ualaka'a in 1980, and the upper section of the Nu'uanu Trail in 1983. While planning and executing those projects, the HSTP developed a very successful trail-building model, using volunteer trail crews coordinated by HSTP leaders.[4]

In 1991, the DLNR again turned to the Sierra Club to build the Maunawili Trail, a demonstration project for Na Ala Hele, the new state trail and access program. The HSTP completed most of that nine-mile route over the next three years. The DLNR and the HSTP also collaborated on the construction of the Maunawili Falls Trail in 1996 and a short connector from the falls trail to the Maunawili Trail in 1998.[5]

Na Ala Hele, Hawai'i Trail and Access System

In late 1986, the Sierra Club and other trail users established a task force to regain access to O'ahu trails that were closed to the public because of the liability concerns of the landowners. Included in the group were the Hawaiian Trail and Mountain Club and the O'ahu Pig Hunters Association.

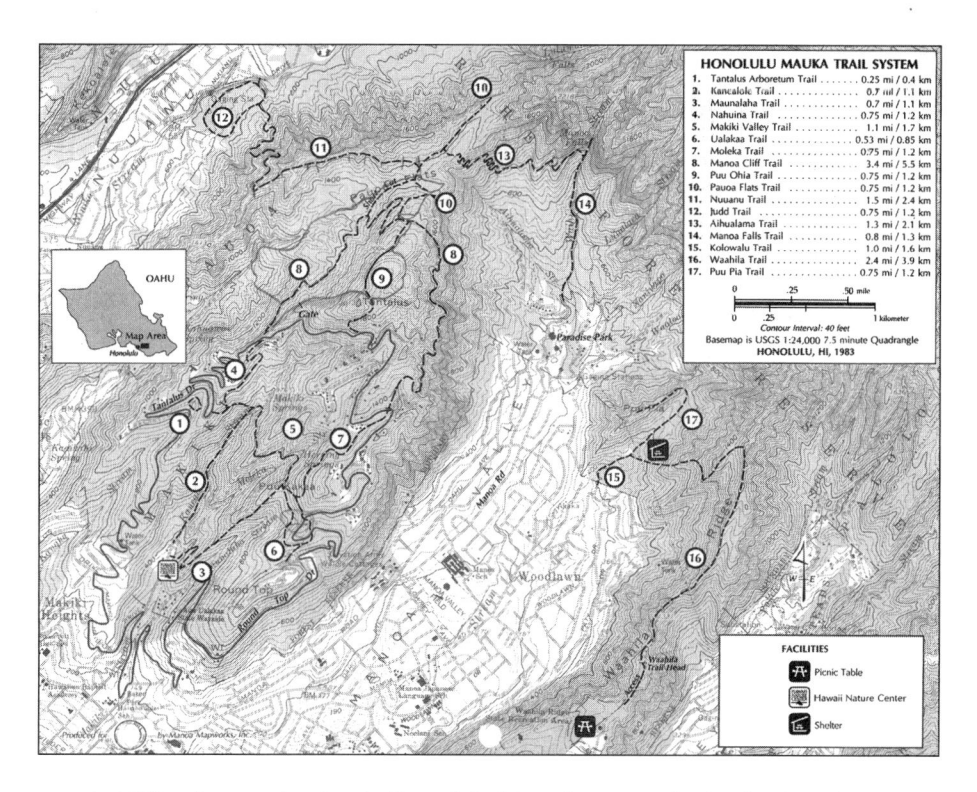

Makiki-Tantalus map showing the five trails built by volunteers under the direction of the Sierra Club, 1983. (State Division of Forestry and Wildlife)

After producing a study describing the trails lost over the years and their history, the task force began discussions with Department of Land and Natural Resources (DLNR), state legislators, and the Honolulu City Council. At the same time, a group of trail advocates on the Big Island became concerned about the rapid increase in land development there and the resulting threat to historic Hawaiian trails and old government roads. The two groups met and joined forces to lobby the state legislature.[6]

Despite initial setbacks, both groups attained their goal in the 1988 legislative session with the passage of a bill creating Chapter 198D, Hawai'i Revised Statutes, which established the Hawai'i Trail and Access System, to be known as Na Ala Hele (trails to go on). The legislation placed Na Ala Hele (NAH) under the Division of Forestry and Wildlife (DOFAW) within the DLNR. In March 1991, the DOFAW completed the NAH Plan, approved by Governor John Waihee in September.[7] The plan described in detail the statewide program objectives, organization, and trail and access management practices. In a nutshell, NAH "wants to ensure adequate public access to coastal and mountain areas consistent with sound conservation principles."[8]

NAH immediately assumed maintenance responsibility for most of the existing DOFAW public trails. On Oʻahu, trail specialist Curt Cottrell organized and coordinated a volunteer program and began restoration of the Keālia, Schofield-Waikāne, Poamoho, and Tantalus area trails. NAH surveyed and constructed the Kuliouʻou Ridge Trail with help from volunteers. Program staff developed excellent strip maps for the more popular Oʻahu trails and erected identification and warning signs on them. NAH also developed an inventory of all Oʻahu trails and access routes, whether on public or private land.[9]

With input from citizen advisory councils, NAH selected one demonstration trail to be built or restored on each major island. The demonstration trail proposed for Oʻahu was the Koʻolaupoko complex on the windward side. From 1991 through 1993, NAH partnered with the Sierra Club, Hawaiʻi Chapter to construct the nine-mile Maunawili Trail from Nuʻunau Pali lookout to Waimānalo at the base of the Koʻolau cliffs. The Sierra Club and NAH later collaborated on the Maunawili Falls Trail in 1996 and a short connector from the falls to the Maunawili Trail to complete the Koʻolaupoko complex in 1998.[10]

Under state NAH program manager Curt Cottrell and Oʻahu trail manager Aaron Lowe, NAH has maintained, improved, and gradually expanded the Oʻahu public trail network over the years. NAH and trail advocates collaborated in negotiations to obtain legal access to the Wiliwilinui, and Mokulēʻia Trails. The major challenge facing Oʻahu NAH and the hiking community remains the Koʻolau Summit Trail complex, which was identified as a series of priority routes in the original 1991 plan. That magnificent network features several remote and run-down trails originally built by the Civilian Conservation Corps in the 1930s. The access and restoration challenges are significant because of the rugged country, endangered species, and complicated public and private land ownership. NAH took the first step by securing access to the Poamoho Trail in 2007.[11]

Hawaiian Trail and Mountain Club

While the Sierra Club concentrated on building graded trails for the DLNR and Na Ala Hele, the Hawaiian Trail and Mountain Club (HTMC) scouted and cleared more rugged routes for its weekly hikes. Some of the HTMC trails were new, but most followed old, rediscovered paths previously used by Hawaiians, *kama'āina* (island-born) hikers, hunters, surveyors, or soldiers.

Richard H. (Dick) Davis and Richard (Dick) Booth were the premier trail blazers for the club after World War II. Davis developed Pu'u Manamana in 1953, Makaua, or Hidden Valley, in 1954, Pauoa Woods in 1956, Pu'u Piei in 1959, Tripler Ridge in 1961, Likeke in 1962, Piliwale Ridge in 1970, and Wai'anae Ka'ala in 1974. He also scouted, marked, and helped construct the Maunawili Trail beginning in 1991. Booth developed 'Ohikilolo in 1953, Kamanaiki with Charles Smith in 1964, Kaunala East in 1968, Tantalus Ramble in 1976, and Wahiawā Hills in 1977.[12]

Other member-created trails were Kaipapa'u by Lloyd Talcott in 1966, Ulupaina by Joyce Davis (Dick's daughter) and Geraldine Cline in 1974, Waikakalaua by David Sanford in 1981, Lua'alaea by Silver Piliwale also in 1981, Waiau by Robert (Bob) Silva in 1986, and Hala Pepe Nui off Waiau by Silva, John Hall, and Gerald Leao in 2005. Hiking legend Albert (Al) Miller specialized in finding precarious routes in the leeward Wai'anae Range. He gave the club Kamaile'unu in 1982 and Pu'u Heleakala and Pu'u o Hulu in 1989.[13]

HTMC trail maintenance crew at the Moanalua (Kamananui) Valley trailhead, circa 2000. Reclining in front, Mabel Kekina. (HTMC Archives)

Chuck Godek and "Skipoles" Erwin Jaskulski concentrated their efforts in Kamananui (Moanalua Valley). With Stuart Ball, the two cleared the middle ridge and power line trails to create the magnificent Puʻu Keahi a Kahoe loop in 1988. In 1990, Godek and Jaskulski also developed the ridge route named after them. In 1995, Ball teamed with Jason Sunada and Gerald Leao to create the Kulepeamoa loop in back of Niu Valley. In 1997, Leao and David Denison cleared the nearby Wailupe loop above ʻAina Haina.[14]

To keep the trails open, the HTMC relied primarily on the hike coordinator. He or she cleared the route with a few friends prior to the scheduled hike or even on the day of the outing. That method worked reasonably well until the 1970s, when invasive species, such as *Clidemia hirta*, began to seriously clog the trails. To address the problem, HTMC member and hike coordinator Mabel Kekina established a separate trail maintenance group in 1985. Armed with machetes, sickles, loppers, saws, and eventually weed whackers, the crew met most Sundays to clear the route of the hike scheduled two weeks later. To encourage participation and camaraderie, Kekina provided delicious snacks *pau hana* (after work). The group soon swelled to about twenty regulars, who have made a huge impact on the Oʻahu trail system. After Kekina's retirement in 2007, the crew continued to be ably led by Michael (Mike) Algiers.[15]

Likeke

What is it about a wooded slope that compels a certain leader to spend hours carving, by ancient method, a wandering trail over its rugged surface?

—Hawaiian Trail and Mountain Club schedule, February 9, 1975

In the late 1950s, the Boy Scouts Council needed a new trail on the windward side to allow the boys to earn their hiking merit badges. The council approached Richard H. (Dick) Davis, a member of the Hawaiian Trail and Mountain Club (HTMC) and volunteer trail builder. Davis agreed to construct the trail, and the Boy Scouts agreed to maintain it. After some searching, Davis selected a contour route at the base of the Koʻolau *pali* (cliff) from the Wilson Tunnel to the old automobile road crossing Nuʻuanu Pali.

Sometime in 1959, Davis started building the trail from the lookout parking lot just outside the tunnel portal. He used a machete and saw to clear the vegetation, and a pick, shovel, and mattock to grade the treadway. He often worked on weekends, sometimes on weekdays after his regular job, and even at night by headlamp. Davis built the trail almost entirely by himself, as he wanted to keep the project a secret.

For the next two years Davis worked into and out of more than ten gulches between the Wilson Tunnel and Nu'uanu Pali lookouts. On the final section, Davis passed an old house site under several mango trees. There he found and followed an abandoned trail winding below the cliffs. While chopping through a hau tangle, he heard a waterfall on his right and routed the trail close to its base. After the waterfall, he cleared past a concrete basin used to settle the sediment in the water from a spring above. Pipes led from the basin to a dairy and workers' cottages below. During the first half of 1961, Davis finally reached the old *pali* carriage road and then the old automobile road, the trail's end.[16]

Mountain man and trail builder Richard (Dick) Davis on the new Maunawili Trail, circa 1991. (Sierra Club, Hawai'i Chapter Archives)

For July 30, the HTMC scheduled a surprise outing.

Fun, games, and surprises for all on a brand new hike to one of the most spectacular panoramas on Oahu—prizes for all events and a special citation to the person who guesses our lunch spot. Phone 746-437 for absolutely no information.[17]

Led by Robert (Bob) Wenkam, the large group admired Dick's handiwork and enjoyed the waterfall and the views of the Koʻolau *pali* and Kāneʻohe Bay. For the second outing on February 4, 1962, the club named the trail Likeke, Richard in Hawaiian, in appreciation for all his hard work.[18]

Over the next four years, Davis continued to improve the grading and width of the Likeke Trail. He dug out a section under the current Pali Highway so that hikers could access the trail from the Nuʻuanu Pali lookout. He then developed a short set of switchbacks to better connect the old *pali* road with the carriage road. Davis also made a number of improvements around the waterfall, which had begun flowing around 1959, when workers building the two *pali* tunnels inadvertently tapped into water-bearing rock. He widened the route to and from the waterfall and created a small pool for wading. He then graded a nearby area to allow hikers to change into their swimsuits.[19]

The HTMC scheduled the Likeke hike regularly over the next several decades. The trail remained the same, but the approach routes varied considerably because of land use changes *makai* (seaward). In 1982, the City and County of Honolulu opened Hoʻomaluhia Botanical Garden and some years later closed the Wilson tunnel parking lot because of the traffic hazard and illegal activities there. With the tunnel access gone, the club incorporated the botanical garden into the hike. Groups started near the Kahua Kuou camping area and climbed through hau tangles to reach the Likeke Trail just below the parking lot. The return followed a connector trail from the waterfall to the equestrian area in the garden. In the early 1990s, the state completed the section of the H-3 freeway between the botanical garden and the Koʻolau golf course, cutting off access to the trail from the Kāneʻohe side. The HTMC, however, soon found several routes underneath the freeway through a culvert and below an elevated section. The return portion followed the old carriage and auto roads and then recrossed the freeway on the golf course access road before entering Hoʻomaluhia through the back gate.[20]

Davis periodically worked on the Likeke Trail until just before his death in the fall of 2004. On Saturday, September 25, about 120 friends and relatives gathered at the HTMC clubhouse for a memorial service and talk story session celebrating Dick's legendary life. Afterward, his daughter Joyce led a smaller group from the golf course up the carriage road and the Likeke Trail to the waterfall. There they scattered his ashes by a boulder where Dick used to sit, smoking his pipe, taking a break from trail building.[21]

Mānana

> Our leader is still clearing and extending the trail—
> this time we may reach another Koolau lookout.
>
> —Hawaiian Trail and Mountain Club schedule,
> October 22, 1967

On a rainy, windy January 8, 1925, territorial forester Charles S. Judd, ranger at large Max F. Landgraf, and four others drove up the ridge between Mānana and Waimano Streams through the sugar cane fields of the Honolulu Plantation Company. The group planned to inspect the vegetation and check for feral pig damage in the nearby ʻEwa Forest Reserve. The six men parked their vehicle in a cane field near the reserve boundary and began hiking *mauka* (inland) along the ridge. After plowing through scratchy uluhe ferns for about a mile, they descended to Mānana Stream and followed it down past the reserve boundary. Judd observed no cattle and very few pigs along the stream above the recently rebuilt perimeter fence. After a steep climb back to the ridgeline, the men reached their vehicle in the late afternoon and were home by 5 p.m.[22]

Thirty-five years later, a consortium of local companies began construction of a housing subdivision on the broad Mānana-Waimano ridge, previously used for growing pineapple. By the summer of 1961, the developers were offering house sites in the first increment and building a community recreation center. Known as Pacific Palisades, the subdivision eventually extended up the ridge to the 960-foot level. From the turnaround at the end of Komo Mai Drive, a one-lane paved road led to a Board of Water Supply tank, providing easy access to the forest reserve for hunters and hikers.

Sometime in 1965, Charles (Charlie) Nakamura and several friends, all members of the Hawaiian Trail and Mountain Club (HTMC), began clearing a trail along the ridge from the water tank toward the Koʻolau summit, about four miles away as the crow flies. On October 3, Nakamura led the first club hike on the Mānana Trail as a substitute for the canceled Puʻu Kawiwi outing.[23]

The HTMC officially scheduled Mānana in 1966 and again in 1967. Each year the hike became longer, as Nakamura and his friends made progress *mauka*. For the October 22, 1967, outing, Nakamura and Herman Medeiros cut a short side trail down to a small pool and waterfall along Mānana Stream about a mile from the summit. Around 1970, the unfinished route became trail number 90 on the State Division of Forestry map. In early 1969, Nakamura finally reached the Koʻolau summit and led club members over the entire six-mile trail on June 1.[24]

In 1967 Kazuo and Misao Yamaguchi, HTMC members and Pacific Palisades residents, began exploring some of the side ridges and gulches off the Mānana Trail. The couple eventually discovered a steep but doable ridge leading down to deep swimming holes and a lovely waterfall along Waimano Stream. On Saturday afternoon, May 25, 1968, the Yamaguchis led the first HTMC hike on the new route, initially called Mānana Stream. In 1972 the club renamed the hike Waimano Pool, which better described its location and attraction. The side ridge became informally and affectionately known as "Cardiac Hill" because of the steep climb on the return.[25]

In the early afternoon of October 17, 1972, Pacific Palisades residents reported smoke along the ridge *mauka* of the subdivision. A fire had started in the dry uluhe ferns near the Mānana Trail less than a mile from the water tank and had advanced slowly toward the Koʻolau summit. Five companies of the Honolulu Fire Department contained the blaze by 6:30 p.m., and one company stayed the night to make sure the fire did not spread.[26] The HTMC hiked Mānana several months later on January 14, 1973. The description of that outing in the schedule noted, "The trail is overexposed, utterly naked, and burned from a recent fire. Charred trees and cinders carpet the ground."[27] The Division of Forestry later replanted the burned area with southern pines and paperbark trees.

The HTMC has regularly scheduled the Mānana and Waimano Pool hikes since the 1970s. On June 20, 1998, the club held its first "super" hike on the Mānana Trail. Led by Dayle Turner and Patrick Rorie, a group of ten stalwarts climbed Mānana, turned south along the Koʻolau summit ridge past the peak of ʻEleao, and descended the Waimano Trail. The weather that Saturday was wet and windy, making for a cool but muddy trip.[28]

With their easy access, both Mānana and Waimano Pool are also popular with individuals, families, and other hiking groups. Because of the distance and difficulty, few hikers take the ridge trail all the way to the summit; most are content to stroll through the lower wooded section out into the open burned area, which is still recovering from the fire. The Boy Scouts occasionally backpack to a covered picnic table about two miles in and camp there for the night. Because of the waterfall and swimming holes, the Waimano Pool hike receives considerably more traffic, especially from local kids.

'Aihualama

> There is no way to describe the great feeling you'll also get, a feeling of satisfaction and exhilaration, which comes from hiking a trail you built yourself.
>
> —Andie Gill, May 1978

At the back of Mānoa Valley in the shadow of Kōnāhuanui peak lies a rugged gulch with a small stream called 'Aihualama. Early Hawaiians blazed a steep path along the left side of the stream to a flat divide, where other trails led up to Kōnāhuanui and down to Pauoa and Nu'uanu Valleys. Over the years the 'Aihualama route probably received only light use, mostly from wood cutters, bird catchers, plant gatherers, and an occasional traveler taking a shortcut to the adjacent valleys.[29]

The 'Aihualama area also figured prominently in a grisly Hawaiian legend. The maiden Kahalaopuna was the beautiful daughter of Kahaukani (Mānoa wind) and Kauahuahine (Mānoa rain). She lived alone at the back of the valley, and the frequent rainbows there were a celebration of her life and beauty. One day Kahalaopuna went walking in 'Aihualama with her suitor Kauhi, a chief of Kailua. Believing her unfaithful, he clubbed her to death in a fit of anger and buried the corpse near the stream. The owl god Pueo saw the murder and the hasty burial. He flew down, retrieved the body, and brought the maiden back to life.

Unfortunately, Kahalaopuna returned to the chief, to whom she had been betrothed by her parents. Again the two walked, this time up the ridge separating Mānoa and Pauoa Valleys. Again Kauhi grew angry and killed her. Pueo then retrieved the body and revived the maiden for a second time. The sequence of events repeated itself again and again in different areas of O'ahu. Eventually the poor owl grew tired from rescuing the maiden so many times and gave up. Luckily, Mahana, another less jealous suitor, revived Kahalaopuna once again with the help of some spirit friends. The two married and lived happily together for a time.

Meanwhile, the king ordered Kauhi to be roasted alive in an *imu* (underground oven). He died horribly, but a tsunami washed his bones out to sea, where he was reincarnated as a shark. Although warned, Kahalaopuna went swimming one day and was devoured by her former suitor. Only the Mānoa rainbows remain to remind us of lovely Kahalaopuna.[30]

On January 9, 1895, the trail along 'Aihualama Stream provided an escape route for royalist rebels fleeing government forces after a skirmish at the back of Mānoa Valley. Led by Samuel Nowlein and Robert W. Wilcox, the royalists had tried to overthrow the recently founded Republic of Hawaii and return Queen Lili'uokalani to her throne. Foiled in their attempt, Wilcox and the rebel remnant crossed from Pālolo to Mānoa Valley and retreated *mauka* (inland) to an area known as "the pen."

> Rocky, wooded ridges enclose it to right and left, and straight back is the black, sheer face of Kōnāhuanui. The rebels were approaching this cul-de-sac at its *makai*, or southern angle, along the stream called 'Aihualama.[31]

About 140 government troops, including 70 sharpshooters, advanced up the valley, found the rebels in "the pen" and attacked during mid-afternoon. With about 50 men, Wilcox quickly formed a strong defensive line, which held for a time. But the sharpshooters eventually flanked his position. In the ensuing disarray some rebels surrendered; Wilcox and others fled up the stream route and over the divide. Several days later Wilcox gave himself up and later received a death sentence, which was commuted to imprisonment by Republic of Hawaii president Sanford B. Dole.[32]

In 1919, the Hawaiian Sugar Planters Association (HSPA) purchased 124 acres in the 'Aihualama area and established a small station there, later known as Lyon Arboretum, to investigate watershed conservation. Shortly afterward the association leased 325 acres *mauka* (inland) of the station for a reforestation project. HSPA crews began planting many different varieties of trees and shrubs to evaluate their potential for watershed restoration. For easier access to the *mauka* section, crews built a trail that switchbacked up the steep slope to the broad divide called Pauoa Flats. Later known as the Arboretum Trail, the route started in back of the HSPA station near the mountain house of former governor George R. Carter.[33]

After the HSPA completed the reforestation study, the Arboretum Trail received less and less use and gradually became overgrown and all but forgotten. About four decades later, in 1977, Lorin Gill, his niece Andrea

(Andie), Ron Nagata, all from the Sierra Club, Gene Renard, a planner with the Division of State Parks, and several others rediscovered and marked the switchback route. From Pauoa Flats the group scrambled down the steep slope, trying to pick out the deteriorated, clogged switchbacks. Eventually, they reached a more level spot where the original trail descended to the arboretum. To bypass Lyon's, the group blazed a new contour route through head-high uluhe ferns to Mānoa Falls. The entire flagged route became the first trail-building project in the new Makiki-Tantalus Recreation Area, established to provide convenient hiking opportunities close to town to reduce gasoline usage.[34]

In early 1978, the State Department of Land and Natural Resources (DLNR) contracted with the Sierra Club, Hawai'i Chapter to build the 1.4-mile 'Aihualama Trail. The project included restoration of the arboretum switchbacks (.75 mile) and construction of the new contour route (.65 mile) connecting the Mānoa Falls Trail with the switchback section. Coordinating the 'Aihualama project was the Hawai'i Service Trip Program (HSTP), the muscular arm of the Sierra Club devoted to trail and fence building and habitat restoration, mostly on the Neighbor Islands. 'Aihualama was the group's first major O'ahu project and its largest and most ambitious undertaking to that date.[35]

Chaired by Andie Gill, the HSTP Steering Committee began planning the project schedule and resources in late spring. The group estimated three hundred man- and woman-days to complete the 1.4-mile trail. Work would start July 8 and finish by the end of August. Volunteer trail crews under HSTP leaders would wield machetes and saws to clear brush and trees, and picks, shovels, rakes, and pulaskis to grade the treadway. Volunteers needed only to be reasonably fit, fifteen years old or older, and bring lunch, water, and heavy gloves. The HSTP would provide tools, refreshments *pau hana* (after work), and a beige/green 'Aihualama T-shirt for all participants. In June, the HSTP held several orientation sessions to familiarize volunteers with the project and the various tools they would be using.[36]

Actual trail work started on July 22. At 8 that morning the first volunteer crew met near the Church of the Crossroads and carpooled to Lyon Arboretum. After signing a liability waiver and listening to a brief safety talk, the group hiked the 0.8-mile Mānoa Falls Trail. At a point just short of the falls, the crew began clearing and grading a path along the rough, rocky hillside. After about five hours of work with a break for lunch, the tired volunteers traipsed back down the falls trail for some well-earned drinks and snacks.[37]

In a similar fashion crews worked on the trail daily through August 8 and then switched to weekends only. Frequently, a second, select crew under Ron Nagata ranged ahead to do chain-saw and other preliminary work. By the end of August volunteers had contributed more than four hundred man- and woman-days to the project, which was still not finished. On September 17, a jubilant trail crew finally completed the last section of the new 'Aihualama Trail. The project had attracted 192 volunteers, ranging in age from fifteen to seventy-five; almost half came out more than once. The DLNR was supportive during the entire project and pleased with the result. O'ahu district forester Herbert (Herb) Kikukawa inspected the new trail several times, as did Joseph (Joe) Souza and Gene Renard of the Division of State Parks.[38]

As of 2010, the 'Aihualama Trail remained a vital link in the Makiki-Tantalus Recreation Area. The switchback route provides access from Mānoa Valley to Pauoa Flats and the Nu'uanu overlook, and connects with trails leading to Tantalus, Hawai'i Nature Center, and Nu'uanu Valley. Na Ala Hele, the state trail and access program, keeps all the Makiki-Tantalus trails in good shape.

Nahuina, Moleka, and 'Ualaka'a

> If you're healthy, over 15, and concerned about outdoor recreational opportunities near urban Honolulu, you're the person we're looking for.
>
> —*Mālama I Ka Honua*, Sierra Club, Hawai'i Chapter newsletter, May 1979

In October 1913, acting governor Ernest A. Mott-Smith established the Honolulu Watershed Forest Reserve to protect the source of the city's water supply. Shortly afterward, the Territorial Forestry Division began reforesting the section of the reserve *mauka* (inland) of its Makiki Station. Forest nurseryman David Haughs set up a small nursery for growing tree seedlings below Pu'u Kākea (Sugarloaf). A trail crew also widened an old route, later called the Makiki Ridge or Maunalaha Trail, from the station to the new nursery.[39]

In the summer of 1915, forestry crews constructed a contour trail connecting the watersheds of Kānealole, Moleka, and Maunalaha Streams with the nursery. Later known as the Makiki Valley Trail, the route was accessible at either end from the Tantalus road and the recently built Round Top road. Linking the Makiki Station with the valley route were the Maunalaha Trail and a dirt road laid out in 1906 to facilitate construction of a water main from springs along upper Kānealole Stream to the Makiki reservoir.[40]

On December 4, 1920, the Hawaiian Trail and Mountain Club (HTMC) first hiked the Makiki Valley Trail. Led by John R. Bisho, the group assembled at Wilder and Makiki Streets on the Punahou streetcar line. The hikers then walked through the Makiki Station and took the valley trail to visit Pu'u Kākea and 'Ualaka'a (Round Top).[41]

Over the ensuing years the Makiki Valley Trail received steady use from hikers because of its short length and proximity to town. The Territorial Forestry Division featured the valley route as trail number 1 at one mile on its 1947 O'ahu map. The trail approach and description read,

> Go up Round Top Drive at end of Makiki Street 3.3 miles to foot of Sugarloaf Hill above Boy Scout camp. Trail starts from left side of road and winds across Makiki Valley to Tantalus Drive. Three branches run down to bottom of valley and road way connecting with Makiki Heights road.[42]

In the second half of 1954, work crews under the Hawaii Employment Program refurbished the valley trail and its branches at a cost of $4,394.34.[43]

In the middle 1970s, during an oil crisis, the State Department of Land and Natural Resources (DLNR) planned several new trails in newly created Makiki-Tantalus Recreation Area to provide easier access to the network, especially by bus, and to better connect the existing routes. The first undertaking was the 1.4-mile 'Aihualama Trail, which gave access to the system from Mānoa Valley. In September 1978, volunteers completed that project, coordinated by the Hawai'i Service Trip Program (HSTP) of the Sierra Club, Hawai'i Chapter.[44] The next three new trails were all short connector routes starting from the Makiki Valley Trail. Nahuina would link with the Kalāwahine Trail, a section of the old Castle Trail built by the HTMC in 1910. Moleka would hook up with the Mānoa Cliff Trail, also constructed by the HTMC, in 1911. The third, 'Ualaka'a, would provide access to 'Ualaka'a State Park.[45]

In early 1979, the DLNR contracted with the Sierra Club to build the Moleka and Nahuina Trails, each about three-quarters of a mile long. The HSTP Steering Committee, chaired by Andrea (Andie) Gill, developed a project plan modeled on the successful 'Aihualama undertaking the summer before. Volunteer crews under HSTP leaders would clear the vegetation and grade the pathway. The HSTP would provide tools, refreshments *pau hana* (after work), and a T-shirt for all participants. Work would run daily from July 14 through July 29 and then shift to weekends only during the first half of August.[46]

At 8 a.m. on Saturday, July 14, the first volunteer trail crew met at the Church of the Crossroads on University Avenue. The leader held a short meeting there to go over the day's work, tool use, and safety practices. The crew then carpooled to a small parking lot on Round Top Drive near the start of the Mānoa Cliff Trail. After stretching their legs, the volunteers unloaded the tools and began building the Moleka Trail. Working downhill, subsequent trail crews made steady progress toward the junction with the Makiki Valley Trail. During construction they unearthed some *pakalolo* (marijuana) plants and had to avoid a beehive in a tree. The volunteers especially enjoyed the lower section around Pu'u Kākea, where they worked in loose cinder rather than the usual mud and rock.[47]

After completing Moleka, the HSTP switched to the Nahuina Trail. Crews started from a small parking lot along Tantalus Drive and again worked downhill toward the Makiki Valley Trail. Along the way, they had to deal with an irate homeowner, a chain saw stuck in a tree trunk, and a tangle of hau branches. By the end of August the volunteers finished Nahuina and rerouted a short section of the valley trail near Tantalus Drive. For November 4, the Sierra Club scheduled a new loop hike made possible by the two new connector trails. Led by Atomman Kim, the group started near the Boy Scout Camp Earhorn and hiked around Pu'u 'Ōhi'a (Tantalus) using the Makiki Valley, Moleka, Mānoa Cliff, Kālawahine, and Nahuina Trails.[48]

In the spring of 1980, the HSTP began planning its fourth Makiki-Tantalus project, the 'Ualaka'a (rolling sweet potato) Trail, again sponsored and financed by the DLNR. Coordinated by Jim Yuen and Roy Ihara, volunteer crews started work in late May and finished the 0.53-mile connector ahead of schedule in late July. Altogether, ninety-six people participated in the project; Silver Piliwale was the oldest at seventy-seven, and Simon Sanidad volunteered the most times. 'Ualaka'a veterans celebrated the completion with a party at 'Ualaka'a State Park.[49]

As of 2010, the Nahuina, Moleka, and 'Ualaka'a Trails remained popular links in the Makiki-Tantalus Recreation Area. The three routes enable various loop hikes starting near the DLNR baseyard (formerly Makiki Station) or from several points along Tantalus and Round Top Drives. The most ambitious loop, called Makiki Tantalizer by the HTMC, incorporates eight different trails while circling Tantalus from the baseyard.

Nu'uanu

> What makes over a 100 people willing to hack uluhe, saw guava, and pick and shovel uncounted tons of earth to make a trail?
>
> —*Mālama I Ka Honua*, Sierra Club, Hawai'i Chapter newsletter, May–June 1983

In 1795, Nu'uanu (cool height) Valley was the site of a pivotal battle in Hawaiian history. That year Kamehameha, chief of the Big Island, invaded O'ahu, landing a large force at Wai'alae. Opposing him was an army massed in Nu'uanu Valley under the direction of Kalanikupule, the son of Kahekili, a Maui chief who had earlier occupied O'ahu. The first engagement took place at Pū'iwa near the present-day Judd Street. Kamehameha attacked the confident defenders, who were protected by a long rock wall. The battle was hotly contested until the invaders brought up a field cannon and trained sharpshooters. The fire from the cannon shattered rocks in the wall, and the sharpshooters killed a key commander. The startled O'ahu warriors broke ranks and retreated up the valley, closely pursued by the attackers. Gradually the retreat turned into a rout. Some defenders escaped up the sides of the valley. Most, including Kalanikupule, made a last stand at Nu'uanu Pali and were killed or driven over the cliff there. With the victory Kamehameha extended his control over all the Hawaiian Islands.[50]

During the battle a fierce skirmish had taken place above Kahuailanawai, a tranquil pool along Nu'uanu Stream. In early 1897, just over a hundred years later, David Haughs set up a small government nursery near the pool to grow tree seedlings to reforest the valley. In the early 1900s local youths renamed the pool or a nearby one Jackass Ginger after a nearby donkey and the surrounding yellow ginger.[51] In 1919, George Po'oloa described a visit to the pool.

> We reach the mauka [inland] part of the woods and there on the Waikiki side of the road is a hau grove and a single lehua tree beside a pool. This is a noted spot in by gone days. It was a place where strangers and natives alike enjoyed themselves stringing ginger leis to bedeck their hats and to wear around their necks.[52]

In 1935, the Civilian Conservation Corps (CCC) began a reforestation project in Nuʻuanu Valley. Crews planted the steep hillside above the pool with Norfolk Island (Cook) Pine seedlings. To access the area, the CCC men undoubtedly developed a contour trail across the slope and improved the makeshift route along the stream by Jackass Ginger pool. On April 6, territorial forester Charles S. Judd joined some Boy Scouts in Nuʻuanu for a tree-planting session. That Saturday morning they dug 190 holes and set Cook Pine seedlings in them.[53]

In 1953, the loop route above Nuʻuanu Stream was officially named the Judd Memorial Trail to honor the forester for his contributions during and before the CCC era. The next year unemployed workers hired under the Hawaii Employment Program cleared and regraded the 0.9-mile loop at a cost of $5,309.06. Starting from Ragsdale Drive, the route contoured through the Judd memorial grove of Cook Pines and then crossed the stream to Nuʻunau Pali Road opposite Reservoir No. 2. The return portion followed the east side of the stream past Jackass Ginger pool back to Ragsdale.[54]

For May 10, 1958, the Hawaiian Trail and Mountain Club (HTMC) scheduled the Judd Memorial Trail as a Saturday afternoon hike. The participants must have enjoyed the short stroll and refreshing swim because the club regularly held the Judd outing during the 1960s and 1970s. The description for the June 6, 1970, hike even mentions an optional scramble up the side of the valley to Pauoa Flats.[55]

Oʻahu forester Herbert (Herb) Kikukawa had always wanted to reopen the old Cooke Trail built from the main reservoir to the Nuʻuanu lookout in 1910. As that path was in restricted watershed, Kikukawa settled on a new route leaving from the Judd loop. On December 19, 1981, Jim Yuen led a hike for the Sierra Club, Hawaiʻi Chapter over the steep grade of the proposed route to connect the Judd and Pauoa Flats Trails. Called the Nuʻuanu Trail, the planned route was the fifth and final project of an ambitious expansion of the Makiki-Tantalus trail system in the 1970s. Yuen was the current chairman of the club's Hawaiʻi Service Trip Program (HSTP), which had coordinated the construction of the four previous trail projects, ʻAihualama, Nahuina, Moleka, and ʻUalakaʻa.[56]

Sponsored and financed by the State Department of Land and Natural Resources (DLNR), phase one of the Nuʻuanu project consisted of a 0.75-mile section from the Pauoa Flats Trail to the rim of Nuʻuanu Valley. In January 1983, HSTP volunteers started clearing and grading from the flats trail around the back of Pauoa Valley. Working weekends only, the trail crews made steady progress and completed the section in June. The arduous project attracted more than 150 volunteers who contributed more than three hundred man- and woman-days. On July 10, the HSTP hosted an all-day picnic to reward the volunteers and project coordinator Gerald Toyomura. On August 7, he led the first Sierra Club hike over the new section.[57]

Phase two of the trail project consisted of another 0.75-mile segment, from the Nuʻuanu Valley rim to a junction with the Judd Trail. The slope was uneven, rocky, and steep and required numerous switchbacks to descend to the valley floor. Because of the difficult terrain, the DLNR elected to hire a contractor to finish the project. Unfortunately, the contractor dug a narrow, humpy treadway, not up to Forestry Division or CCC standards. After serious reworking, phase two was finally completed in 1991.[58]

As of 2010, the Judd Trail was popular with tourists and locals alike. Most walk the short loop, go for a swim in Jackass Ginger pool, and call it a day. A few venture up the Nuʻuanu Trail for a good workout and stunning views of the valley below and Tantalus (Puʻu ʻŌhiʻa) above. Na Ala Hele, the state trail and access program, keeps both trails in good repair.

Maunawili and Maunawili Falls

> Guaranteed sore muscles, tired backs, a blister or two, new friends, clean air, great feeling of accomplishment, your own "piece of the trail"
>
> —*Mālama I Ka Honua*, Sierra Club, Hawaiʻi Chapter newsletter, May–June 1991

In the spring of 1878, Crown Princess Liliʻuokalani, her sister Likelike, and several friends rode horseback over Nuʻuanu Pali to spend a relaxing day at Maunawili Ranch, owned by the Boyd family. As the group was leaving the ranch in the late afternoon, one of her companions, perhaps Colonel James Boyd, received a lei and a warm embrace from a lovely Hawaiian woman. The romantic princess quietly observed the fond farewell by the ranch gate. During the ride back to Honolulu, Liliʻuokalani worked out the haunting melody for a love song and later composed the words at her home, Washington Place. Titled Aloha ʻOe (Farewell to Thee), the composition became a popular and classic song of love and parting. Liliʻuokalani later became queen and the last monarch of the Kingdom of Hawaiʻi.[59]

That same year part-Hawaiian John A. Cummins established a small plantation to grow sugar cane in dry Waimānalo. To supplement pumped water for irrigation, his company, Waimanalo Sugar, began construction of the Maunawili Ditch in 1893. Lined with dirt and cement, the ditch tapped water from *mauka* (inland) tunnels, springs, and streams in Maunawili and Waimānalo. The Maunawili section eventually had twenty flumes and trestles to channel the water to the Olomana Tunnel under Aniani Nui Ridge and into Waimānalo.[60]

On July 23, 1922, the Hawaiian Trail and Mountain Club (HTMC) first scheduled an outing in Maunawili (twisted mountain) Valley. Seven hikers met at the end of the Nuʻuanu streetcar line and walked up the valley and over the *pali* to the windward side. The group hiked to Maunawili Ranch and then along the irrigation ditch. The HTMC repeated the outing in 1924 and 1925, but sometime afterward the ranch was closed to hiking.[61]

In the late 1940s, the HTMC developed a rambling foothill hike incorporating some of the makeshift trails in Maunawili Valley. The loop route often changed from year to year but usually visited the watersheds of Palapū, ʻŌmaʻo, and Maunawili Streams while avoiding the ranch. Highlights included a slippery slide down a stream chute, a tightrope walk on a ditch trestle, and a cooling dip in the spacious pool at the base of Maunawili Falls. With those attractions the hike proved very popular and was scheduled regularly through 1990.[62]

In May 1991, the State Division of Fish and Wildlife within the Department of Land and Natural Resources (DLNR) issued a program plan for Na Ala Hele, the state trail and access system. The plan included a proposed Oʻahu demonstration trail, called Koʻolaupoko. Earlier, HTMC member Richard H. (Dick) Davis had scouted and marked the nine-mile route. It started at Nuʻuanu Pali lookout, contoured around the back of Maunawili Valley at the base of the Koʻolau cliffs, and crossed Aniani Nui Ridge into Waimānalo town. The DLNR contracted with the Hawaiʻi Service Trip Program (HSTP) of the Sierra Club, Hawaiʻi Chapter to construct the first three miles of trail from the horseshoe curve on the Old Pali Road to Maunawili Stream.[63]

The HSTP was the muscular arm of the Sierra Club involved in trail and fence building and habitat restoration. For Koʻolaupoko, the group used the same coordination and construction practices that had proved so successful in five previous DLNR trail projects in the Makiki-Tantalus area. Volunteer crews under HSTP leaders would wield cane knives and saws to clear brush and trees, and picks, pulaskis, and shovels to dig and remove dirt, and hoes to smooth the path. Volunteers needed only to be reasonably fit, fifteen years old or older, and bring lunch, water, and heavy gloves.

The HSTP would provide tools, drinks, and snacks *pau hana* (after work), and a T-shirt for those working three or more days. In June, the HSTP held several orientation meetings to familiarize volunteers with the project and the various tools they would be using.[64]

On May 25, the first volunteer trail crew met at the Church of the Crossroads in Moʻiliʻili. The leader described the day's work, tool use, and safety procedures, and each participant signed a liability waiver. The crew then carpooled to the hairpin turn of the Pali Highway and began clearing and grading toward Waimānalo. About noon the volunteers took a half-hour break for lunch and then resumed work until 3 p.m. After admiring their new section, the trail crew returned to their cars for refreshments and a ride back to town.[65]

Trail construction continued each weekend though the summer and into fall. As work progressed, the HSTP developed additional access routes from Maunawili subdivision to minimize the distance walked to the job site. By early November the crews completed two and a half miles to ʻŌmaʻo Stream. Because of a decline in the number of volunteers, the HSTP extended the schedule into December. On December 14, a jubilant crew reached the three-mile mark past Maunawili Stream. During the summer, prisoners from Oʻahu Correctional Facility constructed a section of trail from Waimānalo.[66]

In 1992, the DLNR contracted with the HSTP for another two miles of the demonstration route, renamed the Maunawili Trail. The first crew hit the trail on May 23, and the last crew of the season finished up in October. Neil Morimoto was the capable coordinator of the phase two project. He worked most weekends, wielding a chain saw, and providing watermelon *pau hana*.[67]

In 1993, the HSTP completed another two miles of the Maunawili project, sponsored and financed by the DLNR. Coordinated by Gina Goodman, crews averaging fifteen people cleared, dug, and graded on weekends that summer and fall. The project attracted 225 volunteers who worked eight hundred man- and woman-days. On November 16, 115 trail builders gathered at the HTMC clubhouse in Waimānalo to celebrate the completion of the third phase. Singled out for their contributions were Goodman, Davis, Vincent Holmes, Ralph Inouye, and others.[68]

By the end of 1993 the Maunawili Trail stretched the entire nine miles from the Pali lookout to Waimānalo. Volunteers coordinated by the HSTP had built seven miles in three phases. The remaining two miles on the Waimānalo side were constructed by prisoners, Boy Scouts, and the Third Battalion, Third Marines from Kāneʻohe Bay. The total cost of the trail was just under $50,000.[69]

Volunteers building the Maunawili Trail, circa 1991. (Sierra Club, Hawai'i Chapter Archives)

During the summer of 1996, the DLNR and the HSTP collaborated on the construction of the Maunawili Falls Trail. Coordinated by Wally Hiraoka, volunteer crews built a 0.8-mile access trail from the Maunawili subdivision to the falls and its popular swimming hole. More than 130 persons participated in the project, with 60 earning a T-shirt for multiple days of work. On the morning of October 5, an opening and dedication ceremony took place at the trailhead with Honolulu mayor Jeremy Harris and DLNR chairman Michael Wilson attending. After the traditional parting of the *maile lei* at 9:45 a.m., about two hundred hikers streamed down the trail toward the falls. On October 26, the trail builders enjoyed a banquet at nearby Luana Hills Country Club. Honored as the top volunteer was HTMC member Richard (Dick) Schmidt.[70]

The HSTP returned to the Maunawili Trail during the summer of 1997. Coordinated by Randy Ching, volunteer trail crews improved the first two miles of that route starting from the hairpin turn. The next summer found HSTP crews constructing a 0.5-mile route linking the falls trail with the Maunawili Trail. On October 11, 1998, the Sierra Club hiked all three trails in celebration of their connection and final completion.[71]

As of 2010, both the Maunawili and Maunawili Falls Trails were well-traveled hiking routes. The falls trail is downright crowded, especially on sunny weekend afternoons. The section of the Maunawili Trail from the hairpin turn to the falls connector is a popular out-and-back outing. The entire nine miles is less often done because of the distance and the complicated car shuttle. Na Ala Hele keeps both trails in good shape.

Notes

Hawaiian Trails

1. Russell A. Apple, *Trails from Steppingstones to Kerbstones* (Honolulu: Bishop Museum Press, 1965), 22, 64–65; Lorrin Thurston, "A Plea for Mountain Trails," *Honolulu Advertiser*, February 26, 1922, section 2, page 1.
2. John Papa Ii, *Fragments of Hawaiian History* (Honolulu: Bishop Museum Press, 1983), 89–98.
3. *The Hawaiian Journal of John B. Whitman, An Account of the Sandwich Islands*, ed. John Dominis Holt (Honolulu: Topgallant Publishing Company, Ltd., 1979), 67.
4. Daniel Tyerman and George Bennett, *Journal of Voyages and Travels* (London: Frederick Westley and A. H. Davis, 1831), I, 432.
5. George A. Byron, *Voyage of the H.M.S. Blonde to the Sandwich Islands in the Years 1824–1825* (London: John Murray, 1826), 140–141.
6. Frederic D. Bennett, *Narrative of a Whaling Voyage Round the Globe from the Year 1833–1836* (New York: Da Capo Press, 1970), I, 202.
7. E. S. Craighill Handy and Elizabeth Green Handy, *Native Planters in Old Hawaii* (Honolulu: Bishop Museum Press, 1991), 445–446.
8. Abraham Fornander, *Fornander Collection of Hawaiian Antiquities and Folklore* (Honolulu: Bishop Museum Press, 1918), V, 314–320.
9. E. O. Hall, "Notes of a Tour Around Oahu," *Hawaiian Spectator*, 1839, 105.
10. Ibid., 106.
11. John A. Cummins, "Around Oahu in Days of Old," *Mid-Pacific Magazine*, September 1913, 233–243.
12. *The Weekly News Muster*, No. 5, 1898.
13. W. F. Martin and C. H. Pierce, *Water Resources of Hawaii 1909–1911* (Government Printing Office, 1913), 174.
14. Charles S. Judd, *Daily Journal 1917*, August 8, 1917, State Archives.
15. Thomas G. Thrum, *Hawaiian Folk Tales* (New York: AMS Press, 1978), 199; "Kaliuwaa-Sacred Falls," *Paradise of the Pacific*, March 1938, 33.
16. Zarel Jones, "Hikers of Hawaiian Trail and Mountain Club Prefer Their Scenics on the Hoof," *Paradise of the Pacific*, July 1925, 26.
17. "Sacred Falls to Be Objective of Hikers Sunday," *Pacific Commercial Advertiser*, June 22, 1920, 2–6.
18. Kermit Kosch, "Conquering Sacred Falls," *Paradise of the Pacific*, April 1934, 7–10.
19. "Sacred Falls Park 350 Acres in Size Planned," *Honolulu Star-Bulletin*, December 10, 1934, 1.
20. Charles S. Judd, *Daily Journal 1934*, December 15, 1934. State Archives.
21. Harry Whitten, "Trail Ways," *Honolulu Star-Bulletin*, February 2, 1952, 22.
22. Harry Whitten, "Trail Ways," *Honolulu Star-Bulletin*. 1950s scrapbook, HTMC Archives.
23. "Nothing Sacred at Sacred Falls," *Paradise of the Pacific*, March 1963, 4.

24. "First Climb above Cliffs at Sacred Falls," *Honolulu Star-Bulletin*, November 16, 1963, 11; Richard H. Davis, interview, July 27, 2001.
25. HTMC hike schedule, February 25, 1978, HTMC Archives.
26. HTMC hike schedule, March 24, 1996, HTMC Archives; Stuart Ball, hike notes, March 24, 1996.
27. Randall W. Jibson and Rex L. Baum, "Assessment of Landslide Hazard in Kaluanui and Maakua Gulches, Oahu, Hawaii Following the 9 May 1999 Sacred Falls Landslide." http://landslides.usgs.gov/recent/archives/1999sacredfalls.php.
28. Merlin Wollenzein, "Merlin and Friends Hawaiian Adventure Site." http://www.merman.us, Activities, Falls, Sacred.
29. "Loaa Kekahi mau Alahele o ke au Kahiko" (Some Old Trails Are Found), *Kuokoa*, February 10, 1922, 3.
30. "Hikers Find Old Hawaiian Trail," *Honolulu Advertiser*, February 6, 1922, 1.
31. *Kuokoa*, February 10, 1922.
32. HTMC hike schedule, June 4 and December 3, 1922, HTMC Archives.
33. HTMC hike schedule, December 11, 1932, HTMC Archives.
34. Charles S. Judd, *Daily Journal 1934*, September 19, 1934, State Archives.
35. Major Roy F. Lynd, "Mountain Trails of Oahu," 1935, and Sergeant Tracy, "Roads and Trails of Oahu," 1939, unpublished pamphlets at the Tropic Lightning Museum.
36. HTMC hike schedule, November 12, 1950, HTMC Archives; Harry Whitten, "Trail Ways," *Honolulu Star-Bulletin*, November 11, 1950, 10.
37. HTMC hike schedule, January 20, 1968, HTMC Archives.
38. HTMC hike schedule, December 11, 1955, HTMC Archives.
39. Erwin N. Thompson, *Pacific Ocean Engineers, History of the U.S. Army Corps of Engineers in the Pacific, 1905–1980* (Honolulu: U.S. Army Corps of Engineers, 1980), 282.
40. HTMC hike schedule, December 11, 1959, and April 15, 1962, HTMC Archives.
41. HTMC hike schedule, February 29, 1964, HTMC Archives.
42. HTMC hike schedule, July 16, 1966, HTMC Archives.
43. HTMC hike schedule, December 4, 1982, HTMC Archives.
44. HTMC hike schedule, October 17, 1998, HTMC Archives.
45. John Papa Ii, *Fragments of Hawaiian History* (Honolulu: Bishop Museum Press, 1983), 96–97.
46. Ross Cordy, *An Ancient History of Waianae* (Honolulu: Mutual Publishing, 2002), 62; J. Gilbert McAllister, *Archaeology of Oahu* (Honolulu: Bernice P. Bishop Museum Bulletin 104, 1985), 116.
47. E. S. Craighill Handy and Elizabeth Green Handy, *Native Planters in Old Hawaii* (Honolulu: Bishop Museum Press, 1991), 468; Gilbert McAllister, *Archaeology of Oahu* (Honolulu: Bernice P. Bishop Museum Bulletin 104, 1985), 119.
48. Gilbert McAllister, *Archaeology of Oahu* (Honolulu: Bernice P. Bishop Museum Bulletin 104, 1985), 117.
49. *Paradise of the Pacific*, August 1889, 4; Bob Krauss, *Historic Waianae* (Norfolk Island, Aust.: Island Heritage, Ltd., 1973), 37–42.
50. Captain W. Ellerbrock, "A Record Mountain March," *Mid-Pacific Magazine*, February 1915, 134–139.
51. "Fifty-One Hikers Visit Makaha Vale," *Honolulu Star-Bulletin*, July 18, 1921, 5.
52. HTMC hike schedule, July 15, 1928, HTMC Archives.
53. Charles S. Judd, *Daily Journal 1929*, March 5, 1929, State Archives.
54. Charles S. Judd to Glenn W. Russ, December 12, 1932, Judd manuscript, State Archives, M-77, Box 1-14.
55. Charles S. Judd, *Daily Journal 1932*, December 11, 1932, State Archives.
56. Charles S. Judd to Captain Raymond G. Sherman, December 12, 1932, Judd manuscript, State Archives, M-77, Box 1-14; Charles S. Judd, *Daily Journal 1933*, January 8, 1933, State Archives.

57. Glenn W. Russ, "Routine Report of the Assistant Forester, October 1932," State Archives, Com 2-36, Judd, Reports, Monthly, Russ; "Trails on the Island of Oahu," *The Sales Builder*, May 1938, 8–9.
58. Harry Whitten, "Trail Ways," *Honolulu Star-Bulletin*, April 24, 1954, Hawaiian Life section, 15.
59. HTMC hike schedule, April 20, 1958, HTMC Archives.
60. HTMC hike schedule, April 14, 1963, HTMC Archives.
61. HTMC hike schedule, December 2, 1973, HTMC Archives.
62. HTMC hike schedule, June 9, 1974, HTMC Archives.
63. HTMC hike schedule, February 29, 1976, HTMC Archives.
64. HTMC hike schedule, January 28, 2007, HTMC Archives.
65. John Papa Ii, *Fragments of Hawaiian History* (Honolulu: Bishop Museum Press, 1983), 97.
66. Oliver Pomeroy Emerson, *Pioneer Days in Hawaii* (Garden City, N.Y.: Doubleday, Doren and Company, Inc., 1928), 70.
67. Charles Wilkes, *Narrative of the United States Exploring Expedition* (Philadelphia: Lea and Blanchard, 1845), IV, 78.
68. John Effinger, "A Tramp Around Oahu," *Paradise of the Pacific*, June 1895, 87–91.
69. Joseph B. Stickney, "Mokuleia," *Mid-Pacific Magazine*, May 1914, 475–477.
70. Major Roy F. Lynd, "Mountain Trails of Oahu," 1935, and Sergeant Tracy, "Roads and Trails of Oahu," 1939, unpublished pamphlets at the Tropic Lightning Museum.
71. T. P. Cadle, "The DePonte Trail," *Paradise of the Pacific*, September 1920, 28.
72. Ibid., 28–29.
73. "Hikers Plan Tramp Across Kaala," *Pacific Commercial Advertiser*, 1920s scrapbook, HTMC Archives.
74. T. P. Cadle, "From Kaena Point to Kaala," *Paradise of the Pacific*, December 1921, 58–60.
75. "Mountain Hikers Retrace Old Trail," *Pacific Commercial Advertiser*, August 7, 1922, 2.
76. "Highest Peak on Oahu Is Climbed," *Honolulu Star-Bulletin*, August 23, 1922, 10.
77. Charles S. Judd, *Daily Journal 1922*, August 30, 1922, State Archives.
78. H. McK., "Surmounting Oahu's Highest Peak Proves Grueling Task for Wahine Mountaineers," *Pacific Commercial Advertiser*, February 8, 1925, 2.
79. Charles S. Judd, "Program for Emergency Conservation Work—Territory of Hawaii, October 28, 1933," State Archives, com 2-12, Brown, ECW, 1933–34.
80. Harry Whitten, "Trail Ways," *Honolulu Star-Bulletin*, November 8, 1952, 3.
81. "Dupont—November 9, 1952," HTMC Archives.
82. "Principal Falls 300 Feet to Death on Hiking Trail," *Honolulu Star-Bulletin*, August 2, 1956, 1; Lorin Gill, interview, April 9, 2008.
83. Harry Whitten, "3-Day Kaala Hike Begins Saturday," *Honolulu Star-Bulletin*, February 18, 1959, 36; HTMC hike schedule, February 21–23, 1959, HTMC Archives.
84. Harry Whitten, "Kaala Hikers Will Ignore New Road," *Honolulu Star-Bulletin*, March 7, 1964, 17.
85. HTMC hike schedule, March 8, 1964, HTMC Archives.
86. John Papa Ii, *Fragments of Hawaiian History* (Honolulu: Bishop Museum Press, 1983), 98.
87. Hawaiian Mission Children's Society, *Missionary Album* (Honolulu: Hawaiian Mission Children's Society, 1969), 64–65.
88. Levi Chamberlain, "Tour Around Oahu, 1928," Sixty-Fifth Annual Report of the Hawaiian Historical Society for the Year 1956, 37.
89. Ibid., 37.
90. U.S. Army, "Island of Oahu Map," 1920s, State Archives, G4382.O2P1(192-).U54.A7.
91. HTMC hike schedule, February 16, 1930, HTMC Archives.
92. HTMC hike schedule, March 5, 1933, HTMC Archives.
93. HTMC hike schedule, March 4, 1934, HTMC Archives.

94. Paul Rosendahl, "Archaeological Inventory and Evaluation Report for Installation Environmental Impact Statement for U.S. Army Support Command, Hawaii," 1977, 2-2-23.
95. Francis Eble, Paul Cleghorn, and Thomas L. Jackson, "Archaeological Investigation at Proposed MK-19 Range Makua Military Reservation, Waianae District, Oahu Hawaii." Final Report, December 1995, 19.

Kama'āina and Club Trails (1842-1922)

1. Mānoa Valley Residents, *Mānoa, the Story of a Valley* (Honolulu: Mutual Publishing Company, 1994), 7-10.
2. John Papa Ii, *Fragments of Hawaiian History* (Honolulu: Bishop Museum Press, 1983), 92.
3. Lorrin Thurston, "A Plea for Mountain Trails," *Honolulu Advertiser*, February 26, 1922, section 2, page 1.
4. Thomas G. Thrum, *Thrum's Hawaiian Annual 1928* (Honolulu: The Printshop Company, Ltd., 1928), 105-106.
5. Lorrin Thurston, "A Plea for Mountain Trails," *Honolulu Advertiser*, February 26, 1922, section 2, page 1.
6. Henry M. Whitney, *The Hawaiian Guide Book* (Honolulu: Henry M. Whitney, 1875), 22-23.
7. "The Valleys Near Honolulu," *Paradise of the Pacific*, December 1888, 6.
8. Mānoa Valley Residents, *Mānoa, the Story of a Valley* (Honolulu: Mutual Publishing Company, 1994), 44, 52, 87.
9. MacKinnon Simpson and John Brizdle, *Streetcar Days in Honolulu* (Honolulu: JLB Press, 2000), frontpiece, 72-73; Ferdinand J. H. Schnack, *Aloha Guide* (Honolulu: *Honolulu Star-Bulletin*, 1915), 119-120.
10. Valerie Noble, *Hawaiian Prophet: Alexander Hume Ford* (Smithtown: Exposition Press, 1980), 43.
11. Ibid., 132
12. Ibid., 132.
13. Ibid., 54.
14. Ibid., 57, 66.
15. HTMC bulletin, July 1910, HTMC Archives.
16. Ibid.
17. Hawaiian Trail and Mountain Club Constitution, 1910, HTMC Archives.
18. Alexander Hume Ford, "Hawaii's Trail and Mountain Club, Its Aims, Progress and Desires," *Pacific Commercial Advertiser*, July 17, 1910, 4; A. Ford, "The Trail and Mountain Club of Hawaii and Its Part in the Pan Pacific Movement," *Mid-Pacific Magazine*, November 1916, 429-431.
19. Alexander Hume Ford, "Hawaii's Trail and Mountain Club, Its Aims, Progress and Desires," *Pacific Commercial Advertiser*, July 17, 1910, 4; "Trail and Mountain Climbers to Start," *Pacific Commercial Advertiser*, July 22, 1910, 7.
20. "Trail and Mountain Club Is Getting Things Going," *Pacific Commercial Advertiser*, July 21, 1911, 3; "Initiation Was Balked by Fog," *Pacific Commercial Advertiser*, June 19, 1911, 9.
21. Alexander Hume Ford, "Hawaii's Trail and Mountain Club, Its Aims, Progress and Desires," *Pacific Commercial Advertiser*, July 17, 1910, 4.
22. "Trail and Mountain Club Is Getting Things Going," *Pacific Commercial Advertiser*, July 21, 1911, 3.
23. William R. Castle to City and County of Honolulu, September 7, 1911, HTMC Archives.
24. Charles S. Judd, "Report of the Superintendent of Forestry, September 1913," *The Hawaiian Forester and Agriculturist*, October 1913, 297.
25. A. Ford, "The Trail and Mountain Club of Hawaii and Its Part in the Pan Pacific Movement," *Mid-Pacific Magazine*, November 1916, 429; J. S. Donaghho, "Mountain Trails near Honolulu" (map), 1915, State and HTMC Archives.

26. A. Ford, "Tramps of the Trail and Mountain Club," *Mid-Pacific Magazine*, June 1915, 581–584.
27. Ferdinand J. H. Schnack, *Aloha Guide* (Honolulu: *Honolulu Star-Bulletin*, 1915), 117–120.
28. R. J. Baker, "A Brief History of the Hawaiian Trail and Mountain Club" (unpublished manuscript, HTMC Archives, 1960), 11.
29. Alexander H. Ford to Charles S. Judd, March 31, 1919, HTMC Archives.
30. R. J. Baker, "A Brief History of the Hawaiian Trail and Mountain Club" (unpublished manuscript, HTMC Archives, 1960), 12.
31. Lawrence H. Daingerfield, "Hawaiian Trail and Mountain Club," in *Thrum's Hawaiian Annual 1920* (Honolulu: The Printshop Company, Ltd., 1920), 92.
32. *The Hawaiian Forester and Agriculturist*, June 1922, 126–133, 146–147.
33. Alexander Hume Ford, "Hawaii's Trail and Mountain Club, Its Aims, Progress and Desires," *Pacific Commercial Advertiser*, July 17, 1910, 4.
34. "To the Manor Born," *Mid-Pacific Magazine*, June 1912, 592–593.
35. "Trail and Mountain Climbers to Start," *Pacific Commercial Advertiser*, July 22, 1910, 7.
36. Alexander Hume Ford, "Hawaii's Trail and Mountain Club, Its Aims, Progress and Desires," *Pacific Commercial Advertiser*, July 17, 1910, 4; "One Day Along a Mountain Trail," *Pacific Commercial Advertiser*, September 10, 1911, 6; J. S. Donaghho, "A Plea for Mountain Trails," *Honolulu Advertiser*, March 2, 1922, 2, 1; R. J. Baker, "A Brief History of the Hawaiian Trail and Mountain Club" (unpublished manuscript, HTMC Archives, 1960), 4; John Hall, "History of the HTMC-Part I," HTMC newsletter, July–September 2004.
37. "Trail and Mountain Club Is Getting Things Going," *Pacific Commercial Advertiser*, July 21, 1911, 3; "Initiation Was Balked by Fog," *Pacific Commercial Advertiser*, June 19, 1911, 9.
38. "Initiation Was Balked by Fog," *Pacific Commercial Advertiser*, June 19, 1911, 9.
39. "One Day Along a Mountain Trail," *Pacific Commercial Advertiser*, September 10, 1911, 6.
40. Charles S. Judd, "Report of the Superintendent of Forestry, September 1913," *The Hawaiian Forester and Agriculturist*, October 1913, 297.
41. Charles S. Judd, *Daily Journal 1918*, October 11, 1918, State Archives; "Report of the Superintendent of Forestry, October 1918," *The Hawaiian Forester and Agriculturist*, October 1918, 447–448.
42. Harold H. Yost, "The Notch in the Ridge," *Paradise of the Pacific*, September 1921, 26.
43. Ibid., 26, 28.
44. "Report of the Superintendent of Forestry, November 1921," *The Hawaiian Forester and Agriculturist*, February 1922, 14–15.
45. *The Hawaiian Forester and Agriculturist*, June 1922, 126–133, 146–147.
46. Charles S. Judd, *Daily Journal 1922*, May 26, 1922, State Archives; *The Hawaiian Forester and Agriculturist*, August 1922, 173, 175.
47. Lawrence Hite Daingerfield, "Climbing Konahuanui," *Paradise of the Pacific*, April 1922, 26.
48. HTMC hike schedule, February 3, 1924, HTMC Archives.
49. Gunder E. Olson, "Project Superintendent's Narrative Report, Honolulu Unit, Island of Oahu, Fourth Enrollment Period, October 1, 1934–March 31, 1935," Talbert Takahama papers.
50. Joseph Neilson, interview, February 11, 2000.
51. Stuart Ball, hike notes, August 11, 1996.
52. "Ukulele Patrol Initiates Victim," *Pacific Commercial Advertiser*, August 7, 1911, 1.
53. "Trail and Mountain Club Is Getting Things Going," *Pacific Commercial Advertiser*, July 21, 1911, 3.
54. Ibid.
55. "Moonlight Picnic Is Lure for Club Hikers," *Honolulu Star-Bulletin*, October 11, 1919, 8.
56. "Boy Scouts to Keep Hikers on Straight Path," *Pacific Commercial Advertiser*, November 1, 1919, second section, 4.

57. HTMC hike schedule, January 14, 1923, HTMC Archives.
58. HTMC hike schedule, August 15, 1926, HTMC Archives.
59. *The Hawaiian Forester and Agriculturist,* October–December 1932, 171.
60. Charles S. Judd, *Daily Journal 1933,* November 12, 1933, State Archives.
61. Charles S. Judd, "Program for Emergency Conservation Work, Territory of Hawaii, Second Enrollment Period: October 1, 1934 to March 31, 1935" (June 7, 1934), 2, State Archives, com 2–12, Brown, ECW, 1933–34.
62. Charles S. Judd, *Daily Journal 1933,* December 13 and 17, 1933, State Archives.
63. Gunder E. Olson, "Project Superintendent's Narrative Report, Honolulu Unit, Island of Oahu, Fourth Enrollment Period, October 1, 1934–March 31, 1935," Talbert Takahama papers.
64. Gunder E. Olson, "Narrative Report—Island of Oahu, Men Working from Homes, Fifth Enrollment Period, April 1 to September 30, 1935," 14, State Archives, Com 2–35, Judd, ECW Reports 1935; Charles S. Judd, "Report of the Territorial Forester for the Calendar Year 1935" (Territory of Hawaii, Board of Commissioners of Agriculture and Forestry, Division of Forestry), State Archives, com 2-35, Reports of the Territorial Forester, 1935–36 Calendar Year.
65. HTMC hike schedule, September 29, 1935, HTMC Archives.
66. Charles S. Judd, *Daily Journal 1935,* April 8, 1935; Charles S. Judd, *Daily Journal 1936,* April 11, 1936; Charles S. Judd, *Daily Journal 1936,* May 1, 1936, State Archives.
67. Division of Forestry, Forest Trail Map of the Island of Oahu (1947).
68. Report of the Board of Commissioners of Agriculture and Forestry of the Territory of Hawaii, Biennial Period ending 6/30/56, 102.
69. Lorin Gill, interview, September 11, 2007.
70. HTMC newsletter, June 1983, HTMC Archives.
71. HTMC hike schedule, October 27, 1990, HTMC Archives.
72. HTMC hike schedule, July 19, 1981, HTMC Archives.
73. Raymond Tabata and John Moriyama, *Manoa Cliffs Trail, Plant Identification Guide and Brief Descriptions for Selected Plants* (Honolulu: Division of Forestry and Wildlife, Department of Land and Natural Resources, 1982).
74. *Mānoa Cliff Trail Plant Guide* (Honolulu: Hawai'i Nature Center, 1996); Jennie Peterson, interview, September 5, 2007.
75. HTMC newsletter, June 1998, HTMC Archives; Jennie Peterson, interview, September 5, 2007; *Kalāwahine Trail Nature Guide* (Honolulu: Hawai'i Nature Center).
76. Mashuri Waite, interview, March 11, 2008; Brandon Stone, interview, March 11, 2008.
77. Gordon A. Macdonald, Agatin T. Abbott, and Frank L. Peterson, *Volcanoes in the Sea* (Honolulu: University of Hawai'i Press, 1983), 442.
78. Nathaniel B. Emerson, *Pele and Hiiaka, a Myth of Hawaii* (Honolulu: *Honolulu Star-Bulletin,* 1915), 104; Mary Kawena Pukui, Samuel H. Elbert, and Esther T. Mookini, *Place Names of Hawaii* (Honolulu: University Press of Hawai'i, 1981), 61.
79. Lorrin Thurston, "A Plea for Mountain Trails," *Honolulu Advertiser,* February 26, 1922, section 2, page 1.
80. "The Valleys Near Honolulu," *Paradise of the Pacific,* December 1888, 6.
81. Alexander Hume Ford, "Hawaii's Trail and Mountain Club, Its Aims, Progress and Desires," *Pacific Commercial Advertiser,* July 17, 1910, 4.
82. "Trail and Mountain Climbers to Start," *Pacific Commercial Advertiser,* July 22, 1910, 7.
83. "Governor Makes a Record Climb," *Pacific Commercial Advertiser,* September 5, 1911, 4.
84. F. Cartwright, "A Stiff Tramp," *Mid-Pacific Magazine,* January 1913, 61.
85. Ibid.
86. Ibid.
87. Charles S. Judd, *Daily Journal 1916,* March 22 and August 26, 1916, State Archives.
88. "Climbers Plan Many Hikes in Present Month," *Pacific Commercial Advertiser,* November 4, 1919, 4.
89. T. P. Cadle, "Perilous Descent on Pali Performed," *Honolulu Star-Bulletin,* December 17, 1921, Society section, 1.

90. *The Hawaiian Forester and Agriculturist*, June 1922, 126–133, 146–147.
91. Charles S. Judd, *Daily Journal 1922*, June 2, 1922, State Archives.
92. HTMC hike schedule, May 1, 1977, HTMC Archives.
93. HTMC hike schedule, July 20, 1986, HTMC Archives.
94. Stuart Ball, hike notes, April 6, 1991.
95. "The Pearl of Honolulu Suburbs," *Paradise of the Pacific*, December 1910, 55–57.
96. "Beautiful Palolo Hill" (advertisement), *Mid-Pacific Magazine*, January 1912, 98.
97. "Trail and Mountain Club Is Getting Things Going," *Pacific Commercial Advertiser*, July 21, 1911, 3.
98. Hawaiian Trail and Mountain Club, guide booklet, circa 1915, HTMC Archives.
99. "T & M Will Hold Pleasant Hikes During December," *Pacific Commercial Advertiser*, Hawaiian Trail and Mountain Club 1920s scrapbook, HTMC Archives.
100. "December Trail Club Schedule Now Arranged," *Pacific Commercial Advertiser*, Hawaiian Trail and Mountain Club 1920s scrapbook, HTMC Archives.
101. "Class A Hike on Sunday Morning," *Pacific Commercial Advertiser*, February 12, 1921, 5; "Some View Say Mountain Fans," *Pacific Commercial Advertiser*, February 14, 1921, 6.
102. "Trail and Mountain Club Off to Scale Mauna Loa," *Pacific Commercial Advertiser*, Hawaiian Trail and Mountain Club 1920s scrapbook, HTMC Archives.
103. Charles S. Judd, *Daily Journal 1925*, September 21, 1925, State Archives.
104. Charles S. Judd, *Daily Journal 1927*, January 27, 1927, State Archives; *The Hawaiian Forester and Agriculturist*, January–March 1927, 7.
105. HTMC hike schedule, October 14, 1928, HTMC Archives.
106. HTMC hike schedule, September 23, 1945, HTMC Archives.
107. Thomas R. L. McGuire, "More Interesting Trails on Oahu," *Honolulu Star-Bulletin*, July 30, 1946, 15.
108. HTMC hike schedule and record, January 22, 1961, HTMC Archives; Erwin N. Thompson, *Pacific Ocean Engineers, History of the U.S. Army Corps of Engineers in the Pacific, 1905–1980* (Honolulu: U.S. Army Corps of Engineers, 1980), 115.
109. HTMC hike schedule, May 20, 1962, HTMC Archives.
110. Gordon A. Macdonald, Agatin T. Abbott, and Frank L. Peterson, *Volcanoes in the Sea* (Honolulu: University of Hawai'i Press, 1983), 433.
111. Mary Kawena Pukui, Samuel H. Elbert, and Esther T. Mookini, *Place Names of Hawaii* (Honolulu: University Press of Hawai'i, 1981), 5, 170, 176.
112. Abraham Fornander, *Fornander Collection of Hawaiian Antiquities and Folk-lore* (Honolulu: Bishop Museum Press, 1918), V, 374.
113. Willis T. Pope, "Geography from the Mountain Tops," *Mid-Pacific Magazine*, May 1911, 541.
114. "Four Girls Climb to Top of Olomana Peak," *Pacific Commercial Advertiser*, March 14, 1921, 5; "Ascent of Olomana Peak Made by Women," *Honolulu Star-Bulletin*, March 15, 1921, 8.
115. "Three Hikers Scale Needle of Olomana," *Honolulu Star-Bulletin*, March 21, 1921, 5; Evelyn Breckons, "The Lure of Oahu's Mountain Trails," *Honolulu Star-Bulletin*, March 26, 1921, Society section, 1.
116. "Hikers Travel Over Olomana: Difficult Feat," *Honolulu Advertiser*, April 20, 1924, 7; HTMC hike schedule, April 17, 1924, HTMC Archives.
117. HTMC hike schedule, August 26, 1945, HTMC Archives.
118. HTMC hike schedule and record, December 26, 1954, HTMC Archives.
119. *A Short History of Schofield Barracks* (Honolulu: Tropic Lightning Museum, 1999), 1.
120. "Ukulele Patrol Is Captured by Cavalry," *Pacific Commercial Advertiser*, 1920s scrapbook, HTMC Archives; "Trail and Mountain Club Is Getting Things Going," *Pacific Commercial Advertiser*, July 21, 1911, 3.
121. R. E. Lambert, "Kaala, the Highest of Them All," *Mid-Pacific Magazine*, September 1915, 289–291.
122. Ruth Eloise Brown, "Topping Oahu's Loftiest Mount," *Paradise of the Pacific*, August 1919, 25.

123. Ibid., 26.
124. T. P. Cadle, "The DePonte Trail," *Paradise of the Pacific*, September 1920, 28–29.
125. "Hikers Go Over Old Trail to Kaala Peak," *Honolulu Star-Bulletin*, March 27, 1922, 9.
126. "Report of the Superintendent of Forestry, November 1923," *The Hawaiian Forester and Agriculturist*, January–March 1924, 15.
127. Charles S. Judd, *Daily Journal 1931*, July 26, 1931, State Archives.
128. Charles S. Judd, "Program for Emergency Conservation Work—Territory of Hawaii," October 28, 1933, 11, State Archives, com 2-12 Brown, ECW, 1933–34.
129. Charles S. Judd, *Report of the Territorial Forester for the Calendar Year 1935* (Territory of Hawaii, Board of Commissioners of Agriculture and Forestry, Division of Forestry), State Archives, com 2-35, Reports of the Territorial Forester, 1935–36 Calendar Year.
130. R. J. Baker, "A Brief History of the Hawaiian Trail and Mountain Club" (unpublished manuscript, HTMC Archives, 1960), 75.
131. Erwin N. Thompson, *Pacific Ocean Engineers, History of the U.S. Army Corps of Engineers in the Pacific, 1905–1980* (Honolulu: U.S. Army Corps of Engineers, 1980), 80; Lieutenant General Robert C. Richardson, Historical Review, U.S. Army Corps of Engineers.
132. Joseph Neilson, interview, February 11, 2000.
133. Richard H. Davis, interview, December 13, 1999.
134. Joseph Neilson, interview, February 11, 2000.
135. HTMC hike schedule and record, January 6, 1952, HTMC Archives; Richard H. Davis, interview, December 13, 1999; Richard Booth, interview, March 11, 2000.
136. HTMC hike schedule, November 9, 1952; HTMC hike schedule, October 23, 1960; HTMC hike schedule, June 9, 1974, HTMC Archives.
137. Ida Elizabeth Knudsen von Holt, *Stories of Long Ago*, rev. ed. (Honolulu: Daughters of Hawaii, 1985), 135–136.
138. Ibid., 142.
139. Ibid., 146–148.
140. Ibid., 150.
141. "Climbers Planning Many Hikes in Present Month," *Pacific Commercial Advertiser*, 1910s scrapbook, HTMC Archives.
142. Charles S. Judd, *Daily Journal 1924*, January 8, 1924, State Archives.
143. United States Geological Survey topographic map 1928, Waipahu quadrangle; Charles S. Judd, *Daily Journal 1929*, April 12, 1929, State Archives.
144. Charles S. Judd, *Daily Journal 1929*, October 3, 1929, State Archives.
145. Charles S. Judd, *Daily Journal 1931*, January 19, 1931, State Archives.
146. Charles S. Judd, *Daily Journal 1931*, February 12, 1931, State Archives.
147. Glenn W. Russ, "Routine Report of the Assistant Forester March 1931," State Archives, com 2-36, Reports, Monthly, Russ; Charles S. Judd to ranger Ralph E. Turner, Jr., March 9, 1931, State Archives, com 2-33, Forest Ranger, Oahu, Turner.
148. HTMC hike schedule, June 7, 1931, HTMC Archives.
149. Charles S. Judd, *Daily Journal 1932*, January 17, 1932, State Archives.
150. Glenn W. Russ, "Routine Report of Assistant Forester, September 1932," State Archives, com 2-36, Reports, Monthly, Russ.
151. Glenn W. Russ, "Routine Report of the Assistant Forester, January 1933," State Archives, com 2-36, Reports, Monthly, Russ.
152. Charles S. Judd, *Daily Journal 1933*, April 23, 1932, State Archives.
153. Charles S. Judd, *Daily Journal 1935*, April 16–17, 1935, State Archives.
154. Charles S. Judd, "Piko Club Song," State Archives, Judd manuscript M-77, Box 1-14.
155. Narrative of May 5, 1935, annual meeting, State Archives, Judd manuscript M-77, Box 1-14.
156. Glenn W. Russ, "Routine Report of the Assistant Forester, September 1936," State Archives, com 2-36, Reports, Monthly, Russ.

157. U.S. Army Corps of Engineers, Specifications, ERA Road and Trail Project OP 13-296 (War Department, 1936).
158. Major General Hugh Drum to Charles S. Judd, December 14, 1936; Frank H. Locey to Major General Hugh Drum, State Archives, com 2-16, Haw Dept 1929–1939.
159. HTMC hike schedule, April 11 and August 29, 1937, HTMC Archives.
160. Vince Soeda, interview, January 14, 2008.
161. HTMC hike schedule, January 26, 1947, HTMC Archives.
162. Joseph Neilson, interview, February 11, 2000.
163. HTMC hike schedule, April 27, 1969, HTMC Archives.
164. The Nature Conservancy of Hawaii, Honouliuli Preserve, Oahu (fact sheet).
165. William Gorst, interview, June 28, 2010; *Honouliuli Preserve Watershed Purchased and Protected*, http://www.tpl.org.
166. *Palehua: A Stone School House*, blogs: Cultural Kapolei, honoluluadvertiser.com.

Sugar Plantation Trails

1. George B. McClellan, *A Handbook on the Sugar Industry of the Hawaiian Islands* (Honolulu: The Hawaiian Gazette Company, Ltd., 1899), 7–10.
2. Annual Report of the Honolulu Plantation Company for the Year Ending 12/31/[19]02, Manager's Report, February 6, 1903, 7, 14; Annual Report of the Oahu Sugar Company Ltd. for the Year Ending September 30, 1900, Manager's Report; Fourth Annual Report of the Waialua Agricultural Company Ltd. for the Year Ending December 31, 1902, Manager's Report, February 16, 1903, 6–7.
3. H. A. Wadsworth, *An Irrigation Census of Hawaii with Some Comparisons with the Continental United States* (Honolulu: Advertiser Publishing Company, 1935), 51–52.
4. H. A. Wadsworth, "A Historical Summary of Irrigation in Hawaii," *The Hawaiian Planters Record* XXXVII, 3 (Third Qtr. 1933): 152.
5. Carol Wilcox, *Sugar Water: Hawaii's Plantation Ditches* (Honolulu: University of Hawai'i Press, 1996), 52–53.
6. H. A. Wadsworth, *An Irrigation Census of Hawaii with Some Comparisons with the Continental United States* (Honolulu: Advertiser Publishing Company, 1935), 51.
7. Ibid., 51.
8. Annual Report of the Oahu Sugar Company Ltd. for the Year Ending December 31, 1904, Manager's Report (rough draft).
9. Annual Report of the Oahu Sugar Company Ltd. for the Year Ending December 31, 1905, Manager's Report, 13.
10. Annual Report of the Oahu Sugar Company Ltd. for the Year Ending December 31, 1911, Manager's Report, January 30, 1912, 5–6.
11. Ibid.
12. Annual Report of the Oahu Sugar Company Ltd. for the Year Ending December 31, 1913, Manager's Report, January 29, 1914, 12–13; Carol Wilcox, *Sugar Water: Hawaii's Plantation Ditches* (Honolulu: University of Hawai'i Press, 1996), 100–102.
13. Charles H. Kluegel, "Engineering Features of the Water Project of the Waiahole Water Company," in *Thrum's Hawaiian Annual 1917* (Honolulu: T. G. Thrum, 1918), 101.
14. Annual Report of the Oahu Sugar Company Ltd. for the Year Ending December 31, 1916, Manager's Report, February 15, 1917, 12–13.
15. Charles H. Kluegel, "Engineering Features of the Water Project of the Waiahole Water Company," in *Thrum's Hawaiian Annual 1917* (Honolulu: T. G. Thrum, 1918), 93; Annual Report of the Oahu Sugar Company Ltd. for the Year Ending December 31, 1915, Manager's Report, February 5, 1916.
16. "Week-End Hikers," *Honolulu Star-Bulletin*, November 27, 1920, section 1, page 8.
17. George T. Armitage, "The Trail That Starts Nowhere," *Paradise of the Pacific*, December 1921, 48.

18. Ibid., 49.
19. Edmund J. Meadows, *Oahu Trail* (pamphlet), circa 1930, HTMC Archives.
20. Annual Report of the Oahu Sugar Company Ltd. for the Year Ending December 31, 1933, Manager's Report, January 19, 1934, 17.
21. Charles S. Judd, "Program for Emergency Conservation Work—Territory of Hawaii," October 28, 1933, 12, State Archives, com 2-12, Brown, ECW, 1933–34.
22. Charles S. Judd, *Daily Journal 1935*, February 20, 1935, State Archives.
23. Charles S. Judd, "Program for Emergency Conservation Work—Territory of Hawaii," October 28, 1933, 12, State Archives, com 2-12, Brown, ECW, 1933–34.
24. Annual Report of the Oahu Sugar Company Ltd. for the Year Ending December 31, 1942, 9.
25. HTMC hike schedule, September 6, 1970, HTMC Archives.
26. HTMC hike schedules, April 9, 1960, and August 31, 1980, HTMC Archives.
27. HTMC newsletter, September 1995; HTMC hike schedule, February 25, 1995, HTMC Archives; John Hall, interview, May 25, 2010.
28. Dayle K. Turner, "Waiahole Ditch," April 10, 2000, http://www2.hawaii.edu/~turner/ohe/.
29. First Annual Report of the Manager and Treasurer of the Waialua Agricultural Company Ltd. for the Year Ending September 30, 1899, Manager's Report, November 14, 1899, 17.
30. Second Report of the Waialua Agricultural Company Ltd. for the Fifteen Months Ending December 31, 1900, Manager's Report, January 28, 1901, 7; H. A. Wadsworth, *An Irrigation Census of Hawaii with Some Comparisons with the Continental United States* (Honolulu: Advertiser Publishing Company, 1935), 52.
31. Fourth Annual Report of the Waialua Agricultural Company Ltd. for the Year Ending December 31, 1902, Manager's Report, February 16, 1903, 6; H. A. Wadsworth, *An Irrigation Census of Hawaii with Some Comparisons with the Continental United States* (Honolulu: Advertiser Publishing Company, 1935), 52.
32. Fifth Annual Report of the Waialua Agricultural Company Ltd. for the Year Ending December 31, 1903, Manager's Report, February 16, 1904, 9–10.
33. Thirteenth Annual Report of the Waialua Agricultural Company Ltd. for the Year ending December 31, 1911, Manager's Report, February 14, 1912, 5.
34. Twenty-First Annual Report of the Waialua Agricultural Company Ltd. for the Year Ending December 31, 1919, Manager's Report, February 10, 1920, 8; Twenty-Second Annual Report of the Waialua Agricultural Company Ltd. for the Year Ending December 31, 1920, Manager's Report, February 14, 1921, 7.
35. "December Trail Club Schedule Arranged," *Honolulu Star-Bulletin*, December 2, 1920, 4.
36. "Sunday Hike to Scenic Opaeula," *Honolulu Star-Bulletin*, April 9, 1911, 9; "Three Buses Needed for Big Hike Outing," *Honolulu Star-Bulletin*, April 11, 1921, 4.
37. "Trail and Mountain Take Trip to Opaeula on Sunday," *Honolulu Star-Bulletin*, July 20, 1925, 3.
38. Charles S. Judd, *Daily Journal 1932*, October 20, 1932, State Archives.
39. U.S. Army Corps of Engineers, Specifications, ERA Road and Trail Project OP 13-296 (War Department, 1936).
40. HTMC hike schedule, August 11, 1946, and July 12, 1953, HTMC Archives.
41. HTMC hike schedule and record, October 17, 1954, HTMC Archives.
42. HTMC hike schedule, July 2, 1972, HTMC Archives.
43. HTMC hike schedule and record, July 8, 1956, HTMC Archives.
44. HTMC hike schedule, August 2, 1964, HTMC Archives.
45. Stuart Ball, hike notes, November 5–7, 1998.
46. First Annual Report of the Manager and Treasurer of the Waialua Agricultural Company Ltd. for the Year Ending September 30, 1899, Manager's Report, November 14, 1899, 17; Second Report of the Waialua Agricultural Company Ltd. for the Fifteen Months Ending December 31, 1900, Manager's Report, January 28, 1901, 7; Fifth Annual Report of the Waialua

Agricultural Company Ltd. for the Year Ending December 31, 1903, Manager's Report, February 16, 1904, 9–10.

47. Fourth Annual Report of the Waialua Agricultural Company Ltd. for the Year Ending December 31, 1902, Manager's Report, February 16, 1903, 6; Sixth Annual Report of the Waialua Agricultural Company Ltd. for the Year Ending December 31, 1904, Manager's Report, February 6, 1905, 5.

48. Eleventh Annual Report of the Waialua Agricultural Company Ltd. for the Year Ending December 31, 1909, Manager's Report, February 12, 1910, 5.

49. Twelfth Annual Report of the Waialua Agricultural Company Ltd. for the Year Ending December 31, 1910, Manager's Report, February 13, 1911, 4; Thirteenth Annual Report of the Waialua Agricultural Company Ltd. for the Year Ending December 31, 1911, Manager's Report, February 14, 1912, 5.

50. Fourteenth Annual Report of the Waialua Agricultural Company Ltd. for the Year Ending December 31, 1912, Manager's Report, 4.

51. Twentieth Annual Report of the Waialua Agricultural Company Ltd. for the Year Ending December 31, 1918, Manager's Report, February 18, 1919, 6.

52. List of Piko Club hikes on General Wells' map, State Archives, Judd manuscript, M-77, Box 1-14.

53. U.S. Army Corps of Engineers, Specifications, ERA Road and Trail Project OP 13-296 (War Department, 1936).

54. HTMC hike schedule, October 31, 1937, HTMC Archives.

55. HTMC hike schedule, June 21, 1969, HTMC Archives.

56. HTMC hike schedule, July 18, 1965, HTMC Archives.

57. Stuart Ball, hike notes, November 5–7, 1998.

58. James H. Chun, *The Early Chinese in Punaluu* (Yin Sit Sha, 1983), 2–6, 13–16, 58.

59. Gwen Allen, "The Man Who Looked Ahead," *Honolulu Star-Bulletin*, December 22, 1956, Hawaiian Life section; Arthur L. Dean, *Alexander & Baldwin, Ltd. and the Predecessor Partnerships* (Honolulu: Alexander & Baldwin, Ltd., 1950), 105–106; "Hawaiian Sugar Plantations History, No 34, Kahuku," *Honolulu Star-Bulletin*, October 19, 1935, 8; Carol Wilcox, *Sugar Water: Hawaii's Plantation Ditches* (Honolulu: University of Hawai'i Press, 1996), 110–111.

60. W. F. Martin and C. H. Pierce, *Water Resources of Hawaii 1909–1911* (Washington, D.C.: Government Printing Office, 1913), 174–177; Hugh M. Polworth, "The Mountain Horse Trails of Hawaii," *Mid-Pacific Magazine*, July 1911, 19; Lorrin Thurston, "Mountain Tramping in Hawaii," *Mid-Pacific Magazine*, November 1920, 2.

61. R. J. Baker, *A Brief History of the Hawaiian Trail and Mountain Club* (1960), 4, HTMC Archives; "Trail and Mountain Club Is Getting Things Going," *Pacific Commercial Advertiser*, July 21, 1911, 3.

62. *Compilation of Records of Surface Waters of Hawaii through June 1950* (Washington, D.C.: U.S. Government Printing Office, 1961), 143; G. K. Larrison, "Division of Hydrography Report, April 13, 1915," *The Hawaiian Forester and Agriculturist*, May 1915, 129.

63. Lawrence Hite Daingerfield, "Mauka Sacred Falls," *Paradise of the Pacific*, April 1921, 7.

64. Charles S. Judd, "Report of the Superintendent of Forestry, September 1923," *The Hawaiian Forester and Agriculturist*, October–December 1929, 144.

65. George M. Collins to Charles S. Judd, November 13, 1923, State Archives, com 2-35, T & M Club.

66. Charles S. Judd, *Daily Journal 1925*, September 17, 1925, State Archives.

67. Charles S. Judd, "Routine Report of the Territorial Forester, June 1928," *The Hawaiian Forester and Agriculturist*, July–September 1928, 113.

68. Charles S. Judd, "Routine Report of the Territorial Forester, November 1928," *The Hawaiian Forester and Agriculturist*, October–December 1928, 158.

69. Charles S. Judd, *Daily Journal 1930*, May 3, 1930, State Archives; Charles S. Judd, "Routine Report of the Territorial Forester, May 1930," *The Hawaiian Forester and Agriculturist*, April–June 1930, 78–79.

70. Charles S. Judd, "Routine Report of the Territorial Forester, July 1930," *The Hawaiian Forester and Agriculturist*, July–September 1930, 118.
71. HTMC hike schedule, November 24, 1929, and September 28, 1930, HTMC Archives.
72. Charles S. Judd, *Daily Journal 1931*, February 17, 1931, State Archives; Charles S. Judd, Notes for Piko Club History, February 17, 1931, State Archives, Judd manuscript, M-77, Box 1-14.
73. Glenn W. Russ, "Routine Report of the Assistant Forester," February 1931, State Archives, com 2-36, Reports, Monthly, Russ, 2.
74. Charles S. Judd, "Routine Report of the Territorial Forester, November 1932," *The Hawaiian Forester and Agriculturist*, October–December 1932, 170; Charles S. Judd, *Daily Journal 1932*, November 14, 16–17, 1932, State Archives; Charles S. Judd, "Routine Report of the Territorial Forester, December 1932," *The Hawaiian Forester and Agriculturist*, October–December 1932, 175.
75. Charles S. Judd, *Daily Journal 1933*, November 19, 1933, State Archives.
76. Charles S. Judd, *Daily Journal 1934*, August 30, 1934, State Archives.
77. Charles S. Judd, *Daily Journal 1934*, October 18, 1934, State Archives.
78. Charles S. Judd, *Daily Journal 1935*, July 14, 1935, State Archives; HTMC hike schedule, May 5, 1935, HTMC Archives.
79. Richard H. Davis, interview, July 27, 2001.
80. Unit History, Pacific Combat Training Center (1945).
81. James H. Chun, *The Early Chinese in Punaluu* (Yin Sit Sha, 1983), 65.
82. HTMC hike schedule, December 22, 1946, HTMC Archives.
83. HTMC hike schedule, August 31–September 1, 1947, HTMC Archives; Division of Forestry, Forest Trail Map of the Island of Oahu (1947); Lorin Gill, interview, January 9, 2007.
84. HTMC hike schedule, January 25, 1981; HTMC newsletter, January 1981, HTMC Archives.
85. Beryl Sawyer, *Confrontation*, HTMC newsletter, April 1981, HTMC Archives.
86. HTMC hike schedule, August 11, 1985, HTMC Archives; Stuart Ball, hike notes, August 11, 1985; HTMC newsletter, July 1987, HTMC Archives.
87. Steve Brown, "Castle Trail Reopens," HTMC newsletter, July–September 2007, 1, HTMC Archives; Stuart Ball, hike notes, December 2, 2008.
88. Annual Report of the Honolulu Plantation Company for the Year Ending 12/31/[19]02, Manager's Report, February 6, 1903, 7.
89. Annual Report of the Honolulu Plantation Company for the Year Ending 12/31/[19]03, Manager's Report, February 1, 1904, 8–9; Annual Report of the Honolulu Plantation Company for the Year Ending 12/31/[19]04, Manager's Report, February 1, 1905, 17.
90. Annual Report of the Honolulu Plantation Company for the Year Ending 12/31/[19]12, Manager's Report, January 27, 1913, 6.
91. Annual Report of the Honolulu Plantation Company for the Year Ending 12/31/[19]15, Manager's Report, January 25, 1916, 6.
92. Annual Report of the Honolulu Plantation Company for the Year Ending 12/31/[19]14, Manager's Report, January 25, 1915, 6.
93. Annual Report of the Honolulu Plantation Company for the Year Ending 12/31/[19]16, Manager's Report, January 22, 1917, 6.
94. Karen Reiko Takemoto, "Unquestionably Lolo" (master's thesis, University of Hawai'i at Mānoa, 1984), 17; Annual Report of the Honolulu Plantation Company for the Year Ending 12/31/31, Manager's Report, January 19, 1932, 10.
95. "Land Shell Hunt by Mountaineers Is Great Success," *Pacific Commercial Advertiser*, April 4, 1920, 4.
96. *Pacific Commercial Advertiser*, Hawaiian Trail and Mountain Club 1920s scrapbook, HTMC Archives.
97. Charles S. Judd, *Daily Journal 1929*, April 17, 1929, State Archives; Glenn W. Russ,

"Routine Report of the Assistant Forester," April 1929, State Archives, com 2-36, Reports, Monthly, Russ.

98. Charles S. Judd, "Program for Emergency Conservation Work, Territory of Hawaii, Second Enrollment Period: October 1, 1934 to March 31, 1935" (June 7, 1934), 2, State Archives, com 2-12, Brown, Corres, ECW, 1933–34.

99. Charles S. Judd, *Daily Journal 1934*, September 25, 1934, State Archives.

100. Gunder E. Olson, "Project Superintendent's Narrative Report, Honolulu Unit, Island of Oahu, Fourth Enrollment Period, October 1, 1934–March 31, 1935," Talbert Takahama papers.

101. Gunder E. Olson, "Narrative Report—Island of Oahu, Men Working from Homes, Fifth Enrollment Period, April 1 to September 30, 1935, 27," State Archives, com 2-35, Reports, ECW Reports 1935.

102. Charles S. Judd, Emergency Conservation Work, Territory of Hawaii, Projects for the Sixth Enrollment Period October 1, 1935 to March 31, 1936, 2, 4, State Archives, com 2-33, ECW, CCC Program 1935–38.

103. HTMC hike schedule, January 26, 1936, HTMC Archives; Harry Whitten, "Trail Ways," *Honolulu Star Bulletin*, February 3, 1951, 24.

104. Annual Report of the Honolulu Plantation Company for the Year Ending 12/31/46, President's Report, April 3, 1947, 1–2; Annual Report of the Oahu Sugar Company Ltd. for the Year Ending December 31, 1946, Manager's Report, February 12, 1947, 7.

105. HTMC hike schedule, July 4–5, 1959, and April 28–29, 1962, HTMC Archives.

106. Robert W. Bone, "Butch, won't you please come home?" *Honolulu Advertiser*, July 2, 1975, D-1.

107. Norman Roberts, "Butch, the Koolau Bear," HTMC newsletter, July–September 2001, HTMC Archives.

108. HTMC newsletter, March 1982, HTMC Archives.

109. Annual Report of the Honolulu Plantation Company for the Year Ending 12/31/[19]02, Manager's Report, February 6, 1903, 7.

110. Annual Report of the Honolulu Plantation Company for the Year Ending 12/31/[19]03, Manager's Report, February 1, 1904, 8–9; Annual Report of the Honolulu Plantation Company for the Year Ending 12/31/[19]04, Manager's Report, February 1, 1905, 17.

111. Charles S. Judd, *Daily Journal 1915*, November 26, 1915, State Archives.

112. Annual Report of the Honolulu Plantation Company for the Year Ending 12/31/[19]15, Manager's Report, January 25, 1916, 6.

113. Annual Report of the Honolulu Plantation Company for the Year Ending 12/31/[19]16, Manager's Report, January 22, 1917, 6, 14; Annual Report of the Honolulu Plantation Company for the Year Ending 12/31/[19]17, Manager's Report, 6.

114. Annual Report of the Honolulu Plantation Company for the Year Ending 12/31/[19]16, Manager's Report, January 22, 1917, 6.

115. Annual Report of the Honolulu Plantation Company for the Year Ending 12/31/[19]18, Manager's Report, January 27, 1919, 6.

116. "52 Hikers Go Up Waimalu Valley," *Honolulu Star-Bulletin*, July 11, 1921, 5; HTMC hike schedules, March 2, 1924, and September 18, 1927, HTMC Archives.

117. Annual Report of the Honolulu Plantation Company for the Year Ending 12/31/46, President's Report, April 3, 1947, 1–2; Annual Report of the Oahu Sugar Company Ltd. for the Year Ending December 31, 1946, Manager's Report, February 12, 1947, 7.

118. Annual Report of the Oahu Sugar Company Ltd. for the Year Ending 12/31/50.

119. HTMC hike schedule and record, April 30, 1961, HTMC Archives.

120. HTMC hike schedule, December 13, 1964, HTMC Archives.

121. HTMC hike schedule, May 21, 1989, HTMC Archives.

122. Stuart Ball, hike notes, June 2, 1991, and others.

123. HTMC hike schedule, July 24, 1999, HTMC Archives.

124. John Hall, interview, May 25, 2010; Stuart Ball, hike notes, April 26, 1992.

Army and Territorial Forestry Division Trails

1. Colonel S. R. Meeken, *The History of Fort Shafter 1898–1974* (U.S. Army Garrison Hawaii, 1974), 4; William C. Addleman, *A History of the United States Army in Hawaii 1849–1939* (Division Headquarters Department, Fort Shafter, 1939), 6; *A Short History of Schofield Barracks* (Honolulu: Tropic Lightning Museum, 1999), 1.
2. Corporal Amos T. Woodruff, "An Army 'Hike,'" *Mid-Pacific Magazine*, February 1911, 117–125.
3. Colonel S. R. Meeken, *The History of Fort Shafter 1898–1974* (U.S. Army Garrison Hawaii, 1974), 6; "Hikers to Tramp Bowman Trail," *Honolulu Star-Bulletin*, September 9, 1921, 5.
4. Brian McAllister Linn, *Guardians of Empire* (Chapel Hill: University of North Carolina Press, 1997), 196; William C. Addleman, *A History of the United States Army in Hawaii 1849–1939* (Division Headquarters Department, Fort Shafter, 1939), 41.
5. Charles S. Judd, "Routine Report of the Territorial Forester, March 1927," *The Hawaiian Forester and Agriculturist*, January–March 1927, 13.
6. Charles S. Judd, "Routine Report of the Territorial Forester, September 1927," *The Hawaiian Forester and Agriculturist*, July–September 1927, 77.
7. Charles S. Judd, "Routine Report of the Territorial Forester, November 1928," *The Hawaiian Forester and Agriculturist*, October–December 1928, 158.
8. Charles S. Judd, "Routine Report of the Territorial Forester, May 1930," *The Hawaiian Forester and Agriculturist*, April–June 1930, 78–79.
9. Charles S. Judd, "Division of Forestry Report, Report of the Board of Commissioners of Agriculture and Forestry for Fiscal Year July 1, 1929 to June 30, 1930," *The Hawaiian Forester and Agriculturist*, July–September 1930, 66.
10. Glenn W. Russ, "Routine Report of the Assistant Forester, July 1931," State Archives, com 2-36, Reports, Monthly, Russ; Charles S. Judd, "Annual Report of the Territorial Forester 1931, *The Hawaiian Forester and Agriculturist*, July–September 1932, 11.
11. Charles S. Judd, "Report of the Territorial Forester, February 23, 1933 for 1931–32," *The Hawaiian Forester and Agriculturist*, January–March 1933, 23.
12. Colonel (ret.) Thomas J. Wells, interview, February 14, 2000.
13. Charles S. Judd, *Daily Journal 1931*, January 19, 1931, State Archives.
14. Charles S. Judd, *Daily Journal 1931*, February 17, 1931, State Archives; Charles S. Judd, Notes for Piko Club history, February 17, 1931, Judd manuscript, State Archives, M-77, Box 1-14.
15. Colonel (ret.) Thomas Wells, interview, February 14, 2000.
16. Charles S. Judd, *Daily Journal 1931*, March 1, 1931, State Archives; Charles S. Judd, Notes for Piko Club history, March 1, 1931, Judd manuscript, State Archives, M-77, Box 1-14; Charles S. Judd, "Pehe'a Kou Piko? Ma'ika'I No!: Piko Club Song," arranged by Captain George L. King, private collection; Mary Judd, interview, August 23, 2002; Colonel (ret.) Thomas Wells, interview, February 14, 2000.
17. Organization Banquet Program, Judd manuscript, State Archives, M-77, Box 2-26.
18. Articles of the Organization of the Piko Club, April 25, 1931, Judd manuscript, State Archives, M-77, Box 2-26.
19. Ibid.
20. Charles S. Judd, *Daily Journal 1931*, February 12, February 20, March 19, April 2, 1931, State Archives; List of Piko Club hikes on General Wells' map, April 23 and June 9, 1931, State Archives, Judd manuscript, M-77, Box 1-14.
21. Captain Arnold W. Shutter, *Excelsior!* General Wells photograph collection, U.S. Army Museum of Hawai'i, Fort DeRussy, Honolulu.
22. Charles S. Judd, *Daily Journal 1931*, July 26, 1931, State Archives.
23. Mary Judd, interview, August 23, 2002; Colonel (ret.) Thomas Wells, interview, February 14, 2000.
24. Charles S. Judd, *Daily Journal 1932*, April 29, May 5, and October 30, 1932, State Archives; Colonel (ret.) Thomas Wells, interview, February 14, 2000.

25. Charles S. Judd to H. A. Mountain, April 21 and July 21, 1933, State Archives, com 2-35, Unemployment Work Relief Commission.
26. Charles S. Judd, *Daily Journal 1933*, March 3 and May 16, 1933, State Archives.
27. Charles S. Judd, *Daily Journal 1933*, May 3 and May 7, 1933, State Archives; Charles S. Judd to Captain George S. Pierce, May 8, 1933, State Archives, Judd manuscript, M-77, Box 1-13; Charles S. Judd, hike announcement to Piko members, April 26, 1933, Judd manuscript.
28. Charles S. Judd, "Division of Forestry Report, Report of the Board of Commissioners of Agriculture and Forestry for the Biennial Period from July 1, 1932 to June 30, 1934"; Charles S. Judd, *Daily Journal 1933*, July 3, 1933, State Archives.
29. W. B. Thomas, "The Wahiawa (Oahu Ditch)," in *Thrum's Hawaiian Annual 1903* (Honolulu: The Printshop Company, Ltd., 1903), 72a–72b; Wahiawa Water Company Report No. 1, Manager's Report to January 31, 1902, 6–8; Wahiawa Water Company Report No. 2 for the Year Ending 12/31/[19]03, 13.
30. Vaughn MacCaughey, "The Mountain Trail from Wahiawa to Kahana," *The Hawaiian Forester and Agriculturist*, December 1910, 356.
31. Ibid., 353–358.
32. Corporal Amos T. Woodruff, "An Army 'Hike,'" *Mid-Pacific Magazine*, February 1911, 119.
33. Ibid., 123.
34. Ibid., 117–125.
35. Vaughn MacCaughey, "The Koolau Mountains between Wahiawa and Kahana, Oahu, *The Hawaiian Forester and Agriculturist*, November 1914, 326, 328.
36. Ibid., 328.
37. Ibid., 325–329.
38. "Hikers Enjoy Trip Over Lofty Range," *Honolulu Star-Bulletin*, July 5, 1920, 6.
39. Lawrence Hite Daingerfield, "The Wahiawa-Kahana Trail," *Paradise of the Pacific*, August 1920, 25–27.
40. William C. Addleman, *A History of the United States Army in Hawaii 1849–1939* (Division Headquarters Department, Fort Shafter, 1939), 38; *The Third Engineers, Schofield Barracks, Hawaii*, assembled from the official records of the Third Engineers by First Lieutenant W. W. Milner and Technical Sergeant M. A. Bales.
41. Thomas R. L. McGuire, "Sauntering With the Trail and Mountain Club Over the Wahiawa-Waikane Pathways on Oahu Island," *Paradise of the Pacific*, June 1924, 6; HTMC hike schedule, April 13, 1924, HTMC Archives.
42. Charles S. Judd, *Daily Journal 1931*, June 8, 1931, State Archives; List of Piko Club hikes on General Wells' map, State Archives, Judd manuscript, M-77, Box 1-14; Richard H. Davis, interview, July 31, 2001.
43. HTMC hike schedule and record, May 13, 1956; HTMC hike schedule, May 24, 1984, HTMC Archives.
44. Eric Vandervoort, *Elepaio*, May 1996.
45. HTMC hike schedule, May 8, 1999, HTMC Archives.
46. S. R. Meeken, *The History of Fort Shafter 1898–1974* (U. S. Army Garrison Hawaii, 1974), 2–4.
47. Executive Order of January 26, 1917, signed by President Woodrow Wilson (describes boundaries and monuments of Fort Shafter).
48. S. R. Meeken, *The History of Fort Shafter 1898–1974* (U. S. Army Garrison Hawaii, 1974), 6.
49. *Men of Hawaii*, edited by George F. Nellist (Honolulu Star-Bulletin, Ltd., 1930), 4, 79.
50. "Hikers to Tramp Bowman Trail," *Honolulu Star-Bulletin*, September 9, 1921, 5.
51. "The Trail and Mountain Club," *Honolulu Star-Bulletin*, 1920s scrapbook, HTMC Archives.
52. "Many Interesting Hikes Planned by T. & M. Climbers," *Pacific Commercial Advertiser*, 1920s scrapbook, HTMC Archives.

53. "Hikers to Tramp Bowman Trail," *Honolulu Star-Bulletin*, September 9, 1921, 5.
54. HTMC hike schedule, June 27, 1927, HTMC Archives.
55. CCC Honolulu Unit Map (October 1, 1935–March 31, 1936), State Archives, G4382. O2K1(1936).U54C5.
56. HTMC hike schedule, November 28, 1937, HTMC Archives.
57. HTMC hike schedule, June 27, 1954, and September 16, 1956, HTMC Archives; "Trails, Hunting & Park Areas, Island of Oahu" (Department of Land and Natural Resources map).
58. HTMC hike schedule, September 9, 1973, HTMC Archives.
59. HTMC hike schedule, December 10, 1995, HTMC Archives.
60. *Mālama I Ka Honua*, Sierra Club, Hawai'i Chapter newsletter, September 1980, Wallaby Watch, September 21, 1980; Harry Whitten, "Trail Ways," *Honolulu Star-Bulletin*, 1950s scrapbook, HTMC Archives.
61. HTMC hike schedule, June 30, 1985, HTMC Archives.
62. Charles S. Judd, "Report of the Superintendent of Forestry, April 1924," *The Hawaiian Forester and Agriculturist*, April–June 1924, 58; Charles S. Judd, *Daily Journal 1924*, April 9, 1924, State Archives.
63. William C. Addleman, *A History of the United States Army in Hawaii 1849–1939* (Division Headquarters Department, Fort Shafter, 1939), 41.
64. HTMC hike schedule and record, November 11, 1924, HTMC Archives; Fred E. Truman, "Trail Knife Cuttings," *Paradise of the Pacific*, February 1926, 30.
65. Charles S. Judd, *Daily Journal 1925*, January 16, 1925; Charles S. Judd, *Daily Journal 1926*, November 17, 1926, State Archives.
66. List of Piko Club hikes on General Wells' map, State Archives, Judd manuscript, M-77, Box 1-14; Glenn W. Russ, "Routine Report of the Assistant Forester, March 1931," State Archives, com 2-36, Reports, Monthly, Russ.
67. List of Piko Club hikes on General Wells' map, State Archives, Judd manuscript, M-77, Box 1-14; Charles S. Judd, *Daily Journal 1933*, February 1, 1933 and May 7, 1933, State Archives.
68. Charles S. Judd, *Daily Journal 1934*, May 18, 1934, State Archives.
69. Charles S. Judd, "Program for Emergency Conservation Work, Territory of Hawaii, Second Enrollment Period: October 1, 1934 to March 31, 1935" (June 7, 1934), 2, State Archives, com 2-12, Brown, Correspondence, ECW, 1933–34.
70. Charles S. Judd, *Daily Journal 1934*, August 30, 1934, and September 5–6, 1934, State Archives; William C. Addleman, *A History of the United States Army in Hawaii 1849–1939* (Division Headquarters Department, Fort Shafter, 1939), 54.
71. Charles S. Judd, *Daily Journal 1935*, June 10, 1935, State Archives; Robert C. Bayless to Charles S. Judd, July 2, 1935, State Archives, com 2-34, ECW, Supt of Foremen, CCC Camp, 1935–41.
72. Charles S. Judd, *Daily Journal 1935*, July 15, 1935, and July 24–25, 1935, State Archives.
73. Robert C. Bayless to Charles S. Judd, August 5, 1935, State Archives, com 2-34, ECW, Supt of Foremen, CCC Camp, 1935–41.
74. HTMC hike schedule, November 17, 1935, and April 2, 1939, HTMC Archives.
75. War Department, Corps of Engineers, U.S. Army, *Waimea and Kahuku quadrangles* (1943), UH Hamilton, G4382.O2s20 1943.v5.
76. HTMC hike schedule, March 9, 1947, and March 2, 1952, HTMC Archives; Harry Whitten, "Trail Ways," *Honolulu Star-Bulletin*, March 1, 1952, 16.
77. Division of Forestry, Forest Trail Map of the Island of Oahu (1947).
78. Stuart Ball, hike notes, May 26, June 3, July 7, September 29, and November 12, 2001.
79. HTMC hike schedule and record, September 28, 2003, HTMC Archives.
80. Charles S. Judd, "Routine Report of the Territorial Forester, September 1927," *The Hawaiian Forester and Agriculturist*, July–September 1927, 77.
81. Charles S. Judd, *Daily Journal 1927*, September 26, 1927, State Archives.

82. Charles S. Judd, "Routine Report of the Territorial Forester, September 1927," *The Hawaiian Forester and Agriculturist*, July–September 1927, 77.
83. HTMC hike schedule and record, December 18, 1927, and January 29, 1928, HTMC Archives.
84. Edmund J. Meadows, *Oahu Trail* (pamphlet), circa 1930, HTMC Archives.
85. Charles S. Judd, "Routine Report of the Territorial Forester, September 1928," *The Hawaiian Forester and Agriculturist*, October–December 1928, 154.
86. Charles S. Judd, "Hiking on Oahu Reveals Beauties of Nature in Friendly Mountains," *Honolulu Star-Bulletin*, May 23, 1936, 3, 1.
87. Charles S. Judd, *Daily Journal 1931*, January 19, 1931, State Archives.
88. Charles S. Judd, "Hiking on Oahu Reveals Beauties of Nature in Friendly Mountains," *Honolulu Star-Bulletin*, May 23, 1936, 3, 1.
89. Charles S. Judd, "Routine Report of the Territorial Forester, August 1932," *The Hawaiian Forester and Agriculturist*, July–September 1932, 159–160; Charles S. Judd to Major General Briant H. Wells, August 2, 1932, State Archives, com 2-16, Exec Sec, Hawaiian Dept; Colonel Adolphe Huguet to Charles S. Judd, August 24, 1932, State Archives, com 2-33, Asst Forester, Russ.
90. U.S. Army Corps of Engineers, Specifications, ERA Road and Trail Project OP 13-296 (War Department, 1936).
91. Charles S. Judd, "Hiking on Oahu Reveals Beauties of Nature in Friendly Mountains," *Honolulu Star-Bulletin*, May 23, 1936, 3, 1.
92. "Hitting the Trail in Hawaii," *The Sales Builder*, May 1938, 10.
93. HTMC hike schedule, May 19, 1957, and March 8, 1959, HTMC Archives; Harry Whitten, "Trail Ways," *Honolulu Star-Bulletin*, May 18, 1957, Hawaiian Life section.
94. HTMC hike schedule, May 3, 1964, HTMC Archives.
95. John Hall, interview, August 5, 2001.
96. "Trail Where Scouts Were Stranded 'Rugged' in Rain," *Honolulu Star-Bulletin*, June 20, 1989, A-7; "The Hike that Became a Survival Course," *Honolulu Advertiser*, June 18, 1989, A-1.
97. Vince Costello, trip record and interview, June 1, 2005.
98. Ibid.
99. Dayle K. Turner, "Pe'ahinai'a," January 18, 1999, http://www2.hawaii.edu/~turner/ohe.html.
100. Kapua Kawelo, interview, April 29, 2005.
101. Charles S. Judd, "Routine Report of the Territorial Forester, April 1931," *The Hawaiian Forester and Agriculturist*, April–June 1931.
102. Glenn W. Russ, "Routine Report of the Assistant Forester, April 1931," State Archives, com 2-36, Reports, Monthly, Russ.
103. Charles S. Judd, *Daily Journal 1931*, April 8, 1931, State Archives.
104. S. N. Hale'ole, *The Hawaiian Romance of La'iekawai* (Honolulu: First People's Production, 1997), 344.
105. Charles S. Judd, *Daily Journal 1931*, April 29, 1931, State Archives; List of Piko Club hikes on General Wells' map, State Archives, Judd manuscript, M-77, Box 1-14.
106. Glenn W. Russ, "Routine Report of the Assistant Forester, June and July 1931," State Archives, com 2-36, Reports, Monthly, Russ; Charles S. Judd, "Report of the Territorial Forester, February 23, 1933 for 1931-2," *The Hawaiian Forester and Agriculturist*, January–March 1933, 22.
107. Charles S. Judd, "Annual Report of the Territorial Forester, 1931," *The Hawaiian Forester and Agriculturist*, July–September 1932, 11.
108. Charles S. Judd, *Daily Journal 1931*, December 31, 1931, State Archives.
109. Charles S. Judd, "Routine Report of the Territorial Forester, September 1932," *The Hawaiian Forester and Agriculturist*, October–December 1932, 162.
110. Charles S. Judd, *Daily Journal 1932*, September 13–14, 1932, State Archives.
111. Charles S. Judd, "Routine Report of the Territorial Forester, October 1932," *The

Hawaiian Forester and Agriculturalist, October–December 1932, 166; Charles S. Judd, *Daily Journal 1931*, October 20–21, 1932, State Archives.

112. Charles S. Judd, *Daily Journal 1933*, June 25, 1933, State Archives; Charles S. Judd to Captain Raymond G. Sherman, December 31, 1932, Judd manuscript, State Archives, M-77, Box 1-14.

113. Charles S. Judd, *Daily Journal 1934*, July 30, 1934, State Archives.

114. Charles S. Judd, *Daily Journal 1935*, March 12, 1935, State Archives.

115. Robert C. Bayless to Charles S. Judd, August 5, 1935, State Archives, com 2-34, ECW, Supt of Foremen, CCC Camp, 1935–41.

116. Richard H. Davis, interview, July 31, 2001.

117. Jesse Palmer, interview, July 23, 2005.

118. Mabel Kekina, interview, April 25, 2005.

119. HTMC hike schedule, June 4, 1995, HTMC Archives.

120. Mabel Kekina, journal, June 12, 1995; Stuart Ball, hike notes, June 12, 1995.

121. Charles S. Judd, *Daily Journal 1932*, March 23, 1932, State Archives.

122. Charles S. Judd, "Routine Report of the Territorial Forester, March 1932," *The Hawaiian Forester and Agriculturist*, July–September 1932, 103.

123. Charles S. Judd, *Daily Journal 1932*, April 13, 20, and 29, 1932, State Archives; Charles S. Judd, "Routine Report of the Territorial Forester April 1932," *The Hawaiian Forester and Agriculturist*, July–September 1932, 107–108.

124. Charles S. Judd, *Daily Journal 1932*, May 5, 1932, State Archives; List of Piko Club hikes on General Wells' map, State Archives, Judd manuscript, M-77, Box 1-14.

125. Charles S. Judd, *Daily Journal 1932*, October 30, 1932, State Archives; Colonel (ret.) Thomas J. Wells, interview, February 14, 2000.

126. Charles S. Judd to General Briant H. Wells, October 30, 1932, Judd manuscript, State Archives, M-77, Box 1-13.

127. Robert C. Bayless to Charles S. Judd, July 12, 1935, State Archives, com 2-34, ECW, Supt of Foremen, CCC Camp, 1935–41.

128. Robert C. Bayless to Charles S. Judd, August 5, 1935, State Archives, com 2-34, ECW, Supt of Foremen, CCC Camp, 1935–41.

129. Charles S. Judd, *Daily Journal 1935*, December 15, 1935, State Archives; Charles S. Judd to Captain Joseph B. Sweet, December 23, 1935, Judd manuscript, State Archives, M-77, Box 1-14.

130. HTMC hike schedule, August 9, 1936, HTMC Archives.

131. Wahiawa Camp Project map, State Archives, G4382.O2K191936.U5; Charles S. Judd, *Daily Journal 1936*, March 23, 1936, State Archives.

132. R. J. Baker, *Diaries 1906–1944*, Bishop Museum, Baker manuscript M516, Box 12.3; HTMC hike schedule, May 17, 1937, HTMC Archives.

133. HTMC hike schedule, December 7, 1941, HTMC Archives; Harry Whitten, "Trail Ways: Hikers Well Recall Fateful Day, December 7, 1941," *Honolulu Star-Bulletin*, December 9, 1950, 10.

134. "Kealia to Mokuleia," June 1, 1952, HTMC Archives.

135. HTMC hike schedule and record, Piko Trail, Makua-Kaena, November 25, 1951, HTMC Archives.

136. HTMC hike schedule, October 30, 1966, HTMC Archives.

137. Charles S. Judd, *Daily Journal 1917*, January 9, 1917, and others, State Archives; Charles S. Judd, *Daily Journal 1924*, January 24, 1924, and others, State Archives.

138. "Cooper Ranch Inn to Be Reopened by Mrs. Iris J. Cullen," *Honolulu Advertiser*, October 25, 1951, 6; "Cooper Ranch Inn Reopens in Hauula," *Honolulu Star-Bulletin*, July 25, 1952, B5; Colonel (ret.) Thomas J. Wells, interview, February 14, 2000; Lucy V. Cooper to Charles S. Judd, April 25, 1932, State Archives, Judd manuscript, M-77, Box 1-13.

139. Charles S. Judd, *Daily Journal 1927*, January 7, 1927, State Archives.

140. Charles S. Judd, "Routine Report of the Superintendent of Forestry, January 1927," *The Hawaiian Forester and Agriculturist*, January–March 1927, 8.

Notes to Pages 141–146

141. Charles S. Judd, *Daily Journal 1931*, March 12, 1931, State Archives; Charles S. Judd, "Notes for Piko Club History," March 12, 1931, State Archives, Judd manuscript, M-77, Box 1-14.
142. HTMC hike schedule and record, June 21, 1931, HTMC Archives.
143. Charles S. Judd, *Daily Journal 1932*, August 9, 1932, State Archives.
144. Charles S. Judd, *Daily Journal 1932*, August 10, 1932, and September 2, 1932, State Archives; Charles S. Judd, "Routine Report of the Territorial Forester, August and November 1932," *The Hawaiian Forester and Agriculturist*, October–December 1932, 159, 171.
145. Charles S. Judd to Glenn W. Russ, December 12, 1932, State Archives, com 2-33, Asst Forester, Russ; Charles S. Judd, *Daily Journal 1932*, December 13, 1932, State Archives; Charles S. Judd, "Routine Report of the Territorial Forester, December 1932," *The Hawaiian Forester and Agriculturist*, October–December 1932, 175; Charles S. Judd, *Daily Journal 1933*, March 9, 1933, State Archives.
146. Charles S. Judd, *Daily Journal 1933*, April 5 and April 9, 1933, State Archives; Charles S. Judd to Lucy V. and Will J. Cooper, April 4, 1933, State Archives, Judd manuscript, M-77, Box 1-13.
147. Charles S. Judd, *Daily Journal 1933*, January 13 and May 16, 1933, State Archives; Glenn W. Russ, "Routine Report of the Assistant Forester, April 1933," State Archives, com 2-36, Reports, Monthly, Russ.
148. Charles S. Judd, *Daily Journal 1933*, March 30, May 16, and May 26, 1933, State Archives; Roger G. Skolmen, *Plantings on the Forest Reserves of Hawaii, 1910–1960* (Honolulu: Institute of Pacific Islands Forestry, U.S. Forest Service, 1970), 45.
149. Charles S. Judd, *Daily Journal 1933*, December 1, 1933, State Archives; Charles S. Judd, *Daily Journal 1934*, May 11, 1934, State Archives.
150. Charles S. Judd, "Program for Emergency Conservation Work, Territory of Hawaii, Second Enrollment Period: October 1, 1934 to March 31, 1935" (June 7, 1934), State Archives, com 2-12, Brown, Correspondence, ECW, 1933–34, 2.
151. Charles S. Judd, *Daily Journal 1935*, January 8, 1935, State Archives.
152. Charles S. Judd, *Daily Journal 1935*, February 7, 1935, State Archives; Gunder E. Olson, "Project Superintendent's Narrative Report, Honolulu Unit, Island of Oahu, Fourth Enrollment Period, October 1, 1934–March 31, 1935," Talbert Takahama papers.
153. Charles S. Judd, *Daily Journal 1935*, March 18, March 28, and September 7, 1935, State Archives.
154. Gunder E. Olson to Charles S. Judd, July 9, 1935, State Archives, com 2-33, ECW, CCC program, 1935–38.
155. HTMC hike schedule, September 12, 1937, HTMC Archives.
156. Division of Forestry, Forest Trail Map of the Island of Oahu (1947).
157. HTMC hike schedule, May 11, 1952, HTMC Archives; Report of the Board of Commissioners of Agriculture and Forestry of the Territory of Hawaii, Biennial Period ending 6/30/56, 102.
158. Division of Forestry, Island of Oahu Recreation Map (1979).
159. HTMC hike schedule, December 10, 1988, HTMC Archives.
160. HTMC hike schedule, March 17, 1990, HTMC Archives.
161. Art Isbell, interview, June 27, 2002.
162. Charles S. Judd, *Daily Journal 1933*, February 1, 1933, State Archives.
163. Charles S. Judd, *Daily Journal 1933*, February 10, 1933, State Archives; Glenn W. Russ, "Routine Report of the Assistant Forester, February 1933," State Archives, com 2-36, Reports, Monthly, Russ.
164. Glenn W. Russ, "Routine Report of the Assistant Forester, February 1933," State Archives, com 2-36, Reports, Monthly, Russ; Charles S. Judd to H. A. Mountain, April 21, 1933, State Archives, com 2-35, Unemployment Work Relief Commission; Charles S. Judd, *Daily Journal 1933*, March 21, 1933, State Archives.
165. Charles S. Judd, *Daily Journal 1933*, April 27, 1933, State Archives.
166. Charles S. Judd, *Daily Journal 1933*, May 3, 1933, State Archives.

167. Charles S. Judd, *Daily Journal 1933*, May 7, 1933, State Archives; Charles S. Judd to Captain George S. Pierce, May 8, 1933, State Archives, Judd manuscript, M-77, Box 1-13; Charles S. Judd, hike announcement to Piko members, April 26, 1933, Judd manuscript.
168. Glenn W. Russ, "Routine Report of the Assistant Forester, May and June 1933," State Archives, com 2-36, Reports, Monthly, Russ.
169. Charles S. Judd, "Program for Emergency Conservation Work—Territory of Hawaii," October 28, 1933, 12-13, State Archives, com 2-12, Brown, Correspondence, ECW, 1933-34.
170. Ibid.; Charles S. Judd, *Daily Journal 1933*, November 23 and December 27, 1933, State Archives.
171. Charles S. Judd, *Daily Journal 1934*, April 27, 1934, State Archives.
172. Charles S. Judd, *Daily Journal 1934*, May 4, 1934, State Archives.
173. Gunder E. Olson to Charles S. Judd, July 9, 1935, State Archives, com 2-33, ECW, CCC program, 1935-38.
174. Charles S. Judd, *Daily Journal 1934*, August 21 and August 28, 1934, State Archives.
175. Charles S. Judd, *Daily Journal 1934*, September 28, 1934, State Archives.
176. HTMC hike schedule, April 14, 1935, HTMC Archives.
177. U.S. Geological Survey, Kahuku quadrangle (1951); Division of Forestry, Forest Trail Map of the Island of Oahu (1947).
178. HTMC hike schedule and record, June 16, 1957, HTMC Archives.
179. HTMC hike schedule, March 12, 1968, HTMC Archives.
180. HTMC hike schedule, October 12, 1969, and May 3, 1970, HTMC Archives.

Civilian Conservation Corps Trails

1. Lawrence M. Judd, radiogram to Harold L. Ickes, July 3, 1933, State Archives, gov 7-26, Judd, Interior, CCC.
2. Charles S. Judd, *Daily Journal 1933*, July 7 and 17, 1933, State Archives; Major General Briant H. Wells to the Adjutant General, July 24, 1933, State Archives, com 2-35, U.S. Army 1913-33.
3. Charles S. Judd to Lincoln L. McCandless, July 19, 1933, State Archives, gov 7-26, Judd, Interior, CCC; Charles S. Judd, *Daily Journal 1933*, July 29, 1933, State Archives.
4. Harold L. Ickes to Lawrence M. Judd, August 2, 1933, State Archives, gov 7-26, Judd, Interior, CCC.
5. Lawrence M. Judd to Harold L. Ickes, September 11, 1933, State Archives, gov 7-26, Judd, Interior, CCC.
6. Charles S. Judd to Glenn W. Russ, October 1, 1933, State Archives, com 2-33, Asst Forester, Russ; Harold L. Ickes, radiogram to Lawrence M. Judd, September 27, 1933, State Archives, com 2-12, Brown, ECW, 1933-34.
7. Charles S. Judd, *Daily Journal 1933*, October 23-24, 1933, State Archives.
8. Charles S. Judd, "Program for Emergency Conservation Work—Territory of Hawaii," October 28, 1933, State Archives, com 2-12, Brown, Correspondence, ECW, 1933-34.
9. Lawrence M. Judd to Harold L. Ickes, November 14, 1933, State Archives, com 2-12, Brown, ECW, 1933-34.
10. Harold L. Ickes, radiogram to Lawrence M. Judd, December 21, 1933, State Archives, com 2-12, Brown, ECW, 1933-34.
11. Charles S. Judd, *Daily Journal 1933*, December 28, 1933, State Archives.
12. Charles S. Judd, *Daily Journal 1934*, January 2, 1934, State Archives; Lawrence M. Judd, radiogram to Harold L. Ickes, January 10, 1934, State Archives, gov 7-26, Judd, Interior, CCC.
13. Joseph B. Poindexter, radiogram to Harold L. Ickes, March 6, 1934, State Archives, gov 8-18, Poindexter, Emergency Relations, ECW.
14. Charles S. Judd, "Program for Emergency Conservation Work—Territory of Hawaii," October 28, 1933, 28, 29, State Archives, com 2-12, Brown, Correspondence, ECW, 1933-34; Charles S. Judd to Major General Briant H. Wells, January 26, 1934; Major General Briant H.

Wells to Charles S. Judd, January 30, 1934, State Archives, gov 7-26, Judd, Interior, CCC; Joseph B. Poindexter to Harold L. Ickes, March 15, 1934, State Archives, gov 8-18, Poindexter, Emergency Relations, ECW.

15. Charles S. Judd, "Program for Emergency Conservation Work—Territory of Hawaii," October 28, 1933, 27, State Archives, com 2-12, Brown, Correspondence, ECW, 1933–34.

16. Ibid., 9–13.

17. See the individual trail chapters for sources on this and subsequent paragraphs on trail building in this section.

18. Charles Gray, "Trailblazers Recall Exciting, Difficult Work 65 Years Ago," *Kaneohe Sun Press*, July 9, 1999.

19. Charles S. Judd, "Program for Emergency Conservation Work, Territory of Hawaii, Second Enrollment Period: October 1, 1934 to March 31, 1935 (June 7, 1934)," 1–2, State Archives, com 2-12, Brown, ECW, 1933–34.

20. Joseph B. Poindexter to Harold L. Ickes, June 16, 1934, State Archives, gov 8-18, Poindexter, Emergency Relations, ECW.

21. A. S. Newman, "Mountain Trails Are Built By Boys in the ECW Camp," *Honolulu Star-Bulletin*, April 14, 1934, 4.

22. Charles S. Judd, "Emergency Conservation Work, Territory of Hawaii, Program for Fifth Enrollment Period from April 1, 1935 to September 30, 1935," State Archives, com 2-33, Judd, ECW, CCC programs 1935–38.

23. Gunder E. Olson, "Narrative Report—Island of Oahu, Men Working from Homes, Fifth Enrollment Period, April 1 to September 30, 1935," 14, State Archives, com 2-35, Judd, ECW Reports, 1935.

24. Charles S. Judd, "Emergency Conservation Work, Territory of Hawaii, Program for Sixth Enrollment Period from October 1, 1935 to March 31, 1936," State Archives, com 2-33, ECW, CCC program, 1935–38.

25. Charles S. Judd, *Daily Journal 1935*, November 22–23, 1935, State Archives.

26. Glenn W. Russ, "Routine Report of the Assistant Forester, March-June 1936," State Archives, com 2-36, Reports, Monthly, Russ.

27. "Charles Judd Dies at 57 in Hospital Here," *Honolulu Star-Bulletin*, June 29, 1939, 1.

28. Charles Sheldon Judd obituary, *Honolulu Star-Bulletin*, June 30, 1939, 1.

29. Press release for the liquidation of the CCC, State Archives, gov 8-18, Poindexter, Emergency Relations, CCC; Report of the Board of Commissioners of Agriculture and Forestry of the Territory of Hawaii, Biennial Period ending 12/31/44.

30. Martha Beckwith, *Hawaiian Mythology* (Honolulu: University of Hawai'i Press, 1979), 340–341.

31. Charles S. Judd, *Daily Journal 1931*, February 20, 1931, State Archives.

32. Glenn W. Russ, "Routine Report of the Assistant Forester, March 1931," State Archives, com 2-36, Reports, Monthly, Russ.

33. Charles S. Judd, *Daily Journal 1932*, January 20, 1932, State Archives.

34. HTMC hike schedule, May 22, 1932, HTMC Archives.

35. Charles S. Judd, "Routine Report of the Territorial Forester, October 1932," *The Hawaiian Forester and Agriculturist*, October–December 1932, 107; Charles S. Judd, *Daily Journal 1932*, October 5, 1932, State Archives.

36. Charles S. Judd, *Daily Journal 1933*, July 11, 1933, State Archives.

37. Charles S. Judd, "Program for Emergency Conservation Work—Territory of Hawaii," October 28, 1933, 10, State Archives, com 2-12, Brown, Corres, ECW, 1933–34.

38. A. S. Newman, "Mountain Trails Are Built By Boys in the ECW Camp," *Honolulu Star-Bulletin*, April 14, 1934, 4; Charles S. Judd, *Daily Journal 1934*, April 24, 1934, State Archives.

39. Charles S. Judd, *Daily Journal 1934*, July 6, 1934, State Archives.

40. Ibid.; Report of the Board of Commissioners of Agriculture and Forestry of the Territory of Hawaii, Biennial Period ending 12/31/34, 18.

41. Charles S. Judd, *Daily Journal 1935*, April 24, 1935, State Archives.

42. Ibid.; HTMC hike schedule, July 14, 1935; Captain Joseph B. Sweet, hike announcement to Charles S. Judd, July 6, 1935, Judd manuscript, State Archives, M-77, Box 1-14.

43. Charles S. Judd, *Daily Journal 1935*, November 3, 1935, State Archives; Captain Joseph B. Sweet, hike announcement to Piko Club members, October 25, 1935, Judd manuscript, State Archives, M-77, Box 1-14.

44. Robert C. Bayless, "Narrative Report of the Wahiawa Camp—Fifth Period," State Archives, com 2-35, Reports, ECW reports, 1935, 1; CCC Project map (4/1–9/30/36), State Archives, G4382.O2N1(1936).U54.C5; Charles S. Judd, *Daily Journal 1936*, April 9 and May 21, 1936, State Archives; Hike announcement to Piko Club members, October 23, 1936, Judd manuscript, State Archives, M-77, Box 1-14.

45. Richard H. Davis, interview, July 27, 2001; Lieutenant General Walter C. Short to Board of Commission, Agriculture and Forestry, June 28, 1941; F. H. Locey to General Walter C. Short, July 5, 1941.

46. Division of Forestry, Forest Trail Map of the Island of Oahu (1947); HTMC hike schedule, September 26, 1948, HTMC Archives.

47. Hawai'i Audubon Society, hike record, May 8, 1955, HTMC Archives.

48. HTMC hike schedule, February 2–3, 1974.

49. HTMC hike schedule, January 22, 1978; HTMC newsletter, March 1978.

50. HTMC hike schedule, April 9, 1978; Harry Whitten, "Palila Recovery Plan," *Honolulu Star-Bulletin*, April 17, 1978, A17.

51. Jim Yuen, interview, April 17, 2006; Stuart Ball, hike notes, September 24, 2000.

52. Edmund J. Meadows, *Oahu Trail* (pamphlet), circa 1930, HTMC Archives; Charles S. Judd, *Daily Journal 1934*, May 1, 1934, State Archives; Charles S. Judd, "Report of the Territorial Forester, February 23, 1933 for 1931–2," *The Hawaiian Forester and Agriculturist*, January–March 1933, 22.

53. HTMC hike schedule, May 8, 1932, HTMC Archives.

54. Charles S. Judd, *Daily Journal 1933*, June 2, 1933, State Archives.

55. Charles S. Judd, "Program for Emergency Conservation Work—Territory of Hawaii," October 28, 1933, 11–12, State Archives, com 2-12, Brown, ECW.

56. A. S. Newman, "Mountain Trails Are Built By Boys in the ECW Camp," *Honolulu Star-Bulletin*, April 14, 1934, 4.

57. Charles S. Judd, *Daily Journal 1934*, May 1, 1934, State Archives.

58. Charles S. Judd, *Daily Journal 1934*, September 8, 1934, State Archives.

59. Charles S. Judd, *Daily Journal 1935*, December 15, 1935, State Archives; Captain Joseph B. Sweet, hike announcement to Piko Club members, December 6, 1935, State Archives, Judd manuscript, M-77, Box 1-14.

60. Charles S. Judd to Captain Joseph B. Sweet, December 23, 1935, State Archives, Judd manuscript, M-77, Box 1-14.

61. HTMC hike schedule, February 17, 1935; Charles S. Judd, *Daily Journal 1935*, May 7–8, 1935, State Archives.

62. Charles S. Judd, *Daily Journal 1936*, June 3, 1936, State Archives; Charles S. Judd to Captain Leroy C. Wilson, June 26, 1936, Judd manuscript, M-77, Box 1-14.

63. War Department, Corps of Engineers, U.S. Army, *Kaena quadrangle* (1943), UH Hamilton, G4382.O2s20 1943.v5; Harry Whitten, "Trail Ways," *Honolulu Star-Bulletin*, May 29, 1954, Hawaiian Life section, 14.

64. Division of Forestry, Forest Trail Map of the Island of Oahu (1947).

65. Harry Whitten, "Trail Ways," *Honolulu Star-Bulletin*, July 22, 1950, 10.

66. HTMC hike schedule, February 20–22, 1965, HTMC Archives.

67. Division of Forestry and Wildlife, Pahole Natural Area Reserve (1994 brochure).

68. Ralph S. Hosmer, "Report of the Superintendent of Forestry, June 14, 1913," *The Hawaiian Forester and Agriculturist*, June 1913, 147.

69. Charles S. Judd, *Daily Journal 1931*, March 19, 1931, State Archives; Notes for Piko Club history, March 19, 1931, State Archives, Judd manuscript, M-77, Box 1-14.

70. Charles S. Judd, "Program for Emergency Conservation Work—Territory of Hawaii," October 28, 1933, 12, State Archives, com 2-12, Brown, Corres, ECW, 1933-34.
71. A. S. Newman, "Mountain Trails Are Built By Boys in the ECW Camp," *Honolulu Star-Bulletin*, April 14, 1934, 4.
72. Report of the Board of Commissioners of Agriculture and Forestry of the Territory of Hawaii, Biennial Period ending 12/31/34, 18.
73. HTMC hike schedule, February 17, 1935, HTMC Archives; Charles S. Judd, *Daily Journal 1935*, May 7-8, 1935, State Archives; Charles S. Judd, "Hiking on Oahu Reveals Beauties of Nature in Friendly Mountains," *Honolulu Star-Bulletin*, May 23, 1936, section 3, page 1.
74. Gwenfread Allen, *Hawaii's War Years* (Kailua: Pacific Monograph, 1999), 240.
75. War Department, Corps of Engineers, U.S. Army, *Kaena quadrangle* (1943), UH Hamilton, G4382.O2s20 1943.v5.
76. Division of Forestry, Forest Trail Map of the Island of Oahu (1947).
77. Harry Whitten, "Trail Ways," *Honolulu Star-Bulletin*, May 29, 1954, Hawaiian Life section, 14; Harry Whitten, "Trail Ways," *Honolulu Star-Bulletin*, HTMC 1950s scrapbook, HTMC Archives.
78. "1st Isle Nike Missile Fired Successfully," *Honolulu Star-Bulletin*, November 8, 1961, 1.
79. HTMC hike schedule and record, May 14, 1961, HTMC Archives.
80. HTMC newsletter, September 1993, HTMC Archives.
81. Charles S. Judd, *Daily Journal 1932*, October 20-21, 1932, State Archives; Charles S. Judd, "Routine Report of the Territorial Forester, October 1932," *The Hawaiian Forester and Agriculturist*, October-December 1932, 166.
82. Charles S. Judd, "Program for Emergency Conservation Work—Territory of Hawaii," October 28, 1933, 10, State Archives, com 2-12, Brown, Correspondence ECW, 1933-34.
83. A. S. Newman, "Mountain Trails Are Built by Boys in the ECW Camp," *Honolulu Star-Bulletin*, April 14, 1934, 4.
84. Charles S. Judd, Notes for Piko Club history, May 27, 1934, Judd manuscript, State Archives, M-77, Box 1-14; Louisa L. and Emma Judd to Major General Briant H. Wells, July 7, 1934, Judd manuscript, State Archives, M-77, Box 1-13.
85. Charles S. Judd, *Daily Journal 1934*, August 15, 1934, State Archives.
86. Charles S. Judd, *Daily Journal 1934*, August 15, 1934, State Archives; Report of the Board of Commissioners of Agriculture and Forestry of the Territory of Hawaii, Biennial Period ending 12/31/34, 18.
87. HTMC hike schedule, May 12, 1935, HTMC Archives.
88. "Emergency Conservation Work, Territory of Hawaii, Program for the Sixth Enrollment Period October 1, 1935, to March 31, 1936," 5, State Archives, com 2-33, ECW, CCC program, 1935-38.
89. Charles S. Judd, *Daily Journal 1935*, November 1, 1935, State Archives.
90. Charles S. Judd, *Daily Journal 1935*, November 6, 1935, State Archives.
91. Charles S. Judd, "Routine Report of the Territorial Forester, November 1935," State Archives, com 2-11, Routine, Div. of Forestry.
92. General Hugh A. Drum to Everett E. Tillett, November 18, 1935; Everett E. Tillett to General Hugh A. Drum, November 22, 1935, State Archives, com 2-33, ECW, Field Supervisor, 1935-40.
93. Charles S. Judd, "Routine Report of the Territorial Forester, November 1935," State Archives, com 2-11, Routine, Div. of Forestry.
94. Charles S. Judd, "Routine Report of the Territorial Forester, February 1936," State Archives, com 2-11, Routine, Div. of Forestry; U.S. Army Corps of Engineers, Specifications, ERA Road and Trail Project OP 13-296 (War Department, 1936).
95. Richard H. Davis, interview, July 27, 2001; HTMC hike schedule, February 24, 1946.
96. Division of Forestry, Forest Trail Map of the Island of Oahu (1947); HTMC hike schedule, March 29, 1964.
97. HTMC hike schedule, January 23, 1983; Stuart Ball, hike notes, January 23, 1983; HTMC newsletter, March 1983.

98. HTMC hike schedule, August 7, 1994; Stuart Ball, hike notes, July 31, 1994, and August 7, 1994.
99. Patrick Rorie, interview, August 29, 2009.
100. Charles S. Judd, *Daily Journal 1926*, October 6, 1926, State Archives.
101. Charles S. Judd to George Ii Brown, October 10, 1926, State Archives, com 2-12, Brown, Judd.
102. Charles S. Judd, "Routine Report of the Superintendent of Forestry, December 1926," *The Hawaiian Forester and Agriculturist*, January–March 1927, 4; Charles S. Judd, "Routine Report of the Superintendent of Forestry, March 1927," *The Hawaiian Forester and Agriculturist*, January–March 1927, 13; Charles S. Judd, *Daily Journal 1927*, January 10, 1927, State Archives.
103. HTMC hike schedule and record, August 8, 1927, and July 29, 1928, HTMC Archives.
104. Glenn W. Russ, "Routine Report of the Assistant Forester, June 1931." State Archives, com 2-36, Reports, Monthly, Russ.
105. Charles S. Judd, *Daily Journal 1932*, September 29, 1932, State Archives.
106. Charles S. Judd, "Program for Emergency Conservation Work—Territory of Hawaii," October 28, 1933, 12, State Archives, com 2-12, Brown, ECW, 1933–34.
107. Charles S. Judd, *Daily Journal 1934*, July 13, 1934, State Archives.
108. Gunder E. Olson, "Project Superintendent's Narrative Report, Honolulu Unit, Island of Oahu, Fourth Enrollment Period, October 1, 1934–March 31, 1935," 2–3, Talbert Takahama papers.
109. Charles S. Judd, *Daily Journal 1935*, February 20, 1935, State Archives.
110. Charles S. Judd, *Daily Journal 1935*, March 20, 1935, State Archives.
111. Gunder E. Olson, "Project Superintendent's Narrative Report, Honolulu Unit, Island of Oahu, Fourth Enrollment Period, October 1, 1934–March 31, 1935," 11, Talbert Takahama papers.
112. Charles S. Judd, *Daily Journal 1935*, March 24, 1935, State Archives.
113. HTMC hike schedule, September 15, 1935.
114. Gunder E. Olson, "Project Superintendent's Narrative Report, Honolulu Unit, Island of Oahu, Fourth Enrollment Period, October 1, 1934–March 31, 1935," 2, Talbert Takahama papers.
115. Charles S. Judd, *Daily Journal 1935*, December 19, 1935, State Archives.
116. Charles S. Judd to Captain J. B. Sweet, December 23, 1935, Judd manuscript, State Archives, M-77, Box 1-14.
117. Charles S. Judd, *Daily Journal 1936*, March 15, 1936, State Archives.
118. Charles S. Judd, *Daily Journal 1936*, September 27, 1936, State Archives.
119. Charles S. Judd to Glenn W. Russ, September 28, 1936, State Archives, com 2-33, Asst Forester, Russ.
120. Richard H. Davis, interview, July 27, 2001.
121. Division of Forestry, Forest Trail Map of the Island of Oahu (1947).
122. John F. Mink, "Rainfall and Runoff in the Leeward Koolau Mountains, Oahu, Hawaii," *Pacific Science*, April 1962, 147–159.
123. HTMC hike schedule, November 23, 1980, February 8, 1987, and June 9, 1991.
124. Nancy Hoffman, interview, April 27, 2006.
125. Nancy Hoffman, interview, April 27, 2006; Patrick Rorie, "Kipapa TM," March 6, 2001. http://www2.hawaii.edu/~turner/ohe/.
126. Dayle Turner, "Kipapa TM," March 24, 2002. http://www2.hawaii.edu/~turner/ohe/; HTMC hike schedule, October 18, 2003.
127. J. Gilbert McAllister, *Archaeology of Oahu* (Honolulu: Bernice P. Bishop Museum bulletin 104, 1985), 176; Lorin Gill, interview, March 7, 2004.
128. J. Gilbert McAllister, *Archaeology of Oahu* (Honolulu: Bernice P. Bishop Museum bulletin 104, 1985), 103.
129. "Hikers Tramp to Little Known Ridge," *Pacific Commercial Advertiser*, February 7, 1921, 2, 4; Thomas R. L. McGuire, "More Trails of Interest to Oahu Hikers," *Honolulu Star-Bulletin*, August 2, 1946, 14.

130. HTMC hike schedule, September 21, 1930, HTMC Archives.

131. Charles S. Judd, "Program for Emergency Conservation Work, Territory of Hawaii, Second Enrollment Period: October 1, 1934 to March 31, 1935 (June 7, 1934)," 2, State Archives, com 2-12, Brown, ECW, 1933–34.

132. Gunder E. Olson, "Project Superintendent's Narrative Report, Honolulu Unit, Island of Oahu, Fourth Enrollment Period, October 1, 1934–March 31, 1935," 5–7, Talbert Takahama papers.

133. Gunder E. Olson, "Narrative Report—Island of Oahu, Men Working from Homes, Fifth Enrollment Period, April 1 to September 30, 1935," 14, State Archives, com 2-35, Judd, ECW Reports, 1935.

134. Gunder E. Olson to Charles S. Judd, July 9, 1935, State Archives, com 2-33, Judd, ECW, CCC program, 1935–38.

135. Charles S. Judd, "Emergency Conservation Work, Territory of Hawaii, Program for Sixth Enrollment period from October 1, 1935 to March 31, 1936," 2, State Archives, com 2-33, ECW, CCC program, 1935–38.

136. Charles S. Judd, *Daily Journal 1935*, October 2, 1935, State Archives.

137. Gunder E. Olson, "Emergency Conservation Work Honolulu Unit's Project Superintendent Narrative Report—Sixth Enrollment Period October 1, 1935–March 31, 1936," State Archives, com 2-33, Asst Forester, Russ.

138. Everett E. Tillett to Charles S. Judd, April 3, 1936, State Archives, com 2-33, ECW, Field Supervisor.

139. Charles S. Judd to Everett E. Tillett, April 6, 1936, State Archives, com 2-33, ECW, Field Supervisor.

140. HTMC hike schedule, May 24, 1936, November 24, 1935, and November 15, 1936.

141. Kenneth J. Thompson, "Memorial Day: Remember the Others," *Honolulu Advertiser*, May 29, 1994, B3.

142. Division of Forestry, Forest Trail Map of the Island of Oahu (1947); Joseph Neilson, interview, February 11, 2000.

143. Nils P. Larsen, "Rededication of the Healing Heiau Keaiwa," Sixteenth Annual Report of the Hawaiian Historical Society for the Year 1951, 7–16.

144. Report of the Board of Commissioners of Agriculture and Forestry of the Territory of Hawaii, Biennial Period ending 6/30/52, 92.

145. Report of the Board of Commissioners of Agriculture and Forestry of the Territory of Hawaii, Biennial Period ending 6/30/56, 102.

146. Richard Booth, interview, March 11, 2000; HTMC newsletter, March 1983.

147. Charles S. Judd, "Program for Emergency Conservation Work, Territory of Hawaii, Second Enrollment Period: October 1, 1934 to March 31, 1935 (June 7, 1934)," 1, State Archives, com 2-12, Brown, ECW, 1933–34.

148. Charles S. Judd, *Daily Journal 1934*, August 8, 1934, State Archives.

149. Charles S. Judd, *Daily Journal 1934*, December 28, 1934, State Archives.

150. Charles S. Judd, *Daily Journal 1935*, March 8, 1935, State Archives.

151. Charles S. Judd, *Daily Journal 1935*, March 30, 1935, State Archives.

152. Robert C. Bayless to Charles S. Judd, July 2 and August 5, 1935, State Archives, com 2-34, ECW, Supt of Foremen, CCC Camp, 1935–41; Robert C. Bayless, "Narrative Report of the Wahiawa Camp-Fifth Period," State Archives, com 2-35, Reports, ECW reports, 1935, 1.

153. Charles S. Judd to Captain Joseph B. Sweet, June 20, 1935, Judd manuscript, State Archives, M-77, Box 1-14; Charles S. Judd, *Daily Journal 1935*, September 1, 1935, State Archives; Charles S. Judd, Route of Paumalu to Laie hike (map), Judd manuscript.

154. HTMC hike schedule, October 6, 1935, HTMC Archives.

155. Daldon Asem, "Wailele," *Paradise of the Pacific*, January 1936, 32.

156. Charles S. Judd, *Daily Journal 1936*, January 3, 1936, State Archives.

157. Richard H. Davis, interview, July 27, 2001.

158. Division of Forestry, Forest Trail Map of the Island of Oahu (1947).

159. HTMC hike schedule, February 22–23, 1953, and December 18, 1960, HTMC Archives.
160. Lorin Gill, interview, March 15, 2006.
161. HTMC hike schedule, March 23, 1986, and February 5, 2006, HTMC Archives; Stuart Ball, hike notes, February 5, 2006.
162. Joseph Neilson, interview, February 13, 2000.
163. Charles S. Judd, "Program for Emergency Conservation Work, Territory of Hawaii, Second Enrollment Period: October 1, 1934 to March 31, 1935 (June 7, 1934)," 2, State Archives.
164. Charles S. Judd, *Daily Journal 1934*, October 11, 1934, State Archives.
165. Charles S. Judd, *Daily Journal 1934*, December 20, 1934, State Archives.
166. Gunder E. Olson, "Project Superintendent's Narrative Report, Honolulu Unit, Island of Oahu, Fourth Enrollment Period, October 1, 1934–March 31, 1935," 3, Talbert Takahama papers.
167. Charles S. Judd, *Daily Journal 1935*, February 24, 1935, State Archives.
168. Gunder E. Olson, "Narrative Report—Island of Oahu, Men Working from Homes, Fifth Enrollment Period, April 1 to September 30, 1935," 23, State Archives, com 2-35, Reports, ECW Reports 1935.
169. Ibid., 22–24.
170. Charles S. Judd, "Emergency Conservation Work, Territory of Hawaii, Program for Sixth Enrollment period from October 1, 1935 to March 31, 1936," 3, State Archives, com 2-33, ECW, CCC program, 1935–38; HTMC hike schedule, November 10, 1935, HTMC Archives.
171. HTMC hike schedule, May 10, 1936.
172. HTMC hike schedule, November 15, 1936.
173. David O. Woodbury, "The High Scalers of Haiku," *Readers Digest*, October 1950, 137–140; Gwenfread Allen, *Hawaii's War Years* (Kailua: Pacific Monograph, 1999), 242.
174. Harry Whitten, "Trail Ways," *Honolulu Star-Bulletin*, October 7, 1950, 14; Joseph Neilson, interview, February 13, 2000.
175. Division of Forestry, Forest Trail Map of the Island of Oahu (1947); HTMC hike schedule, July 31, 1966.
176. HTMC hike schedule, March 19, 1972; Richard Schmidt, interview, July 26, 2006.
177. Charles S. Judd, "Program for Emergency Conservation Work—Territory of Hawaii, October 28, 1933," 10–11, State Archives, com 2-12, Brown ECW.
178. Charles S. Judd, *Daily Journal 1934*, January 27, 1934, State Archives.
179. Charles S. Judd, *Daily Journal 1934*, May 18, 1934, State Archives.
180. Charles S. Judd, *Daily Journal 1934*, July 30, 1934, State Archives.
181. Gunder E. Olson, "Project Superintendent's Narrative Report, Honolulu Unit, Island of Oahu, Fourth Enrollment Period, October 1, 1934–March 31, 1935," Talbert Takahama papers.
182. Charles S. Judd, *Daily Journal 1934*, October 18, 1934, State Archives.
183. Gunder E. Olson, "Project Superintendent's Narrative Report, Honolulu Unit, Island of Oahu, Fourth Enrollment Period, October 1, 1934–March 31, 1935," Talbert Takahama papers.
184. Gunder E. Olson, Narrative Report—Island of Oahu, Men Working from Homes, Fifth Enrollment Period, April 1 to September 30, 1935," State Archives, com 2-35, Judd, ECW Reports 1935.
185. Ibid.
186. Captain Joseph B. Sweet, hike announcement to Charles S. Judd, July 6, 1935, Judd manuscript, State Archives, M-77, Box 1-14; Charles S. Judd, *Daily Journal 1935*, July 14, 1935, State Archives.
187. Colonel (ret.) Thomas J. Wells, interview, February 14, 2000.
188. Glenn W. Russ, "Routine Report of the Assistant Forester, August and September 1935," State Archives, com 2-36, Reports, Monthly, Russ.
189. Gunder E. Olson, Narrative Report—Island of Oahu, Men Working from Homes, Fifth Enrollment Period, April 1 to September 30, 1935," State Archives, com 2-35, Judd, ECW Reports 1935.

190. Charles S. Judd, *Daily Journal 1935,* September 13, 1935, State Archives; Charles S. Judd, "Emergency Conservation Work, Territory of Hawaii, Projects for the Sixth Enrollment Period October 1, 1935 to March 31, 1936," State Archives, com 2-33, CCC Programs 1935-38.

191. Charles S. Judd, *Daily Journal 1935,* November 23, 1935.

192. Charles S. Judd to Captain Joseph B. Sweet, December 23, 1935, Judd manuscript, State Archives, M-77, Box 1-14; Charles S. Judd, *Daily Journal 1935,* December 19, 1935.

193. Gunder E. Olson, "Emergency Conservation Work Honolulu Unit's Project Superintendent Narrative Report—Sixth Enrollment Period, October 1, 1935-March 31, 1936," State Archives, com 2-33, Russ.

194. Glenn W. Russ, "Routine Report of the Assistant Forester, January 1936," State Archives, com 2-36, Reports, Monthly, Russ.

195. Gunder E. Olson, "Emergency Conservation Work Honolulu Unit's Project Superintendent Narrative Report—Sixth Enrollment Period, October 1, 1935-March 31, 1936," State Archives, com 2-33, Russ.

196. Glenn W. Russ, "Routine Report of the Assistant Forester, March-June 1936," State Archives, com 2-36, Reports, Monthly, Russ.

197. Daily Information Sheet, Headquarters, Schofield Barracks, September 14, 1936, Judd manuscript, State Archives, M-77, Box 1-14.

198. Charles S. Judd to Glenn W. Russ, September 28, 1936, Judd manuscript, State Archives, M-77, Box 1-14.

199. Richard H. Davis, interview, July 27, 2001.

200. Gwenfread Allen, *Hawaii's War Years* (Kailua: Pacific Monograph, 1999), 136.

201. HTMC hike schedule, September 2, 1945, HTMC Archives.

202. Harry Whitten, "Trail Ways," *Honolulu Star-Bulletin,* June 9, 1951, 19; "Trail Ways," *Honolulu Star-Bulletin.* 1950s scrapbook, HTMC Archives.

203. Beryl Sawyer, "Summit Trail: July 3-4, 1955," HTMC Archives; HTMC hike schedule, third quarter 1955.

204. Wes Williams, interview, 2002.

205. Harry Whitten, "72nd Birthday Celebrated with 5-Day Koolau Hike," *Honolulu Star-Bulletin,* May 1, 1973, C-8.

206. HTMC hike schedule, February 2-3, 1974, HTMC Archives.

207. HTMC hike schedule, May 29-31, 1976, HTMC Archives; Jim Yuen, interview, May 14, 2002.

208. Harry Whitten, "Hiking the Koolau Summit," *Honolulu Star-Bulletin,* August 27, 1979, A-13.

209. HTMC hike schedule, May 26-28, 1984, HTMC Archives; Stuart Ball, trip notes, May 26-28, 1984.

210. Stuart Ball, trip notes, May 27-29, 1989, and August 19-21, 1989.

211. Stuart Ball, trip notes, May 28-30, 1994.

212. Patrick Rorie, "The Hike of All Hikes, Days 1, 2, and 3," May 27, 29, and June 1, 1998; Gene Robinson, "As Dirty Harry Said . . .," May 27, 1998, both from http://www2.hawaii.edu/~turner/ohe.html.

213. Kapua Kawelo, interview, 2006.

214. Dayle K. Turner, "KST Backpack Trip-Prologue, Days 1, 2, and 3," August 2-4, 1999, http://www2.hawaii.edu/~turner/ohe.html.

215. Dayle K. Turner, "HTMC KST Backpack 2000—Days 1, 2, and 3," May 29-31, 2000, http://www2.hawaii.edu/~turner/ohe.html.

216. Management Plan for the Opaeula Watershed Protection Project, April 1999; Kapua Kawelo, interview, 2006.

217. HTMC hike schedule and record, January 27, 1924, HTMC Archives; Sergeant Tracy, "Roads and Trails of Oahu" (unpublished pamphlet, September 1939); Charles S. Judd, *Daily Journal 1925,* December 8, 1925, State Archives.

218. Charles S. Judd, *Daily Journal 1931,* February 9 and April 22, 1931, State Archives.

219. Charles S. Judd, "Emergency Conservation Work, Territory of Hawaii, Program for Sixth Enrollment Period from October 1, 1935 to March 31, 1936," 5, State Archives, com 2-33, ECW, CCC program, 1935–38.
220. Charles S. Judd, *Daily Journal 1935*, November 12, 1935, State Archives.
221. Charles S. Judd, *Daily Journal 1935*, November 20, 1935, State Archives.
222. Charles S. Judd, *Daily Journal 1936*, January 15 and 23, 1936, State Archives.
223. Charles S. Judd to Captain Joseph B. Sweet, January 24, 1936; Captain Joseph B. Sweet, hike announcement to Piko Club members, January 27, 1936; Charles S. Judd to Major General Briant H. Wells, February 18, 1936, all from State Archives, Judd manuscript, M-77, Box 1-14.
224. Glenn W. Russ, "Routine Report of the Assistant Forester, July and September 1936," State Archives, com 2-36, Reports, Monthly, Russ.
225. Captain Leroy C. Wilson to Charles S. Judd, December 11, 1936, State Archives, Judd manuscript, M-77, Box 1-14.
226. Major General Hugh Drum to Charles S. Judd, December 14, 1936; Frank H. Locey to Major General Hugh Drum, December 16, 1936; Frank H. Locey to Henry C. Wolfe, February 11, 1937, all from State Archives, com 2-16, Hawaiian Dept.
227. Sergeant Tracy, "Roads and Trails of Oahu" (unpublished pamphlet, September 1939); U.S. Army Corps of Engineers, Specifications, ERA Road and Trail Project OP 13–296 (War Department, 1936).
228. James Jones, *From Here to Eternity* (New York: Charles Scribner's Sons, 1951), 12.
229. Thomas R. L. McGuire, "More Trails of Interest to Oahu Hikers," *Honolulu Star-Bulletin*, August 8, 1946, 14; War Department, Corps of Engineers, U.S. Army, *Nanakuli and Waipahu quadrangles* (1943), UH Hamilton, G4382.O2s20 1943.v5.
230. Division of Forestry, Forest Trail Map of the Island of Oahu (1947); Harry Whitten, "Trail Ways: Waianae Range Is Scenic," *Honolulu Star-Bulletin*, February 10, 1951, 12.
231. HTMC hike schedule, April 27, 1969.
232. HTMC hike schedule, June 20, 1954; Harry Whitten, "Trail Ways," *Honolulu Star-Bulletin*, June 19, 1954, Hawaiian Life section, 14.
233. HTMC hike schedule, July 1, 1951.
234. HTMC hike schedule, December 15, 1957.
235. The Nature Conservancy of Hawaii, Honouliuli Preserve, Oahu (fact sheet).
236. William Gorst, interview, June 28, 2010; "Honouliuli Preserve Watershed Purchased and Protected," http://www.tpl.org.

Volunteer Trails

1. "Sierra Club to Have Isle Chapter," *Honolulu Star-Bulletin*, May 10, 1968, A4; *Mālama I Ka Honua*, Sierra Club, Hawai'i Chapter newsletter, May 1969 and November 1969.
2. *Mālama I Ka Honua*, Sierra Club, Hawai'i Chapter newsletter, March 1971 and April 1971.
3. Lorin Gill, interview, January 5, 2009; *Mālama I Ka Honua*, Sierra Club, Hawai'i Chapter newsletter, August 1971, September 1972, May 1974, and June 1976.
4. *Mālama I Ka Honua*, Sierra Club, Hawai'i Chapter newsletter, May 1978, insert; see the individual trail chapters for sources on this and subsequent paragraphs on trail building in this section.
5. Division of Forestry and Wildlife, Program Plan Na Ala Hele, Hawai'i Trail & Access System, II-3, II-11; *Mālama I Ka Honua*, Sierra Club, Hawai'i Chapter newsletter, April–May 1991.
6. *Mālama I Ka Honua*, Sierra Club, Hawai'i Chapter newsletter, April–May 1987; Lorin Gill, interview, January 5, 2009; Curt Cottrell, interview, November 13, 2008.
7. Curt Cottrell, interview, November 13, 2008; *Mālama I Ka Honua*, Sierra Club, Hawai'i Chapter newsletter, April–May and September–November 1988.

Notes to Pages 218–229

8. Division of Forestry and Wildlife, Program Plan Na Ala Hele, Hawai'i Trail & Access System, I-2.
9. Curt Cottrell, interview, November 13, 2008.
10. Division of Forestry and Wildlife, Program Plan Na Ala Hele, Hawai'i Trail & Access System, II-3, II-11.
11. Curt Cottrell, interview, November 13, 2008.
12. Richard H. Davis, interview, July 27, 2001; Richard Booth, interview, March 11, 2000.
13. HTMC newsletter, March 1983, HTMC Archives.
14. Stuart Ball, hike notes, various.
15. Mabel Kekina, interview, March 9, 2009.
16. Richard H. Davis, interview, July 27, 2001; HTMC newsletter, December 1993, HTMC Archives.
17. HTMC hike schedule, July 30, 1961, HTMC Archives.
18. HTMC hike schedule, February 4, 1962.
19. Richard H. Davis, interview, July 27, 2001.
20. Richard H. Davis, interview, July 27, 2001; Stuart Ball, hike notes, various Likeke.
21. Stuart Ball, hike notes, September 25, 2004.
22. Charles S. Judd, *Daily Journal 1925*, January 8, 1925, State Archives.
23. HTMC hike schedule, October 3, 1965, HTMC Archives.
24. HTMC hike schedule, June 19, 1966, October 22, 1967, and June 1, 1969; Department of Land and Natural Resources, "Trails, Hunting & Park Areas, Island of Oahu" (circa 1970).
25. HTMC hike schedule, May 25, 1968.
26. "Palisade Fire Burns Overnight," *Honolulu Advertiser*, October 18, 1972, A-19.
27. HTMC hike schedule, January 14, 1973.
28. HTMC hike schedule, June 20, 1998; Dayle K. Turner, "HTMC Super Hike 1–for the record," June 20, 1998, http://www2.hawaii.edu/~turner/ohe.html.
29. "One Day Along a Mountain Trail," *Pacific Commercial Advertiser*, September 10, 1911, 6; Lorin Gill, interview, March 7, 2004.
30. King David Kalakaua, *The Legends and Myths of Old Hawaii* (Honolulu: Mutual Publishing Company, 1990), 509–522; Lorin Gill, interview, March 7, 2004.
31. Albertine Loomis, *For Whom Are the Stars?* (Honolulu: University of Hawai'i Press, 1976), 164.
32. Ed Towse, *The Rebellion of 1895, A Complete and Concise Account* (Honolulu: Hawaiian Star, 1895), 5–6, 57; "A Brief Record of Rebellion," in *Thrum's Hawaiian Annual 1896* (Honolulu: The Printshop Company, Ltd., 1900), 56–57.
33. Mānoa Valley Residents, *Mānoa, the Story of a Valley* (Honolulu: Mutual Publishing, 1994), 200–201; Lorin Gill, interview, March 7, 2004.
34. Lorin Gill, interview, September 18, 2008; Andrea Gill, interview, October 9, 2008.
35. *Mālama I Ka Honua,* Sierra Club, Hawai'i Chapter newsletter, March 1978, 6.
36. *Mālama I Ka Honua,* Sierra Club, Hawai'i Chapter newsletter, May 1978, insert.
37. *Mālama I Ka Honua,* Sierra Club, Hawai'i Chapter newsletter, July 1978, 3–4; Andrea Gill, interview, October 9, 2008.
38. *Mālama I Ka Honua,* Sierra Club, Hawai'i Chapter newsletter, September 1978, 3; *Mālama I Ka Honua,* Sierra Club, Hawai'i Chapter newsletter, October 1978, 3; Andrea Gill, interview, October 9, 2008.
39. *The Hawaiian Forester and Agriculturalist*, October 1913, 325; "Report of Forest Nurseryman David Haughs," *The Hawaiian Forester and Agriculturalist*, October 1913, 299.
40. "Honolulu Watershed Planting," *The Hawaiian Forester and Agriculturalist*, July 1915, 189; Lorin Gill, interview, March 7, 2004.
41. "December Trail Club Schedule Now Arranged," *Pacific Commercial Advertiser*, 1920s scrapbook, HTMC Archives.
42. Division of Forestry, Forest Trail Map of the Island of Oahu (1947).

43. Report of the Board of Commissioners of Agriculture and Forestry of the Territory of Hawaii, Biennial Period ending 6/30/56, 102.
44. *Mālama I Ka Honua,* Sierra Club, Hawai'i Chapter newsletter, October 1978, 3.
45. "New Trails on Makiki-Tantalus," *Mālama I Ka Honua,* Sierra Club, Hawai'i Chapter newsletter, May 1979, HSTP reader.
46. *Mālama I Ka Honua,* Sierra Club, Hawai'i Chapter newsletter, April, June, and July–August 1979, HSTP reader; Andrea Gill, interview, October 28, 2008.
47. *Mālama I Ka Honua,* Sierra Club, Hawai'i Chapter newsletter, July–August 1979, HSTP reader; Andrea Gill, interview, October 9, 2008.
48. Andrea Gill, interview, October 9, 2008; New Tantalus Loop, November 4, *Mālama I Ka Honua,* Sierra Club, Hawai'i Chapter newsletter, November 1979.
49. *Mālama I Ka Honua,* Sierra Club, Hawai'i Chapter newsletter, April, May, and October 1980, HSTP reader.
50. "Battle of Nuuanu," in *Thrum's Hawaiian Annual 1899* (Honolulu: The Printshop Company, Ltd., 1900), 107–112.
51. Harry Whitten, "Trail Ways," *Honolulu Star-Bulletin,* 1950s scrapbook, HTMC Archives; Neil Bernard Dukas, *A Pocket Guide to the Battle of Nu'uanu, 1975* (Honolulu: Mutual Publishing, 2010), 52–53; Mary Kawena Pukui, Samuel H. Elbert, and Esther T. Mookini, *Place Names of Hawaii* (Honolulu: University Press of Hawai'i, 1981), 58, 66.
52. George Pooloa, "Na Pana Kaulana o na Inoa o Ka Mokupuni Oahu," *Ke Aloha Aina,* February 1, 1919 (English translation in Elspeth P. Sterling and Catherine C. Summers, *Sites of Oahu* (Honolulu: Bishop Museum Press, 1997), 311).
53. Roger G. Skolmen, *Plantings on the Forest Reserves of Hawaii, 1910–1960* (Honolulu: Institute of Pacific Island Forestry, U.S. Forest Service, 1970), 45; Charles S. Judd, *Daily Journal 1935,* April 6, 1935, State Archives.
54. Mary Kawena Pukui, Samuel H. Elbert, and Esther T. Mookini, *Place Names of Hawaii* (Honolulu: University Press of Hawai'i, 1981), 58; Report of the Board of Commissioners of Agriculture and Forestry of the Territory of Hawaii, Biennial Period ending 6/30/56, 102; Division of Forestry, Forest Trail Map of the Island of Oahu (circa 1960).
55. HTMC hike schedule, May 10, 1958, and June 6, 1970, HTMC Archives.
56. *Mālama I Ka Honua,* Sierra Club, Hawai'i Chapter newsletter, April–May 1981; Lorin Gill, interview, October 30, 2008; Jim Yuen, interview, November 1, 2008.
57. *Mālama I Ka Honua,* Sierra Club, Hawai'i Chapter newsletter, December 1982, May–June 1983, July–August 1983, September–October 1983.
58. Lorin Gill, interview, October 30, 2008; Jim Yuen, interview, November 1, 2008.
59. Lahilahi Webb and Virginia Dominis Koch, informants, http:/www.huapala.org/Aloha/Aloha.Oe.html.
60. H. A. Wadsworth, *An Irrigation Census of Hawaii with Some Comparisons with the Continental United States* (Honolulu: Advertiser Publishing Company, 1935), 55; Carol Wilcox, *Sugar Water: Hawaii's Plantation Ditches* (Honolulu: University of Hawai'i Press, 1996), 111.
61. HTMC hike schedule, July 23, 1922, HTMC Archives.
62. HTMC hike schedule, May 22, 1948.
63. Division of Forestry and Wildlife, Program Plan Na Ala Hele, Hawai'i Trail & Access System, II-3, II-11; Richard H. Davis, interview, July 27, 2001; *Mālama I Ka Honua,* Sierra Club, Hawai'i Chapter newsletter, April–May 1991.
64. "Build a Trail This Summer," *Mālama I Ka Honua,* Sierra Club, Hawai'i Chapter newsletter, June–July 1991, insert.
65. Ibid.
66. *Mālama I Ka Honua,* Sierra Club, Hawai'i Chapter newsletter, August–September 1991, October–November 1991, December–January 1991–1992, and February–March 1992.
67. *Mālama I Ka Honua,* Sierra Club, Hawai'i Chapter newsletter, April–May 1992, August–September 1992, October–November 1992, and December–January 1992–1993.

68. *Mālama I Ka Honua,* Sierra Club, Hawai'i Chapter newsletter, June–July 1993, August–September 1993; "Hearty Trailbuilding Party," *Mālama I Ka Honua,* Sierra Club, Hawai'i Chapter newsletter, December–January 1993–1994.
69. Curt Cottrell, interview, November 13, 2008.
70. *Mālama I Ka Honua,* Sierra Club, Hawai'i Chapter newsletter, July–September 1996, October–December 1996, and January–March 1997.
71. *Mālama I Ka Honua,* Sierra Club, Hawai'i Chapter newsletter, April–June 1997, July–September 1997, October–December 1997, April–June 1998, July–September 1998, and October–December 1998.

Index

Agee, Hamilton P., 121
Agriculture and Forestry, Board of, 42, 103, 151–152, 163, 212
Ahrens, August, 72–73
Ahrens Ditch. *See* Waiawa Ditch
Akina, Stanislaus, 25
Alexander, William D., 30
Algiers, Michael, 90, 189, 220
Anahulu Trail, 173–174
Armitage, George T., 74–75
Army, U.S.: cooperation with Territorial Forestry, 106–110; Fifth Cavalry of, 60; Fort Shafter surveying by, 117; Hawaiian Division of, 106; Hawaiian pack train of, 202; Nineteenth Infantry of, 120, 175; O'ahu defense plan of, 103, 106; O'ahu surveying of, 102; Second Volunteer Engineers of, 102; Third Engineers of, 18, 68, 79, 83, 115, 120, 128, 175, 210, 212; Thirteenth Artillery of, 123; Twentieth Infantry of, 102, 112–113; Twenty-seventh Infantry of, 122; Unit Jungle Training Center of, 89
Au, Randall, 129

Baker, R. J., 8, 36, 38, 59, 121, 139
Balch, John A., 37
Ball, Stuart, 90, 100, 125, 175, 205, 208, 220
Ballentyne, Gustav C., 60
Ballentyne, Watson, 60
Bayless, Robert C., 138, 151, 166, 187, 210–211

Bennett, Frederick D., 3–4
Bingham, Hiram, 29
Bisho, John R., 36, 38, 79, 229
Bishop, Hubert K., 73
Bishop Estate, 6, 84, 86–87, 89–90, 104, 132, 176, 207, 209
Blacow, Chester E., 49
Blaich, Beryl, 70
Booth, Phil, 76
Booth, Richard, 43–44, 76, 116, 129; trailblazing by, 18, 47, 68, 148, 185, 213, 219
Bowman, Donald S., 103, 117–118
Brackenridge, J. D., 20
Breckons, Evelyn A., 36, 58
Breton, Roger, 208
Brown, E. Herrick, 36
Brown, George Ii, 151
Brown, Gilbert, 37, 40, 49, 60
Brown, Jo Anne, 205
Brown, Ruth E., 61
Bryan, E. H., Jr., 140
Bryan, Kenneth C., 126
Bryan, William A., 44, 114
Bryan's mountain house, 80, 126, 128–129, 131
Burt, Matt, 131
Bush, William, 58, 87
Butch the bear, 96–97
Byron, George A., 3

Cadle, Thomas P., 11, 13, 21–23, 36, 42, 52, 58, 61–62
Campbell Estate, 69, 213–214
Camp Wells, 110, 146–148
Carter, George R., 226

Cartwright, F., 48, 50–51
Castle, James B., 6, 34, 84–85
Castle, William R., 30–31, 33–35, 38–39, 40, 42, 45, 85
Cayetano, Benjamin, 59
Chamberlain, Levi, 26–27
Ching, Randy, 237
Civilian Conservation Corps (CCC): crew working hours of, 155; Honolulu Unit of, 151; organization of, 151–152; reduction in work force of, 156; trail crew composition of, 153; trail crew safety of, 155–156; Wahiawa Camp of, 151–157. *See also* Emergency Conservation Work
Cline, Geraldine, 18, 163–164, 205–206, 208, 219
Coflin, L. W., 166
Collins, George M., 55, 126
Conklin, Gay, 97
Cooke, Anna Rice, 34, 40
Cooke Trail, 34–35, 40, 44
Cooper, Henry E., 34, 40
Cooper, Lucy V., 141
Cooper, Will J., 141, 143
Cooper Ranch Inn, 87, 107, 110, 128, 133, 141–142, 144
Cooper Trail, 34, 40
Costello, Vince, 130–131
Cottrell, Curt, 218
Cowes, Walter, 40, 60
Crosson, John L. H., 24–25
Cummins, John A., 6, 234

Daingerfield, Lawrence H., 23, 37, 42, 52, 64–65, 86, 111, 114–115
Davis, Joyce, 219
Davis, Richard H.: accident on Ka'ala of, 63; campout leading by, 25, 96, 168, 202–203; Likeke Trail building by, 220–222; Maunawili Trail scouting and building by, 234; picture of, 221; trailblazing by, 9, 18, 53, 56, 77, 135, 140, 189, 213, 219
Denison, David, 220
de Ponte, Frank, 21

De Ponte, Mary, 22
Dickey, Charles H., 39
Dillingham Airfield, 25, 170–171
ditches, irrigation: access trails for, 71–72; cabins along, 72; components of, 71; construction of, 71–72; list of, 71; surveys for, 70–71
Dole, Sanford B., 226
Donaghho, John S., 23, 36–37, 39, 42, 44–45, 62, 111
Dresner, Edward, 24
Drum, Hugh A., 124, 174, 212
Drum Drive. *See* Wahiawa-Pupukea Trail
Duerst, Fred, 14, 129

Effinger, John, 21
Ellerbrock, William T. H., 16–18
Emergency Conservation Work (ECW): application for, 149–150; approval of, 150–151; assignment of responsibility for, 151; disbanding of, 157, 160; enactment of, 149; first enrollment period of, 152–154; fourth enrollment period of, 156–157; reduction in funding of, 156–157; second enrollment period of, 154–155; third enrollment period of, 155–156; trail map of, 158–159
Emergency Relief Appropriation Road and Trail Project, 128, 212
Emerson, John S., 19–20
Emerson, Ursula, 19–20
Emma, Queen, 6
Emory, Kenneth, 211
Escherich, Peter, 215
Ewart, George R., III, 87, 108, 133

Farrington, Wallace R., 42, 53, 120
Fechner, Robert, 150, 154
Feldman, Jay, 181
Firebreak Trail, 62–63, 209–210
Ford, Alexander Hume: founding of the Hawaiian Trail and Mountain Club by, 31, 33–34; hiking by, 49, 112–113; picture of, 32, 36; promoting *kama'āina* trails, 34–37,

39; reviving the Hawaiian Trail and
Mountain Club, 37
Forestry, Territorial Division of: cooperation with U.S. Army of, 106–110; reduced appropriations for, 111; trail building by, 110; war on feral pigs by, 104, 106
Forestry and Wildlife, State Division of, 25, 144, 148, 168, 214, 217
Fraser, Dexter, 111
Frazier, Thomas, 143–144
Frear, Walter F., 30–31, 33, 35–37, 40, 49
Freeman, David, 170
Fullaway, David T., 41

Gibb, James, 91, 99
Gill, Andrea, 225–227, 229
Gill, Lorin T., 47, 56, 83, 89, 215–216, 226
Godek, Chuck, 206, 220
Godek-Jaskulski hike, 220
Goodale, William W., 78, 82
Goodman, Gina, 235
Gowen, James C., 211–212
Grieg, Thelma, 55, 81, 171

Ha'ikū Stairs, 193
Hala Pepe Nui hike, 219
Hālawa-'Aiea hike, 185
Halfway House, 45
Hall, Edwin O., 5–6
Hall, John B., 77, 101, 129, 219
Hansbrough, Vernie, 58
Haughs, David, 228
Hau'ula-Papali hike, 144
Hawaiian legends: of 'Aihualama, 225–226; of Helemano, 160; of Ka'au Crater, 48; of Kalauao, 181–182; of Kaliuwa'a (Sacred Falls), 4–5; of Kawiwi, 15; of Olomana, 57
Hawaiian Sugar Planters Association, 41, 79, 99, 104, 117, 120, 126, 226
Hawaiian Trail and Mountain Club (HTMC): centennial of, 38; clubhouse of, 13; constitution of, 33–34; decline of, 36; founding of, 31–33; Hui Alo Pali of, 21–22; members of, 33; partnership with Kaimuki Land Company, 35;
reactivation of, 37; trail construction by, 34–35; trail maintenance by, 220; trail map published by, 36; Ukulele Patrol of, 40, 49, 50, 60
Hawaiian trails: disappearance of, 4; to Ka'au Crater, 48; of leeward O'ahu, 1, 3; in Mānoa and Pālolo Valleys, 29; map of, 2; on Mau'umae Ridge, 54; to windward O'ahu, 3–4
Hawaii Employment Program, 8, 47, 144, 185, 229, 232
Hawaii National Guard, 103, 117
Hawai'i Reserves, Inc., 136, 189
Haylett, Beverley, 97, 205
Helemano Ditch, 71
Helemano hike, 161
Hidden Valley hike. See Makaua Valley hike
Hiraoka, Wally, 237
Hoffman, Nancy, 181
Hokuloa, 69
Holmes, Vincent, 235
Holt, Walter W., 178
Honolulu Plantation Company, 70–71, 91, 96, 98, 100, 223
Honolulu Unit. See Civilian Conservation Corps
Honouliuli Preserve, 69, 213–214
Huguet, Adolphe, 128
Hui Alo Pali. See Hawaiian Trail and Mountain Club
Hui O Mālama I Ka 'Āina, 181

Ickes, Harold L., 149–151, 154
Ihara, Roy, 230
Ii, John Papa, 1
'Iliahi Ridge hike, 77
Inouye, Ralph, 235
Irwin, William G., 50
Isbell, Art, 144

Jaskulski, Erwin, 220
Jones, Glenn W., 53
Jones, James, 209
Jorgenson, Jorgen, 73
Judd, Albert F., 7, 55

Judd, Charles S.: article written by, 128; career of, 103; cooperation with U.S. Army of, 106–110; death of, 157; Emergency Conservation Work involvement of, 149–157; forest inspections by, 7, 13, 17, 23, 55, 65, 79, 87, 92, 99, 121, 126, 128, 133–134, 172, 177; forest reserve management by, 103–104; hiking attire of, 109; hiking ban in Mānoa and Pālolo Valleys by, 41–42; picture of, 66, 105; planting by, 67, 137–138, 143, 176, 232; trail scouting and inspections by, 41, 46, 62, 66, 88, 93, 120, 123, 127, 133–135, 137, 141–143, 145–147, 160–163, 166–167, 169, 173–174, 177–179, 184, 187, 190, 194–195, 200–201, 210–211, 223; war against feral pigs by, 104, 106
Judd, Charles S., Jr., 188
Judd, Emma, 147, 173
Judd, Lawrence M., 108, 149
Judd, Louise, 137, 173, 188
Judd Memorial Trail, 232

Ka'aikukai Cabin, 65–67, 69, 211, 213
Ka'aikukai-Nānākuli traverse, 66
Ka'aikukai Trail, 66–67, 69
Ka'ala-Mokulē'ia Trail, 23–24, 152–153, 166
Ka'ala Natural Area Reserve, 35
Ka'ala Road, 25
Kahalepuna, Lawrence, 129
Kahana Bay Trail, 103, 115
Kahanahāiki-Mokulē'ia Trail, 27
Kahana Trail, 76, 153
Kahekili, Chief, 231
Kahuku cabin, 204–206
Kahuku Plantation Company, 84–85, 121, 132, 147, 187
Kaimuki Land Company, 35, 49, 54
Kaipapa'u cabin, 87–88, 195
Kaipapa'u hike, 219
Kākuhihewa, Chief, 182
Kalakaua, King, 39, 70
Kalanianaole, Prince Jonah K., 33
Kalanikupule, Chief, 231
Kalauao hike, 182, 185–186

Kalo'i Gulch Trail, 64–66
Kaluakauila Trail, 139, 169
Kamanaiki hike, 219
Kamananui Ditch. See Kawainui Ditch
Kamapua'a, 4–7, 9, 86
Kamapua'a hike, 9
Kamehameha, King, 231
Kamehameha Schools-Bishop Estate. See Bishop Estate
Kānehoa-Hāpapa hike, 213–214
Kapalama hike, 215
Kaua hike, 213–214
Kaukonahua Ditch. See Mauka Ditch
Kaukonahua Gulch Trail, 108
Kaunala East hike, 148
Kaunala West hike, 148
Kaupakuhale Ridge hike, 24
Kaupakuhale route, 19, 21, 61
Kawaihāpai-Ka'ena Point hike, 27
Kawaihāpai-Mokulē'ia hike, 27
Kawaiiki Ditch, 78–79, 82, 172
Kawailoa cabin, 175, 202, 204, 207
Kawailoa Gulch Trail and hike, 83–84
Kawainui Ditch, 71, 78–79, 82, 84
Kawelo, Kapua, 130, 132, 207, 209
Keaīwa *heiau*, 182, 185–186
Keaīwa Heiau State Park, 185–186
Keālia cabin, 139
Kekahuna, J., 143–144
Kekina, Mabel, 135–136, 206, 219–220
Kikukawa, Herbert, 228, 232
Kim, Atomman, 230
Kim, Steve, 130
King, Myrtle, 27, 165
Kīpapa Ditch, 71–72
Kiyota, Wallace S., 173–174
Knudsen, Ida E., 64
Koolau Agricultural Company, 84
Ko'olaupoko Trail, 218, 234
Koolau Railway, 7, 84, 112, 132, 187
Kosch, Kermit, 7
Kraebel, Charles J., 41–42
Kuaokalā Access Road, 168, 171
Kukuiala cabin, 137, 139, 165–167, 170
Kulepeamoa hike, 220
Kuokoa, 1, 15, 19
Kuolani-Waianu hike, 76
Kupehau Trail, 68, 213

Laie Plantation, 84
Land and Natural Resources, State Department of, 132, 209, 214, 216–217, 227, 229, 232, 234
Landgraf, Ernest W.: on Castle, 88; on Kaunala, 145–147; on Koʻolau Summit, 122–123, 195–200; on Maʻakua Ridge and Hauʻula, 142–143; on Mānoa Cliff, 45; on Piko, 137; on Poamoho, 161; trail crew of, 110, 194
Landgraf, Max F.: forest inspections by, 17, 79, 86, 92, 133–134, 172, 223; Piko Club member, 108; planting by, 55, 176, 211; trail scouting and inspections by, 87–88, 93, 104, 110, 123, 126–127, 137, 141–143, 145–147, 160–162, 174, 177–178, 184, 187, 190, 194–195, 211
Lanipō-Wiliwilinui hike, 56
Leao, Gerald, 77, 100–101, 219–220
Lidman, Inger, 144
Likelike, Princess, 233
Liliʻuokalani, Queen, 226, 233
Lippincott, J. B., 73
Lloyd, James W., 151
Locey, Frank H., 212
Lowrey, Frederick D., 79, 134, 172, 186
Luaʻalaea hike, 219
Lyon, Harold L., 41, 121
Lyon Arboretum, 204, 226–227

MacCaughey, Vaughn, 111–112
Mākaha-Kaʻala hike, 18
Makaleha-Keālia Trail, 152
Makapuʻu-Tom Tom hike, 13–14
Makaua Valley hike, 219
Makiki Tantalizer hike, 44, 47, 230
Mākua-Kaʻena Point hike, 139
Mākua Mountain Trail, 28
Malcolm, James, 96
Mann, James B., 126
Marconi-Kuliouou hike, 14
Marconi Pass Trail, 13
Marconi-Tom Tom hike, 13
Marines, U.S. Third, 235

Masuyama, Lynne, 208
Matthewman, John A., 83, 138–139, 174, 188
Māui (demigod), 48
Mauka Ditch, 71, 111–112, 116
Maunawili Ditch, 234
Maunawili hike, 234
McCandless, Lincoln L., 99, 138, 150, 167
McCandless Ditch. See Waimalu Ditch
McCluskey, Robert, 166
McEldowney, George A., 120–121, 126
McGuire, Thomas R. L.: article written by, 55; forest inspections by, 13, 43, 86, 143; as Hawaiian Trail and Mountain Club guide, 42, 54, 66, 74, 85–87, 92, 115, 127, 182; as *kāhuna lapaʻau*, 185; picture of, 12, 36; Piko Club member, 108; planting by, 182; trail scouting and inspections by, 11, 46, 104, 126, 145, 147, 178–179, 201, 211
McKenzie, Arthur W., 162, 173
Meadows, Edmund J., 17, 87, 98, 127, 161, 182
Medeiros, Herman, 224
Mendes, Nicholas, 79, 87, 104, 132–134, 161, 172
Mendonca contour trail, 137, 165–166
Merrill, Lyndon D., 62
Mersino, Ed, 176
Miller, Albert, 206, 219
Mink, John F., 180
Mizuno, Robert, 216
Mokuleia Airfield. See Dillingham Airfield
Mokulēʻia Firebreak Road. See Kuaokalā Access Road
Molony, J. S., 73
Moon, Carole, 206
Morimoto, Neal, 235
Moriyama, John, 47
Motomura, Hiroshi, 215–216
Mottl, Michael J., 9
Mott-Smith, Ernest A., 228
Mountain, Harold A., 151
Mutual Telephone Company, 37, 68

Na Ala Hele: demonstration trails of, 218; establishment of, 216–217; trail administration by, 144, 148, 228, 233, 237; trail restoration by, 47, 65, 171, 218
Nagata, Ron, 216, 227–228
Nakamura, Charles, 18, 223–224
Nature Conservancy, The, 69, 180, 213
Neilson, Joseph, 14, 43, 63, 68, 119, 124, 189, 192
Newman, A. S., 170
Ng, Wing, 44
Nike-Hercules missile site, 14, 168, 171
Nowlein, Samuel, 226

Oahu College. See Punahou School
Oʻahu Forest National Wildlife Refuge, 180, 208
Oʻahu Natural Resources Program, 69, 130–131, 207, 209, 214
Oʻahu Pig Hunters Association, 216
Oahu Sugar Company, 70–72, 76, 96, 100, 176, 211
ʻOhikilolo hike, 219
Olomana (warrior), 57
Olson, Gunder E., 135, 143, 152, 155, 157, 178; Emergency Conservation Work project reports by, 46, 93, 144, 147, 183, 191
Opaeula Artillery spur, 128
ʻŌpaeʻula Ditch, 71, 78–80, 82, 126
ʻŌpaeʻula Watershed Protection Partnership, 132, 208
Ortman, Charles, 58
OʻShaughnessy, Michael M., 73
Osmun, Russell A., 62, 109
Owen, Zon, 89

Paʻalaʻa Uka Pūpūkea Road. See Wahiawa-Pupukea Trail
Pahamoa, John, 87, 104
Pahole Natural Area Reserve, 140, 168
Palama Uka, 80, 83, 131
Pa Lehua, 64–65, 67–68
Pa Lehua Artillery Spur, 68, 212
Palmer, Jesse, 135
Palolo-Manoa Drainage Reservation, 42, 53

Pankiwskyj, Kost, 206
Papali Trail, 144
Pardee, Austin M., 112–113
Patton, George S., Jr., 167, 179, 188, 200
Peterson, Jennie, 47
Pierce, George S., 128, 142
Piko Club: annual meeting of, 67, 110; founding of, 106–108; hikes of, 108–109; last hike of, 211; marathon of, 210; members of, 108; organization articles of, 108; organization banquet of, 108; yell, 109
Piliwale, Silver, 14, 164, 204–207, 216, 219, 230
Piliwale Ridge hike, 219
Plunkett, Robert, 87, 104, 110, 132–133, 141–142
Poamoho cabin, 161–165
Poindexter, Joseph B., 154–155, 174
Polworth, Hugh M., 84
Pope, Willis T., 56–57
Postl, Anton, 185
Potter, Colin, 96, 98
Punahou School, 29–30
Punaiki Trail, 110, 141–144, 154, 194
Punaluʻu Ditch, 7, 84
Punaluʻu Store, 89–90
Puʻu Heleakala hike, 219
Puʻu Kaʻaumakua hike, 116
Puʻu Kahuauli hike, 118
Puʻu Kawiwi hike, 18, 224
Puʻu Keahi a Kahoe hike, 220
Puʻu Manamana hike, 219
Puʻu o Hulu hike, 219
Puʻu Piei hike, 219
Puʻu Uau hike, 182

Quinn, Buster H., 162

Reeves, Jack, 53
Reidford, Kenneth, 40, 60
Renard, Gene, 227–228
Rich, William, 20
Richardson, Julius L., 16
Riley, William R., 117
Robinson, Gene, 206–207
Rocha, Tony, 65

Index

Rodrigues, Manuel, 174
Rohrer, Joby, 130–132, 207, 209
Rohrmayr, Steve, 18
Roosevelt, Franklin D., 149
Roosevelt, Theodore, 31
Rorie, Patrick, 77, 100, 116, 125, 131, 206–207, 209, 224
Rosendahl, Paul, 28
Rowell, William E., 39, 44, 84–85
Russ, Glenn W.: Civilian Conservation Corps involvement of, 150–152, 154–155; forest inspections by, 17, 87, 92, 128, 133–134, 160–161, 170; Piko Club member, 108; reports by, 198, 200; trail scouting and inspections by, 137, 145–146, 162, 166–167, 173, 190, 195, 210

Sanford, David, 202, 219
Sanidad, Simon, 205, 230
Sawyer, Beryl, 89, 202–203
Scheerer, Cedric E., 16
Schmidt, Richard, 53, 193, 237
Schuyler, Walter F., 65
Schuyler Trail, 65
Sekiguchi, Nao, 58
Sewell, Harold, 65, 67–68
Shaw, Jessie, 114
Sherman, Raymond G., 106, 108, 150
Short, Walter C., 163
Sierra Club, Hawai'i Chapter: establishing of, 215; Hawai'i Service Trip Program of, 215–216; High School Hikers program, 215; newsletter, 215; trail building by, 216, 227–230, 232–237; wallaby watches of, 119
Silva, Robert, 219
Sky Line Trail, 62–63
Smith, Charles, 25, 81, 219
Smith, James, 58
South Hālawa Trail, 154, 190
Souza, Joseph, 228
Stanton, Charles A., 54
Stickney, Joseph B., 21, 25
Stone, Brandon, 48
Strona, Paul, 205
Summerall, Charles P., 103, 115, 120

Sunada, Jason, 206, 220
Super, Paul, 49–50
Suzuki, Ken, 206
Sweet, Joseph B., 88, 162, 174
Swezey, Otto H., 79, 99, 115

Tabata, Raymond, 47
Talcott, Lloyd, 56, 80, 83, 219
Tantalus Ramble hike, 44, 47, 219
Tarleton, Albert H., 49
Taylor, M. D., 115
Thompson, H. L., 121
Thurston, Lorrin A., 30–31, 33, 37, 42
Tillett, Everett E., 156, 174, 184, 210–211
Toyomura, Gerald, 233
Tracy, Clifton H., 173
Tripler Ridge hike, 219
Truman, Fred E., 55, 60, 121
Trust for Public Land, 69, 214
Turner, Dayle, 15, 77, 100, 116, 125, 131, 207–208, 224
Turner, Lorna, 89
Turner, Ralph E., Jr., 17–18, 67, 110, 136–138
Tyerman, Daniel, 3

Uchida, Deborah, 206
Ukulele Patrol. See Hawaiian Trail and Mountain Club
Ulupaina hike, 219
Uncle Tom's cabin, 178–181, 200–201
Unemployed Workers Relief Commission, 110, 142, 145, 151
United States Exploring Expedition, 20

Vachon, Joseph P., 128
Valentino, Ralph, 165
Vandervoort, Eric, 116
von Holt, Heinrich M., 64–65, 67–68

Wahiawa Camp. See Civilian Conservation Corps
Wahiawā Hills hike, 219
Wahiawa-Pupukea Trail, 79–80, 83–84, 124, 128–129, 175
Wahiawa Water Company, 111, 161
Waiāhole Ditch, 73, 75, 77, 211

Waiahole Water Company, 73–74, 96, 100
Wai'alae Ridge hike, 54–55
Waialua Agricultural Company, 22, 70–71, 78, 82, 111, 126, 134, 172–173
Waialua Sugar Company. *See* Waialua Agricultural Company
Wai'anae Ka'ala hike, 18, 219
Wai'anae Kai hike, 17–18
Waianae Sugar Company, 16
Wai'anae Waterworks hike, 18
Waiau Ridge hike, 92
Waiau Trail, 101, 219
Waiawa Ditch, 71–75
Waiawa Trail, 75, 177–179, 200
Waikakalaua Ditch, 71–72
Waikakalaua hike, 219
Wailele Trail, 124, 135, 154, 186–188
Wailupe Loop hike, 220
Waimalu Ditch, 71, 99, 101
Waimanalo Sugar Company, 6, 13, 234
Waimano Ditch, 91, 96
Waimano Home, 92–93
Waimea Trail, 156–157, 174
Waipi'o hike, 176–177
Waite, Mashuri, 48
Warner, Thelma. *See* Grieg, Thelma
Weiner, William M., 133
Wells, Briant H.: career of, 106; and cooperation with Territorial Forestry, 106, 109–110; Emergency Conservation Work involvement of, 149–151; hiking attire of, 109; memorial tree planting by, 137–138; picture of, 107; Piko Club president, 17–18, 67, 173; reconnaissance hikes by, 66, 108–109, 115–116, 122, 141, 169
Wells, Mrs. Briant H. (Mary), 17, 108, 137
Wells, Thomas J., 79, 134–135, 137, 161, 172, 198
Wenkam, Robert, 202, 215, 222
Whisenand, Adeline, 80
Whisenand, George, 24
Whitman, John B., 3
Whitten, Harry, 25, 124, 202, 216
Whittle, Joseph, 139
Widemann, Hermann, 15
Wilcox, Robert W., 226
Wilkes, Charles, 20
Williams, Weston, 203–204
Willison, Rose, 58
Wilson, Albert A., 111, 161
Wilson, Leroy C., 201, 211
Wilson, Roland O., 170
Wingate, E. C., 151
Wollenzein, Merlin, 10–11
Wright, George F., 7

Yamaguchi, Kazuo, 224
Yamaguchi, Misao, 224
Yamane, Charlotte, 135, 209
Yost, Harold H., 41
Yoza, Thomas, 125, 208
Yuen, Jim, 47, 97–98, 165, 175, 189, 205, 230, 232